FAR-FLUNG LIN

CW01082500

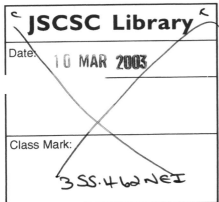

India became independent and was no longer the jewel in the crown, seemed an irrelevancy when the fate of the world apparently was being decided in Europe by the United States and the Soviet Union.

The inevitable consequence of this was that graduate students flocked—pushed by the trade winds of funding and 'relevancy'—to the more fashionable approaches to British defence policy advocated by such historians as Michael Howard, Brian Bond and, later, Paul Kennedy. These young scholars wrote books in which the words 'empire and imperial defence' took on a different meaning. As this movement caught the tide of the expansion of universities in the halcyon days of the 1960s and 1970s, it produced works that threatened to exorcize the 'old' school of imperial history from the canon. The lessons of Corbett, Laughton, Knox, the Colomb brothers, Richmond, the intellectual founts of British naval and imperial history, that clearly demonstrated the undeniable ties between commerce, diplomacy, finance, national will and military and naval power, were ignored.[6]

A second consequence was the decline of naval history. As the Royal Navy had existed to serve and protect the British Empire, when the latter was deemed a matter not to be discussed in polite society, studies of the navy reduced themselves to battle accounts, operational histories, examinations of technological minutiae and great-man biography.[7] At their very best, such studies were aimed at explaining how Britain prepared for war and fought against Germany: the naval race, steam and continuing technological change, blockade, convoy, Jutland, main fleet to Singapore and the great betrayal became the only prototypes for naval writing. Lost were the connections between diplomacy and naval force, imperial requirements and command of the sea, economics and imperial defence. In the shadow of the Battle of the Atlantic, Pearl Harbor, the sinking of the *Repulse* and the *Prince of Wales*, Midway and Operation Overlord, Mahanian dogma regarding command of the sea—itself a derivative of Clausewitz and Jomini's pernicious emphasis on land warfare—became paramount. The subtler vision of a British way in warfare, espoused by such imperial thinkers as Corbett, was lost.

The essays that follow join together the separated aspects of what was once encompassed within imperial history. They deal with the relationships between domestic politics and defence; the links between diplomacy, economics and finance; the need to maintain imperial communications to defend imperial frontiers; the adaptations in strategy caused by technological advances; the changes in the mechanisms for strategic planning; and the interconnections between perceptions and policy.

It is the latter theme that is the subject of Karl Revells' look at the Crimean War. Revells reinforces much of what recent scholarship has said about that conflict, but emphasizes the way in which the faulty perceptions of the efficacy of naval power—the legacy of Trafalgar—held by the political elite in Britain muddled the imperial strategy of the naval professionals.[8] John Beeler, starting with the *loci classici* provided by Schurman and Tunstall, traces the development of imperial defence strategy in a period of rapid and profound technological and ideological change. The adaptation to steam and the protection of free trade churned up a number of specialists whose views of the future were listened to, often with scepticism, by both government and defence professionals. For both Beeler and Revells, personality and ideas were at the centre of imperial events.

Nicholas Lambert, utilizing archives on three continents, shows how the Empire itself played into imperial defence. Focusing on the Far East before the First World War, Lambert reveals the complex relationship between Britain and her Pacific Dominions—Australia, Canada and New Zealand. Lambert clearly demonstrates that Britain was willing to share the strategic planning in the Far East with the Dominions if they were willing to accept the responsibility of helping to defend their own interests. While not a master–servant relationship, clearly Britain held the central position in this pre-Commonwealth defence partnership, especially in naval matters.

The First World War posed new problems for imperialists. The rise of new powers, such as the United States, not only created threats to the existing Empire itself but also made it necessary to factor their strength into the new equation for post-war imperial defence. David French speaks directly to this matter. Would the anti-imperial United States prove to be more than a temporary, wartime 'associated power', or would it be only, as the Second World War revealed, an 'ally of a kind'?[9] Coupled with the rise of new peripheral powers came the collapse of other existing empires—particularly the Ottoman and Russian ones. This provided new opportunities and imperatives for the expansion of the British Empire. However, this expansion created the possibility of imperial overstretch, replete with its own dangers. In his examination of imperial defence in India and the Middle East, Keith Neilson confirms that imperial defence was considered against all comers, including wartime allies.

In the environment of pacifism and disarmament that followed the First World War, imperial defence faced enemies from without and within. John Ferris links naval strategy, political will and economic and industrial capability to suggest why the Royal Navy's ability to defend the Empire rested on a fragile base. Pared to the bone by those who believed that the Great War had ushered in an era of peace and harmony through international co-operation for security, the Royal Navy maintained its supremacy only by tying its building programmes to domestic stability. Its mission, however, remained as it had always been: the defence of the far-flung lines of the Empire. This was not the only way that the Royal Navy ensured that it could survive and still fulfil its tasks. Orest Babij illustrates that the professional heads of the Royal Navy had a surprising suppleness in their dealings with their political and public masters. Realizing that their maximum demands for ships could never be granted in the existing political climate, the sea lords negotiated shrewdly and ruthlessly in order to maintain what they perceived to be the essential sinews of empire: a navy second to none.

Tying together many of the themes touched on above, Greg Kennedy traces the complex web of British imperial policy in the Far East in 1935. British imperial defence and economic interests in that region were dependent upon maintaining a subtle balance between the regional realities, great power politics and imperial imperatives. Kennedy's piece thus illustrates a central tenet of British imperial defence: the differences between the defence policy of an empire and that of a sovereign nation state.

All of the above would come as no surprise to Donald Schurman. Schurman's approach to imperial defence was, above all, an intellectual one. His concentration on individuals, their ideas and the institutional memory that ensured that these ideas became part of British imperial defence policy shaped his writing and teaching. Donald is an 'ideas man' in all aspects of his life. Lesser-known aspects of his scholarly career, at least to those who think him primarily a naval historian, are his work on the Disraeli project and his writings on the Anglican church in Canada.[10] In both of these endeavours, his unique approach to history—the study of personality and ideology—are evident. This methodology has permeated the study of naval history in Canada, for Donald was the founder of the serious study of maritime history in that country from his posts at Queen's University and the Royal Military College of Canada.[11] On either side of the Rideau, as well as on both sides of the Atlantic, Donald Mackenzie Schurman has made an indelible mark on his chosen field. It is the editors' pleasure and honour to present what follows as a tribute to and acknowledgement of his contribution to scholarship.

NOTES

1. Schurman has made his own partial explanation, see his 'Imperial Naval Defence: Then and Now', in K. Neilson and E.J. Errington (eds), *Navies and Global Defence* (Hamden, CN, 1995), pp 9–23.
2. There is a nice typology in John Darwin, *The End of the British Empire* (London, 1991). For an excellent historiographical discussion and debate, P. J. Cain and A. G. Hopkins, *British Imperialism. Innovation and Expansion 1688–1914* (London, 1993), pp 5–17.
3. J. Gallagher and R. E. Robinson, 'The Imperialism of Free Trade' *Economic History Review*, 2nd ser., 6 (1953).
4. This sort of thinking is epitomized by Paul Kennedy, *The Rise and Fall of the Great Powers: Economic Change and Military Conflict from 1500 to 2000* (New York, 1987); Correlli Barnett, *The Collapse of British Power* (London, 1972); Aaron Friedberg, *The Weary Titan. Britain and the Experience of Relative Decline, 1895–1905* (Princeton, 1988); Bernard Porter, *The Lion's Share. A Short History of British Imperialism 1850–1970* (London, 1975); Keith Robbins, *The Eclipse of a Great Power. Modern Britain 1870–1975* (London, 1983); Max Beloff, *Britain's Liberal Empire 1897–1921* (London, 1969); Bradford A. Lee, *Britain and the Sino-Japanese War, 1937–1939: A Study in the Dilemmas of British Decline* (Stanford, 1973); and Christopher Hall, *Britain, America and Arms Control, 1921–37* (London, 1987).
5. The cornerstone of such analysis is Michael Howard's seminal work, *The Continental Commitment: The Dilemma of British Defence Policy in the Era of Two World Wars* (London, 1972). Others in this mould include John Gooch, *The Plans of War: The General Staff and British Military Strategy c. 1900–1916* (London, 1974); Brian Bond, *British Military Policy between the Wars* (Oxford, 1980); N. H. Gibbs, *Grand Strategy* Vol. I, *Rearmament Policy* (London, 1976); H. Montgomery Hyde, *British Air Policy between the Wars 1918–1939* (London, 1976); W. Wark, *The Ultimate Enemy. British Intelligence and Nazi Germany 1933–39* (Ithaca, NY, 1985).
6. Such thinkers and their ideas of Empire are central to Schurman's work: see his 'Imperial Defence, 1868–1887' (Ph.D. dissertation, Cambridge, 1955); *Education of a Navy. The Development of British Naval Strategic Thought 1867–1914* (Chicago, 1965) and Julian S. Corbett, *1854–1922: Historian of British Maritime Policy from Drake to Jellicoe* (London, 1981).
7. For a perceptive account of the problems with the writing of naval history, see John B. Hattendorf, 'Ubi Sumus? What Is the State of Naval and Maritime History Today?' in John B. Hattendorf, ed, *Ubi Sumus? The State of Naval and Maritime History* (Newport, RI, 1994), pp 1–9 and many of the articles in this collection, particularly those on Britain, Canada and the United States.
8. The best modern account is Andrew Lambert, *The Crimean War. British Grand Strategy against Russia, 1853–56* (Manchester, 1990).
9. Christopher Thorne, *Allies of a Kind: The United States, Britain and the War Against Japan, 1941-1945* (New York, 1978).
10. The Letters of Benjamin Disraeli (Toronto, 1982–); Donald M. Schurman, *A Bishop and His People: John Travers Lewis and the Anglican Diocese of Ontario 1862–1902* (Kingston, Ont., 1991).
11. For Schurman's influence in Britain, see N. A. M. Rodger, 'Britain', in Hattendorf, ed, *Ubi Sumus?*, p 43; for his influence in Canada, see Marc Milner, 'The Historiography of the Canadian Navy: The State of the Art', in ibid, p. 85 n. 14; and for his influence in the United States and in navalist circles generally, see his contribution in James Goldrick and John B. Hattendorf, eds, *Mahan is Not Enough. Proceedings of a Conference on the Works of Sir Julian Corbett and Admiral Sir Herbert Richmond* (Newport, RI, 1993) and the effect of his ideas in the discussions.

Perception in the midst of chaos

KARL REVELLS

Q: What is the difference between the fleet in the Baltic and the fleet in the Black Sea?
A: The fleet in the Baltic was expected to do everything and did nothing; the fleet in the Black Sea was expected to do nothing and did it.
(*Punch*)

Mr Punch's answer to his riddle underscores the misunderstanding and intolerance with which the British public viewed the Royal Navy's performance during the Russian War, 1854–1856. Indeed, the suggestion that the Baltic fleet was charged with the primary mission in the war highlights the public's ignorance of the Crimea's significance in the Allies' strategy. This ignorance was juxtaposed in the popular mind with the impression that, at best, the war was a tale of wasted sacrifice and heroism, of woe and tragedy, of Florence Nightingale—the Angel of Mercy—and of the immortalized Charge of the Light Brigade. Overwhelmed by the overbearing sense of gloom and doom that emitted from the Crimea, the public seemed to lose interest in and sight of the importance of Britain's naval operations during the conflict and readily assumed that the fleets 'did nothing'. What is most curious about this attitude was its obvious negation of reality.

Throughout the war, the British Cabinet never lost sight of the fact that, in the absence of a large army, Britain had to rely principally on the Royal Navy and its Allies' military forces to accomplish its war goals. Thus, out of necessity, the conflict for Britain was essentially a naval war. Curiously, there seems to have been little appreciation of this fact by the British public. The cause of this omission is an intriguing problem and, one which raises in its wake a host of complementary questions: What was the British public expecting from this war? Was there any correlation between its expectations and reality within the campaign theatres? Perhaps, of greater importance, how did popular perception of the war effort succeed in condemning the Navy's operations to virtual anonymity in the public's mind at the time and in the historiography of the war since then?

An answer to these questions would require a full review of Britain's naval operations during the war—an impossibility given the limited length of this chapter. Nevertheless, a brief overview of the Royal Navy's campaign season in the Baltic and Black Sea theatres combined with an analysis of the reaction to some of the more prominent and newsworthy events of the conflict will help to illustrate the public's perception of reality. Moreover, measuring these perceptions against the factors and forces which combined to form these singular events will demonstrate that the British public had a very distorted and simplistic view of what actually occurred in the operational theatres. Indeed, one could argue that because of the environment in which they lived, the observers of the war could not distinguish between reality and a mere perception of it.

THE ADMIRALTY'S ACHIEVEMENTS: A BRIEF OVERVIEW

The problems that confronted the Admiralty at the inception of the war were daunting, for Russia's coasts bordered on four major bodies of water: the White, Baltic and Black Seas and the northern Pacific. Each of these became an instant theatre of operations for the Royal Navy which had to mount blockades of Russian ports, protect British commerce in the region and be on alert for possible attacks at sea. In addition, the Admiralty was charged with organizing the logistical arrangements for the expeditionary forces that were being sent to the East in ever increasing numbers.

The First Lord, Sir James Graham, shouldered the responsibility for mobilizing Britain's available naval resources to meet these demands. Most pressing was the need to commission a fleet for the Baltic where the Tsar maintained a large fleet capable of wreaking havoc on Britain's shores and trade if allowed to enter the North Sea. By reassigning ships from the Atlantic and home squadrons, and by commissioning ships in refit or off the construction blocks, Graham was able to produce a fleet on short order. Manning this fleet, however, presented a greater problem, for Britain's maritime commerce had siphoned off a great number of experienced seamen; new recruits were difficult to attract given the navy's reputation for harsh discipline and conditions. In desperation, the Admiralty was forced to draw on its lists of officers and seamen on half-pay or on pension; it also transferred able-bodied men from ships with full complements. When the fleet, commanded by Vice-Admiral Sir Charles Napier, sailed from Portsmouth for the Baltic on 11 March 1854, a good number of its ships were undermanned or heavily complemented by inexperienced crews.[1] Graham employed similar methods to cover the needs of the other operational theatres. Thus, a detachment of three steamers from Napier's fleet was assigned to maintain watch in the White Sea. Solving the needs of the Pacific theatre proved more taxing given the length of Russia's Pacific coastline. As a stop-gap measure, a squadron under the command of Rear-Admiral David Price was created out of contingents from the Pacific and China Squadrons. The operational needs in the Black Sea were met directly by ships of the Mediterranean fleet, under Vice-Admiral Sir James Dundas, which had been anchored in the Euxine since late September 1853. Dundas was warned not to expect reinforcements in the near future as Graham's drafts to fill the Baltic fleet had been so heavy that the home ports were depleted of ships.[2] By stretching his resources, therefore, Sir James was able to produce creditable naval forces for each of the four theatres of operations from a peacetime establishment.

Throughout the war, the Tsar's fleets never actively challenged the Allies' command over the Black and Baltic Seas. Though this deprived the fleet commanders of an opportunity to engage the Russians in battle, it did provide them the opportunity to harass virtually unimpeded Russia's lines of communication in either ocean. Thus, in the Black Sea, a squadron under Dundas' second-in-comand, Sir Edmund Lyons, was despatched in May 1854 to the Circassian and Georgian coasts to encourage local rebellions against Russian overrule in the region and to drive the Tsar's troops from the eastern shores of the Black Sea. The port of Odessa was attacked to loosen Russia's grip on the western shore. Aside from maintaining a constant watch on Sevastopol, Dundas was ordered to hang on the flank of the Turkish army which was poised in Bulgaria to repel a Russian crossing of the Danube.[3] This arrangement tied the fleet's operations directly into those of the Allied armies. Dundas' movements at sea would soon largely parallel those of Britain's expeditionary forces on land. Hence, when Lord Raglan, the commander of the force, shifted his troops to Varna in June, Dundas anchored his fleet within ready distance in neighbouring Balchik Bay.

The same arrangement held in mid-September when, prompted by their governments, the Allied armies invaded the Crimea. Dundas' ships provided a screen of security for the armies as they were convoyed to their landing zone at Kalamita Bay. Given the lack of intelligence respecting Russian troop movements, the fleet prudently shadowed the armies' advance along the coast on to Sevastopol. This close support proved most beneficial on 20 September when the Russians attacked the Anglo–French armies at the Alma River. Caught in unfavourable terrain by enfilading fire, the Allies suffered heavy casualties. Dundas volunteered the services of the fleet's surgeons to assist the army's medical staff and drafts of seamen were used to carry large numbers of sick and wounded soldiers from the battlefield to the hospital ships thereby saving many lives. Unfortunately, this achievement was overshadowed by the decision of Prince Menshikov, the Russian commander, to sink seven of his own warships across the mouth of Sevastopol harbour to deny access to the Allied fleets. The Russian admirals had preferred to attack the Allied fleets directly but their protests had been overruled. Their ships sank as Dundas' fleet appeared off Sevastopol on 23 September.[4]

Menshikov's decision, though seemingly irrational to naval observers at the time, completely changed the nature of the war in the Black Sea. The ships in the Allied fleet were now useless as far as the reduction of Sevastopol was concerned for there could be no major naval engagements nor any attempt to dash quickly into the harbour to help take the fortress by storm. Combined with his earlier opposition to launching the invasion on such short notice and with insufficient intelligence, the incident all but sealed Dundas' fate as commander of the fleet. An irate Graham officially reprimanded him for having spent too much time at the Alma thereby allowing Menshikov the freedom to sink his own ships![5] However unfair these charges may appear, Menshikov's decision did confine the Allied line-of-battle ships to their anchorages for the duration of the war. Moreover, the naval guns and crews from the sunken warships were added to Sevastopol's already formidable batteries. As a result, while there was a perennial shortage of gunpowder throughout the siege, Sevastopol's defence did not suffer from a want of large guns and skilled crews to operate them. A long siege now seemed inevitable.

The fleet settled down to its new role as auxiliary to the army's operations. A squadron under Lyons was assigned to Balaklava harbour to provide immediate security and support for Raglan's army which was encamped on the surrounding hillsides and plains. The bulk of the fleet lay anchored in nearby Kazatch Bay, a natural but undeveloped harbour. In addition to reconnaissance patrols, the fleet assumed management of the harbours in Balaklava and Constantinople and thereby controlled the logistical arrangements between the Crimea and Britain.

The first opportunity for the Anglo–French fleet to engage in a more active role came on 17 October. In conjunction with the armies' simultaneous bombardment of the Russian defence works, the fleets launched an attack on Sevastopol's seaward batteries. While the pace of the firing was furious, the bombardment achieved little and the heavy damages suffered by the fleet confirmed Dundas' view that ships' guns were no match for the massive stone-encased walls of the fortress.[6] The fleet now turned its attention more closely to helping the land attack succeed; Dundas authorized the disembarkation of ships' guns and crews as well as Marines—the so-called 'Naval Brigade'—to bolster Raglan's understrength forces.

The landing was timely for, on 25 October, Menshikov launched a surprise attack on Balaklava which, in spite of the confusion reigning in the British camp, was repulsed bravely by Raglan's troops. Nevertheless, the heavy losses considerably weakened Raglan's already overstretched forces. Eleven days later (5 October), Menshikov launched a second massive attack against the British lines at the Inkerman ridge. This attack was also repulsed but with such heavy losses that the Allied commanders were forced to reassess their position and decided to cancel their own attack scheduled for 8 October.

The grim prospect of a long winter siege now became reality. Locked in by inclement weather, the fleet confined its activities to sorting out the chaotic and congested conditions in Balaklava harbour, to conveying the sick and wounded to hospitals in Constantinople, and to reinforcing the activities of the Naval Brigade onshore. Fortunately, because of its self-contained logistics system, the fleet avoided the tragedy and suffering that plagued Raglan's forces encamped only a few miles from its anchorage. Indeed, were it not for the fleet's efforts to restore order in the army's chaotic logistical system, Raglan's forces probably would have suffered even greater losses by winter's end. Nevertheless, the fleet's efforts were overlooked because of the sensationalistic press coverage given to the army's plight during the harsh winter of 1854–55. Moreover, the navy's operations in the Baltic did little to divert attention from the debacle in the Crimea.

The Admiralty's operations in the Baltic were governed by a much higher sense of public expectation. Indeed, Sir Charles Napier had been selected to command the fleet by Graham on the basis that he possessed the 'Nelson Touch'. Unfortunately, Sir Charles was also known to be difficult, self-promoting and 'too fond of demonstrations on shore, of Dinners and Speechifying'— Sir James decided to take his chances.[7] The fleet sailed for the Baltic on 11 March amidst high hopes and great public fanfare. Alarmed somewhat by these exaggerated expectations, Sir Charles warned his well-wishers that they should 'not expect too much'. Nevertheless, en route to the Baltic, he raised both fear and hope within the fleet with strongly worded signals implying that battle, gore and death awaited it. He drilled his gun crews excessively to the point that the Admiralty had to caution him against running his stocks of shot and powder too low. These antics reinforced his image as a swashbuckling seadog amongst his subordinates; their expectations for action rose accordingly.[8]

These high hopes proved shortlived. It soon became apparent that Napier had little faith in his crews—his reports home were filled with complaints about the shortage of seamen or their inexperience and the inefficiency of his officers. These diatribes seemed to mask another problem. Having rushed into the Baltic, Napier now seemed reluctant to proceed to the Gulf of Finland where the Tsar's premier fleet lay anchored. Rumours alleging that the Russian fleet was divided between its bases at Helsingfors and Kronstadt merely accentuated the crews' bloodlust and Sir Charles' apparent unwillingness to unleash it. Whilst he had entered the Baltic on 21 March, Napier anchored off Hangö, at the mouth of the Gulf of Finland, only on 20 May – a fortnight after it had been free of ice. Sir Charles blamed the delays on the presence of bad weather.[9]

Earlier in mid-April, Napier had despatched a squadron of steamers to patrol the Gulf of Riga and the Estonian and Latvian coasts. He now directed another squadron to blockade the towns along the Finnish coast up to the Ålands archipelago. Frustrated by the long delays and anxious to cut their mark, the officers involved in this operation performed their duties with excessive zeal. In the first week alone, forty-six vessels and large amounts of shipbuilding material were destroyed. The landing parties also antagonized the local Finnish population by indiscriminately confiscating or destroying property. This led to an ambush and firefight at Gamla Carleby on 7 June in which several seamen were killed and injured. A fortnight later, the same ships' companies launched an unauthorized attack on the Russian fortress at Bomardsund.[10] While these actions were undertaken for self-promotional reasons, they illustrate clearly the growing frustration in the fleet with Napier's reluctance to undertake attacks against Russian targets.

Under mounting pressure from Graham, Sir Charles drew up on 20 June a list of options which outlined the fleet's prospects of attacking Russia's fortresses at Bomarsund, Sweaborg and Kronshtadt. He actively discouraged the idea of attacking the latter two naval bases, particularly Kronshtadt, which he felt presented too formidable a challenge given his limited resources. A close-in survey of the fortress a week later confirmed this view.[11] This report cleared the way for an attack on the only feasible option—Bomarsund. Between 8 and 16 August, Napier, in conjunction with his French counterpart, Admiral Parseval, launched a combined assault and bombardment of the fortress. The fortress was captured on 15 August with minimal Allied losses. News of the assault was welcomed in Britain for it amounted to the Allies' first major success against Russia—a good prelude to the much expected attack on Sevastopol. Indeed, many in the Cabinet believed that the operation proved that Russian troops and fortresses could not withstand a concentrated naval attack.[12] Immediately, Graham renewed his pressure on Napier to reconsider the possibility of attacking Sweaborg. To placate the First Lord, Napier, in conjunction with Parseval and Generals Neil and Jones, two engineering liaison officers attached to the combined fleets, conducted a second reconnaissance of Sweaborg. The engineers reported very favourably on the prospects of attack thereby raising expectations in London for an assault on the fortress. Sir Charles was forced to dampen this enthusiasm on the grounds that it was too late in the season, and that the engineers' views represented military rather than naval considerations.[13] Indeed, a joint naval council held on 12 September readily supported this assessment. In any case, Parseval, who shared Napier's views, had ordered some of his ships home and detached yet another squadron five days later. The possibility of launching the attack was a moot point. Following his original instructions, Napier ordered his sail-of-line ships to proceed to Kiel as the weather began to change.[14]

The news of these withdrawals, combined with Napier's harsh criticism of the engineers' reports, convinced Graham that Sir Charles was deliberately abandoning his command to forestall the possibility of launching any late operations. Correspondence between the two men deteriorated into a series of reprimands and acrimonious responses. Napier became convinced that he was being made a scapegoat by the Admiralty, and particularly by Graham, to assuage the public's outcry for victories. His communiqués became high-strung and accusatory if not altogether threatening. Finally, on 22 December, the Admiralty ordered Sir Charles to strike his flag—the naval lords had had enough of Napier's 'indiscreet letter writing'.[15]

The Admiralty had no intention of repeating the mistakes it made in the Baltic in the forthcoming season. While censuring Napier for his unacceptable behaviour, the naval lords were fully aware that his criticism of the fleet's material shortcomings were justified and that they had limited its offensive capabilities. Accordingly, Graham enacted an emergency construction programme, the 'October Plan', to rectify most of the obvious shortages. Provision was made for the construction of forty gunboats, twenty mortar vessels and five armoured floating batteries. While these vessels alone would not make up all of the fleet's needs for blockading purposes, the Admiralty hoped that, coupled with a number of similar ships promised by the French Government, the flotilla would allow the fleet to attack, and possibly demolish, Kronshtadt.[16]

British production, however, was unequal to the set quotas. As the Admiralty's shipyards were already overburdened with refitting and repair work as well as normal construction, the new projects had to be farmed out to private builders ensuring further delays. The shortage of steam plants in Britain hamstrung the construction programme as the Admiralty was competing directly with the private sector. In addition, a good number of vessels and equipment originally destined for Baltic service were channelled off to the Black Sea. It was hardly surprising, therefore, that at the start of the summer campaign season of 1855, the Baltic fleet had received only fifteen gunboats and a similar number of mortar vessels, together with the promise of two floating batteries —a far cry from Graham's original estimates.[17]

The construction problems at home were compounded by the fact that the French Government back-pedalled on a number of its commitments. The quotas set in the October Plan had been premised on the assumption that France would provide twenty steam gunboats and ten mortar vessels for Baltic operations.[18] Once these arrangements had been concluded, however, it became apparent that the French Government began to waver on its commitments. Depressed by the news emanating from the Crimea, Napoleon III expressed a strong desire to withdraw his naval forces from the Baltic altogether and to use them instead in the Black Sea. As the new year progressed, it became obvious that he considered the Baltic a mere sideshow to Crimean operations and had no intention of providing gunboats for the Baltic. The protests of Sir Charles Wood, Graham's successor at the Admiralty, fell on deaf ears. As Lord Cowley, the British Ambassador in Paris confirmed, 'The fact is the Emperor's thoughts are all concentrated upon the Black Sea; the North interests him very little.' To all intents and purposes, an assault on Kronshtadt in 1855 was a dead issue.[19]

This provided little consolation for the Baltic Fleet's new commander, Rear-Admiral Richard Dundas, who was very conscious of the high expectations and pressure under which Napier had operated and which, ultimately, ruined his career. As *The Times* warned ominously, 'no doubt he (Dundas) knows that he has to do more than Napier. If he does not accomplish more, he will certainly find himself next November under orders to lower his flag...'.[20] A dark cloud hung over Dundas' flagship, the *Duke of Wellington*, as it sailed from Spithead bound for the Baltic on 20 March.

Upon on his arrival at Faro Sound on 8 May, Dundas immediately organized surveys of Riga and the Helsingfors–Sweaborg complex. Formidable new batteries had been constructed at both sites and on the islands surrounding the latter fortress. A fortnight later, Dundas surveyed Kronshtadt where his observations confirmed Napier's assessment that it was impregnable. The channels leading into the fortress had been mined with 'infernal machines' and its landward defences had been considerably strengthened against a land-based attack. All incoming ships would be heavily exposed to enfilading fire, making a close-inshore attack extremely risky. As Sulivan observed, 'the more we see of this place, the less likely it is that we can do or even attempt anything'.[21]

Dundas also informed the Admiralty that he could not mount effective blockades of the major ports and coastline in the Gulfs of Bothnia, Finland and Riga without more ships, preferably steam-powered cruisers. His means were enhanced somewhat by the arrival of the French squadron under Rear-Admiral Penaud on 1 June. The French commander quickly pointed out, however, that he expected no reinforcements by way of gunboats or floating batteries.[22] Thus, in spite of the fact that a small flotilla of block-ships, gunboats, and mortar vessels was then en route to the fleet's anchorage at Nargen, it was apparent once again that the season's operations were going to be governed by material constraints. As if to emphasize this point, eight of the fourteen gunboats which Graham had allocated specifically for Baltic service were making their way at that moment to the Crimea in support of combined operations in the Sea of Azov.[23]

In reality, the situation was hardly better in the Black Sea where the fleet, now under Lyons' control, would soon find its operations dominated by French operational priorities. In mid-February, the Admiralty ordered Sir Edmund to occupy the Sea of Azov once the ice broke up and before Russia had an opportunity to resupply the Crimea from that source. The success of the operation would hinge on the Allies' ability to overcome the strategic fortress at Kerch which controlled access into the sea. Lyons requested the army commanders to lend him 10–12,000 troops for a fortnight to take Kerch and other Azov fortified towns. Canrobert refused and Raglan was unable to spare sufficient troops to make up the difference. Under orders from Paris, Canrobert also refused several requests by Raglan to launch immediate assaults on Sevastopol's outlying defences.[24]

It took another three months of endless haggling and several false starts before Lyons was finally able to sail for Kerch on 22 May. The breakthrough came when Canrobert was replaced by General Pelissier who, defying Napoleon III's direct orders, loaned Sir Edmund the required troops. The expedition which swept the Azov in search of supplies that could bolster Russian resistance in the Crimea was immensely successful. In just four days, the Azov squadron destroyed 246 vessels and at least 5 million rations of corn and flour. These results were enhanced further by raids against Taganrog, Ghiesk and Marienpol. After the gloom of winter, the news from the Azov created an air of renewed faith and exhilaration in official circles in London. Even the Queen could 'really think of *nothing* else'.[25]

The euphoria, however, proved short-lived. Inspired by the moment, the Admiralty ordered Lyons to extend his operations against Anapa and other Russian fortresses on the Circassian and Georgian coasts. Napoleon III, however, incensed by Pelissier's insubordination and consumed by the idea of

launching a major inland campaign to envelope Sevastopol, refused to sanction
other diversionary raids. His recall of the French troops from the Azov seriously hampered the effectiveness of the squadron's operations.[26]

For his part, Pelissier was now intent on demanding his pound of British
flesh in return for his earlier co-operation. As the Cabinet would learn much to
its despair, this meant that once again the fleet's operations would have to take
a back seat to the land campaign. More important, it meant that the battlefield
would be covered with blood and human debris as Pelissier stubbornly followed his single-minded dream of capturing Sevastopol and a field marshal's
baton by launching a series of costly assaults on Sevastopol's external defences
in late May and June. These failures, particularly the disastrous assault on the
Malakoff and Redan batteries on 18 June, combined with Raglan's sudden
death a week later, overshadowed whatever hope the easy gains made in the
Sea of Azov had created. With operations in the Crimea so obviously dependent on French manpower and completely at the mercy of Napoleon III's or
Pelissier's whims, the Cabinet's highest hopes remained focused in the Baltic
where, despite material shortages, the Admiralty still retained the upper hand
in the combined fleets' movements.

In the meantime, Dundas and his colleagues had chosen initially to limit
their fleet's activities to manning a strict blockade of the Finnish and Russian
coasts while searching for alternative targets to Kronshtadt. With this priority
in mind, the fleet's surveyor, Captain Sulivan, performed another close survey
of Sweaborg and its island defences. Although the fortress had been considerably strengthened since the first survey in May, Sulivan was convinced that it
could be attacked successfully by prudent positioning of the ships. With so few
options to consider, Dundas adopted the proposal. Admiral Penaud preferred to
bombard the adjoining fortified town of Helsingfors instead but he was overruled by a joint council of the naval commanders.[27]

The attack on Sweaborg, begun on 10 August, lasted two days, during
which time the fleet's steamers and gunboats coupled with the mortar vessels
concentrated their fire on Gustavfard and Vargon islands destroying most of
the building complexes within the protective walls. On the second day, the
British mortars failed, considerably reducing the effectiveness of the bombardment on Swarto island and the attack as a whole which was abandoned on 13
August. In addition to the damage inflicted on the islands, French intelligence
reported that Sweaborg's dockyard and stores were destroyed, that all the powder magazines had been blown up, and that twenty-three vessels had been
burnt with a similar number severely damaged.[28] The comparative ease with
which the Allies had attacked the Tsar's second largest fortress in the Baltic
dealt a significant blow to the prestige of the Russian Government.

Predictably, the early reports of the assault encouraged optimism in London
that Sweaborg could be reduced completely. As a result, on 21 August, the
Admiralty despatched sixteen mortars and a large supply of shells to the fleet.
Dundas, however, had already sent the mortar vessels home believing that they

would no longer be useful. Consequently, he informed the Admiralty that no further major operations could be undertaken because of the lateness of the season. The arrival of the new equipment would cause embarrassment and rouse unjustified expectations at home. Accordingly, the Admiralty recalled the ships, thereby accepting that, aside from the continuation of the blockade and minor actions, the campaign in the Baltic was at an end. Once again the Cabinet switched its attention to the Black Sea.[29]

In the interim, the Azov squadron, under Commander Sherard Osborn, had continued to wreak havoc in Sevastopol's lines of communication. The squadron destroyed stocks of dried fish and grain as well as bridges linking the region to the Crimean peninsula. On one particular raid against Taganrog on 6 August, a stack of forage and grain between 50 and 80 feet high and covering a square mile was destroyed.[30] These attacks were beginning to have a telling effect on Sevastopol's defence, particularly the growing shortage of powder and ammunition. Pellisier's strategy of attrition was also beginning to take its toll as the continuous bombardments of Sevastopol's outer trenches and batteries were exacting high Russian casualties.

To slow the Allies' advance, Prince Gorchakov, Sevastopol's new commander, launched an assault on 16 August across the Chernaia River against the northernmost sector of the Allied lines. Alerted by the timely arrival of intelligence from London warning of the impending attack, the French and Sardinian troops defending the lines inflicted between eight and ten thousand losses on Gorchakov's troops.[31] Coming as it did within a week of the Sweaborg bombardment, the Russian defeat greatly increased the Allies' enthusiasm for a general assault on Sevastopol. Napoleon III gave Pelissier a free hand to press on with his plans and the Allies maintained their steady bombardment of the Russian defenceworks in preparation for the final assault set for 8 September.

It was the success of the French assault on the Malakoff battery on that day which convinced Gorchakov to withdraw from the beleaguered fortress. The simultaneous British attack on the Redan battery was decimated by Russian gunfire and failed. The outcome was greeted with dismay in London reinforcing as it did the image of French superiority and British incompetency. Fearing that the French would also take the Redan battery, Clarendon complained, 'Now I suppose the French . . . will have a double-crow over us and we may expect heartburnings and recriminations.'[32]

The French success at the Malakoff also deprived Lyons of any hope he may have entertained for a final showdown with the remainder of the Russian Black Sea fleet, for Gorchakov ordered the sinking of the remaining warships and merchantmen in Sevastopol harbour. Thus, in spite of the continuing success of the raids in the Sea of Azov and a successful bombardment of and combined operation against the Russian fortress at Kinburn on 17 October, Sir Edmund never achieved the great naval victory that he believed destiny owed him. From this point onwards, the French showed great reluctance to proceed with further operations in the Black Sea and only lukewarm interest in a possible attack against Kronshtadt in the coming season. Rather, Napoleon III's attention was now focused on the proceedings in Vienna where an end to the war was being negotiated.

In spite of the mistakes committed, the material shortages encountered and the French tendency to play down the value of naval operations and to resist Britain's requests for further combined operations, Britain's naval operational achievements were considerable. The Admiralty had been able to mount operations in four theatres of war separated by some 4500 miles at the greatest point. In addition to mounting blockades in these regions covering thousands of miles of coastline, the Navy launched, or aided in, successful attacks against two of Russia's three principal naval fortresses, kept her naval forces completely blocked in their ports and caused serious dislocation of the Russian economy. In addition, the navy helped to keep Raglan's army alive during the terrible winter of 1854–55. Though it did not deliver another grand victory like Trafalgar, the Royal Navy's achievements using an essentially peacetime establishment, were hardly inconsequential. Given this realization, one is inclined to ask why then were these achievements so casually overlooked during a war that received an enormous amount of coverage both in the press and in subsequent historiography?

PERCEPTION AND REALITY

The Royal Navy's actions were inclined to be overlooked for one essential reason—they lacked colour. As the press complained at the time, the fleet's activities were unattended by sufficient bloodletting and losses to be noteworthy or pleasing.[33] Groomed in the mythology of the last great war and of Nelson's legendary naval victories, the public had come to expect similar success from their naval contemporaries. Alas, the popular heroes of the day, the flamboyant Sir Charles Napier and Sir Edmund Lyons, failed to deliver. The public felt duped, and in its frustration turned on its heroes and then dismissed them from common memory. Thus superficially, the Royal Navy's essential problem was that it entered the war in the shadow of Nelson's legacy and, when the war ended in 1856, it left no legacy of its own.

In their search for an explanation of the fleets' seemingly lacklustre performance, critics overlooked the fact that human behaviour is governed as much by irrational as by rational motives. They were inclined to view the behaviour of individuals as either acceptable or unacceptable and judged accordingly. Thus, Napier was criticized for his 'inaction'; superficially, it seemed that he deliberately avoided undertaking any major assaults against the Russians. It was presumed that he did this consciously from choice, irrespective of the impact it would have on his career and those of his followers. As Delane, the editor of *The Times*, warned him, 'For your own sake then, and for that of your friends who have so long supported you and asserted your claims, do make an effort, cease to find difficulties—any old woman can find them.'[34] Delane and other critics failed to consider whether there were other, less obvious factors behind Sir Charles' behaviour, which seemed so totally at odds with his public image. Indeed, had they troubled themselves to do so, their understanding of events in the Baltic would have been considerably enhanced and their criticism softened.

Within a week of sailing from Portsmouth, Napier was at odds with his superiors. Issued with conflicting instructions from the Admiralty and the Foreign Office, Sir Charles prematurely sailed his fleet through the Belts leading into the Baltic Sea. This action confirmed fears within the Cabinet that the touchy old admiral was inclined to act rashly, without authorization, and had to be reined in. For his part, Napier was annoyed at the mild reprimand he received, yet he assumed from the incident that he was not expected to undertake any independent action without first clearing it with the Admiralty.[35] Thus, while the Cabinet fully expected Sir Charles to rush headlong towards Russia looking for a fight, he surprised and frustrated everyone by refusing to act without clearing his every move. Though it went largely unnoticed at the time, his apparent hesitance to act was an early indication that Sir Charles was also undergoing a severe personal crisis.

In the weeks that followed, Napier seemed reluctant to approach the Russian coast and was almost obsessed with bad weather or heavy fog, yet his captains appeared untroubled by the same conditions. Privately, his subordinates began to complain of Sir Charles' inability to maintain order in fleet manoeuvres, his indecisiveness and his inclination to find fault in his senior captains. The fleet's surveyor observed that Napier seemed 'very nervous, afraid of the land, and, I think, seems weighed down with the responsibility (he always has a nervous twitching of his lips and face), and yet will not be easily advised by those around him but will have his own way'.[36] Clearly, Sir Charles was suffering from depression. This was well evident during an inshore survey of Sweaborg on 30 June, when he fell 'directly asleep' in his deck chair and nodded incessantly during a discussion that followed. The incident contributed further to the feeling that it was impossible 'to hope for much from a leader in his condi-tion'.[37] Indeed, as a close confidante intimated, Napier was troubled throughout his professional career by simultaneous notions of his own grandeur and achievement and a nagging lack of self-confidence. From his correspondence it is apparent, too, that he was obsessed with the fear that his enemies were out to ruin his reputation and honour.[38] While he had been able to keep these conflicts under control in the past, the stress caused by his assignment in the Baltic accentuated his condition and allowed it to overcome him. Thus, his difficult, highly-strung, and erratic behaviour were all symptoms of his depressed state.

There is little doubt, too, that Napier's decision to oppose an assault on Sweaborg was heavily influenced by his despondency. He had already made up his mind in mid-June that he would not attack the fortress; rejecting Neil's and Jones' reports in late August and resisting pressure from London thereafter were mere formalities. Indeed, it was not until Sulivan made a detailed survey of Sweaborg in late September that the technical and physical reasons against an attack could be verified.[39] Since in reality there were no major targets for Napier to attack, his 'inactivity' was therefore largely the result of his mental and emotional instability.

Given these observations, the question naturally arises: was Sir Charles fit to command the Baltic Fleet? The Admiralty certainly would not have appointed Napier had it foreseen the problems that arose. Nevertheless, initially there were no obvious indications that he was suffering from mental or emotional problems. The only objections of substance raised against his appointment were based on his difficult character and his past outspoken criticism of the Admiralty. No one doubted Sir Charles' courage under fire or his competence to command a fleet. Moreover, from a naval perspective, none of his actions warranted his removal from command. Even his decision to resist attacking Sweaborg, though based on inconclusive evidence, was perfectly sound. It was not the decision that the public, ignorant of Napier's personal crisis, wanted to hear, however, and consequently he was crucified publicly for his 'inaction'.

The public's perception of the Admiralty's operations in the Black Sea was equally distorted. Dundas was extremely unpopular in both public and official circles because he dared question the Cabinet's wisdom of invading the Crimea without sufficient resources or intelligence concerning Russia's military forces in the region. In contrast, Lyons was idolized by the public and the Cabinet and particularly by Graham, who relied on him to enforce his operational priorities. Indeed, Newcastle, the war minister, went so far as to encourage Raglan to encourage a mutiny against Dundas if he thought it would expedite the assault on Sevastopol![40] It was popularly believed that if anyone could bring success in the Crimea, it was Sir Edmund, who bore an uncanny likeness to the great Nelson. This open prejudice against Dundas and bias towards Lyons strongly influenced the way operations in the Black Sea were conducted and events were later interpreted. The results were often disastrous.

Following the flank march to Balaklava, Lyons had all but usurped Dundas' authority within the fleet by his natural elan and by his deliberate efforts to subvert the latter's authority. Indeed, Sir Edmund enjoyed a special status amongst the Allied commanders which allowed him to have an inordinate say in the army's operations. Sensing that the siege was bogging down, Lyons prodded the generals to bombard Sevastopol as a prelude to attacking the fortress. Anxious to play a part in the action, he also volunteered the combined fleets' services to launch a simultaneous attack on Sevastopol's seaward-facing batteries. Neither Dundas nor his French counterpart Admiral Hamelin thought the attack wise or prudent given the strength of the stone-encased batteries. Sir Edmund also pressed Dundas to land the Naval Brigade to help bolster Raglan's artillery units.[41]

The assault launched on 17 October began in confusion when, early that morning, Admiral Hamelin and General Canrobert requested that the combined fleets be repositioned further south and at a greater distance from their targets. From this position, the fleets could cover only a portion of the target, but they would be less exposed to direct fire from Sevastopol's batteries. Dundas protested against these last minute changes, but was forced to concede when Hamelin threatened to act alone. Lyons created a major scene over the changes and, to please both parties, Dundas allowed Sir Edmund to attack Sevastopol's northern defence works with his squadron as originally planned while he stood with the rest of the fleet on Hamelin's van.[42]

Lyons' attack resulted in near disaster as his squadron was raked by devastating crossfire from the fortress' batteries. Dundas was forced to release more ships to help deflect the fire from the beleaguered squadron. One ship, the *Albion*, was reduced to a 'wreck' and, along with another, had to be sent to Constantinople for repairs. The *London* was forced to withdraw from the engagement after being set on fire three times while the *Rodney* ran aground during the action and had most of her rigging shot away. Lyons' flagship, the *Agamemnon*, caught fire twice and was hit 240 times. In comparison, the damage suffered by the Russian forts was nominal. Tragically, the attack had been in vain. Unbeknown to the admirals, the generals had called off their bombardment some two hours before the fleets went into action when a chance Russian shot scored a direct hit on a French magazine, and touched off a massive explosion causing high casualties.[43]

In his official report of the action, Dundas consciously played down the damage suffered by the fleet, fearing that the Russians would claim the setback 'as a victory'. And, while he praised Lyons' conduct of the inshore attack, he generously made no mention of Sir Edmund's insubordination.[44] Unfortunately, the prejudice against him in Britain was running so high that it completely distorted the public's perception of these events. Even those critical of the war, like the diarist Greville, complained, 'If Lyons had been in command, he probably would have declined to make it (the attack), and he could have ventured to exercise his own discretion, which Dundas could not.' Indeed, even Graham, who favoured the attack, blamed the fiasco on Dundas' decision to loan the Naval Brigade to Raglan. Few questioned whether the attacks should have been undertaken in the first place, and all seemed intent on blaming Dundas for Lyons' personal initiatives![45]

Thus, Hamelin's decision to reposition his fleet produced some rather baffling results. First, it totally distorted the public's perception of why the attack failed. Second, it drove yet another nail in Dundas' coffin as commander of the fleet. Third, it offset Lyons' planned attack and may have been responsible for reducing the effectiveness of the combined fleets' firepower thereby practically ensuring the failure of the attack. Conversely, it could equally be argued that, by forcing the fleet's redeployment, he spared it even greater damage and loss. After all, even Dundas' flagship, the *Britannia*, suffered seventy hits and was set ablaze in spite of its great distance from Sevastopol's batteries.[46]

The attack produced another unexpected result. In spite of its failure, it convinced Sevastopol's defenders that the Allies were priming for a major assault against them soon and forced them to look for ways to forestall it. This was the logic behind Menshikov's attack on Balaklava a week later. Designed to disrupt the momentum of the Allies' preparations, the attack caused a great deal of alarm, panic and confusion in the British camp where it soon became apparent that there was very little central control over the direction of the battle as each British unit fought to save itself. This was especially so of the ill-fated charge of the Light Brigade where the delivery of a garbled message led to such tragic and immortalized results. Though it was insufficiently realized at the time, Balaklava demonstrated that Britain's leaders were slowly losing control of the war effort.

Nowhere was this more evident than in Menshikov's massive second attack against the British positions on the Inkermann Ridge on 5 November which pre-empted the Allies' own planned assault by three days. Curiously, Menshikov had been forced to alter his original plans at the last minute by an order from St Petersburg which directed him to concentrate his attack on the Inkermann. While his superiors had no way of realizing this, Raglan had reduced his forces in the region a few days earlier to reinforce other sections of his lines in preparation for the Allied attack. Chance, therefore, had cast Menshikov a lucky die and, though his attack was very poorly co-ordinated and failed to evict the Allies from their defences, it inflicted sufficient casualties in the Allied camp to convince Canrobert and Raglan to abandon their own assault.[47] This ensured that the siege would run its painful course throughout the winter and, also, that the fleet's operations would be tied directly to that siege for the duration of the war.

The two battles were viewed with great alarm in Britain as concern for the heavy casualties far exceeded any euphoria generated by the brave defence put up by Raglan's troops. As Clarendon lamented: 'Everyone is downhearted about the victory (if it was one) and feels that another such attack, would finally smash us, and then will come the monster catastrophe—a horrible compound of Afghanistan and Corunna'.[48]

An unnerving premonition of doom dominated the British perception of their war effort at this stage. Given the emotional sensations these unfortunate incidents aroused, occurring as they did in quick succession, it is easy to understand why observers were inclined to overlook the important services the Royal Navy provided during the war even in spite of the mishaps.

Noticeably, all of these events were touched off by rational human choices, yet the consequences were all chaotic from Britain's perspective. When in their turn, these results were exposed to uncontrollable natural forces, in particular inclement weather, the very existence of Britain's expeditionary forces would be threatened. Nine days after the Battle of Inkermann, a storm with hurricane force winds ravaged the Allied camps, stripping away tents and shelters, and reduced the battlefield, roads and the bivouac areas into a sea of mud. The accompanying high seas destroyed thirty laden transports and three warships anchored in an exposed roadstead outside Balaklava harbour. Three hundred seamen and tons of warm clothing, supplies of food, forage and equipment which Raglan's Army now desperately needed were lost at sea.[49]

The storm, which signalled the start of a particularly hard winter, could not have occurred at a worse time. The transports had been anchored outside the harbour because Menshikov's attacks on Balaklava and the Inkermann had forced its evacuation. Since then, all semblance of order in the crowded port collapsed into chaos—there was a chronic shortage of berthing space. Balaklava harbour was too small to contain the traffic necessary to meet the army's logistic needs. Here again, fate had dealt Britain another unfortunate blow, for when the decision to undertake the flank march was made, Lyons, recognizing the difficulty of unloading heavy military equipment in an open roadstead, rushed in before the French and claimed the harbour for Britain's use. Despite the fact that Sir Edmund's own flagship could barely navigate its way into the harbour, the Cabinet was elated with his far-sighted coup.[50]

Lyons' action led, in turn, to other unplanned consequences. To maintain control over the harbour, Raglan was forced to man the most difficult sector of the Allied defence lines in spite of his numerically inferior forces; he thereby unwittingly exposed his troops to the brunt of Menshikov's attacks. In contrast, the French, with superior forces occupied defence lines which safely abutted the sea on one end and the British trenches on the other. Moreover, forced to fend for themselves for landing facilities, the French, quite by accident, discovered Kamiesch Bay which, though less protected, offered ample space for the loading and unloading of transports. In gratitude, the French nicknamed Kamiesch the 'Bay of Providence', for it served their needs well during the winter; in contrast, the name Balaklava became synonymous with filth, disorder, and the stench of neglect and death.[51]

Attempts to reverse the chronic problems in the harbour were handicapped because the casualties suffered by the army during Menshikov's attacks prevented Raglan from sparing the manpower needed to help clear unloaded cargo. Moreover, in its efforts to quickly compensate for these losses and those suffered as a result of the storm, the Government only served to increase the chaos in Balaklava as scores of transports descended on a harbour designed originally to serve a sleepy holiday and fishing village. Thus, as literally hundreds of tons of material sat idly on the docks or in the holds of idle transports, Raglan's army slowly perished of exhaustion, cold, or disease on the heights overlooking the congested harbour. This was the image of the war which most dominated the public's impression of the war and which has strongly influenced the historiography of the conflict. Noticeably, it was not the series of interconnected actions leading up to this unfortunate state of affairs which caught the public's attention; rather, all that mattered was the chaotic result.

PERCEPTION ON A HIGHER PLANE

From these observations it is obvious that the British public had a simplistic perception of what occurred in the campaign theatres during the Russian War. Much of what they understood about specific events was based on press reports, hearsay, and whatever could be gleaned from their correspondence with relatives involved in the war. Collectively, these sources tended to emphasize the more sensational occurrences without providing the public with an in-depth understanding of the way individual incidents randomly combined to create these events. Such knowledge would probably have generated more sympathy for the difficulties involved in fighting the war. Without it, the public's inclination to focus on what was going wrong or what was not happening far exceeded its concern for what went right or what was being achieved. The predominance of the sensational and the negative accentuated the public's crisis of expectation—it had expected great things at the outset of the war and suffered anguish and disappointment instead.

Beyond the lack of visible achievements, however, there was a deeper, more fundamental factor affecting the public's attitude—its expectations had also been conditioned by the positivistic intellectual trends of the day. The literate public's conception of their world and universe was greatly simplified by the tendency of contemporary economists, scientists and philosophers to reduce the behaviour of all phenomena to highly mechanistic laws, principles and theorems. Indeed, war itself was being subjected during this period to the same mechanistic-based investigation by European military theorists like Clausewitz and Jomini and, later, the highly influential American naval theorist, Alfred Mahan.

Coupled with this trend was the mesmerizing effect which Britain's material achievements of the past century had on Britain's leaders and the public. There can be no doubt that the hopes of the nation at large were founded on the imagined advantages that Britain's industrial and technological superiority would provide over Russia. Indeed, the mid-Victorians were very conscious of the lead their country possessed in these fields, more especially because of the recent attention drawn to it by the Great Exhibition in Hyde Park in 1851 where Britain's industrial and technological achievements were put on display for the world to admire.

Thus, the British public was highly conscious that the war it was about to enter represented a new age in warfare, one that would be governed as much by superior scientific and technological knowledge and capability as by the traditional reliance on courage in the face of enemy fire. And, indeed, when onlookers had gathered at Portsmouth to send off Napier's fleet to the Baltic, it was not the calibre of the individuals controlling these machines that impressed them so much as the sheer numbers and size of the steam-powered warships, with their ominous-looking armaments and the clouds of smoke billowing from their smokestacks. It is significant in this respect that the Admiralty's hopes in the Baltic in the following year were pinned almost entirely on the types of armament and steam-powered warships it had been able to muster. There was very little appreciation at that time that while technology changes the way wars are fought, it does not change the essentially chaotic nature of war itself.

This reality, brought home by war correspondents reporting the carnage, the mishaps, the missed opportunities, and the frustrations on the scene, presented the public with an image of a war which was altogether different from the one that it believed was its natural right to expect. It was inconceivable that this cumulative wealth, material strength, and knowledge had not allowed Britain's forces to overcome easily any obstacles that tradition-bound and industrially under-developed Russia created during the war. Exasperation with this situation was well captured by Palmerston who, during a Cabinet meeting called to discuss the army's desperate plight, angrily exclaimed: 'But why should this be?'[52] No one could provide him or the public with a satisfactory answer. And, in anger, the public turned against specific individuals, against a defective 'system', and against its leaders— the Aberdeen Government— in the search for someone or something to blame for its confusion and disappointment. Somewhere in this emotional melee, the importance of the Royal Navy's operations was lost.

The British public failed to see meaning in the war because it consciously rejected the opportunity to do so and, in the process, its perception of events was extremely distorted. It did not consider that human behaviour is governed as much by irrational as rational motives, or that machines, too, can break down or have their own limitations. Appreciating this would have allowed the war effort to be seen more realistically and discourage the inclination to examine events as disjointed, isolated entities rather than as parts of a larger complex whole. The public would have been more prepared to accept that all choices and decisions when combined randomly with other acts, can produce negative, as well as positive, results and, sometimes, may even lead to total chaos and disaster. It would have appreciated also the role which natural forces, such as the weather, might have on the development of events. Finally, it would have realized that this process of random combination never really stops; with Hegelian logic it continues to roll onwards creating yet new combinations in the process.

The public lacked a broader intellectual framework for interpreting the events which unfolded and which, ultimately, were responsible for obscuring its perception of the navy's role in the conflict. That framework which physicists today collectively refer to as the 'science of complexity' accepts incidents of chaos as regular phenomena in nature alongside elements of order. As this brief account illustrates, both elements were abundant in the Russian War. Utilizing this new intellectual framework would help to make the phenomenon of war more understandable while, at the same time, emphasizing that it is, by far, the most chaotic and complex of all human endeavours.

NOTES

1. 'Memo on the recall of Pensioners', Sir James Graham, 6 February 1854 and 'Notification,' 20
    Feb. 1854, Admiralty Papers, 1/5632, [Public Record Office]; A. Otway, *Autobiography and
    Journals of Admiral Lord Clarence Paget* (London, 1896), pp 78–9; H.N. Sulivan (ed.), *Life and
    Letters of the late Admiral Sir Bartholomew James Sulivan* (London, 1896), p 121; G.B. Earp,
    The History of the Baltic Campaign of 1854 (London, 1857), pp 13–4.
2. Russell to Graham, 15 Jan. 1854, Graham Papers, MS. 44, [University Library, Cambridge].
3. D. Bonner Smith and A.C. Dewar, *Russian War, 1854. Baltic and Black Sea Official
    Correspondence* (London, 1943), pp 258–9, 246–8, quoting: 'Orders issued by Vice-Admiral
    Dundas,' 1 May 1854, Enclosure in No. 16; Newcastle to Lord Commissioners, 29 Mar. 1854,
    No. 3; Lord Commissioners to Dundas, 30 Mar. 1854, No. 5.
4. Ibid, pp.319–22. Quoting: Dundas to the Secretary of the Admiralty, 21, 23, and 24 Sept. 1854,
    Nos. 55, 57–8; J. Curtiss, *The Russian Army under Nicholas I, 1822–1855* (Durham, 1965),
    p 332.
5. Bonner Smith and Dewar, *The Russian War, 1854,* pp 338–9. Quoting: Secretary to the Admiralty
    to Dundas, 13 Oct. 1854, No. 68.
6. Ibid., pp 325–6, 339–40. Quoting: Dundas to the Secretary to the Admiralty, 3 and 18 Oct. 1854,
    Nos. 62 and 69; Lyons to Dundas, 1 Oct. 1854, Dundas Papers, MS. 60/018/DND 11, [National
    Maritime Museum]; Dundas to Graham, 18 Oct. 1854, Graham Papers, MS. 45.
7. Graham to Clarendon, 6 Oct. 1853, Clarendon Papers, Dep. C4, [Bodleian Library, Oxford];
    Graham to Clarendon, 8 Mar. 1854, Graham Papers, MS. 44.
8. H.N. Williams, *The Life and Letters of Admiral Sir Charles Napier, K.C.B. 1786–1860* (London,
    1917), p 261; Otway, *Autobiography and Journals of Admiral Lord Clarence Paget*, pp 80–4;
    Berkeley to Napier, 4 Apr. 1854, Napier Papers, Add. MS. 40,024, [British Library].
9. H.N. Williams, *Life and Letters of Admiral Napier*, pp 265–72; G.B. Earp, *The Baltic Campaign*,
    pp 136–7; A. Otway, *Autobiography and Journals*, pp 87–8, 91–5; D. Bonner Smith, *The Russian
    War, 1854,* pp 50, 54–5. Quoting: Napier to Secretary to the Admiralty, 18 Apr. and 20 May
    1854, Nos. 11 and 14.
10. Sulivan (ed), *Life and Letters of the late Admiral Sir Bartholomew James Sulivan*, p 295; A.
    Otway, *Autobiography and Journals*, p. 97; W.L. Clowes, *The Royal Navy. A History from the
    Earliest Times to the Present* (London, 1901), IV, p 417; Bonner Smith and Dewar, *Russian War,
    1854,* pp 63–80, 82–5. Quoting: Napier to Secretary to the Admiralty, 18 Jun. 1854, No. 21a and
    enclosure 5, and Hall to Plumridge, 22 and 23 Jun 1854, enclosures 3 and 4 in No. 23a
11. Earp, Baltic Campaign, pp 186–7; H.N. Williams, *Life and Letters of Admiral Napier*, pp 304–5;
    H.N. Sulivan, *Life and Letters*, p 189; Bonner Smith and Dewar, *The Russian War, 1854*, pp 85–7.
    Quoting: Sulivan to Napier, 28 Jun. 1854, enclosure in No. 24.
12. Palmerston to Clarendon, 22 and 23 Aug. 1854, Clarendon Papers, Dep. C15; Graham to Napier,
    15 and 22 Aug. 1854, Napier Papers. Add. MS. 40,025; G.B. Earp, **Baltic Campaign**, p 394; J.
    Martineau, *The Life of Henry Pelham, Fifth Duke of Newcastle 1811–1864* (London, 1908),
    pp 163– 4. Quoting: Newcastle to Raglan, 21 Aug. 1854.
13. Bonner Smith and Dewar, Russian War, 1854, pp 111–2, 115–8. Quoting: 'Report of
    Brigadier-General Jones on Sweaborg,' 27 Aug. 1854, enclosure in No. 33, and Niel to D'Hilliers,
    1 Sept. 1854, enclosure 2 in No. 35; Napier to Secretary to the Admiralty, 29 Aug. 1854,
    ADM[miralty Papers] 1/5625, [Public Record Office].
14. Bonner Smith and Dewar, *The Russian War, 1854*, pp 121–3, 125–30. Quoting: Napier to the
    Secretary to the Admiralty, 13, 18, and 19 Sept. 1854, Nos. 39 and enclosure, and 42 and enclo-
    sures.
15. Graham to Aberdeen, 5 Oct. 1854, Aberdeen Papers, MS. 43, 191, [British Library]; Napier to
    Berkeley, 10 Oct. 1854 and Napier to Graham, 6 Nov. 1854, Napier Papers, 30/16/12; H.N.
    Williams, *Life and Letters of Admiral Napier*, pp 378–9, 384; Bonner Smith and Dewar, *The
    Russian War, 1854*, pp 12–2, 187–8. Quoting: Napier to the Secretary to the Admiralty, 13 Sept.
    1854, No. 39; Secretary to the Admiralty to Napier, 22 and 26 Dec. 1854, Nos. 95 and 97.
16. 'Memorandum by Sir James Graham, 30 Sept. 1854, ADM 1/5632; J. Baxter, *The Introduction of
    the Ironclad Warship* (Hamden, 1968), pp 70–6.
17. W.L. Clowes, *The Royal Navy*, IV, p 478.
18. J. Baxter, *Introduction of the Ironclad Warship*, pp 70–6.
19. Cowley to Clarendon, 11 Nov. 1854, Cowley Papers, F[oreign] O[ffice] Papers] 519/4 [Public

Record Office]; Wood to Cowley, 14 and 16 May 1855, and Cowley to Wood, 21 May and 20 Jun. 1855, Halifax Papers, Add. MS. 49562 and 49555 respectively, [British Library].

20. *The Times*, 20 Mar. 1855.
21. H.N. Sulivan, *Life and Letters*, pp 291–6; D. Bonner Smith, *The Russian War, 1855. Baltic Sea Official Correspondence* (London, 1944), pp 59–61. Quoting: Dundas to Secretary to the Admiralty, 4 Jun. 1855, No. 14.
22. Dundas to Wood, 21 May, 4 and 13 Jun 1855, Halifax Papers, Add MS 49533.
23. W.L. Clowes, *The Royal Navy, IV* p 478.
24. A.C. Dewar, *Russian War, 1855. Black Sea Official Correspondence* (London, 1944), pp 72–4. Quoting: Secretary to the Admiralty to Lyons, 19 Feb. 1855, No. 23; Wood to Lyons, 9 Mar. 1855, Halifax Papers, Add MS 49562; G. Douglas and G. Ramsay, *The Panmure Papers* (London, 1908), I, pp 120–4, 130–1, 141–2. Quoting: Stewart to Panmure, 24 and 26 Mar. 1855 and Raglan to Panmure, 27 Mar. and 3 Apr. 1855.
25. A.C. Dewar, *Russian War, Black Sea 1855*, pp.173–6. Quoting: Capt. Lyons to Rear-Admiral Lyons, 29 May 1855, Enclosure in No. 86, and Lyons to Secretary to the Admiralty, 2 Jun. 1855, No. 87; G. Douglas, *The Panmure Papers*, p 207. Quoting: The Queen to Panmure, 23 May 1855.
26. Wood to Lyons, 1 and 4 Jun. 1855, Halifax Papers, Add MS 49562; B. Gooch, *The New Bonapartist Generals* (The Hague, 1959), pp 208–9; T. Martin, *The Life of His Royal Highness the Prince Consort* (London, 1877), III, pp 291–3. Quoting: Prince Albert to Baron Stockmar, 7 Jun. 1855
27. Dundas to Wood, 31 Jul. 1855, Halifax Papers, Add MS 49553; H.N. Sulivan, Life and Letters, pp 307–8, 315–20.
28. W.L. Clowes, *The Royal Navy, IV*, p 497.
29. D. Bonner Smith, *The Russian War, 1855. Baltic Sea*, pp 240, 215–6, 243. Quoting: Secretary to the Admiralty to Dundas, 21 and 27 Aug. 1855, Nos. 62a and 62c, and Dundas to Secretary to the Admiralty, 21 and 27 Aug. 1855, Nos. 60 and 68.
30. A.C. Dewar, *Russian War, Black Sea*, 1855, pp 208–11, 213, 224–5. Quoting: Lyons to Secretary to the Admiralty, 7, 10 and 30 Jul. 1855, Nos. 115 and enclosures, 117, and 125.
31. J. Curtiss, *Russia's Crimean War* (Durham, 1979), pp 440–4; B. Gooch, *New Bonapartist Generals*, pp 240–2.
32. F.A. Wellesley, *Secrets of the Second Empire. Private Letters from the Paris Embassy* (London, 1929), p 82.
33. Berkeley to Napier, 22 Aug. 1854, Napier Papers, Add MS 40025 [British Library].
34. *The Times*, 13 Sept. and 4 Oct. 1854; Sulivan, *Life and Letters*, p 263; H.N. Williams, *Life and Letters of Admiral Napier*, pp 360–1. Quoting: Delane to Napier, 4 Oct. 1854.
35. H.N. Williams, *Life and Letters of Admiral Napier*, pp 277; D. Bonner Smith, *Russian War, 1854*, p 46. Quoting: Secretary to the Admiralty to Napier, 2 Apr. 1854, No. 2; and Napier to the Secretary to the Admiralty, 1 Apr. 1854, No. 8.
36. H.N. Williams, *Life and Letters of Admiral Napier*, pp 266–72; P.H. Colomb, *Memoirs of Admiral the Right Honorable Sir Astley Cooper Key* (London, 1898), p 233; A. Otway, *Autobiography and Journal*, pp 87–8, 97; H. Keppel, *A Sailor's Life under Four Sovereigns* (London, 1899), II, pp 225–6; H.N. Sulivan, *Life and Letters*, p 138.
37. J. Moresby, *Two Admirals. A Record of Life and Service in the British Navy for a Hundred Years* (London, 1909), pp 153, 160.
38. See for example: H.N. Williams, *Life and Letters of Admiral Napier*, pp 78, 369, 378–9.
39. Bonner Smith and Dewar, *The Russian War, 1854*, pp 132–4. Quoting: Napier to Secretary to the Admiralty, 25 Sept. 1854, No. 46.
40. J. Martineau, *Life of Henry Pelham*, pp 166–7. Quoting: Newcastle to Raglan, 9 Oct. 1854.
41. B.S. Mends, *Life of Admiral Sir William Robert Mends* (London, 1899), pp 158, 160; Raglan to Dundas, 13 and 15 Oct. 1855, and Lyons to Dundas, 10 Oct. 1854, Dundas Papers, MS 60/018/DND 11; Bonner Smith and Dewar, *The Russian War, 1854*, pp 325–6. Quoting: Dundas to Secretary to the Admiralty, 3 Oct. 1854, No. 62.
42. S. Calthorpe, *Letters from Headquarters; or, the Realities of the War in the Crimea* (London, 1856), I, pp 285–8; L.G. Heath, *Letters from the Black Sea during the Crimean War 1854–55* (London, 1897), pp 83–4; B.S. Mends, *Life of Admiral Mends*, pp 167, 181–2.
43. Ibid., pp 442–4; Bonner Smith and Dewar, *The Russian War*, 1854, pp 339–45. Quoting: Dundas to Secretary to the Admiralty, 18 Oct. 1854, No. 69; W.L. Clowes, *The Royal Navy, IV*, pp 439–40; A.W. Kinglake, *The Invasion of the Crimea* (Edinburgh, 1863–75), III, p 424.

44. Dundas to Graham, 18 Oct. 1854, Graham Papers, MS. 45.
45. L. Strachey and R. Fulford, *The Greville Memoirs 1814–1860* (London, 1938), VII, p 199; Bonner Smith and Dewar, *The Russian War, 1854*, pp 345–7. Quoting: Secretary to the Admiralty to Dundas, 23 Oct. 1854, No. 71.
46. W.L. Clowes, *The Royal Navy, IV*, p 444.
47. J. Curtiss, *Russia's Crimean War*, p 232; S. Calthorpe, *Letters from Headquarters*, I, pp 398–99.
48. F.A. Wellesley, *Secrets of the Second Empire*, p 63.
49. Christie to Secretary to the Admiralty, 18 Nov. 1854 ADM 1/5631; Bonner Smith and Dewar, *The Russian War, 1854*, pp 360–70. Quoting: Dundas to Secretary to the Admiralty, 17 Nov. 1854, no. 88 and enclosures.
50. Airey to Christie, 27 Oct. 1854, Milne Papers, MLN 156/1, [National Maritime Museum]; B.S. Mends, *Life of Admiral Mends*, p 150; Newcastle to Russell, 7 Oct. 1854, Russell Papers, 30/22/11/E.
51. E. Hamley, *The War in the Crimea* (London, 1891), p 80; L.G. Heath, *Letters from the Black Sea*, p 70; B.S. Mends, *Life of Admiral Mends*, pp 150, 176.
52. Duchess of Argyll, *George Douglass Eighth Duke of Argyll, Autobiography and Memoirs* (London, 1906), I, p 516.

Steam, strategy and Schurman imperial defence in the post-Crimean era, 1856–1905

JOHN BEELER

INTRODUCTION

In the wake of defining works by Donald M. Schurman and W.C.B. Tunstall on the subject of Victorian imperial defence, another survey of the topic—in a volume honouring the former, no less—may strike readers as carrying coals to Newcastle or, perhaps more apposite, carrying coals to New South Wales.[1] The cliché seems doubly appropriate: not only is it applicable to any attempt to retrace the defining voyages of the acknowledged masters of the field, it is remarkably apt in a purely literary sense as well, given the centrality of coal and coal depots to nineteenth century imperial defence.

Appropriate clichés or not, recharting seas already surveyed in such thorough fashion by Schurman and Tunstall leaves subsequent literary mariners, if not at a complete loss for words (a rare occurrence indeed amongst historians), then at least at a loss for new insights and fresh perspectives on the subject. Hence, what follows is often, perforce, a reiteration of the work done so capably by my distinguished predecessors. At the same time, however, it will attempt a few novel tacks, either by focusing on topics which Professors Schurman and Tunstall dealt with only in passing, or, in a few instances, by reassessing their conclusions in light of more recent scholarship. And, if all else fails, one can always fall back on the last traditional port of refuge for historians with nothing new to say: the historiographical essay.

CONVENTIONAL WISDOM

Although this essay deals principally with British imperial defence policy during the second half of the nineteenth century, it may be useful to start with a few more general observations about strategic policy as a whole, before turning to the specific topic of imperial defence. On the overall strategic level, it is traditionally posited that the period 1856–1905 witnessed a gradual trend from strategic dispersal world-wide to concentration in European—ultimately home —waters.[2] Concurrently, the composition of the fleet shifted from one in which small, 'non-fighting' vessels—the maritime police force—played a major and highly visible role, to one in which, by 1900 at the very latest, capital ships (armoured cruisers and pre-dreadnought battleships) predominated.

There has been, in addition, another observation—one might almost say a charge—frequently made of post-Crimean British naval policy, namely, that until the era of Mahan the navy's strategic conceptions were, as N.A.M. Rodger has phrased it, 'not so much misguided as non-existent'.[3] Specifically, several authors have argued that the confusion wrought upon ship design by rapid technological change, from the introduction of steam line-of-battle ships in the late 1840s until the emergence of the standard pre-dreadnought design at the end of the 1880s, caused British naval planners—both civilian and professional—first of all to concentrate on tactical and technological considerations to the almost complete exclusion of larger strategic concerns: ships were designed and built, it has been alleged, on the basis of their envisioned tactical role, but without reference to their strategic one.[4] Secondly, several authors also stress the tendency of Admiralty planners to design ships on the basis of their peacetime, constabulary role, rather than for more warlike ends, saddling Britain with a fleet which, until the very end of the century, was suitable enough for gunboat diplomacy, but which was greatly wanting for such duties as the interdiction of commerce raiders.

There is also a general consensus among modern authorities that the advent of steam was quickly perceived to have negated the efficacy of the traditional strategy of close blockade, leaving the home islands—and the Empire—prey to invasion: a 'bolt from the blue', made possible by a source of power independent of the wind. This contemporary belief was summed up in the phrase, attributed to both the Duke of Wellington and Lord Palmerston, that 'steam has bridged the Channel', and that Britain's naval supremacy was no longer proof against invasion.[5] The chief consequence, it is usually argued, was that for much of the mid and late-Victorian era—until the 1890s—Britain's traditional reliance on the navy was supplanted by the ascendance of land-based defensive schemes, for both the home islands and the Empire: the triumph (albeit temporary) of military strategists over navalists, of the 'brick and mortar school' over the 'blue water school'. Arthur Marder's assessment may be taken as representative of modern views: '[t]he purely military views of the "brick and mortar" school dominated after 1860, and defensive policy was based on the assumption of a formidable lightning invasion against which the navy alone, concentrated at home in a defensive attitude, would be ineffective.'[6]

In at least three respects, however, this received wisdom should be tempered substantially. First of all, attention-grabbing as the exploits of the maritime constabulary often were, the small vessels of gunboat navy were not the bulwark of Britain's national and imperial defence. As Paul Kennedy has reminded us, the true foundation of British naval power and foreign policy influence in the nineteenth century was the battle fleet, and it was the battle fleet, not gunboats, which acted as a deterrent, and which formed the first line of defence, for both the home islands and the Empire.[7] That its role in the post-Crimean era was almost entirely deterrent—and hence unobtrusive and largely unremarked—should not obscure its importance to Britain's world position, national, or imperial security.

Secondly, it is curious, even alarming, how little Donald Schurman's works on the formulation of imperial defence strategy seem to have been appreciated by many other British naval historians. A quick perusal of his dissertation should be enough to disabuse students of the notion that British strategic planning during the era was 'not so much misguided as non-existent'. Indeed, he convincingly demonstrates that by the mid-1870s—the depths of the 'Dark Ages' of the Victorian Navy according to at least two authorities[8]—the Admiralty, in particular First Naval Lord Sir Alexander Milne, was systematically considering the potential threats to British commerce and territorial possessions in the event of war and advancing practical recommendations to secure the necessary counter measures.

Finally, it must be stressed that for all the attention that the 'brick and mortar' school has received, the navy was clearly and consistently the first and the principal line of defence, both of the home islands and of the Empire, and this was no less true of 1860 or 1870 than it was of 1890 or 1900. Indeed, in December 1867, First Lord Henry Thomas Lowry Corry, to whom Milne served as principal professional advisor, sounded a note very similar to that played by the 'blue water' school in the post-Mahanian era in a memorandum for the consideration of the Cabinet, a memorandum which succinctly spelt out the overarching strategic imperatives of the navy in wartime, a memorandum very difficult to reconcile with the alleged ascendance of the brick and mortar school:

> If we cannot command the Channel and the coast of Ireland, we are open to invasion. If we cannot command the Mediterranean, we are cut off from our direct line of communication with India ... In addition to the force required for the maintenance of our superiority at home and in the Mediterranean, we should have to provide for the protection of our colonial, commercial and political interests, in the Baltic, in North America, the West Indies, the Pacific, the Indian, Australian and China Seas....[9]

Moreover, so far from passively acquiescing to military domination or even failing to develop a coherent naval strategy, the Admiralty seems to have given careful thought to the problems technology wrought on the traditional strategy of close blockade and, it has been recently suggested, evolved an alternative strategy and built the vessels required to implement it.

Andrew Lambert has put forward the argument that, owing to short range and high maintenance requirements of steam vessels—to which one could add doubts about the efficacy of the traditional blockade from the late 1850s onward—and the centrality of supply bases owing to technological change,

'Britain saw the overseas bases of her rivals as an early target for offensive operations....'[10] Indeed, argues Lambert, '[b]etween 1856 and 1890 coastal warfare dominated naval policy,' not only for the British, but for the United States, France and Russia as well. As far as the British navy was concerned, 'the majority of ... battleships built between 1870 and 1890 (13 out of 22) were low freeboard turret ships with very high levels of protection, fully enclosed gun mounting and the heaviest artillery. In the absence of a serious naval challenge these ships would fight forts, indeed, they were quite unsuited to open ocean combat.'[11]

In addition, Britain built several shallow-draft ironclads which were passed off as 'coast defence vessels' but which were, there can be no doubt, viewed by their designers at the Admiralty as offensive weapons, specifically intended for attacking coastal fortifications and naval arsenals. In urging the construction of several such vessels in 1866, Controller of the Navy, Vice-Admiral Sir Robert Spencer Robinson, stated that they were 'intended either for coast defences, or the attack of shipping in an enemy harbour'.[12] In an equally explicit acknowledgement of the offensive role of the so-called 'coast defence' ships, First Naval Lord Sir Sydney Dacres complained of the deficient stability of one of the type, noting '[t]he ship only half meets the purposes for which she was ordered for she could hardly be trusted across the Channel to attack an Enemy's port—much less venture to the Baltic.'[13] In short, the Royal Navy developed an alternative strategy to the close blockade, an alternative built around destroying enemy vessels before they could utilize their ability to evade blockaders. The 'coast defence' battleships, along with gun- and later torpedo boats were, in the words of Lambert, 'the cutting edge of British strategy, their function ... to destroy fleets sheltering inside their bases....'[14]

THEORY VERSUS PRACTICE: THE EVOLUTION OF IMPERIAL STRATEGY

Much has been written of the consequences for British security following from the construction of Depuy de Lome's steam battle fleet in the late 1840s and early 1850s, but, with the exceptions of Schurman and Tunstall, historians have focused primarily on the consequences as they pertained to national (that is, home) rather than colonial or imperial defence.[15] In many respects, it is true, there could be no distinction between the two spheres: a French steam battle fleet which managed to evade a blockading British squadron was, at least in theory, a menace to the Colonies as much as it was to the home islands. The traditional policy of close blockade was as important a factor in imperial as it was in national defence. But it is likely the concentration of historical scrutiny on national defence, at least in the period before 1889, simply reflects the priorities of contemporaries: the home islands were, in the first and last analysis, of greater significance than the Colonies and, more importantly, the peril to them was the greatest owing to the geographic proximity of the threat.[16]

It must also be stressed that imperial defence was bedevilled by several other factors in the second half of the nineteenth century. The accretion of the Empire, obviously, increased the scope of the Navy's obligations. Likewise, the growth of rival colonial empires, accompanied after 1890 by the emergence of Japan, the United States and Germany as naval powers of consequence, in addition to the more traditional Franco-Russian naval threat, multiplied potential threats to imperial security. But for most of the period 1856–1905, in particular the years prior to the passage of the Imperial Defence (1888) and Naval Defence (1889) Acts, the chief wellspring of problems for the defence of the Empire, as it was for the home islands, was rapid technological change, especially the supplantation of sail by steam.

The technological revolution which took place between the late 1840s and the late 1880s had profound consequences for the nature and capabilities of the tools with which Britain had to maintain its world-wide security. In one respect, but in only one, did technological change have a liberating effect: it *did* free vessels from the vagaries of the wind, although by simultaneously freeing the ships of rival navies it vastly complicated the tasks of the Royal Navy, and gave rise to the series of invasion scares which characterized the eras 1847–62 and 1882 onwards. In other respects, the consequences of technological transformation were uniformly debilitating, at least in the strategic sphere. At the same time that steam freed ships from reliance on the wind, it tied them to coal depots and colliers. For that matter, steamships could not keep the sea for weeks, much less months, at a time in the manner that sailing ships could, a fact fraught with consequences both for the maintenance of a naval blockade and for oceanic—or imperial—defence. And while iron (and eventually, steel) hulls were far more durable than hulls of wood, they also required cleaning far more frequently.

Likewise, the incidence of maintenance, both routine, like scraping the hull, and major, like replacing boilers, increased dramatically after 1850, especially after sails began to be abandoned outright on some vessels in the 1870s. Sailing ships had been largely self-sufficient units, their radius of action restricted only by their draught and their endurance circumscribed only by food and water for the crew. Their wholly steam-powered successors were continually—and to contemporaries, alarmingly frequently and expensively—reliant on the coal depot, the graving dock, and the repair yard. In short, by 1870, at the very latest, not only did it cost Britain far more to keep an adequate force at sea, even in peacetime: it was far more difficult to keep that force at sea, and the ships of which it consisted were vastly inferior to sailing ships in terms of range, endurance, and self-sufficiency. This, along with the related blockade quandary, was the cardinal complication for British imperial defence planners in the post-Crimean era.

It was this conjunction of largely technological factors, combined with the appreciation that defence of Empire and of the intervening sea lanes, rather than the construction of 'Fortress England,' was the key to both national and imperial security, which formed the foundation on which Royal Marine Artillery Captain John Charles Ready Colomb's theories of imperial defence were erected. What Colomb did, quite simply, was figure out what sort of strategic network or logistical infrastructure would have to be established, maintained, and defended to permit a steam-powered navy to undertake operations of the same global scope that had routinely been performed by the sailing navy in the eighteenth and early nineteenth centuries.

Both Schurman and Tunstall have stressed the importance of Colomb's work, beginning with 'The Protection of our Commerce and the Distribution of our War Forces Considered,' published in 1867. Schurman remarks that by 1867 there was 'a body of doctrine available on the connection between Empire trade, coal and defence' which 'had been outlined ... by Capt. J.C.R. Colomb....'[17] Prior to Colomb's work the phrase, to say nothing of the concept of, 'imperial defence' lacked currency in Britain. Defence overseas was conceived in terms of colonial, rather than of imperial defence. The distinction is important; colonial defence implied local defence—the protection of individual colonies; imperial defence, by way of contrast, was global. It encompassed the defence of individual colonies, to be sure, but more importantly it meant the defence of the sea lanes between the far-flung parts of the Empire, defence of the trade which passed along those sea lanes, and the defence of the naval bases and coal depots on which the defenders of the sea lanes depended.

There were two key aspects to imperial defence. Most crucially, the best defence for British possessions overseas and the sea lanes was preventing enemy forces from escaping from port in the first place. Hence, blockade, or some alternative like coastal assault, was central to imperial, just as it was to national defence. Secondly, it had to be presumed that even if British blockaders kept enemy battle fleets bottled up in port, individual enemy ships would unavoidably escape, just as they had in the days of sail. Against these marauders it would be necessary to defend the sea lines of communication, a task which had traditionally been performed by smaller units of the Royal Navy, while capital ships laid siege to enemy ports.

But, emphasized Colomb, whether blockading or interdicting commerce raiders, the most important tasks of imperial defence were *naval* in nature. In contradistinction to the military theorists of the 'brick and mortar' school, Colomb saw the navy as the key element in his imperial security scheme. Beyond Canada and India, no part of the Empire was susceptible to landward attack by other than indigenous peoples, *unless enemy troops were first transported by sea*. Control the sea lanes, he argued, and local colonial defence would largely take care of itself. It was the navy and the navy alone which could keep enemy threats to the Empire and, equally important, enemy threats to British commerce, at bay. Hence, concluded Colomb, 'large fleets should be concentrated in the Channel and Mediterranean areas [for blockade duty], and detached squadrons must cover the rest of the Empire.'[18]

Colomb also grasped what no previous naval or imperial strategist had appreciated: 'the fact that modern trade movements and modern security depended on the constant abundance and availability of coal.'[19] Steam warships required constant resupply and frequent maintenance to a degree which their sailing forebears had not, and for the machine-age Royal Navy a comprehensive world-wide system of naval bases and coal depots was a logistical necessity. The success of the detached squadrons which Colomb envisioned patrolling the sea lanes of the globe 'would depend on the security of the base of operations selected for each. Hence the importance of wartime availability of coal supplies which would enable the squadrons to operate effectively while at the same time denying these coaling facilities to enemy cruisers.'[20] Colomb advocated the creation of a comprehensive network of bases, encompassing Halifax, Bermuda, Bahamas, Jamaica, and Antigua on the North America and West Indies station, Gibraltar and Malta in the Mediterranean, Suez and Aden on the Mediterranean route to India, Trincomalee, Bombay, and Cape Comerin in Indian waters, Singapore and Hong Kong in the Far East, and King George's Sound in Western Australia.[21] To these essential bases, he added several more, whose security was a matter of somewhat less urgency: Sierra Leone, Ascension, St Helena, Simons Bay (Cape Colony), Mauritius, the Falklands, Sydney, and Fiji, the last of which was not a British possession until 1875.[22]

In respect of these naval bases and coaling stations, however, some form of local defence was necessary. Were the bases to be defended by the squadrons they supplied, the ability to patrol the sea lanes would be severely hampered, if not wholly negated: 'Colomb felt that the defence of Imperial bases should not be the sole duty of the Navy since such a responsibility would detract from the fleet's duty of trade protection at sea...the defence of the bases should be an army responsibility.'[23] The army was, therefore, to play a subordinate role in imperial defence; the navy was, as it had traditionally been, the first and most important bulwark.

Of the importance of Colomb's pioneering work there can be no question; Schurman sums it up neatly in noting that although 'he only indicated particular paths tentatively he did lay down his general principles authoritatively,' and these 'principles...were eventually accepted by the United Kingdom Government...'[24] Tunstall more sweepingly observes: '[t]he first satisfactory and comprehensive statement of the problem of imperial defence was made by Sir John Colomb ... who in 1867 published a remarkable pamphlet in which he laid down those general principles of imperial strategy which guide British defence policy to-day.'[25]

But although Colomb is properly credited with having produced the first systematic consideration of the problems associated with imperial defence in the age of steam, and for establishing the theoretical framework in which imperial security policy was debated and formulated for at least the next half century, he was 'outside the loop', and his influence, regardless of the soundness of his views, was transmitted purely through unofficial channels. The practical implementation of imperial defence schemes rested in the hands of administrators at the Admiralty and in the War Office, which leads back to the figure of Admiral Sir Alexander Milne, First Naval Lord from 1866 to 1868 and again from 1872 to 1876, and the first Admiralty insider to address the problems which had exercised the mind and pen of Colomb.

Milne is the central figure in British naval administration during the mid-Victorian era. In addition to his two stints as First Naval Lord, he served at the Admiralty in a subordinate capacity from 1847 to 1859, through repeated changes of Ministry, at a time when naval lords were routinely chosen with reference to their political loyalties. That Milne remained at the Admiralty for such a long stretch, despite the prevailing governmental instability, is doubtless a testimony to the esteem in which his professional and administrative abilities were held.[26] More importantly, he was alive to the problems of colonial defence as early as the late 1850s, when still a Junior Naval Lord. The French invasion scare of 1858–62 prompted widespread fears of war in Britain, in turn spurring Milne to reflect on the consequences wrought by the transformation of the battle fleet. Among his papers is an Admiralty memorandum from June 1858 devoted to the problem of ensuring coal supplies in wartime, especially with regard to the Colonies.[27] At about the same time, as Bryan Ranft has noted, Milne 'warned the Prime Minister [Palmerston or Derby] that the French threat to ships carrying industrial raw materials as they approached home waters was almost as serious as the danger of invasion,' prompting Ranft to label him 'the pioneer of professional naval thought about the protection of shipping....'[28]

By the 1870s, moreover, Milne was beginning to consider imperial defence in a thorough and systematic fashion. In late 1874 he turned his attention and energies to the practical considerations which would be necessary to place the navy in a state of strategic readiness, producing a series of memoranda which directly addressed imperial defence. In his 'Paper Relative to Unarmoured Ships, and Proposal for an Establishment' he calculated the minimum force requisite for imperial and commercial defence at thirty frigates, twenty-five to thirty first-class corvettes, thirty second-class corvettes, forty-five sloops, sixty gun vessels, and sixty gunboats, adding ominously that this force of upwards of 250 small units would require considerable augmentation as soon as war threatened.[29] At the same time, as Schurman notes, Milne began to give full consideration to the changed circumstances wrought by the technological transformation of the navy's *matériel*, especially with regard to the pressing need for coal. 'Coaling stations,' he stated unequivocally, 'would be the great problem in a future war and they must be maintained and extended....'[30] 'We could,' Milne wrote, 'get no coal except from our own Colonies, where new depots would have to be established....'[31]

Milne was, Schurman acknowledges, very much 'pro-Empire' and anti 'Fortress England' in his approach to defence strategy, and it is plain that it was he who, between 1872 and 1876, took the first decisive steps towards formulating a coherent plan—as opposed to Colomb's general strategic principles

—for imperial defence, and who worked out the number and the nature of the vessels required to implement it. That his efforts were not acted upon immediately owed to a set of circumstances over which the Admiralty had little control.

Despite the lack of immediate action on Milne's recommendations, the subject of imperial defence was not allowed to sink into obscurity in the wake of his retirement in 1876. Indeed, at his inspiration the Admiralty turned over the question of local defence for coaling stations and naval bases to the War Office, since, as the navy saw it, the duty was rightly the Army's responsibility. Thus, in early 1875, Colonel Sir William Jervois, assistant Inspector-General of Fortifications, produced a memorandum which concurred with Colomb's and Milne's ideas of fixed local defence, leading Schurman to remark that Jervois 'firmly grasped the first Naval principle of Imperial Defence: that "the fleet is required for cruising, and cannot be kept in harbour to guard its own supplies".'[32]

Schurman terms the Jervois Memorandum 'a landmark in the history of Imperial Defence.' Not only did Jervois adopt the division of service duties laid out by Colomb, he extended Milne's reasoning, drawing up a list of naval bases considered to be inadequately defended, and providing suggestions for their security, in terms not only of fixed defences, but also of manpower and, not least of all, cost.[33] Moreover, despite Jervois' subsequent reassignment to Singapore, his memorandum was printed for the consideration of Disraeli's Cabinet and accepted by the Inspector-General of Fortifications by December of 1875. 'This memorandum and its general acceptance in the War Office meant that a rational concept of the true nature of Imperial Defence had gained the dignity of Departmental support.'[34]

If there was a turning point for the fortunes of imperial defence, however, it came with the Eastern Crisis of 1875–78, centred on apparent Russian designs in the Balkans, which reached the level of a war scare in the early months of 1878. The war scare 'clearly caught the British Empire woefully unprepared for coaling station defence though both the War Office and the Admiralty had previously recognized this as extremely important in any future war.'[35] More substantively, it led to the appointment of, first, the Colonial Office's ad hoc Colonial Defence Committee in 1878, followed by the Royal Commission on Colonial Defence in 1879. The former, chaired by Alexander Milne, produced five reports on the fortification of specific ports, and served in an advisory capacity to the colonial office until its dissolution in April 1879.

Little resulted directly from the committee's reports; the scope of its inquiry had been restricted, and even had it not been, the 'lack of any systematic knowledge of local colonial conditions and lack of any spare ordnance at home made [its] recommendations almost ludicrous.'[36] Yet the efforts of the committee were not without benefit; by its very deliberations it 'explored the problems involved in Imperial Defence,' the circumstances surrounding its creation 'had so impressed' its members that 'they ... were prepared to admit that Home Defences should take second place to...overseas needs' and that, on the most immediate level, 'some sort of permanent investigating committee was needed...'[37]

Chiefly on the impetus of the Colonial Secretary, Sir Michael Hicks Beach, a Royal Commission was substituted for another committee on the subject, this body chaired by Lord Carnarvon, and including among its members the prominent navalist Thomas Brassey (until his appointment to the Admiralty in 1880) and, once again, Alexander Milne, but not, despite his desire, J.C.R. Colomb.[38]

Carnarvon's Commission, or, to better convey the scope of its inquiry, the Commission appointed 'to make enquiry into the condition and sufficiency of the means of the naval and military forces provided for the defence of the more important sea-ports within our Colonial possessions and dependencies' collected evidence and deliberated until early 1882, despite the indifference-verging-on-hostility towards the subject of its inquiry of several members of the Gladstone Government which took office in 1880.[39] During its existence it also produced three reports. The first, drafted very hastily, dealt principally with Britain's dependence on its overseas trade and defences at the Cape of Good Hope, the second with the naval dimension of imperial defence and Australasia, and the third with the defence of imperial bases elsewhere. For several years the reports remained unpublished, save for a handful of copies distributed to the members of the commission and high-level politicians. Only in 1887, in conjunction with the Colonial Conference, were the first and second reports and extracts from the third made public.

Schurman ably sums up both the strengths and weaknesses of the commission's accomplishments. On the positive side, it defined naval strategy 'in a truly modern sense,' and unequivocally 'represented the triumph of the ideas of the officially spurned Captain J.C.R. Colomb.' 'British Naval strategy,' the commissioners stated, 'depended on the assurance of adequate coal supplies for our own Navy, wherever it might be operating, and the denial of coal supplies to the ships or fleets of the enemy.'[40] On a more practical level, the reports of the commission, in particular the recommendations made for the defence of individual ports, formed the basis for the implementation of imperial defence policy for the next decade and more. The Commissioners advocated the expenditure of £2,507,386 on the fortification of coaling stations and colonial ports—in particular Singapore, Mauritius, Jamaica, Barbados, Antigua, Aden, Sierra Leone and the Falklands—along with the establishment of many more coaling stations and the necessity of 'maintaining not only a fleet sufficient in number and in power to give absolute security to the sea-board of the United Kingdom, but also fast and powerful vessels so stationed as to be ready at the commencement of hostilities to deal with the enemy's ships in more distant seas.'[41]

On the other hand, Schurman criticizes the commission on a number of counts: its conception of strategy was not always consistent, and its choices for fortification were often debatable.[42] Most crucially, however, he charges that 'the Commissioners felt that they knew better than the Admiralty how naval war should be conducted:' 'this lack of respect for Admiralty views, or ... lack of any sustained attempt to discover what Admiralty opinion really was, marked and marred the whole Report.'[43] But, on the whole, the three reports of the Carnarvon commission 'did at least represent a reasonable approximation of what was necessary for the security of the British Empire .... The basic requirement of a world girt with a chain of secure bases which would enable the Royal Navy to act almost anywhere was provided for....'[44] Tunstall's evaluation is similarly laudatory: '[t]he first and third Reports of the Carnarvon Commission are of special importance because they lay down general principles of imperial defence conceived on a governmental basis and with full knowledge of the facts....'[45]

It would be several years, however, before the commission's recommendations were implemented on any substantive level; the reluctance of the second Gladstone ministry (1880–85) to undertake expensive projects of any sort, much less those pertaining to military or naval preparations, caused first a delay in recognition of the commission's work and then, when Carnarvon himself chided the Government to spur action—concurrent with the alarm raised by Stead's revelations in the 'Truth about the Navy' series (1884)—the Liberals produced a much watered-down proposal for erecting permanent fortifications which involved the expenditure of only £891,000 (later revised upwards to £976,760), much of it to be born by colonial governments.[46] Yet in the wake of the Stead alarm, and the potential menace posed by a new class of Russian armoured cruisers, a new Colonial Defence Committee was created (1885), this a permanent organization, whose existence went far to ensure continuity and coherence in the formulation and implementation of imperial defence policy.[47] Moreover, small though the sum allotted for imperial defence by the Gladstone Government was, at least in comparison with the Royal Commission's recommendations, it enabled work on Aden, Trincomalee, Columbo, Hong Kong, the Cape, Mauritius, Jamaica and St Lucia to be taken in hand.

Progress was slow: by 1888 Thomas Brassey reported in the second *Naval Annual* (for 1887) that work on fortifications had begun at Trincomalee, Columbo, Singapore, Mauritius, Simon's Bay (Cape), St Helena and Sierra Leone, although the War Office's belated decision to switch from muzzle to breech-loading ordnance—made in the early 1880s but plagued by delays, difficulties, and poor designs—meant that guns for most of these works would, as in the case of Ceylon, 'probably be years late.'[48] Two years later, in the 1890 *Naval Annual*, Brassey could still point out that 'Gibraltar requires considerable improvements, with a view to increased facilities for giving succour to the Navy in case of war.' At Hong Kong a few guns had been mounted, but 'Lord Carnarvon has recently felt himself justified in remonstrating on the insufficiency of the armaments of Hong Kong, especially in guns of the more powerful calibres.'[49] Aden, too, was not judged secure 'against the attack of a small squadron.' Elsewhere, however, the picture was brighter, and Brassey detailed the arrangements at Malta, Bombay, Kurachee [sic], Columbo, Singapore, St Helena, Sierra Leone, and both of the Cape anchorages in terms suggesting confidence, if not complacency.[50]

There were, furthermore, by the late 1880s other factors contributing to the rising status of imperial defence; in 1887 London hosted the first Colonial Conference, whose deliberations were largely taken up with matters related to imperial security, especially its cost and how the financial burden was to be divided between the parent country and the colonies, a question for which no mutually satisfactory solution was devised.[51] The subsequent Imperial Defence Act of 1888 embodied some of the agreements reached at the conference, most notably the decision to strengthen the Australian squadron, and it authorized the expenditure of £2,600,000 for harbour and coaling station defence.

The era also witnessed the growth of navalist agitation in the press, exemplified by the appearance of Brassey's *Naval Annual* beginning in 1886, and culminating in 1890 with the appearance of the first of Mahan's *Influence of Sea Power* volumes. In addition, the comments of Admirals Richard Vesey Hamilton, W.M. Dowell and Frederick Richards on the naval manoeuvres of 1888, published in the *Parliamentary Papers* the following year, spurred further public outcry: 'they reported unanimously that the Navy was too weak to take the offensive by blockade against even a single enemy and at the same time carry out all the multifarious duties which would inevitably be thrust upon it in war.'[52] 'No time should be lost,' they stated, in placing Britain's 'Navy beyond comparison with that of any two powers.'[53] This 'Report of the Three Admirals,' as it became known, along with concurrent agitation in Parliament spearheaded by Lord Charles Beresford, produced the Naval Defence Act of 1889, which invested the 'Two Power Standard' with legally binding status and funded the construction of eight first-class battleships, thirty-eight cruisers, and twenty-four other vessels. By 1889, therefore, both the naval and the military aspects of imperial defence had been addressed in a comprehensive fashion, although completion of the works sanctioned by the Imperial Defence and Naval Defence Acts would stretch well into the nineties.

Aside from the tangled question of funding and direction of imperial defence forces—which this essay will scrupulously skirt—there were other matters which still evaded resolution beyond 1890, chief among them the lack of co-ordination in imperial defence arrangements. It was not simply a matter of inter-service rivalry; the Colonial Office was a third agency with direct involvement in overseas defence, and Schurman's dissertation admirably illustrates the many problems which dogged the Carnarvon Commission—to select but a single example—as a consequence of want of co-operation, co-ordination, and often simple communication between the War Office, the Admiralty, and the Colonial Office.[54]

It was this want of co-ordination which in 1888 prompted the appointment of a Royal Commission 'to enquire into the Civil and Professional Administration of the Naval and Military Departments and the Relationship of those Departments to each other and to the Treasury,' chaired by the Liberal Unionist Lord Hartington. The commission 'found that there was never any regular communication between the War Office and the Admiralty nor had either department considered its material requirements or defence plans in relation to the other.'[55] Its reports, released in 1889 and 1890, called for the establishment of a co-ordinating body, consisting of cabinet ministers and professional advisors from both services which could 'authoritatively determine the requirements of the two services in accordance with a concerted plan of imperial defence.'[56] This recommendation, Tunstall emphasizes, 'was clearly a demand for what eventually emerged as the Committee of Imperial Defence.'[57]

Yet it would be several years before the chief recommendations of the Hartington report were taken in hand. Only with the retirement of the Duke of Cambridge as Army Commander-in-Chief in 1895 was the Government capable of moving to implement reorganization of the command structure of the armed services. And, unfortunately for the proponents of co-ordinated imperial defence, Rosebery's Liberal Government, which was enabled to undertake the task, seems to have been motivated principally by the desire to secure greater political control over the War Office, with the obstreperous duke finally out of the way. The new structure, Sir Henry Campbell-Bannerman, then Secretary for War, claimed, followed the 'main principles' of the Hartington Commission report, but in fact it left the formation of an advisory council for imperial defence no closer to realization than had been the case when the report was released.

Later in 1895, following the change of government, Prime Minister Lord Salisbury authorized the creation of the Defence Committee of the Cabinet, 'perhaps', suggests Tunstall, 'as a salve to conscience for ignoring the recommendations of the Hartington Commission.'[58] If so, it was no more than a salve, however, since although 'apparently intended to provide some means of co-ordinating the conflicting policies of the Admiralty and the War Office ... it seems to have concerned itself mainly with adjusting the Service [budget] estimates before they came before the full Cabinet, and with settling the conflicting financial claims of the Navy and Army.'

It was only following the army's embarrassing performance in the Boer War that decisive steps were taken to address the want of co-ordination, both between the services, and between professionals and their civilian overseers, that the war had so disastrously revealed. The Elgin Committee, established to hold an inquiry on the conduct of the war, 'revealed a condition of affairs which outraged public feeling throughout the Empire.'[59] The upshot of the committee's report was the formation of the War Office (Reconstitution) Committee in November 1903, consisting of Viscount Esher, Admiral Sir John Fisher, and Colonel Sir George Sydenham Clarke. The committee produced three reports in early 1904, in which it moved well beyond the scope of its brief, not merely contenting itself with drafting plans for restructuring the War Office. Indeed, claimed the commission, War Office reform would be futile 'unless associated with provision for obtaining for the use of the Cabinet all the information required for shaping national policy in war and for determining the necessary preparations in peace ... the Cabinet had in 1899 no adequate means of obtaining reasoned opinion on which to set up a war policy.'[60] The committee thus recommended not only the establishment of a War Office Council, but also a Department for the Defence committee, to be chaired by the Prime Minister. On 4 May 1904 the latter body, styled the Committee of Imperial Defence, was created, inheriting and expanding the duties of the earlier Colonial Defence Committee and Defence Committee of the Cabinet.[61] Its membership consisted of, aside from the Prime Minister, the Lord President, the Secretary of State for War, the First Lord of the Admiralty, the Commander-in-Chief, the First Naval Lord, and the Directors of Naval and Military Intelligence. The Empire finally had a co-ordinating body including professional advisors from both services as well as the most relevant members of the Government.

SUMMING UP

A great deal more could be said of imperial defence in the post-Crimean era. This essay has not touched on the question of convoy versus interdiction strategies for the protection of maritime commerce, nor on what Schurman terms 'the problem which came to dominate [imperial defence] thinking—the question of what financial or manpower contribution the various parts of Britain overseas should make to this scheme.'[62] This neglect is rationalized owing to constraints of space, plus, as Schurman notes, the latter was an imperial political question, rather than a defence question *per se*, and even given Clausewitz's dictum regarding the extension of politics, its exclusion seems warranted. Those in search of a discussion of the issue are hereby recommended to Tunstall's essays in the *Cambridge History of the British Empire*.[63]

On the narrower level of security policy itself, a recitation of the often tortuous and usually torpid evolution of British imperial defence strategy in the early steam era almost inevitably conveys with it the impression that the British were unconscionably slow in perceiving the threat to their Empire and the intervening sea lanes, and slower still to act on their perceptions. It was, after all, almost two decades after the decision to build steam battleships was made that J.C.R. Colomb first enunciated his general principles of imperial defence strategy, it was a further seven years before the Admiralty began systematic consideration of the subject, another five before the appointment of a major commission to examine it, and almost another decade before the recommendations of that commission began to be carried out on a significant scale. In the meantime, navalists like the Colomb brothers, Rear-Admiral Sir John

Hay, Admirals Geoffrey Phipps Hornby and Alexander Milne, the young John Fisher, and others, repeatedly decried the lack of preparation for war and the defencelessness of the Empire, leading many more recent analysts to portray British performance in somewhat less than flattering terms.

With the overall slow pace of formulation and implementation there can be no dispute. Equally true, there were shortcomings in the structure and personnel of the crucial departments—not to mention their relations with each other—and an overall unwillingness on the part of the Government—whether Conservative or Liberal—to embark on lavish expenditure for imperial defence. These points are beyond contention. But there were other factors which bore on the subject which should be considered before critiquing either Government or individuals too pointedly.

First and foremost, the nature of technology, from the 1840s through the late 1880s, seriously hampered efforts to implement a coherent naval strategy. At the risk of repetitiousness, the foremost problem of imperial defence in the post-Crimean era was that the two traditional methods of commanding the sea: blockade and commerce-raider interdiction seemed to have been rendered vastly more complicated, more prone to failure, and more fraught with danger by the advent first of steam and then torpedoes. The dilemma for the British therefore was two-fold, and for both dimensions they had to find alternatives or solutions. In the case of blockade, an alternative had to be found. In the case of the circumscription of ships' ranges foisted upon the navy by the switch to steam, the solution likewise was twofold. The first element, expounded by Colomb and acted upon beginning in the late 1880s, was the creation of a comprehensive network of well-defended coaling stations and naval bases.

The second, equally crucial, element was the creation of a steam navy capable of operating on the high seas. It has generally been assumed that this navy, or at very least the technological means to create it, existed by 1870.[64] They did not. Many naval historians have concluded that the advances in steam technology which were incorporated into naval designs in the late 1860s and early 1870s—most notably the compound engine, the cylindrical boiler and the surface condenser—should have enabled the Royal Navy to dispense with sails. As Stanley Sandler puts it, 'developments in the marine engine itself doomed sail... The success of surface condensers made possible higher steam pressures, and by 1870 the compound or double expansion engine had been developed... The Board of Admiralty could thus hardly plead technological hindrances to the abolition of masts and sails.'[65] That the Admiralty failed to act promptly on the changed technological circumstances, it has been widely concluded, was a manifestation of conservatism, foot-dragging, a backwards-looking mentality or some other equally pernicious obstructionist influence.

Put simply, however, subsequent critics of the Admiralty's policy towards steam during the 1870s and early 1880s have failed to comprehend fully the existing state of technology on both the theoretical and practical levels. The adoption of the compound engine, cylindrical boiler and surface condenser made it possible, even desirable, to dispense with sails in some types of vessel, specifically those warships designed for service in European waters, which could, and did, beginning with the *Devastation* (authorized 1869), dispense with their rig.[66] But, as then Director of Naval Ordnance, Arthur Hood, summed up the situation in 1873: although the *Devastation* type of mastless breastwork monitor was 'by far the most powerful fighting machines in the world for European waters, yet I do not think they are well adapted for making long sea voyages, or in fact for keeping the sea as ocean cruisers for a lengthened period....'[67]

The *Devastation* carried up to 1,800 tons of coal, enough for a radius of 9,200 miles at five knots, 4,700 miles at ten knots, and 2,700 miles at full speed (12.5 knots). This range was adequate, it has been stressed, for crossing the Atlantic both ways without refuelling, albeit at a modest five knots. But even short-term operations in American waters would have required the presence of a nearby coaling station. Moreover, the *Devastation*, a low-freeboard vessel, was unsuited for service in the rough waters of the North Atlantic, even had its range been far greater. The *Devastation*'s successors, from the *Dreadnought* onwards, benefited from the introduction of the compound engine, yet it is a mistake to conclude, as Sandler and many others have, that this novelty should have signalled the prompt death-knell of sails. With its range of 5,700 miles at 10 knots, the *Dreadnought* was no more suited for service on the Pacific Station, in the Far East, or in the Indian Ocean than the *Devastation*, even with a comprehensive, world-wide system of coaling stations in place. Only with the transition to the triple expansion engine and the water-tube boiler, both of which were widely utilized in the Royal Navy after 1885, could the service afford to dispense with sails in virtually all its warships. It was these two advances—themselves made possible by the transition from iron to steel construction—not those of the late 1860s and early 1870s, which made a truly world-wide steam navy possible.

There was, furthermore, another dimension to the sail–steam situation in the 1870s and early 1880s which few modern writers have examined, that being the practical matter of day-to-day operations under steam. The maintenance problems attendant on the wholesale switchover, especially boiler upkeep, made the employment of purely steam vessels overseas a virtual impossibility until a network of support bases was in place. In addition, the theoretical maximum pressure in the cylindrical boilers in use throughout the 1870s was upwards of 90 psi, but owing to rapid corrosion and deterioration—largely a consequence, ironically, of the surface condenser, which made it possible to use fresh, rather than salt, water in the boilers—it was not uncommon for ships with boilers only three or four years old to keep pressure at one third to one half that level, with consequences for efficiency and economy of coal consumption which may easily be imagined.[68]

The upshot of this technological quandary was what one author has called 'the bizarre, ill-assorted vessels' of the late 1860s, 1870s and early 1880s, in particular the armoured cruisers which were incapable of cruising under steam for more than a few days: the *Shannon*, the *Nelson* and the *Northampton*. That these ships would have been hapless in their intended wartime roles of commerce-raider interdiction there can be no doubt, but rather than viewing their defects as manifestations of Admiralty conservatism or of chief constructor Nathaniel Barnaby's supposed incompetence, they may be more appropriately seen as the unhappy but necessary consequences of the state of technology during the 1870s. The cruisers of the 1870s were inadequate for the tasks they would have had to perform in the event of war, but they were by and large— at least in terms of their engines and boilers—the best designs which could be evolved at the time, given the strategic imperatives under which the navy overseas had to function. For the Royal Navy was a world-wide force, not a regional or a local one, and ships designed for imperial duties might be dispatched to any remote region of the globe for weeks or even months, whether or not there was a coaling station conveniently close at hand. In the mid-Victorian era those coaling stations were too few in number and too far between, and even had they not been, the state of maritime steam technology would not have permitted the wholesale abandonment of sailing rig that many naval historians believe should have been made.

Perhaps most crucially, however, while navalists could point to the vulnerability of the Empire, and of the want of cruisers to protect sea lanes and commerce, the truth was that from 1856 to the passage of the Naval Defence Act there was very little from which the Empire or British commerce required defending. For most of the era the actual foreign threat to the countries of the Empire and to the sea lines of communication which connected them was virtually non-existent. Naval alarmists could decry the defencelessness or near defencelessness of virtually all of the Empire, as well as the vast volume of merchant shipping which would require protection in the event of war, but for the whole of the pre-Mahanian period, with the arguable exception of the years 1858–62, when France appeared to be mounting a substantial challenge to British naval hegemony, there were no rivals worthy of serious consideration.[69] Britain maintained a two power standard or something very close to it throughout the era.[70]

The same was true with regard to the *guerre de course* threat. It is regularly alleged that the Russian imperial navy led the way in developing the armoured cruiser, whose principal role would have been commerce raiding, but the vessels in question—the *General Admiral* and the *Gerzog Edinburghski*—were as ill-suited in terms of range and speed under steam for chasing merchant vessels as the British counter designs were for catching them. Much is also made of the French *Jeune Ecole*, which actively preached the gospel of commercial warfare, but the theories of Theophile Aube, the leader of the school, only gained cognizance after 1885, and never became official doctrine within the republican navy.[71] As Arthur Marder notes wryly, '*Jeune Ecole* theories were from time to time in the ascendant at the Ministry of Marine.'[72] As of 1886, the French navy had 'only a single modern cruiser for commerce raiding,' and this lone vessel—the *Sfax*—was still a year from completion. Moreover, in the larger dimension of naval strategy, it is doubtful that the *guerre de course* could have succeeded in 'starving Britain into submission,' no matter how numerous an enemy cruiser force might have been, prior to the advent of the submarine/torpedo combination. During the mid-Victorian era it is beyond dispute that there was not a navy in the world capable of so doing, nor of seriously disrupting the sea lines of communication between parent country and colonies.

It was not merely owing to the want of suitable vessels either, although it tends to be forgotten that the same technological factors which circumscribed the performance of British cruising vessels acted upon those of her rivals as well: '[i]n the steam age oceanic cruising required vast amounts of fuel, a nightmare for fleets without an adequate chain of bases. Only Britain had these bases, and high grade steam coal.'[73] Perceptive contemporaries appreciated the fact too: in 1889 no less an authority than Thomas Brassey admitted 'we find the resources of our neighbours for the conduct of naval operations in distant waters slender indeed in comparison with those which we command.'[74]

Finally, there was a political/ideological aspect to the apparent lack of priority afforded imperial defence prior to the late 1880s, that being provided by the Declaration of Paris (1856), which outlawed privateering and prohibited attacks on neutral shipping, save that carrying 'contraband of war.' Many politicians, not only Manchester Radicals and Gladstonian Liberals, assumed that these bans would be operative in wartime:

> In the eighties the protection of commerce seemed so insoluble a problem [on a theoretical level] that even Arthur Forwood, the great Liverpool shipowner, [ardent imperialist Sir Charles] Dilke and [Thomas] Brassey ... saw the transfer of British commerce to the flag of a war the only solution.[75]

In the words of Paul Kennedy, 'most people' concluded that neutral shipping would remain inviolable in wartime, and even Lord Salisbury, hardly the most naive or idealistic politician of the era, observed in 1871 that the Declaration of Paris 'had made the fleet "almost valueless" for anything other than preventing invasion.'[76]

Under this conjunction of circumstances the reluctance of political leaders, regardless of their party affiliation—although there is no question that the Gladstonian Liberals were the more parsimonious in terms of defence spending —to embark on expensive projects seems not merely rational, but prudent. Despite length of time between the introduction of major steam warships and the implementation of a comprehensive scheme of imperial defence, it is not entirely fair, much less accurate, to conclude that Britain was simply slothful in its treatment of imperial security. In some respects—the fortification of coaling stations, for instance—more rapid action might have been possible, but the insignificance of the threat to the Empire neither warranted nor induced haste. In others—the nature of maritime steam technology in the 1870s especially— prompt and successful action was, on a practical level, impossible. Donald Schurman opens his dissertation with the observation: '[t]here can be little doubt, viewing the question of Empire defence from the vantage point of the present day, that the attention paid to defence problems during the years 1868 to 1887 was hardly commensurate with the growth and population of the Empire.'[77] Again, the point is beyond dispute. The lack of attention was, how- ever, commensurate with the paucity of threats to Empire and connecting sealanes, and this standard of judgment is arguably more appropriate to con- temporary circumstances than Schurman's retrospective appraisal.

CONVENTIONAL WISDOM REDUX

In the conclusion of his dissertation, Schurman assesses the contributions, both positive and negative, made by individuals towards formulating an imper- ial defence policy between 1868 and 1887. J.C.R. Colomb, naturally, receives very high marks, as does William Jervois.[78] Not surprisingly, the only praise earned by Gladstone falls into the 'damning with faint' category: 'Gladstone and the Liberals must be given a kind of inverted credit, since the very antipa- thy of the Government of 1868–74 to the Empire and the armed forces pro- duced a reaction in favour of the continuance of the Empire that was a basic requirement to making plans to defend it.'[79] Carnarvon's role is judged in somewhat more ambivalent terms: Schurman attributes to him 'defects of judg- ment,' but concludes that through his chairmanship of the Royal Commission on Colonial Defence and tireless pro-Empire efforts, his 'share in the emer- gence of the concept of Imperial Defence might well be described as decisive.'[80] Curiously, Alexander Milne is only mentioned in passing in this summing up. Despite his pivotal position at the Admiralty from 1872 to 1876, his chairmanship of the ad hoc Colonial Defence Committee, and his subse- quent membership in Carnarvon's commission, Schurman goes no further than noting that Milne was 'the earliest member of the Board [of Admiralty] to be aware that coal would be a problem in future wars.'[81] This assessment is in keeping with his generally critical take on the First Naval Lord.

Schurman first takes Milne to task over his insistence that ships designed for tasks of imperial defence carry sailing rig. As the First Naval Lord put the mat- ter in one of his memoranda of 1874, the

> coal question will, in any future war, be one of the great difficulties which the Admiralty will have to meet; it therefore becomes necessary that our ships should retain their sailing power and be handy under canvas; for there will be some intervals of time when coal may be entirely wanting.[82]

Such pronouncements lead Schurman to charge that Milne was 'anti-sail,' that 'his dislike for steam is discernible...,' and elsewhere he expresses some surprise that 'the personal story of the rearguard action of sailors [Milne among them] who believed in sail against the new steam navy (1868–1878) has never been properly recounted.'[83]

In this respect however, Schurman missed the boat. Although it is indisputably true that Milne was wrong in maintaining that sails would be necessity for imperial cruisers in 'any future war,' his erroneous prediction seems to have obscured the fundamental fact that at the time he wrote those words he was correct. Schurman further claims that 'the sail-steam controversy ... so far as the Merchant Navy was concerned had already been settled' by 1874, apparently buttressing his contention that Admiralty officials were dragging their feet. This assertion is also disputable. In 1871 the British merchant marine was overwhelmingly sail-powered: of some 5.6 million tons of merchant shipping, 4.3 million were sailing vessels and only 1.3 million steamers.[84] As of 1878, the year that Schurman marked as ending the navy's 'rearguard action against steam,' the merchant marine had 4.1 million tons of sailing vessels to 1.9 million tons of steamers. Only in 1883 did steamships achieve parity (3.6 million to 3.3 million).[85] There may have been an 'anti-steam' clique within the officer corps as a whole; there was not a senior officer who served at the Admiralty during the 1870s, with the possible exception of Lord Gilford, who could be so labelled, least of all Alexander Milne. Milne and his colleagues had an intimate understanding of the limitations of contemporary technology, an understanding which many who have subsequently passed judgment on their actions and thoughts have not shared.

Schurman is, if anything, more critical of Milne's performance as a member of the Carnarvon commission, even suggesting that the failure of the commission to take full cognizance of Admiralty policy and opinion was not pointed out by Milne in his dissenting opinion to some of its findings 'since it would indicate incompetence on his part....'[86] Elsewhere Schurman veers off into the realm of speculation: from the evidence given to the commission by First Naval Lord Admiral Sir Astley Cooper Key, he posits, 'Milne must have realized at once ... that he had been sleeping, and probably he was accused by his ex-colleagues at the Admiralty of betraying the service.'[87] At best, he is willing to concede that Milne 'was a blunt old sailor', yet even this observation is tempered by the remark 'he knew a great deal about this great defence problem, but his mind lacked precision.'[88] The charge of want of precision seems hard to sustain, however, given the very precise calculations of requisite naval strength that Milne routinely produced at the Admiralty. Perhaps the effects of age—Milne was born in 1809—and ill-health, as Schurman suggests, reduced his influence in the deliberations of the Carnarvon commission, but there is substantial evidence that Milne had a clear conception of the subject and was forceful in enunciating his views.[89]

That the navy's views were not accorded the same weight as those of the army in the course of the commission's deliberations seems to be attributable to several factors, among them Lord Carnarvon's own reliance on General John Lintorn Simmons for professional advice, his lack of regard for Milne personally, the Admiralty's failure to make its case forcefully, and, not least of all, because the matter of coaling station defence was, in the first and last analysis, more a matter of army than of navy concern. That the Admiralty was somewhat insular in its handling of imperial defence strategy may have in part simply been a consequence of the fact that its role was in itself—assuming local defence to have been the responsibility of the army—largely insular.

Schurman's assessment of Milne, and the tendency to play down the import of his contributions to imperial defence policy as it evolved might, in short, be tempered somewhat. The three reports of the commission bore the hallmarks of Milne's views on imperial defence, the second stating emphatically that

> [w]ith regard to the permanent defence of Your Majesty's Colonial possessions, we may observe that there is an impression in the minds of many that the navy ought to afford permanent protection to all of them. The Royal Navy is not maintained for the purpose of affording direct local protection to sea-ports or harbours, but for the object of blockading the ports of an enemy, of destroying his trade, attacking his possessions, dealing with his ships at sea, and may we add in preventing an attack in great force against any special place. It is by the efficient performance of these duties that our commerce and colonies will best be protected. Our sea-ports must rely for their immediate defence on local means, leaving Your Majesty's navy free to act at sea.[90]

Additionally, the commission vented its views on the requisite measure of British naval strength in another pronouncement which might have come from Milne's own pen:

> your Commissioners deem the commercial interest to be so great and the paramount importance of its protection so great, especially in the supply of food and raw materials, that they consider Her Majesty's Government ought not to rest satisfied with our fleet being merely on a comparative equity with those of other nations, which has [sic] few Colonies and but a limited trade; but that our navy should be decidedly superior to that of all other nations not only in our ironclad fleet for home defence as well as any service which might arise in the Mediterranean ... but that in fast and well-armed cruisers we ought most decidedly to be considerably in advance of any nation, especially in regard to the speed and armament of our ships.[91]

Milne, it is true, was no theoretician like J.C.R. Colomb, yet his contributions to the evolution of British imperial defence policy were arguably more substantive. Indeed, Bryan Ranft credits Milne with having evolved 'the germ of the worldwide naval strategy which was the core of Britain's defence posture for the rest of the century and in support of which she was eventually to go to war with Germany....,' and that 'Milne's attempt to quantify the task, and his realization of the logistical problem presented by dependence on coal, marked a definite beginning of systematic thought to meet the new conditions.'[92]

That, Ranft aside, Milne has not generally been recognized for his efforts may be a consequence of Schurman's generally critical portrayal, but it may also be related to the fact that Milne was not a publicist; his efforts were largely behind the scenes, his most crucial writings took the form of confidential memoranda and were seen by few eyes beyond Admiralty House. Colomb, on the other hand, was a tireless promoter of his imperial defence scheme, using such forums as the Royal Colonial Institute and the Royal United Services Institute, as well as the press, to deliver his message. Milne's efforts lacked the public dimension of Colomb's or those of later navalists like Beresford, Stead, and Fisher.

In so far as the Carnarvon Commission failed to take proper cognizance of the navy's point of view, Schurman appears far nearer the mark in suggesting that 'behind all the failure to determine Admiralty opinion lay the attitude of the Admiralty itself.'[93] On this matter the evidence is much more substantial. Throughout the period 1856–1905 (and beyond, for that matter) there were discernable deficiencies in the Admiralty's attitude towards the formulation of policy and strategy. Bryan Ranft, for instance, has made a telling case study of the Admiralty's failure to develop even the most rudimentary convoy system until Britain faced the spectre of starvation in 1917, and even Andrew Lambert, less critical than most, has remarked that '[n]aval issues were not debated in the round, largely because there was no need, but also from a marked aversion among the officers of the age to engage in theoretical speculation.'[94]

Some of the Admiralty's shortcomings stemmed from the nature of the department's administrative structure: it lacked anything like a professional staff to consider strategic problems until the creation of the Foreign Intelligence Department by Lord Northbrook in 1882. That body was renamed the Department of Naval Intelligence in 1886, which better conveys the scope of its activities. But other problems with the Admiralty, especially between 1876 and 1889, may be more appropriately attributed to personal factors.

The naval lords were, in theory, responsible in concert with the First Lord for the formulation of strategic policy. Milne's own tenure as First Naval Lord from 1872 to 1876 amply demonstrated that the system could function in this fashion, given a conscientious First Naval Lord who was capable of seeing the big picture. Unfortunately, Milne's successors, in particular Astley Cooper Key (First Naval Lord, 1879–85) and Arthur Hood (1885–89), lacked Milne's breadth of vision, tending instead to immerse themselves in administrative details. N.A.M. Rodger goes as far as uncharitably terming Cooper Key 'a born administrator, if by that is meant someone who loves work and hates decisions'.[95] To the extent that either of them considered strategic policy at all, they seem to have done so only in the vaguest and most unmethodical manner, at least as is evidenced by their respective testimony to the Carnarvon (Cooper Key) and Hartington (Hood) Commissions. Ranft provides a telling synopsis of the former's evidence:

> Asked for an estimate of the number of warships required to protect essential convoys, he gave the revealing reply, 'I could not answer that question without a great deal of thought and inquiry.' Milne's attempts at quantification do not seem to have been followed up.[96]

In short, Cooper Key's testimony demonstrated 'an alarming poverty of thought by the professional head of the Admiralty,' and, 'in light of the rambling and imprecise nature of his evidence, it is not surprising that the Commission could make no specific recommendation about the naval forces required and contented itself with the general judgement "that the strength of the Navy should be increased with as little delay as possible".'[97]

But despite the criticism that the Admiralty, or Cooper Key, or Hood deserve, it should not be postulated, as several have, that the navy or the Admiralty were devoid of any strategic notions whatsoever. So far from designing vessels without reference to their intended strategic role, the disparate collection of vessels—the force derisively dismissed as 'the fleet of samples'—which made up the Royal Navy in the 1860s, 1870s and 1880s, were conceived and constructed with very clear strategic aims, from the coast assault vessels designed to provide a decisive alternative to the close blockade, to the sail–steam cruisers designed for imperial duties.[98] These designs, and the rest evolved by the Admiralty were themselves explicit testimony to the degree to which naval planners took strategic roles into consideration. That many of these vessels—especially the imperial cruisers—are seen in retrospect as failures, combining the worst qualities of sail and steam, should not be taken as an indication of short-sightedness or some worse sin; they were the unavoidable consequences of the state of technology in this crucial transitional period, when steam was reliable and valuable enough to be a necessity on all vessels, but before the technological breakthroughs of the 1880s—water-tube, high pressure boilers and triple expansion engines—coupled with the extension of the network of coaling stations and naval bases (not to mention submarine telegraph cables) made it possible for sails to be abandoned on all but a handful of small vessels. As Arthur Hood stated in an 1873 memorandum to Milne, the Admiralty should be guided as to the types and characteristics of the vessels it designed 'by a consideration of the nature of service...' they 'will be required to perform...'[99] The navy of the mid-Victorian era furnishes overwhelming evidence that Hood's policy was followed.

One final observation: most studies which focus on imperial defence tend, perhaps inevitably, to focus on the periphery, on the Empire itself, and on the sea lanes between colonies and parent country. Insofar as the centre comes into play, it is treated as the nexus from which strategic policy emanated. In closing, therefore, it seems worth stressing that the blockade or assault of European naval arsenals was by far the most important element of imperial defence. All that related to coaling stations and commerce-raiding interdiction was a sideshow, or several sideshows, for naval planners took for granted that the navy would, as it had in the past, keep the major fleet units of hostile forces bottled up in port, or else destroy them before they could escape. With regard to surface vessels, the events of the First and Second World Wars unambiguously confirmed the wisdom of this assumption.

Perhaps the study of imperial defence, at least in the nineteenth century, has become a bit too insular or parochial, concentrating on the peripheries to the detriment of the larger framework. Imperial strategy was, in the final analysis, only one element of British grand strategy, along with national security, commerce protection, and, ultimately, the commitment to intervention on the Continent. None of these facets can or should be divorced from the others or from the larger context. Just as nineteenth century imperial strategists decried the tendency to view defence matters from the insular view of individuals colonies, so should we, in taking stock of their accomplishments, keep in mind that imperial defence was but one element of the overarching net of British grand strategy.

NOTES

1. The principal works on the subject by Schurman are his unpublished but widely-cited Ph.D. Dissertation, 'Imperial Defence, 1868–1887: A study in the decisive impulses behind the change from "Colonial" to "Imperial" defence' (Sidney Sussex College, Cambridge; 1955) and his subsequent *The Education of a Navy: The Development of British naval strategic thought, 1867–1914* (London: Cassell, 1965). Tunstall's contributions to the study of Imperial defence are found chiefly in his essays in the *Cambridge History of the British Empire* (Cambridge, 1940, 1959): 'Imperial Defence, 1815–1870,' vol. 2, 807–41; 'Imperial Defence, 1870–1897,' vol. 3, 230–54; and 'Imperial Defence, 1897–1914,' vol. 3, 563–604.
2. Much attention has been given — by A. J. Marder and others — to the narrowing strategic concentration which took place after 1890, and, especially, during the Fisher era, but this can be viewed as the culmination of a process which began in the late 1860s. See C.J. Bartlett's 'Mid-Victorian Re-appraisal of Naval Policy,' Kenneth Bourne and D.C. Watts (eds.), *Studies in International History: Essays Presented to W. Norton Medlicott, Stevenson Professor of International History at the University of London* (London, 1967).
3. N.A.M. Rodger, 'The Dark Ages of the Admiralty, 1869–1885, Part I, Business Methods, 1868–74,' *Mariner's Mirror* 62, 1(1975), p 331.
4. For instance, see Theodore Ropp (Stephen Roberts, ed.), *The Development of a Modern Navy: French Naval Policy, 1871–1914* (Annapolis, 1987), pp 26–28, 33–41; N.A.M. Rodger, 'British Belted Cruisers,' *Mariner's Mirror* 64, 1(1978), pp 23–35; 'The Design of the Inconstant,' *Mariner's Mirror* 61, 1(1975), pp 9–22, and 'The Dark Ages of the Admiralty, 1969–1885, Part II: Change and Decay, 1774–80,' *Mariner's Mirror* 62, 1(1976), pp 33–46, especially 40–46; Schurman, *Education*, pp 3–5.
5. See, for example, I.F. Clarke, *Voices Prophesying War, 1763–1984* (London, 1970), pp 22–29 passim. Clarke notes that the famous letter from Wellington to Sir John Burgoyne, which was subsequently published only served to confirm the worst fears that the days of Britain's insular security were over; for the Duke had said that, apart from the Dover area, there was not a spot on the coast on which infantry might not be thrown on shore at any time of the tide, with any wind, and in any weather(p 23).

See also Michael Partridge, *Military Planning for the Defence of the United Kingdom, 1814–1870* (New York, 1989), chapters 1 and 2.

6. Arthur J. Marder, *The Anatomy of British Sea Power: A History of British Naval Policy in the Pre-Dreadnought Era, 1880–1905* (New York, 1940), p 67.

7. Paul Kennedy, *The Rise and Fall of British Naval Mastery* (reprint ed., London, 1994, originally published 1976), p 167.

8. N.A.M. Rodger, 'The "Dark Ages" of the Admiralty, 1869–1885', *Mariner's Mirror*, 61 and 62 (1975 and 1976); Oscar Parkes, *British Battleships, 'Warrior' 1860 to 'Vanguard' 1850: A History of Design, Construction and Armament* (London, Seeley, 1957).

9. H.T.L. Corry, 'Memorandum for the Consideration of the Cabinet,' Printed, Confidential, 2 Dec 1867, Milne Papers, MLN/143/3/10 [National Maritime Museum, Greenwich].

10. Andrew Lambert, 'The Royal Navy 1856–1914: Deterrence and the Strategy of World Power,' p 13. I am indebted to Dr Lambert for permission to cite his yet-unpublished paper.

11. Ibid., p 14.

12. 'Augmentation of the Naval Force, in Ships and Stores' (Copy), 9 Aug 1870, ADM 1/6159 [Public Record Office, Kew].

13. Remarks of Dacres, 12 Dec. 1871, ADM 138/64 (Ship's Cover for H.M.S. *Glatton*) [National Maritime Museum, Woolwich Collection].

14. Lambert, p 14.

15. For instance, Clarke, *Voices Prophesying War*; Andrew Lambert, *Battleships in Transition: The Creation of the Steam Battlefleet, 1815–1860* (London, 1984); C.I. Hamilton, *The Anglo-French Naval Rivalry, 1840–1870* (Oxford, 1993); Partridge, *Military Planning*. Schurman and Tunstall are notable exceptions.

16. See especially I. F. Clarke's opening chapter, in which he details the 'break-in' mentality.

17. Schurman, *Education*, pp 16–35. An entire chapter is devoted to Colomb and his writings.

18. Schurman, 'Imperial Defence,' p 44.

19. Ibid., p 47.

20. Ibid., pp 44–45.

21. Ibid., p 45.

22. There were a few other important bases as well, such as Esquimalt (Vancouver).

23. Schurman, 'Imperial Defence,' p 45.

24. Ibid., p 46.

25. Tunstall, 'Imperial Defence, 1815–70,' p 838; Schurman, ibid., pp 41–47.

26. It was probably a testimony to his political neutrality as well. When he came to the Admiralty in 1847 one of his conditions was that he be spared from dealing with any matters of a political nature. Twenty-four years later, when Milne's name was vetted for First Naval Lord, First Lord of the Admiralty G.J. Goschen reported to Prime Minister William Gladstone that Milne was 'politically neutral'. 'Abstract of Measures introduced by Sir Alexander Milne while at the Admiralty,' (Printed), MLN/145/5/2; Goschen to Gladstone, 27 October 1872, Gladstone Papers, Add Mss 44161, fol. 217 [British Library, London].

27. Schurman, 'Imperial Defence,' p 35. The memorandum was dated 10 June 1858.

28. Bryan Ranft, 'The protection of British seaborne trade and the development of systematic planning for war, 1860–1906,' in Ranft (ed.), *Technical Change and British Naval Policy 1860–1939* (London, 1977), p 2.

29. Milne to Board of Admiralty, 'Paper Relative to Unarmoured Ships and Proposal for an Establishment,' Printed, Confidential, Dec. 1874, Milne Papers, MLN/144/3/1.

30. Schurman, 'Imperial Defence,' p 54.

31. Milne to Board of Admiralty, 'Position of Cruising Ships for Protection of Trade,' Printed, Confidential, Dec 1874, Milne Papers, MLN/144/3/1.

32. Schurman, 'Imperial Defence,' p 59. Jervois' paper was formally titled 'Memorandum by Colonel Sir W.F.D. Jervois, K.C.M.G., C.B., R.E., with reference to the defenceless condition of our Coaling Stations and Naval Establishments Abroad.' Carnarvon Papers, PRO 30/6/122 [Public Record Office].

33. He believed that the bases he listed—Port Royal, Antigua, Ascension Island, Simon's Bay, Port Louis (Mauritius), Trincomalee, Singapore, Hong Kong, King George's Sound (Western Australia), Esquimalt (Vancouver), and the Falklands (presumably Port Stanley)—could be made secure at a total expense of £950,000, and that the cost should be borne by the imperial government, rather than by the individual colonies, since it was, he maintained, 'essential for Imperial

interests.' See Schurman, ibid., pp 56–60.

34. Ibid., p 61.
35. Ibid., p 127.
36. Ibid., pp 122–23.
37. Ibid., pp 127, 135, 136–38.
38. Schurman, *Education*, p 30. See also pp 32–35 for Colomb's unceasing efforts, and 'Imperial Defence,' p 143 for his attempt to gain a seat on the Carnarvon Commission. Colomb remained a vocal and tireless proponent of his theories until his death in 1909, and his efforts were repaid with the Carnarvon Commission, whose appointment was, Schurman maintains, 'along the lines' he suggested.
39. 'Report of the Royal Commission appointed to make enquiry into the condition and sufficiency of the means of the naval and military forces provided for the defence of the more important sea-ports within our Colonial possessions and dependencies' (commonly known as the Carnarvon Commission), Printed, Confidential, Carnarvon Papers, PRO 30/6/131. For an able published summary of the proceedings and Reports of the Carnarvon Commission, see Donald C. Gordon, *The Dominion Partnership in Imperial Defense, 1870–1914* (Baltimore, 1965), pp 62–67.
40. Schurman, 'Imperial Defence', p 173.
41. 'Colonial Ports and Coaling Stations, and to consider the Apportionment of the cost of such Defences,' appendix to 'Proceedings of the Colonial Conference, at London, with Appendix [relating to Legal Questions, Posts and Telegraphs, Life Saving at Sea, Pacific Islands, Australian Defences, and Carnarvon Commission on Imperial Defence];' *Parl. Papers* (microprint edition), 1887 [c.5091], LVI, 917.
42. Schurman, 'Imperial Defence', pp 167, 182, 185. He notes, by way of example, that the Commission 'indicated some lack of sympathy [appreciation?] with their own evaluation of the strategic importance of coal', and, regarding their strategic judgment, he terms their recommendations for the Cape 'particularly unsatisfactory'.
43. Schurman, 'Imperial Defence', p 185.
44. Ibid., p 212.
45. Tunstall, 'Imperial Defence, 1870–1897', p 23.
46. Schurman, 'Imperial Defence', pp 213–29.
47. As Schurman notes, it was still 'heavily weighted in favour of the War Office,' rather than the Admiralty, containing five members from the former department and only one from the latter. Schurman suggests that this is another example of a 'failure to place naval functions in their proper relation to imperial defence', but given that most of the Committee's work concerned local defences, that is, military works, War Office predominance would seem logical. On the Russian cruisers—the *Rurik* and its half-sister—see Tunstall, 'Imperial Defence, 1870–1897', p 235; Roger Cheasneau and Eugene Kolesnik (eds.) *Conway's all the World's Fighting Ships, 1860–1905* (London: Conway Maritime Press, 1979), pp 67, 189. The British designed the *Powerful* class in response to the *Rurik*.
48. Schurman, 'Imperial Defence', 239–40, citing Brassey's *Naval Annual*, 1887, pp 55–59.
49. Brassey, *Naval Annual*, 1890, pp 81, 87.
50. Ibid., pp 79–91.
51. See Tunstall, 'Imperial Defence, 1870–1897', pp 237–41.
52. Ibid., p 243.
53. 'Extracts from the Report of the Committee on the Naval Manoeuvres, 1888, with the Narrative of the Operations, and the rule laid down for conducting the same,' *Parl. Papers*, 1889, L [c. 5632], pp 29–31.
54. Schurman, `Imperial Defence,' pp 156–61, 205–12.
55. W.S. Hamer, *The British Army: Civil–Military Relations 1885–1905* (Oxford, 1970), p 139.
56. Ibid.
57. Tunstall, 'Imperial Defence, 1870–1897,' p 252.
58. Ibid., p 566.
59. 'Report of the Royal Commission on the War in South Africa,' *Parl. Papers*, 1904, XL (c.1789), p 15.
60. 'Report of the War Office (Reconstitution) Committee, Pt. I,' *Parl. Papers*, 1904, VIII [c.1932], p 3.
61. Tunstall, 'Imperial Defence, 1897–1914,' 573. The latter Committee had, it is true, been reconstituted in 1902, 'so as "to survey as a whole the strategical military needs of the Empire,"' and the

Prime Minister regularly attended its meetings from this point forward.

62. Schurman, 'Imperial Defence,' p 25.

63. See also Schurman, *Education*, p 29 and 'Imperial Defence,' pp 65–73, 241–59.

64. See, for instance, Stanley Sandler, *The Emergence of the Modern Capital* : Delaware, 1979); Schurman, 'Imperial Defence'; Oscar Parkes, *British Battleships, 1860–1950* (London, 1957); Rodger, 'British Belted Cruisers;' George Ballard, *The Black Battlefleet* (a collection of *Mariner's Mirror* articles from the 1930s, Annapolis, 1980).

65. Sandler, ibid., pp 86–87.

66. The last major British armoured unit to be designed with a sailing rig was H.M.S. *Inflexible*, which was laid down in 1873. It is not fully clear why the *Inflexible* bore sails, although evidence in the ship's cover indicators that her designers anticipated the possibility that she might serve east of Suez.

67. Memorandum by Hood to Milne, 5 Feb 1873, Confidential, Milne Papers, MLN/144/1/3.

68. See Mary Augusta Egerton, *Admiral of the Fleet Sir Geoffrey Phipps Hornby, G.C.B. A Biography* (Edinburgh, 1896), pp 205–06. Admiral Geoffrey Phipps Hornby wrote First Lord George Ward Hunt in 1876 'The *Monarch*, Captain Seymour, has burnt since leaving Malta 331 tons [of coal], while this ship has burnt 160; and, I believe, this fairly represents the difference between steam at 60 lb. to [sic] steam at 16 lb.' The subject of boiler deterioration was also a regular feature of Parliamentary debates over the Navy during the 1870s, and generated the appointment of a Committee to consider the subject. See Great Britain, *Hansard's Parliamentary Debates*, 3rd Ser., 215 (1873), col. 61; 218 (1874), 854; 238 (1878), cols. 1429, 1453. A.E. Seaton, author of a standard contemporary text on marine engineering, described the problem: 'Boilers, especially those in H.M. Navy, showed signs of premature decay, such as was not customary with those receiving water from a jet condenser. It was found to be due to the highly corrosive power of redistilled water on the bare surface of the iron, and to the impossibility of keeping a protective scale on the surface when such water was used.' A.E. Seaton, *A Manual of Marine Engineering: Comprising the Design, Construction, and Working of Marine Machinery* (London, 1907), pp 228–29. For a modern survey of the problems surrounding maritime steam technology during the mid-Victorian era, see K.T. Rowland, *Steam at Sea: A History of Steam Navigation* (Newton Abbot, 1970), especially pp 106–36.

69. John Beeler, 'A "One Power Standard?" Great Britain and the Balance of Naval Power, 1860–1880', *Journal of Strategic Studies*, 15, 4(1992), pp 550–67.

70. Ibid., pp 569–70; Lambert, 'The Royal Navy 1856–1914,' pp 28–29; George Modelski and William R. Thompson, *Seapower in Global Politics, 1493–1993* (Seattle, 1988), pp 78.

71. Ropp, *Development of a Modern Navy*, pp 155–80.

72. Marder, *Anatomy*, p 87.

73. Lambert, 'The Royal Navy 1856–1914,' p 11.

74. Brassey, *Naval Annual*, 1888–9, p 231.

75. Marder, *Anatomy*, p 89.

76. Kennedy, *Naval Mastery*, p 199.

77. Schurman, 'Imperial Defence,' p 1.

78. Ibid., pp 266–68.

79. Ibid., p 266.

80. Ibid., p 270.

81. Ibid., pp 268–69.

82. Milne, 'Position of Cruising Ships for Protection of Trade,' Printed, Confidential, December 1874, Milne Papers, MLN/144/3/1.

83. Schurman, 'Imperial Defence,' pp 32, 52.

84. Great Britain, *Statistical Abstract for the United Kingdom* (London): 23 (1876), p 96; 37 (1890) p 157.

85. Moreover, merchant vessels operating on regular schedules and/or between commercial ports with coal supplies faced fewer problems in making the switchover than many naval vessels, which might be called upon to operate for weeks or even months at a time out of range of a coal depot.

86. Schurman, 'Imperial Defence,' p 205.

87. Ibid., pp 207–8.

88. Ibid., p 207.

89. Milne to Carnarvon, 28 Nov 1879, cited in ibid., p 148. Indeed, Schurman acknowledges that Milne twice informed Carnarvon on his views regarding the scope of the inquiry, the second time

volunteering an explicit synopsis of the task of imperial defence, in which
he put forward the following important points: first, that since an enemy could be
blockaded in Europe, the Commission's calculations need only be based on the
threat of a small squadron or single raiding vessels; second that the problem of
local volunteers and Militia to man the forts was very important; third, that in
matters where colonial defence contribution was hoped for, previous consultation
with those concerned would render cooperation more likely.

90. 'Second Report of the Commission to inquire into the State of the Defences of the more important
     Colonial Ports and Coaling Stations, and to consider the Apportionment of the cost of such
     Defences,' appendix to 'Proceedings of the Colonial Conference, at London, with Appendix [relat-
     ing to Legal Questions, Posts and Telegraphs, Life Saving at Sea, Pacific Islands, Australian
     Defences, and Carnarvon Commission on Imperial Defence];' *Parl. Papers* (microprint edition),
     1887 [c.5091], LVI, p 918.
91. 'First Report of the Royal Commission appointed to make enquiry into the condition and sufficien-
     cy of the means of the Naval and Military forces provided for the Defence of the more important
     sea-ports within our Colonial Possessions and Dependencies,' 9 Jul. 1881, Confidential, Printed,
     Carnarvon Papers, PRO 30/6/5.
92. Ranft, p 2.
93. Schurman, 'Imperial Defence,' p 208.
94. Lambert, 'The Royal Navy, 1856–1914,' p 19.
95. N.A.M. Rodger, *The Admiralty* (Lavenham, Suffolk, 1979), p 113. Rodger adds: 'An essentially
     weak man, he crowded his desk, his day and his mind with comforting trivia, and carefully
     excluded anything so unsettling as policy.'
96. Ranft, p 3.
97. Hood's evidence to the Hartington Commission was of a similar dubious quality. See Ranft, p 7.
98. Rodger, 'Dark Ages, Part II,' p 43.
99. Hood to Milne, 5 Feb 1873, Confidential, Milne Papers, MLN/144/1/3.

Economy or empire?

The fleet unit concept and the quest for collective security in the Pacific, 1909–14

NICHOLAS LAMBERT

The efforts by Great Britain before the First World War to forge a system of collective security with the self-governing Dominions for the defence of their common maritime interests have been largely ignored by historians. Indeed, the formation of Australian and Canadian navies in 1909 and 1910 barely rates a mention in most standard accounts. Arthur Marder, for instance, devoted just one line to the 'offer of some dreadnoughts by some of the Dominions' in 1909 which he dismissed as a 'by-product' of the navy scare.[1] Such attitudes are attributable to the presumptions that Britain's defence policy was driven by an anti-German imperative, and that questions of imperial defence in peripheral regions such as the Pacific were by comparison regarded as insignificant. The standard political and diplomatic accounts of the period reinforce this impression.[2] Generally, the negotiation of a naval treaty with Japan in 1902 is held to mark the end of Britain's 'splendid isolation'.[3] The renegotiation of the Anglo-Japanese Alliance in 1905 for another ten years is generally regarded as sufficient explanation for imperial defence policy east of Suez.[4]

The parentage of these 'daughter' navies has been studied in more detail in the Dominions.[5] Many writers of these studies, however, have tended to focus upon naval development in the context of emerging national identities.[6] All share one common weakness; namely a superficial treatment of the British side of the story and of the relationship between imperial policy and naval policy in general. The standard interpretation of the Admiralty's views is that Britain's naval leadership remained steadfastly opposed to the creation of independent colonial navies. Even the best works on the subject insist that throughout this period the Admiralty remained wedded to the strategic formula of 'one ocean, one empire, one navy'.[7] When in 1909 the decision was taken to form the Royal Australian and Royal Canadian Navies, it is argued the Admiralty co-operated only reluctantly and provided little encouragement.[8] This simply was not the case.

While Sir John Fisher was First Sea Lord (from 1904 and 1910) the Board of Admiralty maintained that the formation of local navies was inevitable and tried to persuade the British Government that it would be a mistake to stand in the way.[9] As early as 1906, the admirals recognized that the creation of a 'national' navy had assumed a 'political complexion' in the Commonwealth of Australia.[10] Documents from this period show that the majority of senior Admiralty officials did not object to the idea of a Dominion Navy, and expressed themselves willing to support any reasonable plan. Unfortunately their definition of reasonable usually involved the expenditure of comparatively large sums.[11] At that time the Australians were unable or unwilling to allocate more than a 'token' sum, sufficient to pay for a couple of small ships manned by a handful of reservists.[12] The Admiralty, meanwhile, consistently refused to have anything to do with what they termed 'sentimental navies'.[13] Such forces, they argued with justification, would be more a source of weakness than strength to the empire. Dominion politicians (and many subsequent historians) mistakenly interpreted their negative remarks as amounting to no more than obstruction.[14]

In July 1909, however, the Admiralty suddenly conceived an ambitious and coherent plan to serve as the basis for a system of naval defence designed to protect all imperial interests in the Far East. In effect, they proposed to re-establish a large British fleet in the Pacific. More importantly, the Admiralty also devised an acceptable formula for Britain and her Colonies to share the incidental expenditure. At the Imperial Defence Conference the 'fleet unit' concept was put forward as the model for adoption by Dominions that wished to create navies of their own. That the Admiralty was planning in mid-1909 (at the height of the 'navy scare'!) to send a significant proportion of its newest warships to the Pacific does not fit easily into the theory that Britain's naval leadership at this time was fixated by the growing German fleet. This article will attempt to address this lacuna by examining the attitude towards Britain's defence commitments in the Pacific held by the Board of Admiralty *as distinct* from the views of the Cabinet or Foreign Office. It will show that the Admiralty possessed a far broader strategic outlook than previously suspected, belying the notion that questions of imperial defence were being more or less ignored at this time.

* * *

Many assessments of Britain's strategic position in the Far East during this period fail to take proper account of the nature of naval operations that then prevailed. Until the end of the nineteenth century, the Pacific squadrons of all the principal naval powers were comprised of gunboats and cruising vessels—perhaps supported by an old battleship—and were organized to police seaborne trade and protect commercial interests.[15] At the turn of the century, however, the situation changed. Russia, Japan and France began stationing first class naval units in the region. By 1900, the Russian squadron at Port Arthur had grown into a fleet of six modern battleships.[16] Despite the formidable costs involved, the British Government believed it had no alternative but to follow suit. The simultaneous development of the side-armoured cruiser compounded the Royal Navy's growing difficulties in defending a sprawling global empire.[17] These fast, long range, and well protected new model warships were specially designed by the French for raiding commerce. Overnight they rendered obsolete all existing trade protection vessels.[18] By 1902, the British state was already struggling to finance the construction of battleships to maintain the Two Power Standard, build adequate numbers of armoured cruisers, and at the same time respond to the threat to imperial interests in the Far East. Largely because of financial limitation, the Admiralty agreed as an interim measure to the suggestion of a naval treaty with Japan.[19]

The early months of the Russo-Japanese War which began in February 1904, quickly revealed the vulnerability of old ships when matched against new, and the foolishness of handicapping a squadron comprised of modern warships with obsolete craft. When in October 1904, Sir John Fisher was appointed Senior Naval Lord, he immediately recalled from overseas all cruisers 'too old to fight and too slow to run away'.[20] Shortly afterwards, despite fierce criticism, he also brought home the five battleships of the China squadron. In their place, Fisher had planned to re-equip the station fleets with modern armoured cruisers.[21] But he was only half way through redistributing the fleet when the strategic situation in the Pacific dramatically changed. In May 1905 the Russian Fleet was annihilated at Tsushima. Shortly thereafter France and the United States recalled their modern battleships and cruisers to home waters. As a result, except for the Japanese navy, the Pacific became virtually deserted of modern armoured warships. In the autumn, the British Government renegotiated and extended the naval treaty with Japan until 1915. Finally, at the end of 1905, a radical Liberal ministry came to power in Britain with the declared intent of cutting naval expenditure to pay for social reform.[22] With no obvious threat to British interests in the Pacific, and not wanting to appear profligate, the Admiralty suspended the dispatch of new ships to the Far East. Obviously, to have kept a large fleet on the China station would have invited accusations of extravagance and probably had led to even more severe cuts in the navy budget.

The logistical difficulties in operating a naval force in the Pacific during this time have been scarcely realized by some historians. Without a plentiful supply of steam coal, a fleet, however imposing on paper, could not be operated effectively.[23] The vast majority of coal used by all naval squadrons in the Pacific was mined in Wales and was transported to the region in British colliers. The only 'local' coals suitable for naval purposes came from Westport, New Zealand.[24] Except for Britain, no other major naval power kept large stocks in the Far East. Without access to British coal, therefore, navies could mount a sustained offensive in the Pacific with no more than three or four large armoured ships.[25] Under the Liberal Government, the Admiralty endeavoured to exploit and develop what might be termed its 'hidden strengths'. Considerable sums were expended on maintaining large coal stocks (300,000 tons at Hong Kong alone)[26] and modernizing the docks at key naval bases east of Suez to take the new generation of large armoured warships then under construction.[27] In the process, the Royal Navy developed the unique capability to dispatch at short notice significant numbers of reinforcements to its station fleets in the Far East. In addition, the Admiralty quietly expanded its intelligence-gathering capability in the region, and also tightened its grip on the flow of information into and out of the region by sponsoring a network of British-controlled wireless telegraph stations.[28]

It is therefore essential that any analysis of defence policy in the Pacific must be looked at in the context of the new conditions of naval warfare resulting from recent changes in naval technology, as well as any constraints imposed by domestic political considerations. Furthermore, it must be recognized that the main threat to British imperial interests came from first class armoured cruisers preying upon merchantmen; not a battle fleet covering an invasion fleet.[29] The Admiralty was quite justified to argue that:

> the known intentions of our possible enemies quite preclude the hope
> that the ill-armed unprotected second and third class cruisers, which
> have recently been removed from the fighting fleet, would have been
> of any real service as commerce protectors. The announced intention
> of France is to employ upon 'the guerre de course' her fastest and
> finest armoured cruisers.[30]

The sums of money earmarked by the Dominions for the formation of their own navy would have covered the annual maintenance (but not the building cost) of one or possibly two big cruisers. Hence the Admiralty's view that the Dominions were simply not 'disposed to take up the matter of defence in earnest'.[31] Needless to say, a navy comprised of one or two ships was just not viable. It may be argued that from the Dominions' perspective, money and politics were all important: that the technological and strategic considerations were not relevant to the formation of Dominion navies. Maybe so, but this argument ignores certain facts. Most importantly, the British Admiralty consistently refused to help the Dominions 'play the game' by any rules except their own; secondly, colonial politicians were always anxious to obtain a seal of approval from the Royal Navy for their schemes; and finally, the formation of any sort of affordable local navy depended upon co-operation by the British to provide the ships, designs, instructors and technical support.

The question of imperial naval policy was forced into prominence in March 1909, after the Prime Minister of Great Britain, H.H. Asquith, and the First Lord of the Admiralty, Reginald McKenna, announced the Liberal Government's intention to lay down immediately four new dreadnoughts under the 1909 programme, and *possibly* another four later in the year. Britain's naval supremacy, they explained to the House of Commons, was threatened by the steady growth of the German high seas fleet. On 22 March, the New Zealand Cabinet telegraphed an offer to assume financial responsibility for building one, and possibly two, first class battleships.[32] A week later, the Canadian Parliament passed a resolution recognising 'the duty' of Canada 'to assume in a larger measure the responsibilities of national defence'.[33] On 15 April, the Prime Minister of the Australian Commonwealth telegraphed his willingness to lend support for the mother country.[34] But despite strong public pressure to match the New Zealand offer,[35] he proposed instead to build a flotilla of twenty-odd destroyers, completely independent of the Royal Navy.[36] Not surprisingly, the British Cabinet greeted all these gifts with delight. Some ministers speculated whether the colonial ships might be built 'in substitution of the [four contingent] ships which we ourselves, or shall, propose to build'.[37]

The Admiralty, by contrast, was far less sanguine at the possibility of being given 'free' ships. As to the more concrete proposition advanced by the Australians, which the Colonial Office thought to be 'a very good offer',[38] with reservations the Admiralty agreed to co-operate.[39] It did not seem to matter much as the destroyers would contribute little to imperial defence.[40] Besides, commented Rear-Admiral Alexander Bethell, the Governor-General of Australia had warned that 'owing to the unsettled condition of politics here no great reliance should be placed on these proposals as a final expression of Australian opinion.'[41] After reflecting on all the offers, the Admiralty insisted it needed to hear much more before expressing any further opinion, and suggested the best course would be to summon representatives from each nation to London for a conference. On 30 April invitations were issued to all colonial heads of government. The Admiralty's caution was quickly shown to be well founded. As the atmosphere of crisis subsided, dispatches from the Governors-General of both Australia and Canada informed London that 'their' politicians were becoming more reticent about giving away money.[42] The Canadian Prime Minister, Sir Wilfrid Laurier, was reported to be especially reluctant to divert money from 'much needed public works' and the construction of 'transcontinental railways'.[43] Whether these were his true motives is doubtful. As Lord Grey (in Ottawa) reminded the British Government, Laurier was an avowed pacifist who regarded armaments 'with all the horror of a man who sees in them only the advancing shadow of impending national bankruptcies'.[44] This did not surprise the Admiralty.[45]

The offers from the Dominions to assist with naval defence of the Empire did not result in the reappraisal of British naval policy in the Pacific.[46] In fact a review had been underway since the beginning of the year. This had been prompted by a complaint from Vice-Admiral Hedworth Lambton, commanding the China squadron, that the coastal defences protecting the naval base at Hong Kong were seriously inadequate.[47] He had remarked to the Governor-General of the Colony that 'Great Britain had lost command of the sea in the Far Eastern waters' and that consequently the colony could no longer rely upon the Navy to protect it from invasion. The Admiralty was not amused at having to calm a minor panic at the Colonial Office. 'Under existing conditions in the Far East', wrote Rear-Admiral Edmond Slade, the outgoing Director of Naval Intelligence, Lambton's assessment was preposterous. If a couple of submarines could be spared from home waters, he minuted, 'the apprehension which has arisen as to the sufficiency of the present defences would be to a great extent allayed'.[48] The future, Slade admitted, was however less certain.[49] Unfortunately the matter did not end here. The Secretary of State for the Colonial Office, who had also been sent a copy of Lambton's complaints, passed the matter on to the Colonial Defence Committee (CDC).[50] After considering his arguments at a meeting held on 28 January 1909,[51] the CDC concluded that 'Admiral Lambton's letter raises important issues which materially affect the fundamental strategic principles upon which the system of imperial defence is at the present time based'.[52] To the Admiralty's fury,[53] the majority of members voted to refer the matter to the Committee of Imperial Defence (CID). The CID was slow to reply.[54] Between March and June, Prime Minister Asquith (who was chairman of the CID) was preoccupied with the more immediate problem of holding his Cabinet together during the navy scare. In addition, much of his time was taken up by listening to Admiral Lord Charles Beresford's complaints against Fisher's naval administration.[55] So it was not until 29 June 1909 that the Prime Minister found the time to convene a meeting.[56]

On 2 July 1909, Admiral Sir John Fisher reported to a friend that 'last Tuesday [29 June] we had to deal in Defence Committee [CID] on the defence of Hong Kong with an insidious military scheme fostered by a silly Admiral to provide for the British Navy being wiped out! It's really damnable!'[57] In their position paper, the Admiralty pleaded that the 'picturesque sentences' used by Admiral Lambton to set forth his case could 'scarcely be taken seriously'.[58] So long as the Government maintained the Two Power Standard, the Admiralty claimed, the navy could guarantee the defence of all British defended ports around the world. At the meeting Rear-Admiral Alexander Bethell, the new DNI, outlined the navy's reinforcement strategy. Within twenty-four days, he claimed, the entire Mediterranean fleet could reinforce the China squadron.[59] 'We could', he added, 'even if we were engaged in war with Germany, send out twenty battleships to Hong Kong, with a proper proportion of armoured cruisers'.[60] All present were satisfied that 'so long as the Anglo-Japanese Alliance remained in force the British possessions in the Far East are secure'. But what if Japan renounced the alliance? It was also pointed out by Lord Crewe, the Secretary of State for the Colonies, Viscount Esher, and Admiral of the Fleet Sir Arthur Wilson, that in times of strained relations the government of the day might not want to risk dispatching reinforcements for fear of precipitating conflict. They argued that a significant naval presence must be retained in China. At the close, the CID resolved to take a middle course. The Admiralty was instructed to strengthen the China squadron 'before the termination of the alliance'. At the same time the defences at Hong Kong would be improved 'to enable the fortress to hold out for a period of one month'.[61] Subsequently, a more detailed assessment by the CDC calculated that increasing the garrison by even a battalion was impracticable. 'Reliance must therefore be placed upon the action of the British fleet', they concluded, 'to render the fortress secure from such forms of land attack as Japan might bring to bear against it should the Anglo-Japanese alliance be terminated'.[62] The Admiralty was happy to oblige.

As an afterthought the CID also suggested it might be sensible to consider the defence of the Far East in light of the imminent establishment of Dominion naval forces.[63] On 2 July a sub-committee of the CID was appointed to study if and how the Dominion naval forces might best contribute to the naval defence of the Pacific.[64] Considering the Imperial Conference was scheduled to open on 28 July, the reader may think it a little surprising that nothing had been worked out before this time! But this was the case. On 17 June, Sir Charles Ottley, secretary of the CID, had sent a letter to McKenna expressing his anxiety that 'time is short' and that he had yet to be sent any memoranda from the Admiralty or the Colonial Office 'on the question of colonial naval co-operation'.[65] The Colonial Office, apparently, had refused to make any decisions until after the meeting of the CID on the 29th.[66] The Admiralty's opinion was still harder to gauge. At this time the Board was preoccupied with a number of important issues. Yet it does seem that Britain's naval leaders recognized that unless they put forward a coherent plan at the Imperial Conference, the Dominions would never be dissuaded from building themselves 'little twopenny-halfpenny navies.' Even critics of local navies within the service accepted that 'the experiment had to be tried only to make people realize that it would never be efficient'.[67] In addition, the Board acknowledged that 'something had to be done to meet Australian and New Zealand nervousness who did not like being with no large armoured ships in the Far East ... it is the dread of the Japanese which is at the bottom of the matter'.[68]

The direction of the Admiralty's thinking on the character of the force they eventually hoped to establish in the Far East was heavily influenced by recent technological developments. In July 1908, the newly commissioned 'battle cruiser' HMS *Indomitable* steamed straight across the Atlantic Ocean at an average speed of 25 knots.[69] This proved the reliability of the turbine engine to propel a large armoured warship over distances of several thousand miles at high speed. The previous generation of reciprocating engines fitted to armoured cruisers could not be run at high speed for any length of time. Despite costing almost two million sterling each, Sir John Fisher advocated the battle cruiser as the ideal type of warship for Dominion navies.[70] Also in 1908, the oil-fired turbine-driven HMS *Swift* began her trials. Although saddled with the nomenclature of 'destroyer', she was designed to fulfil the missions assigned to craft which were later known as 'light cruisers',[71] (although technical difficulties and opposition to the type from within the service delayed their introduction in large numbers until 1913). Finally, the Royal Navy had recently completed its chain of wireless telegraphy stations covering the Far East. Linked to their well-established network of 'agents' in most foreign ports, the Admiralty was now better able to exploit its intelligence and vector trade protection vessels into the vicinity of raiders. 'It was not generally realised how recent inventions had revolutionised naval warfare', Fisher later stressed at the Imperial Conference. 'The need for the smaller class of cruisers was greatly diminished by the invention of wireless telegraphy'.[72]

Shortly after his retirement from the service at the end of 1909, Rear-Admiral Reginald Bacon presented an extraordinary paper to The Institute of Naval Architects.[73] Bacon, it should be noted, had recently served as Director of Naval Ordnance and, until he accepted the directorship of the Coventry Ordnance Works, had been destined to assume the post of Controller and Third Sea Lord the following April.[74] Bacon started his lecture by announcing that the development of long-range torpedoes now exposed battleships to effective attack by smaller vessels.[75] 'Not only is the battleship itself open to attack by small craft which it cannot engage on equal terms, but it is powerless to protect any form of vessel against the attacks of such craft'. He went on to predict that the big-gun warship of the future would carry only light armour protection because new capped projectiles 'could penetrate any thickness of armour that could be practically mounted in a ship', and would possess high speed for tactical and strategic reasons.[76] Bacon, of course, was describing the battle cruiser concept. But perhaps the most revealing aspects of the paper were the references to tactics. If battleships were formed into a traditional close order line of battle, Bacon reasoned, they would be left extremely vulnerable to torpedoes. 'It is far easier to hit one of twelve ships with a torpedo than to hit a singe ship aimed at', he declared. Therefore:

> we may reasonably expect that the huge monsters of the future will always be accompanied by torpedo craft of the highest seagoing speed as defensive and offensive satellites. The battleship as now known will probably develop from a single ship into a battle unit consisting of a large armoured cruiser with attendant torpedo craft. Line of battle, as we now know it, will be radically modified, and the fleet action of the future will, in course of time, develop into an aggregation of duels between opposing battle units. The tactics of such units open up a vista of most exhilarating speculation.[77]

The significance of this paper was that Bacon was well known to be a close 'confidant' of Admiral Fisher. Between 1905 and 1907, he had served as his principal assistant. It is, therefore, likely that Bacon's paper encapsulated at least part of Fisher's vision. Fisher privately admitted as much.[78] And certainly this was the impression of the civilian inventor, Arthur Pollen. The day after the lecture he wrote to a friend:

> We have the First Lord's word for it that the lecturer of yesterday enjoyed the fullest confidence of the Board of Admiralty less than a year ago. The portentous question that faces us, therefore, is this: is this balderdash about non-combatant battleships just his own extemporised opinion or has he unconsciously revealed to friend and foe at last

that imponderable and unknown quantity, the mind of the British Admiralty?[79]

Fisher's enthusiasm for the battle cruiser type is now unquestioned.[80] Yet no-one can deny his radical ideas on force structure and tactics were regarded as controversial by most of Britain's naval leaders. Even some of his allies thought them inappropriate for North Sea requirements. But there is no doubt that his modular fleet 'system' was eminently suited for the strategic conditions of the Pacific where the principal mission was trade protection; distances were vast; and for logistical reasons navies could not deploy more than a handful of large armoured ships for any length of time.

Fisher's theories withstand close scrutiny. Until the development of light cruisers fitted with geared turbines and burning oil fuel (during the First World War), it was impractical to build small cruisers for oceanic trade protection duties.[81] Smaller coal-burning vessels simply could not compete with large armoured cruisers. They had neither the guns and armour to fight; nor the speed and endurance to run away. For instance, the cruising radius (at ten knots) of an Indomitable and a Bristol class cruiser were roughly similar— about 6000 miles. But when proceeding at twenty-five knots, the Indomitable could steam 3,100 miles without refuelling whereas the coal-eating Bristol would manage only 260 miles.[82] 'Like ants', Fisher often privately explained to friends, small cruisers 'will all be eaten up by one "Indomitable" armadillo, which puts out its tongue and licks them all up! (The bigger the ant, the more placid the digestive smile!)'[83] And 'on the wide Ocean one Indomitable owing to her immense superiority of speed in a sea-way — (waves that are like mountains to destroyers are nothing to her!) would overtake and lick up one after the other'.[84]

In the memorandum circulated to the Dominions explaining how they might best co-operate with the Royal Navy in the defence of the Pacific, for the first time the Admiralty publicly conceded 'that in defining the conditions under which the naval forces of the Empire should be developed, other considerations than those of strategy must be taken into account'.[85] At the same time, if Dominion navies were going to become efficient and thus make a positive contribution to the naval defence of the Empire, then it was essential they remain closely linked with the Royal Navy. Interchangeability was the key to efficiency. The Admiralty therefore proposed that any nation 'desirous of creating a navy should aim at forming a distinct fleet unit' built around a battle cruiser and supported by twelve smaller warships of specific types.[86] The reader will immediately recognize the term 'fleet units' as being synonymous with Admiral Bacon's 'battle units'. According to William Graham Greene, the Assistant Secretary at the Admiralty, the idea of proposing fleet units for the Dominion navies owed much to Admiral of the Fleet Sir Arthur Wilson.[87] It was Arthur Wilson's endorsement of the battle cruiser type in the CID which led to the recommendation that colonial navies should be built around a 19,000 ton battle cruiser rather than just 5,000 ton light cruisers as many at the Admiralty had originally envisaged.[88] Sir John Fisher had good reason to be euphoric.[89] For most of the summer, he had been fighting a losing battle with the rest of the Board over whether 'the eight' capital ships of the 1909 programme should be laid down as battleships or battle cruisers.[90] In effect, each 'fleet unit' was intended to be a navy in miniature, and serve as the nucleus for further growth. In peace, each would be independent;[91] but in wartime identical 'units' would be combined to serve as components or modules of a multi-national imperial Pacific fleet.[92] Obviously, for the scheme to work it was essential for all the navies to share the same equipment and tactical doctrine; their personnel were subject to the same laws of discipline and training methods.

In 'selling' the fleet unit concept at the Imperial Conference the Admiralty sailed a different tack. When Reginald McKenna first 'tentatively' outlined the fleet unit concept to the Dominion representatives he emphasized that when forming a navy 'the first thing you have to consider is personnel'. The effectiveness of a warship depended very largely upon the efficiency of her crew. It was thus essential, he explained, to attract top quality recruits.

> I venture to put it to you that it is no use starting with half-a-dozen destroyers or half-a-dozen submarines, or any individual type of vessel which, in the long run, cannot give you all grades of officers and men. If you are going to enlist men into the Navy you must offer them a future, and you will never get men to enlist if they know that when they are over 30 years of age perhaps, the possibility of rising in the service is gone. We, therefore, have to start upon the basis of the smallest fleet unit which will offer to both officers and men a career in life.[93]

In other words, 'if any Dominion desires to build up a navy of its own, that navy must be of a certain size'.[94] The Admiralty had calculated that not less than 2,000 men would satisfy 'this fundamental condition'.[95] Upon this foundation, local training schools could be set up and a life-career structure established with 'prospects likely to attract and keep the right class of candidate'.[96] If the Dominions started with this number of men, McKenna promised, then the Admiralty would arrange a system of constant exchange and interchange of men and warships with the Royal Navy.[97] As a final incentive, the Royal Navy offered to 'lend any portion of the unit and any portion of the personnel which a Dominion Government did not find itself equal to bearing'.[98] It was upon this basis, therefore, that the Admiralty insisted that each navy should start with one battle cruiser, three light cruisers, six destroyers and three submarines.[99]

In all, the Admiralty proposed that four 'units' be provided for the Pacific, one by Canada (based at Vancouver), one by Australia (at Sydney), and two by the Royal Navy (at Hong Kong and Singapore). The China unit would be partially subsidized by New Zealand. The Board further conceded that 'the requirements of the China station could not be met by a fleet unit alone', and therefore would be bolstered by five old cruisers and several gunboats.[100] Originally, the Admiralty had intended to demand that the Indian Government finance *at least* one complete fleet unit instead of the measly sum of £100,000 a year.[101] (India's military budget was over £20 millions.) But for some as yet unknown reason before the conference the Admiralty was instructed to stop harassing Calcutta until 'the political atmosphere was better suited for fresh claims upon the Indian Government'.[102] On the last day of the conference, McKenna outlined the Admiralty's ultimate ambition:

> The ideal which we have in view is that in any danger of war these units, which are all ships of the newest and best type, extremely fast, of large coal carrying capacity and consequent large radius of action, would be able to unite, and would offer a resistance to any possible enemy of such a kind as would enable the Admiralty to have the necessary time for reinforcing the Fleet by ships from home or from the Mediterranean station. The result of the scheme ... will be greatly to strengthen our force in the Pacific, ensuring safety in any conceivable state of affairs, and at the same time affording relief to the Home Government, while offering a basis upon which Dominion navies may be built up in the future.[103]

Looking further ahead, the Admiralty was confident of extracting a contribution from a unified South Africa,[104] and also hoped that all nations would bear the cost of establishing a model naval base at Singapore.[105]

Turning to the money. Each unit would require an investment of £3.7 millions to build, and cost between £600,000 and £700,000 a year to run. This sum, it should be noted, was approximately double the amount either Canadian or Australian politicians had budgeted for a local Navy.[106] But, remarkably, it was considerably lower than the annual running costs of existing station fleets. The Australia squadron for instance, comprising ten old cruisers, cost over £900,000 per annum.[107] The magnitude of the saving was largely due to the newer warships requiring considerably fewer personnel and less maintenance. Thus, trumpeted McKenna, the advantage to us of the fleet unit concept 'is a double one'. We will 'obtain both a saving in money and should get a superior force to what we have in Eastern waters at the present time'.[108]

Negotiations to hammer out final settlements were conducted privately with each Dominion. This took time. Colonel Foxton, the chief representative for Australia, was taken aback by the scope of the fleet unit concept and immediately telegraphed home for instructions.[109] Several days later, he tried to explain to McKenna that when his Prime Minister had offered the mother country a 'dreadnought', the gift 'did not comprehend the maintenance of the vessel as well as the original cost'.[110] As it was, raising £2 million for a battle cruiser was a formidable undertaking for the Commonwealth.[111] Much as his

Government liked the fleet concept, Foxton explained, Australia wanted to begin their navy with just light cruisers and destroyers. His chief adviser 'Captain' William Creswell was also pushing him in this direction. But the Admiralty demurred. 'It would be a waste of money to provide small vessels unless they were supported by an "Indomitable"', replied Fisher. Light cruisers 'would not be able to deal unaided with the more powerful hostile commerce-destroyers' that might reasonably be expected to raid Australian waters, where-as the battle cruiser would catch and sink any vessel afloat.[112]

After bargaining that lasted for most of August, Foxton finally agreed that Australia would adopt the fleet concept in its entirety; but only after the British Government agreed to pay for all maintenance costs over £500,000.[113] (Ultimately the Australian Parliament voted to bear the whole cost.)[114] By contrast, New Zealand was easy to satisfy. After just one short meeting Sir Joseph Ward, their Prime Minister, agreed to increase the New Zealand subsidy and also pay the interest and sinking fund on the cost of one battle cruiser. In return, the Admiralty promised to base several Royal Navy manned modern light cruisers and destroyers at Auckland.[115] The New Zealanders, apparently, were not at all keen to see the Southern Seas policed solely by 'their Australian sister'.[116] With the South African representatives there was some talk of financing the cost of building another battle cruiser, but nothing materialized.

'As you may expect', Greene reported to Edmond Slade, the former DNI, 'Canada is half-hearted. She may provide a few cruisers; nothing more.'[117] While the Canadians approved the concept of 'fleet units' in principle, they claimed it was not appropriate to their needs and asked for alternative schemes to be worked out.[118] Their Minister of Marine, Mr Louis Brodeur, justified this stance by pointing out 'that a large section of the population of Canada took no interest in naval developments, and if the Dominion Government tried to go too fast at the beginning, opposition would be aroused which might result in nothing of practical value being done'.[119] Accordingly, he refused to guarantee spending more than £400,000 per annum.[120] Brodeur proposed to limit Canada's initial contribution to the recruitment of some 2000 personnel and asked the Admiralty if they could spare two old cruisers for training purpos-es.[121] Much to their embarrassment, (and doubtless the Admiralty's delight) the modesty of the Canadian proposals was criticized by nearly all the other colonial representatives.[122] The 'Canadians', Colonel Foxton noted acidly, 'propose to begin own navy without at present deciding on its ultimate compo-sition or sphere of activity'.[123] Brodeur was particularly stung at being pub-licly told off by the South Africans that his 'proposition of a local navy is based purely and simply on sentiment, and that such a local force would be inefficient'.[124] Although to be fair, it must be said that the 'navy issue' in Canadian politics was a highly complex and divisive subject for both political parties—and, many believed, best left alone.[125] Among the electorate there was no real interest in navies except that perhaps it might be 'a nice thing to have'.[126] Furthermore, perhaps McKenna should have been more discreet in expounding the idea of combining 'units' into an imperial Pacific fleet.[127] Such a scheme would never have appealed to 'Sir Wilfred Laurier, who would see "the vortex" of militarisation in it'.[128]

'On the whole things went off better than we expected', Greene wrote to Slade on 10 September.[129] The Admiralty's proposals had successfully defused the growing antagonism between Britain and the Dominions over the issue of imperial defence in the Pacific, and solved a string of long-standing and seemingly intractable defence problems. The most significant result of the 1909 Conference, was a compact to re-establish the Royal Navy's Pacific fleet, 'to which Canada, Australia and Great Britain should contribute their share'.[130] The Pacific Fleet was seen by all parties as a force capable of providing a minimum level of protection for imperial interests in the Far East, at an affordable price, which would stay permanently in the Pacific and remain independent of any changing defence requirements elsewhere in the Empire. From the Admiralty's perspective the scheme was a masterpiece of political compromise. Shortly after his retirement in early 1910, Fisher confided in his friend Lord Esher:

> I am so surprised how utterly both the Cabinet and the Press have so failed to see the *'inwardness'* of the new *'Pacific Fleet'*. I had a few momentous words with Sir Joseph Ward (the Prime Minister of New Zealand). *He saw it!*[131] It means *eventually* Canada, Australia, New Zealand, the Cape (that is, South Africa), and India *running a complete Navy!* We manage the job in Europe. They'll manage it against the Yankees, Japs, and Chinese, as occasion requires out there![132]

In another letter to a journalist friend he wrote:

> *The keel is laid* (though no-one knows it) of that great Pacific Fleet ... so don't go blazing away a want of something which is truly coming, but you can 'cocker it up' by judicious phrasing to keep our Pacific children to their task. The 3 'New Testament' ships, with their attendant satellites, will be in the Pacific in 1913. That marks the first step.[133]

Not everybody was happy with the new Pacific Fleet. Several senior British diplomats expressed their uneasiness at the prospect of giving 'bumptious' colonial politicians warships with which 'to play romps for which Her Majesty's Government would be ultimately responsible to foreign powers'.[134] And internal Admiralty memoranda show that some officers had misgivings at dispatching so many modern warships to the Pacific at a time when Germany was challenging the Royal Navy's superiority in home waters. Neither Bethell nor Captain Herbert King-Hall (Director of Naval Mobilisation) could see how the Royal Navy could spare modern light cruisers or destroyers from the home fleets. In January 1910, the Admiralty considered instead sending several older ships to the Far East.[135] Though they recognized that 'any such weakening of the fleet in the Far East would be looked upon by Australia and New Zealand as a want of faith on the part of the Admiralty'.[136] Integrity seems to have prevailed. None the less, documents dated from the end of 1910, show that except for substituting seven destroyers (of which there was a chronic shortage in home waters) the Board resolved to stick by their promises.[137]

The most serious objections to the Pacific Fleet were raised by the economist wing of the Liberal Party. In July 1910, Winston Churchill, the Home Secretary, who the previous year had led the opposition within Cabinet to the navy's demands for eight 'dreadnoughts', circulated a memorandum which more or less denounced the 'Navy Scare' as having been a sham. Why, he asked, was the Admiralty now going 'to send the two colonial "dreadnoughts" to the Pacific'?[138] When they were offered to the British Government:

> it was understood by everyone that these ships were to aid us in maintaining the command of the sea by a supreme battle fleet for decisive action. We are told now that these ships, which were declared eighteen months ago to be the vital units of naval strength, are not wanted in the North Sea, but can safely be dispatched during the critical years to the other end of the world ... ships needed for service in Australasian waters need certainly not be the largest or the strongest class. Older battleships or smaller cruisers could perfectly well discharge all the necessary naval duties.[139]

Churchill appears not to have known that the Admiralty intended also to send the Royal Navy battle cruiser *Indomitable* to Hong Kong.[140] Although nothing immediate came out of Churchill's complaint, readers should take note of his remarks because in October 1911, he succeeded Reginald McKenna as First Lord of the Admiralty.

In February 1911, Churchill again queried the Admiralty's intention to send battle cruisers to the Pacific, during a Cabinet discussion on the size of forthcoming naval estimates.[141] The dispatch of several old ships in lieu of the battle cruisers, he declared, would be quite sufficient for the 'colonials' defence requirements.[142] And 'if the 2 colonial dreadnoughts could be retained in Home Waters', Churchill reasoned, 'the preponderance [over Germany] which Mr McKenna considers necessary in 1913 and 1914 could be attained by the construction of 8 instead of 10 ships in the two years 1911 and 1912'.[143] Dropping two battleships (each costing £2.5 million) would reduce the level of naval estimates below £44 million, a total which was 'above the utmost' the 1909 'People's' budget 'was expected to sustain'.[144] In turn, this would alleviate fiscal worries caused by the fact that the social reforms introduced by the Liberals under the 1908 and 1909 budgets, were proving to be much more costly than anticipated.

This time Churchill found considerably more sympathy for his views. The Liberals first targeted the construction budget.[145] After much prodding McKenna, to the annoyance of the sea lords, trimmed two light cruisers (saving about half a million) from the programme but refused to go any further.[146] This was not enough. Yet after the debacle of 1909, the economist wing of the Cabinet was reluctant to engage the Admiralty head on over battleship construction. Accordingly, a sub-committee of Cabinet was formed to scrutinize the other votes of the navy budget. Particularly attractive in Churchill's eyes was the extravagant number of ships kept overseas which cost the British taxpayer £5 million.[147] As an example he suggested that the defence of British interests in the Mediterranean did not require a battle fleet and could safely be left to a single cruiser squadron.[148] Explaining his reasoning, the Home Secretary preached that history taught 'the sea is all one' and that the key to naval warfare was concentration of forces in the decisive theatre with the object of annihilating the main enemy fleet in battle.[149] Thus 'the maintenance there of such a strong and costly subsidiary establishment is inconsistent with accepted modern naval theory' developed by Captain Alfred Mahan.[150] The Board of Admiralty, however, remained unmoved. And McKenna, much to Churchill's chagrin, did nothing 'but raise difficulties and resist'.[151]

When Churchill discovered the Admiralty was planning to send the British-owned HMS *Indomitable* out to the Far East he immediately insisted she be retained in home waters. McKenna found it impossible to refute his argument that a modern battle cruiser was not really needed in the Far East. Latest intelligence reports indicated that Japan's 'dreadnought' programme was being retarded by their weak fiscal position.[152] McKenna's uncompromising stance was further undermined at the end of March by the unexpected news from the Foreign Secretary, Sir Edward Grey, that Japan was anxious to renegotiate and renew the Naval Alliance.[153] Grey easily persuaded the Cabinet that it would be 'disastrous' for Britain (and especially the Liberal Government's financial policy!) to give up the treaty.[154] On 30 March, the Cabinet voted to extend the treaty with Japan up to 1921. In view of the marked improvement in the strategic situation in the Pacific, the First Lord now conceded 'he might utilise two smaller [and older] armoured cruisers for the "Indomitable" as representing the East Indies Unit'.[155] McKenna, however, did not pluck up the nerve to tell Sir Arthur Wilson, the First Sea Lord, until 6 July.[156] 'I remember being told something about this', Wilson reacted, 'but I dismissed it from my mind as too absurd for serious consideration'.[157] In no uncertain terms the First Sea Lord went on to tell McKenna that he was 'strongly opposed' to retaining *Indomitable* or asking the Dominion governments for permission to postpone the despatch of their battle cruisers to the Far East, fearing such actions might dampen their enthusiasm and jeopardize the contribution of additional warships, as well as compromising 'our position in China'.[158] The timing of McKenna's awkward confession was significant. During the previous month, June 1911, the heads of all the self-governing Dominions were still in London after attending the 1911 Imperial Conference. Had the Cabinet's deliberations been leaked to the colonial politicians, the Government would have been severely embarrassed.[159]

Before any final decision was taken on the composition of the Pacific Fleet, McKenna was ousted from the Admiralty. During August 1911, political manoeuvring by the Secretary of State for War, Richard Haldane, succeeded in discrediting the Admiralty administration in the eyes of the Prime Minister.[160] At the end of October, the arch-economist Winston Churchill was given the portfolio of First Lord of the Admiralty. Within a month, the obstinate Sir Arthur Wilson was replaced as First Sea Lord by supposedly more compliant Admiral Sir Francis Bridgeman.[161] Only days after taking office, Bridgeman confided to a friend that already 'Churchill is strongly on the economy drive—I trust he will not go too far'.[162] Among his junior staff, the new First Lord quickly acquired the reputation of being 'a young man in a hurry and what is more he is—in his opinion—a heaven born strategist'.[163]

Once established in Whitehall, Churchill immediately initiated a review of the number and disposition of ships in commission.[164] As had been shown, before he took control at the Admiralty, Winston Churchill had consistently tried to cut or at least contain British naval expenditure as much as possible in order to release funds for domestic social reforms. As yet he did not seem concerned by rumours of an impending expansion of the German fleet. But at the same time he recognized that the Royal Navy's numerical superiority over Germany in numbers of battleships could not be compromised. The Liberals had to maintain a fig leaf of naval respectability in order to avoid political criticism.[165] He therefore chose again to propose a rationalisation of the overseas squadrons. Once again senior Admiralty officials refused even to consider such ideas. On 1 November, Rear-Admiral Alexander Bethell (still DNI) directly challenged the validity of Churchill's textbook naval strategy:

> The theory of the sea being all one has its limitations as far as the necessity for defending outlying possessions is concerned and does not hold good unless you can get at your enemy to destroy him in the decisive waters—it might be months before we could meet and defeat the German Fleet. It depends upon them and the pressure we are able to bring to force them to come out and fight. Meanwhile our possessions in the Mediterranean would be in danger ... I think also the British public would insist on an attempt being made to keep open our large trade.[166]

As to cutting the Pacific Fleet, Bethell reminded Churchill 'we are under a *promise* to Australia and New Zealand to maintain a fleet of a definite strength in the East divided between the East Indies and China stations and they will no doubt protest if we do not carry out our obligation'.[167] Churchill, however, was unmoved. A fortnight later Bethell was banished to command the East Indies squadron.[168] The following week the Director of Naval Mobilisation, Rear-Admiral Herbert King-Hall, was also sent overseas. At the end of 1911, the new team at the Admiralty prepared to bring home the battle squadron from Malta in the new year.[169]

On 18 January 1912, Churchill directed that 'every ship possible should be brought home from Australian waters', and ordered that a request should be sent to the New Zealand Government asking for their battle cruiser to be kept in European waters.[170] Again, at this stage Churchill was not responding to any intensification of the Anglo-German naval race. Towards the end of the month the First Lord approached the Colonial Office to enlist the support of the newly-promoted Secretary of State, Lewis 'Loulou' Harcourt.[171]

> I do not think anyone can doubt that the arrangements made in 1909 with Australia were not very satisfactory so far as British naval interests were concerned. The whole principle of local Navies is, of course, thoroughly vicious, and no responsible sailor can be found who has a word to say in favour of it.[172]

'I do not expect that there is any chance of inducing Australia to let us have [their] battle cruiser', Churchill lamented, but would the Colonial Office use their influence with the New Zealand Government to authorize the release of their ship from the Pacific fleet?[173] Harcourt, recognising a political quagmire when he saw one, replied that he would not approach the New Zealand Government before consulting the rest of Cabinet. Churchill immediately withdrew his request. In April the First Lord renewed his request.[174] On 1 May the Admiralty was notified they could keep HMS *New Zealand* in home waters.[175]

At the end of January, the First Lord notified Harcourt that he expected very soon representatives from the newly-elected Canadian Government would be visiting London to discuss their naval policy. The Admiralty had reason to believe that instead of expanding the Royal Canadian Navy, Canada might be persuaded to build '2 or 3 of the finest vessels in the world' and present them to the Royal Navy. And if the Canadians could be steered in this direction the Admiralty would be grateful.[176] Harcourt replied that he thought such an offer was very unlikely. 'Amongst the Canadian public', he told Churchill, 'a contribution of money or ships to the imperial navy is even more unpopular than a "tin-pot" navy of their own'.[177] This assessment was a little harsh. Harcourt knew full well that the Canadian Government was contemplating building a flat unit. In a letter dated 16 May, the new Canadian Prime Minister Robert Borden *reminded* Lewis Harcourt that his Cabinet envisaged building '2 full units, one for the Pacific and the other for the Atlantic'. 'Speaking for myself,' Borden added, 'I would not be afraid to advocate such a policy now, or such modifications as the Admiralty might recommend.'[178] But that came later.

Churchill's dream of presenting his Party with a reduction in naval expenditure was destroyed on 31 January 1912, by confirmation that Germany intended to amend her fleet law.[179] For several months the Admiralty had been anticipating some acceleration in German battleship construction.

> From the general indications which they had previously received they were inclined to think that the new construction would be its most seri-

ous feature. But on examining the text they found that ... the increases
of personnel and the increases in the vessels of all classes maintained
in full commission constituted a new development of the very highest
importance .... compared to this predominant fact, any alteration of the
tempo of the proposed additional new construction appeared a comparatively small thing.[180]

Under the new law the establishment of the German navy was forecast to rise
from 66,700 in 1912 to 101,500 men by 1920, thereby allowing a third
squadron of eight battleships to be kept in full commission all year round.[181]
In 1912, the Royal Navy kept only sixteen fully manned battleships in home
waters. Everyone agreed that the larger number of warships in full commission
across the North Sea left the Admiralty few options. Accordingly the
Admiralty announced that they planned to increase the number of commissioned battleships in home waters from sixteen to thirty-three. What the Board
concealed, however, was that the Germans, perhaps unknowingly, had scored a
direct hit on one of the Royal Navy's most vulnerable spots. Finding the additional ships was not a major problem. The navy had a large reserve of battleships in good condition. The difficulty was finding enough trained men to provide all these ships with full complements of active service ratings. Since
1907, the Royal Navy had never kept more than twenty-eight battleships in full
commission at any one time. As each new battleship was completed, an old
ship was placed in reserve and her crew turned over. In the short run the navy
could not make up their personnel shortage by simply increasing recruitment.[182] The Royal Navy's 'dreadnoughts' were designed to be manned by
skilled crews: considerably more than half the complement was supposed to
comprise 'higher rates' of six to eight years service since entry.[183] The
Admiralty had no alternative, therefore, but to recall the Mediterranean battle
squadron in order to free skilled personnel required to man the new 'dreadnoughts' completing. Of course, for financial reasons Churchill had intended to
do this anyway.[184]

    The story of how the Cabinet reacted to the Admiralty's decision to evacu-
ate the Mediterranean is too well known to need recounting in detail.[185]
Basically, nearly every other Department of Government expressed objections,
insisting that such a major change of policy could not be decided by the
Admiralty unilaterally. At the end of April the Prime Minister was persuaded
to allow the naval redistribution evaluated by the CID. In May, Asquith,
accompanied by Churchill and other naval representatives,[186] convened a preliminary meeting at Malta in order to consult Field Marshal Lord Kitchener,
the Consul-General of Egypt, who was an acknowledged expert on the Near
East. Kitchener presented a formidable case based on the need to uphold
British prestige in the region.[187] This, he insisted, depended upon the Royal
Navy maintaining a battle squadron at Malta. His view was strongly endorsed
by the Foreign Office. Faced with the embarrassing prospect of having his pol-

icy overruled, Churchill—on the spur of the moment—offered to station two 'prestigious' battle cruisers at Malta. When Sir Francis Bridgeman (who was back in England) was first telegraphed the details of 'The Malta Compromise', he was angry at not having been first consulted.[188] But after Churchill returned and explained the situation more clearly, Bridgeman was forced to admit 'the question of prestige (about which Lord Kitchener makes a strong point) had a great deal in it'.[189] For the moment, he agreed, the two battle cruisers should be sent.[190] Indeed, he confessed, 'if the policy of bringing the battleships home *can* be satisfied with these two battle cruisers—we shall have got out of a serious difficulty very cheaply'![191]

The Admiralty was not to escape so lightly. After two further meetings of the CID during July, but this time attended by most of the senior members of the Government, Churchill was pushed into stationing yet more capital ships (and their crews) in the Mediterranean. Ultimately he agreed that by 1915 a squadron of eight 'dreadnoughts' would be returned to the Mediterranean. In the interim, not two but four battle cruisers would be kept at Malta, and Churchill had to promise that even in the event of war with Germany they would not be recalled 'unless to meet some unlikely and unforeseeable emergency'.[192] The formula was finally endorsed by the Cabinet on 16 July.[193] The warships ordered to the Mediterranean in 1912 were all ships built originally for the imperial Pacific fleet. Churchill not only lost the two Canadian fleet units, but the two battle cruisers he 'sacrificed' at Malta were both stripped from the British fleet units destined for East of Suez. He admitted as much in a Cabinet memorandum. 'The argument for sparing these', Churchill wrote, 'is that the late Board of Admiralty had proposed to send *Indomitable* to China, and to let *New Zealand* go there too. We have stopped *Indomitable* and we have been allowed to keep *New Zealand*. We are therefore two to the good on these'.[194] The British officers commanding squadrons in Pacific waters were not warned of this reversal in policy. As late as 31 December 1912, the C in C China squadron was expecting to be sent the *Indomitable* any day.[195]

Part of the reason why Churchill surrendered so easily to pressure from the CID was because he believed he had managed to secure the gift of three additional 'dreadnoughts' from Canada.[196] By coincidence, the new Dominion Prime Minister, Robert Borden, was in London over the summer to discuss naval policy. Ignoring the advice of his sea lords, Churchill induced Borden not to build two 'fleet units' but instead to offer the Royal Navy money to buy three dreadnoughts. The cost of maintaining these ships, however, would fall to Great Britain. 'Canada it is true might find the ships', Bridgeman pointed out, 'but we must find the men and officers or at any rate most of them. This means a further addition to our personnel (vote A) and there is no getting out of it!'[197] In other quarters there was considerable doubt whether the Canadian ships would ever materialize. 'I am quite sure', Asquith confided to Harcourt, 'that Borden will find himself in stormy waters the moment he launches his naval proposals, whether in his Cabinet, or in public'.[198] This assessment was quickly proved accurate. In October, Borden telegraphed Churchill that he was already encountering difficulties. By January 1913, the Admiralty was seriously considering the implications of seeing the Canadian ships being postponed or lost altogether.[199]

* * *

On 14 October 1913, Churchill wrote that as far as he was concerned 'the fleet unit policy of 1909 has been abandoned'—but was unwilling to admit this outside the Admiralty.[200] While he may have acknowledged that 'the Dominions have a right to have the whole situation arising out of the abandonment re-examined' and discussed at a conference, he seemed more interested in taking such an opportunity to 'impress' upon the colonials 'the true strategic considerations on which the empire is conducted', that is, his theory of 'one-ocean, one-navy'.[201] As subsequent correspondence clearly shows, Churchill never had any intention of apologising to the Dominions for failing to consult them beforehand. He also refused to accept that the Admiralty had ever been bound by a 'compact'.[202] Churchill always maintained that the composition of the fleet was a matter for the Admiralty alone 'except so far as they may be guided by the *spirit* of the arrangements' made in 1909.[203]

Alas, space prevents the telling of the fascinating story of the steady deterioration in relations between Britain and the Dominions between 1912 and 1914. Suffice to say that by July 1914, a serious rift had opened between the British Government and the Dominions caused by the Admiralty reneging on its promises. The New Zealand Government was left seething at being fobbed off with antiquated cruisers (some of which were known by the Admiralty to be unserviceable) instead of the modern ships promised to them in 1909.[204] 'That the Dominions have not been treated fairly by the Admiralty regarding naval defence matters is undeniable', complained the New Zealand Prime Minister on 14 July 1914. 'The agreement of 1909 has been ignored and explanations [given] which do not meet the situation'.[205] Even the Governor-General had to agree: 'I think this Government have a legitimate grievance'.[206] The Admiralty's relations with the Australians were even worse.[207] In April 1914 'Loulou' Harcourt was warned by a friend in Sydney that 'there is undoubtedly a strong feeling of resentment here first at the suggestion that Japan shall protect us and next because the Indian and Chinese squadrons have not been brought up to the strength of the Australian.'[208] For Winston Churchill to claim 'that Japan safeguards them in the Pacific is simply gall and woodworm to the Australians on whom the Asiatic danger has been worked for all its worth for many years'.[209] Similar sentiments were echoed by Admiral Sir George King-Hall, commanding the Royal Navy's Australia squadron (1911–13).

> It is bad policy to throw cold water on the efforts of a young, and rising nation, in taking measures for their own defence, it might do harm: whereas if encouragement is given, and sympathy, they will place con-

fidence in the old country, and be ready to place their defence forces certainly and always at our disposal, and if we act wisely, we become more and more amalgamated with the Home Forces.[210]

The only good news, from the imperialist perspective, was that by 1914 the fleet unit concept appeared to be developing a momentum of its own in the Dominions. Canada, Australia and New Zealand were all considering whether to persevere with the scheme independently of Britain. In early 1913, Borden's Cabinet had began to reconsider their original plan 'to establish and maintain one or more fleet units', a formula which was much more likely to appeal to Canadian nationalist sentiment. In March that year, Churchill was warned that if Canada did finally present the Royal Navy with some dreadnoughts, they might well be recalled shortly thereafter 'to form part of such unit or units'.[211] And in the summer of 1914 the resolve was growing in Wellington to demand the return of the battle cruiser *New Zealand* and form a joint navy with the already completed Australian fleet unit.[212]

Winston Churchill displayed little sympathy towards the 'colonials' defence worries; it could be argued that he appeared interested in the Dominions only for what he could get out of them. To save a comparatively trifling sum, or for some other short term interest, Churchill, as First Lord of the Admiralty, with the backing of the Liberal Cabinet, dismantled a highly imaginative and surprisingly popular system of collective security designed to protect imperial interests in the Pacific. Possibly he simply failed to take imperial defence seriously and thus was guilty only of possessing a too narrow strategic outlook. This was Lord Esher's view.[213] Was the omniscient Churchill really such a myopic strategist? Intriguingly, a statement made by Admiral of the Fleet Earl Beatty to a Cabinet committee in 1924 suggests maybe not. In February that year, Beatty recalled that 'our traditional naval policy in the past had been to maintain sufficient naval Forces to protect our commitments and interests in all parts of the world'. But from 1905, he testified, this policy was 'departed from' and warships were recalled to home waters. 'Early in 1914 it had been recognised, however, that this departure from our traditional policy was a mistake and steps were being taken to reinforce our Eastern Fleet by battle cruisers, when war broke out.'[214] Possibly he was mistaken. Much of Beatty's statement in 1924 was factually inaccurate, and he was moreover a notorious apologist for the perceived failings by the Royal Navy before and during the First World War. And yet, an Admiralty file dating from early 1914 shows that plans were certainly afoot to break up the home fleet battle cruiser squadron (under Beatty's command) into smaller units.[215] Why, the papers do not say.[216] It is therefore impossible to establish for certain whether Churchill's strategic outlook did expand on the eve of war. Yet it can hardly be denied that when war began in August 1914, the British naval forces stationed in the Pacific were not equal to the tasks imposed upon them,[217] or that the Dominions' enthusiasm for naval co-operation had been severely damaged by Churchill. His

high-handedness had tilted the balance of overseas opinion some distance
away from the ideal of the broad imperialism thought to be achievable in 1909,
towards the separatism and self-reliance in naval and imperial affairs many had
so strenuously tried to avert.

NOTES

1. Arthur Marder, *From the Dreadnought to Scapa Flow*, (5 vols; (Oxford, 1961–69) pp i, 179, 214.
    (hereafter cited as *FDSF*.)
2. George Monger, *The End of Isolation: British Foreign Policy 1900–1907* (London, 1963); Aaron
    Friedberg, *The Weary Titan: Britain and the Experience of Relative Decline, 1895–1905*
    (Princeton, 1988), pp 189–208; Paul Kennedy, *Strategy and Diplomacy* (Fontana Press, 1984),
    pp 111–160; Paul Kennedy, *The R55 and Fall of the Great Powers: Economic Change and
    Military Conflict From 1500–2000* (New York, 1987) pp 224–233; see also: Keith Neilson, '
    "Greatly Exaggerated": The Myth of the Decline of Great Britain before 1914', *International
    History Review*, 13 (1991), pp 661–680, Zara Steiner, *Britain and the Origins of the First World
    War* (London, 1977) pp 31–36.
3. For an excellent account of the origins of the alliance see Ian Nish, *The Anglo-Japanese Alliance*,
    (London, 1966), pp 174–238.4.   Nicholas Lambert, 'The Opportunities of Technology: British
    and French Naval Strategies in the Pacific, 1905–1909', in Nicholas Rodger, ed, *Naval Power in
    the Twentieth Century* (London, 1996). In press.
5. Gilbert Tucker, *The Naval Service of Canada* (Ottawa, 1952); Nicholas Meaney, *The Search for
    Security in the Pacific* (Sydney, 1976); Ian McGibbon, *Blue Water Rationale: the Naval Defence
    of New Zealand, 1914–42* (Wellington, 1981).
6. The exception is Avner Offer, *The First World War: an Agrarian Interpretation* (Oxford, 1989)
    pp 206–208. Offer's brief explanation of the Admiralty's and Dominions' motives is broadly cor-
    rect, although I disagree with his assertion that 'such an order of battle was well beyond the capac-
    ity of the British treasury', for reasons which will become apparent below.
7. Donald Gordon, *The Dominion Partnership in Imperial Defence, 1870–1914* (Baltimore, 1965).
8. Donald Gordon, 'The Admiralty and Dominion Navies, 1902–1914', *Journal of Modern History*,
    33 (1961), pp 407–422. Roger Sarty, 'Canadian Maritime Defence, 1892–1914', *Canadian
    Historical Review*, 71, 4 (1990), pp 462–490, p.477; Robert Gowen, 'British Legerdemain at the
    1911 Imperial Conference: The Dominions, Defence Planning, and the Renewal of the
    Anglo-Japanese Alliance', *Journal of Modern History*, 52 (1980) pp 385–413.
9. Minutes of the 88th meeting of the C.I.D., 16 May 1906, Lord Tweedmouth speaking, CAB 2/1
    [Public Record Office, Kew]; see also Fisher to Admiral Reginald Henderson, 10 Feb 1914, in
    *Fear God and Dread Nought: The correspondence of Admiral of the Fleet Lord Fisher of
    Kilverstone*, ed by Arthur Marder, (3 vols; London, 1952–59), ii, p 266, note 1. (hereafter cited as
    FGDN.)
10. Captain Charles Ottley (DNI) to Colonial Office, 20 Jul 1906, f.65, CAB 17/77.
11. Minutes (14 Aug 1908) by Greene, on docket 'Draft letter to the Colonial Office', ADM 1/7949
    [Public Record Office, Kew]. Mr.William Graham Greene was the assistant secretary of the
    Admiralty, a civil service post. Traditionally, the Admiralty's administrative correspondence with
    Commanders in Chief overseas and other departments of Government had always passed through
    the civilian M branch. Accidentally, therefore, before the formation of independent dominion
    navies, Greene acquired a certain expertise and knowledge of 'colonial navies' not possessed by
    naval officers.
12. A local flotilla comprising six destroyers and nine submarines would cost `at least' 346,000 per
    annum which was considerably more than the sum for which the Australians had budgeted: for
    which, see Admiralty to Alfred Deakin via Colonial Office, 20 Aug 1908, ADM 1/7949; also see:
    memorandum by the DNI, 'Australian Naval Defence Force', Slade, 15 Jun 1908, Slade Mss, reel
    1 [Admiral Edmond Slade Papers, National Maritime Museum, Greenwich].
13. Proceedings of the Imperial Conference (1909), CAB 18/12A, 'Dominion No.15', p 73,
    Mr. Merriman speaking; Sir Joseph Ward speaking; Mr.Brodeur speaking.
14. Minute (7 Nov 1907) by Captain Edmond Slade (DNI) on 'M branch remarks—Australian Naval
    Agreement', by Greene, 30 Oct 1907, ADM 1/7949, 'Australia' (C.O. 20 Nov 1907).

15. Much of the argument used and evidence cited in the next three paragraphs can be found in: Lambert, 'The Opportunities of Technology'.
16. 'Navy Estimates', Goschen, 31 Jan 1899, CAB 37/49/7; Letters from Goschen (First Lord) to Hicks Beech (Chancellor of the Exchequer), 17 Dec 1897, 6 Jun 1898, 20 Jul 1898, 21 Jul 1898 (two letters) and 4 Feb 1899, Hicks Beech Mss, D2455, PCC/83, [Sir Michael Hicks Beech Papers: Gloucester Record Office].
17. Jon Sumida, *In Defence of Naval Supremacy: Finance, Technology and British Naval Policy, 1889–1914* (London, 1989), pp 19–21; Nicholas Lambert, 'Admiral Sir John Fisher and the Concept of Flotilla Defence', *Journal of Military History*, (October 1995), 59/4, pp 639–60.
18. 'Navy Estimates 1901–1902', Selborne, 17 Jan 1901, CAB 37/56/8; 'Memorandum' [Distribution of the Fleet], Selborne, 6 Dec 1904, CAB 37/73/159.
19. Nish, *The Anglo-Japanese Alliance*, pp 174–184; Kerr to Selborne, 5 Oct 1901, f.41, Selborne Mss, 26. [Earl Selborne Papers: Bodleian Library, Oxford].
20. Sumida, *In Defence*, pp 18–28; Ruddock Mackay, *Fisher of Kilverstone* (Oxford, 1973) pp 306–318.
21. Nicholas Lambert, *A Revolution in Naval Strategy: the Influence of the Submarine Upon Maritime Strategic Thought*, (forthcoming monograph).
22. Lambert, 'The Opportunities of Technology'.
23. 'Australian Defence', Ottley, Apr 1906, ADM 1/8905; in 1913 Vice Admiral Patey complained that, when burning coal from Newcastle, Australia, his flagship, the battle cruiser *Australia*, could steam at only 22 knots, whereas when burning Welsh coal she was capable of 27 knots.
24. 'The Fleet Coaling Service – Memorandum showing the general position on 1st February 1907', pp 1–21, ADM 1/7934.
25. J.H.Maurer, 'Fuel and the Battle-fleet: Coal, Oil, and American Naval Strategy, 1898–1925', *Naval War College Review,* (1981), pp 60–77.
26. NID 751, 'Annual Statement of requirements, Resources, and Proposed Method of Supply of Coal, 1904–05', ADM 231/42; ADM 231/44, 1905–06; NID806, 1906–07, ADM 231/46; NID829, 1907–08, ADM 231/48; Report on 'The Fleet Coaling Service', 1.2.07, ADM 1/7934.
27. 'Navy Estimates Committee 1908/09: Expenditure under Navy Works Act, 1895–1905', [Jan 1908], Tweedmouth Mss, File on 1908/09 Estimates [Earl Tweedmouth Papers: Naval Library, Ministry of Defence, London]; 'Future Battleship Building', Tweedmouth, 21 Nov 1907, and Appendix B – Statement showing total estimated cost as shown in "The Navy Works Act 1905", and as subsequently revised, and the expenditure to October 31, 1907', 19 Nov 07, all in CAB 37/90/101.
28. Paul Kennedy, 'Imperial Cable Communications and Strategy, 1870–1914', in Kennedy, P., ed., *The War Plans of the Great Powers, 1880–1914*, (London, 1985), pp 75–98; also see Hicks-Beech Mss, D2455, PCC/83, Goschen to Hicks Beech, 13 Dec 1898.
29. Memoranda by the CDC: 'General Scheme of Defence: Australia', No. 362M, 15 May 1906; 'Principles of Imperial Defence', No. 348M, 2 Aug 1905; 'Principles of Imperial Defence', No. 417M, 7Jul 1910; 'Australia: Scale of Attack', No. 429M, 24 Feb 1911, all in CAB 8/5.
30. Fisher to Balfour, enclosing remarks on Admiral Cyprian Bridge's article, 'Criticisms of Recent Naval Reform', f.17, Balfour Papers, Add Mss 49711, [Arthur Balfour Papers: British Library, London].
31. Minute (19 Apr 1909) by Mr. William Graham Greene, ADM 116/1100B.
32. Governor General of New Zealand to Crewe, 22 Mar 1909, f.3, ADM 116/1100B.
33. Proceedings of Imperial Conference (1909), CAB 18/12A, Dominions No. 15, p.4, Lord Crewe speaking.
34. Telegram, Dudley (Governor General of Australia) to Crewe (Secretary of State for the Colonies) 15 Apr 1909, f.19–21, ADM 116/1100B.
35. Joint telegram from Governors of New South Wales and Victoria to Crewe, 4 Apr 1909, f.12, ADM 116/1100B.
36 . Telegram, Dudley to Crewe, 15 Apr 09, and letter, Colonial Office to Admiralty, 16 Apr 1909, f.17–21, ADM 116/1100B; see also Nicholas Meaney, *The Search for Security in the Pacific*, pp 133–141.
37. Edward Grey (Foreign Secretary) to Lewis Harcourt, Apr 1909, Harcourt Mss, f.33, dep.441. [Lewis Harcourt Papers: Bodleian Library, Oxford].
38. Minute (16 Apr 1909) by A.B.K., on telegram, Dudley to Crewe, 15 Apr 1909, and Just to Sir Francis Hopwood, 18 Apr 1909, all f.247, CO 418/70/12859 [Colonial Office Papers: Public Record Office, Kew].

39. Draft letter, Admiralty to Colonial Office, (Not Sent) May 1909, and minute thereon (5 May 1909) by Greene, f.28, ADM 116/1100B; for details of the Australian scheme of 15 Apr 1909, see: letter, Dudley to Crewe, 12 Apr 1909, f.90–94, ibid.

40. Minute (16 Jun 1909) by Bethell, on docket 'Naval and Military Defence of Australia', f.124, ADM 116/1100B.

41. Telegram, Dudley to Crewe, 19 Apr 1909, f.32, ADM 116/1100B; and Minutes (19 Apr 1909) by Greene, (23 Apr 1909) Anderson, and (23 Apr 1909) Bethell, on docket 'Naval Forces of Australia', dated 16 Apr 1909, f.23, ADM 116/1100B.

42. Dudley to Crewe, 22 Jul 1909, f.399; and Lord Grey (Governor General of Canada) to Crewe, 11 May 1909, f.99, both ADM 116/1100B.

43. Lord Grey was even more scathing about Mr.Brodeur, the Canadian Minister for Marine and Fisheries, for which see: Lord Grey (Governor General of Canada) to Sir Wilfred Laurier, 30 Mar 1909, f.174, Asquith Mss 21 [H.H.Asquith Papers: Bodleian Library, Oxford].

44. Lord Grey to Crewe, 11 May 1909, f.99; and minutes (2 Jun 1909) by Greene, and (2 Jun 1909) Bethell, f.102, both in ADM 116/1100B.

45. Minutes (2 Jun 1909) by Greene, and Bethell, ibid.

46. Gordon, *The Dominion Partnership*, p 233.

47. Lambton to Sir Fred. Lugard (Governor-General, Hong Kong) 25 Nov 1908, and 'Remarks by D.N.I.' on M038/09, Rear-Admiral Slade, 3 Feb 1909, ADM 1/8890.

48. 'Remarks by D.N.I.', on M038/09, by Rear-Admiral Edmond Slade, 3 Feb 1909, ADM 1/8890.

49. Ibid.

50. 'Hong Kong – Standard of Defences', CDC memo No.440M, ADM 1/8890.

51. Minutes of CDC meeting on 28 Jan 1909, item 9, CAB 7/8.

52. 'Standard of Defences at British Defended Ports in Distant Seas', CDC No.405M, 7 Apr 1909, CAB 8/5.

53. 'Dissent by D.N.I.', p 10, ibid.

54. Minute (24 Apr 1909) by Greene, on telegram Lambton to Admiralty, 22 Mar 1909, ADM 1/8890.

55. 'Report and Proceedings of a sub-Committee of the Committee of Imperial Defence appointed to inquire into certain questions of Naval Policy raised by Lord Charles Beresford', CAB 16/9.

56. Minute (12/5109) by Just to Hopwood, CO 537/353/15918

57. Fisher to J.A. Spender (editor of *Westminster Gazette*), 2 Jul 1909, Spender Mss, f.67, Add Mss 46390 [J.A.Spender Papers: British Library]; and Minutes of 102nd meeting of the CID, 29 Jun 1909, CAB 2/2: n.b. Item 1, 'The Standard of Defences at British Defended Ports in Distant Seas'

58. 'Defences of Hong Kong', 18 Jun 1909, CID No.59–C, CAB 38/15/9.

59. Minutes of 102nd CID, 29 Jun 1909, Admiral Bethell speaking, CAB 2/2.

60. Ibid. For an explanation of how this would be possible see: Lambert, 'The Opportunities of Technology'; and Lambert, 'Admiral Sir John Fisher and the Concept of Flotilla Defence', Journal of Military History, 59/4 (October, 1995), 639–60.

61. Minutes of 102nd meeting of CID, 29 Jun 1909, conclusions, CAB 2/2.

62. 'Hong Kong – Standard of Defences', CDC No.440M, paragraph 21, ADM 1/8890.

63. Minutes of 102nd meeting of CID, 29 Jun 1909, CAB 2/2.

64. This was clearly an inter-departmental committee whose remit was not confined to military/strategic questions: the members were, Lord Fisher (CID); Lord Crewe (CO); Lord Morley (Secretary of State for India); Sir Charles Hardinge (FO); Mr Haldane, General Sir William Nicholson and General Sir John French (WO); Mr McKenna, Admiral Sir Arthur Wilson, Admiral Alexander Bethell (Admiralty): 'Papers on the Imperial Conference of 1909" Appointment of sub-committee, terms of reference, CAB 17/78.

65. Ottley to McKenna, 19 Jun 1909, f.3a, MCKN 3/7 [Reginald Mckenna Papers: Churchill College, Cambridge]·

66. Lambert, 'Admiral Sir John Fisher'.

67. George Strickland to Battenberg, 4 Nov 12, Battenberg Mss, MB1/T21/157 [Admiral of the Fleet Prince Louis of Battenberg Papers: University of Southampton].

68. Greene to Slade, 23 Oct 09, Slade Mss, reel 1; see also Proceedings of Imperial Conference, 'Dominions 17' (10 Aug 1909), CAB 18/12A, remarks by Sir John Fisher, p 6.

69. Fisher to White, 15 Aug 1908, *FGDN*, ii, 189.

70. Fisher to Yexley, 1 Aug 1909, *FGDN*, ii, 258. N.B. Fisher was a very close friend of G.L. Garvin, the editor of *The Observer*, and frequently co-operated in the content of his editorials for which see: Alfred Gollin, *The Observer and G.L.Garvin, 1908–1914* (London, 1960).

71. HMS *Swift* displaced 2,500 tons; Memorandum: 'Remarks on H.M.S. Swift as far as I, Rightly or Wrongly, Comprehend Her', (by her commanding officer) Capt. John Dumaresq to Fisher, 27 Jul 1910, FP4278, FISR5/17; For Fisher's enthusiasm for 'Super-Swifts' see: Churchill to Fisher, 3 Dec 1912, FP546, FISR1/11 [Admiral of the Fleet Lord Fisher Papers: Churchill College, Cambridge].

72. 'Proceedings of a Conference at the Admiralty on Tuesday, 10 August 1909', Sir John Fisher speaking, Dominions No.17, CAB 18/12A.93. Proceedings of Imperial Conference (1909), CAB 18/12A, Dominions No. 15, p 63, Mr. McKenna speaking.

73. Sumida, *In Defence,* p 256.

74. Fisher to McKenna, 14 Nov 1909, MCKN3/4.

75. For Bacon's assessment .of the revolutionary implications for the 21-inch torpedo Mk.2, see: Minutes (both 17 Dec 1908) by Capt. Reginald Bacon and Capt. Bernard Currey, on memorandum 'As to Allowance of 21-inch Torpedoes in Ships', (G18176/8) f.34, Ships Covers 224; for more general assessment of the torpedo threat see: Lambert, 'Flotilla Defence'.

76. Quoted in Sumida, *In Defence*, pp 256-7.

77. Rear Admiral Reginald Bacon, 'The Battleship of the Future', *Transactions of the Institute of Naval Architects,* 52 (1910), pp 1–9.

78. Sumida, *In Defence*, pp 256–57.

79. Draft of Letter sent by Arthur Pollen to editor of *Morning Post*, 18 Mar 1910, Pollen Papers, PLLN3/6, [Arthur Pollen Papers: Churchill College, Cambridge] cited in Sumida, *In Defence*, p 286, note 387. I am indebted to Professor Sumida for bringing this document to my attention.

80. Sumida, *In Defence*, pp 51–61, 100, 158– 62, 256– 61, 289– 95.

81. For the best explanation of British cruiser policy see the following memoranda: 'The Strategic Aspects of Our Building Programme, 1907', by Charles Ottley, 7 Jan 1907, Crease Papers, box 3, [Captain Thomas Crease Papers: Naval Library, Ministry of Defence, London]; 'Recent Admiralty Administration', by Charles Ottley and Julian Corbett, Crease Papers, box 3; Minutes of secret meeting held at the Admiralty entitled 'Saturday, 2nd December, 1905', section two on mercantile cruisers, Crease Papers, box marked Prints.

82. Figures taken from 'Information Required by Director of Commonwealth Naval Forces', Engineer-in-Chief, 22 Sept 1909, f.50, Ships Covers 224 (Australia and New Zealand), [National Maritime Museum, Brass Foundry, Woolwich, London]. If the Bristol steamed at 22 knots her endurance extended to 1,200 miles; for irrefutable evidence that battle cruisers really could steam these distances see: Fisher to Arnold White (Journalist) 15 Aug 1908, *FGDN*, ii, 189.

83. Fisher to Yexley, 1 Aug 1909, *FGDN* ii, p 258.

84. Fisher to Churchill, 6 Nov 1911, f.16, Chart13/2 [Sir Winston Churchill Papers: Chartwell Trust, Churchill College, Cambridge].

85. 'Imperial Conference on Defence — Admiralty Memorandum', 20 Jul 1909, p.1, CAB 37/100/98; also Proceedings of Imperial Conference (1909), Dominions No.15, p 5, Lord Crewe speaking, CAB 18/12A; see also original. 'Admiralty Memorandum', submitted to the CID, dated 13 Jul 1909, CAB 17/78.

86. Ibid, p 2, para 5.

87. Greene to Slade, 23 Oct 1909, Slade Mss, reel 1.

88. Minute (16 Jun 1909) by Bethell, on docket 'Naval and military Defence of Australia', f.124, ADM 116/1100B.

89. Fisher to Esher, 13 Sept 1909, *FGDN* ii, p 266.

90. Lambert, 'Admiral Sir John Fisher and the Concept of Flotilla Defence', pp 643–45.

91. Greene to Slade, 10 Sept 1909, Slade Mss, reel 1.

92. 'Imperial Conference on Defence – Admiralty Memorandum', McKenna, 20 Jul 1909, CAB 37/100/98 (Hereafter cited as 'Admiralty Memorandum'); Proceedings of Imperial Conference (1909), CAB 18/12A, Dominions No.15, p 34, McKenna speaking.

93. Proceedings of Imperial Conference (1909), CAB 18/12A, Dominions No. 15, p 63, Mr. McKenna speaking.

94. Ibid.

95. Ibid, pp 34–5, 63–5, McKenna speaking.

96. 'Memorandum from Admiralty', dated 11 Aug 1909, p 1, Australian Archives, B197, 1894/6/131, [Australian Archives, Canberra]. Hereafter cited as A.A. (notes courtesy of Bob Nicholls).

97. Telegrams, Foxton to Deakin, 4 Aug 1909, 5 Aug 1909 and 20 Aug 1909, A.A.. (notes courtesy

of Bob Nicholls.); and Proceedings of Imperial Conference (1909), CAB 18/12A, Dominions No. 15, pp 70–1.

98. Proceedings of Imperial Conference (1909), CAB 18/12A, p 36, Mr. McKenna speaking.
99. Ibid, p 64, McKenna speaking.
100. Minute (24 Feb 1910) by Greene, 'Earlier papers about constitution of Eastern Fleet in General and New Zealand division in particular', ADM 116/1270, f.8.
101. In July 1906, the Admiralty 'suggested' that India should increase her subsidy to the Navy from 100,000 to 1.5 millions per annum; see memoranda: 'Indian Contribution to Navy Funds', Admiralty to India Office, Jul 1906, Naval Necessities, Vol 3, Naval Historical Branch.
102. Greene to Slade, 19 Jul 1910, Slade Mss, reel 1; See also file of correspondence between the India Office MSS, L/MIL/7/3410 (India Office Library, London).
103. Proceedings of the Imperial Conference, CAB 18/12A, Dominions No.15, pp 82–83, 64, McKenna speaking.
104. Greene to Slade, 10 Sep 1909, Slade Mss, reel 1; Proceedings of Imperial Conference (1909), CAB 18/12A, pp 36–7, McKenna speaking.
105. Greene to Slade, 23 Oct 1909 and 25 Jan 1910, Slade Mss, reel 1.
106. CAB 18/12A; also 'Memorandum from the Admiralty', dated 11 Aug 1909, A.A.; The first cost of warships for fleet unit, 3,695,000; depreciation on warships, (20 year life, interest at 3%) 259,000; personnel, 177,000; ship maintenance, 173,000.
107. In January 1909, the Australia station consisted of one first class, three second class, and six third class cruisers, manned in peacetime by a total of 3,237 men, figures compiled by Nicholas Lambert.
108. Proceedings of the Imperial Conference (1909), CAB 16/12A, Dominions No. 17, p.65, McKenna speaking.; cost of Australia station, £900,000.
109. Telegram, Foxton to Deakin, 4 Aug 1909, A.A. (notes courtesy of Bob Nicholls.)
110. 'Notes of the Proceedings of a Conference at the Admiralty on Tuesday, 10 August 1909', Dominions No. 17, CAB 18/12A, pp 4–7.
111. Telegram, Deakin to Foxton, 6 Aug 1909, A.A. (notes courtesy of Bob Nicholls.)
112. 'Notes of the Proceedings of a Conference at the Admiralty on Tuesday, 10 August 1909', Dominions No. 17, CAB 18/12A, pp 4–7.
113. Proceedings of the Imperial Conference, CAB 18/12A. Dominions No. 15, p 82, McKenna speaking.
114. Greene to Just, 23 Jan 1911, t9, CO 418/95.
115. 'Notes of the Proceedings of a Conference at the Admiralty on Wednesday, 11 August 1909', pp 8–11, Proceedings of Imperial Conference (1909), CAB 18/12A. The 'cost' of the battle cruiser to the New Zealand Government was £150,000 per annum.
116. Proceedings of Imperial Conference (1909), CAB 18/12A, Dominions No. 17, p. 9, Sir Joseph Ward speaking; for evidence that Australia was keen to establish a joint ANZAC unit see: Telegram, Deakin to Foxton, 12 Aug 1909, and letter from Foxton to Sir Joseph Ward, 13 Aug 1909, A.A. (notes courtesy of Bob Nichols.)
117. Greene to Slade, 10 Sep 1909, Slade Mss, reel 1.
118. 'Notes of the Proceedings of a Conference at the Admiralty on Monday, 9 August 1909', Dominions No. 17, CAB 18/12A, pp 1-3.
119. Ibid, p 3.
120. The Admiralty was asked to prepare two alternate schemes, one costing £400,000 p.a. and another at £600.000, see: 'Notes of the Proceedings of Conference at the Admiralty, Monday 9 August 1909', CAB 18/12A, Dominions No. 17, p 1.
121. Telegram, Foxton to Deakin, 9 Aug 1909, A.A. (notes courtesy of Bob Nicholls.); For suggestions that Brodeur negotiated a secret deal with McKenna see: Nigel Brodeur, 'L.P.Brodeur and the Origins of the Royal Canadian Navy', in Boutilier, J, ed, *The Royal Canadian Navy in Retrospect* (Vancouver, 1982) chapter 2.
122. For the Admiralty's disgust see: Greene to Slade, 25 Jan 1910, Slade Mss, reel 1.
123. Telegram, Foxton to Deakin, 6 Aug 1909, A.A. (notes courtesy of Bob Nicholls.)
124. Proceedings of Imperial Conference (1909), CAB 18/12A, Dominions No. 15, p 74, Brodeur speaking.
125. Sarty, 'Canadian Maritime Defence', p 478–86.
126. Michael Hadley and Roger Sarty, *Tin-Pots and Pirate Ships: Canadian Naval Forces and German Sea Raiders, 1880–1918*, (McGill – Queen's University Press, 1990) p.15.
127. Proceedings of Imperial Conference (1909) CAB18/12A, Dominions No.15, pp.35–38, Mr

McKenna speaking.

128.   Phrase used at the time of the 1911 Imperial Conference in a letter from H. Just (Permanent Undersecretary at Colonial Office) to Harcourt, 31 Jan 11, Harcourt Mss, dep.592.
129.   Greene to Slade, 10 Sep 09, Slade Mss, reel 1.
130.   Ibid.
131.   Proceedings of Imperial Conference (1909), CAB18/12A, Dominions No.15, pp.68–70, Sir Joseph Ward speaking: on p.70, he refers to a 'naval defence system'.
132.   Fisher to Esher, 13 Sep 09, FGDN ii, 266.; for Rear Admiral Jellicoe's view (Third Sea Lord) see: Report of naval Mission to Australia (1919), p.4, by Admiral Jellicoe, Jellicoe Papers, Add Mss 49048.
133.   Fisher to Fiennes, 14 Apr 10, FGDN, ii, 321.
134.   Lord Grey to Harcourt (Colonial Secretary), 19 Dec 10, Harcourt Mss, f.125, dep. 483.
135.   Minutes (25 Jan 10) by Bethell, and (4 Feb 10) by G.King-Hall, on "Pacific Fleet— provision and disposition of" ADM116/1270, f.5–8.
136.   Minute (24 Feb 10), by Greene, f.8–9, ibid.
137.   'Estimate of Manning Requirements of the Navy up to 1914', N branch, printed Nov 1910 (but dated July 1910), table 7 showing British Fleet in China and Australia, Battenberg Mss, MB1/T7/40B. In 1914, the China station would comprise of two fleet units plus two county class armoured cruisers (1902 vintage) and seven river gunboats. The manpower of the China squadron would rise from 4,651 in Jul 1910, to 5,075 in Apr 1914.
138.   'Naval Expenditure', Winston Churchill (Home Secretary), 15 Jul 10, p.3, CAB 37/103/32.
139   Ibid, pp 3–4.
140.   See also 'Reply to Mr. Churchill's Memorandum', McKenna, 17 Oct 10, CAB 37/103/57.
141.   'Navy Estimates', McKenna, 16 Feb 11, CAB 37/105/12. The Admiralty was asking for more than £15 million for new construction; £13,320,00 for old programmes, and £1,740,000 for the 1911/12 programme.
142.   'Secret' [Naval Expenditure], Churchill, 3 Feb 11, CAB 37/105/7; also see Churchill to Crewe, 14 Feb 11, Lloyd George Papers, C/3/15/3 [Lloyd George Papers: House of Lords Records Office].
143.   'Secret' [Naval Expenditure], Churchill, 3 Feb 11, CAB 37/105/7.
144.   Churchill to Lloyd George, 12 Jul 12, cited in Randolph Churchill, Winston S. Churchill: Young Statesman, 4 volumes (London, 1967–69) companion 3, p 1613; 'Navy Estimates', McKenna, 16 Feb 11, CAB 37/105/12.
145.   Ibid.
146.   For the reference to the formation of the Cabinet sub-committee and McKenna's concession of two cruisers see: memoranda, 'Navy Estimates, 1911–12', McKenna, 16 Feb 11, p 4, CAB 37/105/12; for the Admiralty's annoyance see report of conversation with Vice-Admiral Francis Bridgeman (Second Sea Lord) in: Sanders to Balfour, 14 Feb 11, Add Mss 49767, f.99.
147.   Asquith to the King, report of Cabinet meeting, 1 Mar 11, Asquith Papers, box 6; and Churchill to Lloyd George, 14 Feb 11, Lloyd George Papers, C/3/15/4 [David Lloyd George Papers: House of Lords Record Office, London].
148.   'The Mediterranean Fleet', Churchill, 15 Mar 11, CAB 37/105/27.
149.   Ibid.
150.   Ibid.
151.   Churchill to Lloyd George, 14 Feb 11, Lloyd George Papers, C/3/15/4.
152.   MacDonald (Ambassador to Japan) to Foreign Office, 13 Jun 10, FO 371/918/24689 [Foreign Office Papers: Public Record Office, Kew].
153.   Ian Nish, Alliance in Decline: A study in Anglo-Japanese Relations, 1908–23 (London, 1972) pp 46, 54–59.
154.   Minute (not dated) by Edward Grey on memorandum by Sir Arthur Nicholson dated 16 Jan 1911, FO 371/1140/1827.
155.   For a summary of McKenna's thoughts on the Pacific Fleet in 1911 see: memoranda 'Naval Policy For the Pacific', Greene, 17 Jan 13, f.66–68, ADM 116/1270.
156.   McKenna to Wilson, 6 Jul 11, f.54, MCKN 3/22.
157.   Wilson to McKenna, 10 Jul 11, f.57, MCKN3/22.
158.   Ibid.
159.   Robert Gowen, 'British Legerdemain at the 1911 Imperial Conference', pp 410–411.
160.   Nicholas d'Ombrain, 'The Imperial General Staff and the Military Policy of a Continental

Strategy during the 1911 International Crisis', in *Military Affairs*, (now *The Journal of Military History*) 34, 3(1970), pp 88–95.

161. For the complex reasons surrounding Bridgeman's selection see: Nicholas Lambert, 'Admiral Sir Francis Bridgeman', in Murfett, M., ed, *The First Sea Lords: From Fisher to Mountbatten* (Praeger: Westport, 1995).

162. Bridgeman to Fisher, 4 Dec 11, Fisher Papers, FP547, FISR1/11.

163. Capt. Osmond de Brock to Slade, 28 Dec 11, Slade Mss, reel 1.

164. Churchill to Battenberg, 18 Nov 11, Battenberg Mss, MB1/T9/46.

165. Jon Sumida, 'Churchill and British Sea Power: the Politician and Statesman as an Advocate and Antagonist of Royal Navy Expansion, 1908–1929', in Sir Winston Churchill, Europe, the Empire, and the United States, ed. Alister Parker (London, 1995).

166. Memorandum signed by Alexander Bethell dated, 1 Nov 11, CHART21/20, f.12a.

167. Ibid.

168. Churchill to Battenberg, 19 Nov 11, Battenberg Mss, MB1/T9/43.

169. Churchill to Battenberg, 26 Dec 11, Battenberg Mss, MB1/T10/58; and Battenberg to Churchill, 20 Nov 11, cited in Mark Kerr, *Prince Louis of Battenberg, Admiral of the Fleet* (Longman Green & Co: London, 1934) p 233.

170. Minute (18 Jan 12) by Churchill, 'China and Australia Squadrons', First Lords Minutes, p 6–7. [First Lords Minutes 1911–1915: Naval Historical Branch, Ministry of Defence, London].

171. Just to Harcourt, 27 Jan 12, Harcourt Mss, f.111, dep.468.

172. Churchill to Harcourt, 29 Jan 12, Harcourt Papers, f.113, dep.468.

173. Churchill did, nevertheless, try to gain control of the Australian unit: Esher to Spender, 5 Jun 12, f.80, Spender Papers, Add Mss 46392; and Donald Gordon, `Admiralty and Dominion Navies', p 414, note 31.

174. Harcourt to Churchill, 1 Feb 12, Harcourt Mss, dep.468, f.121.; and Churchill to Harcourt, 11 Feb 12, f.124, ibid.

175. Churchill to Harcourt, 2 Apr 12, Harcourt Mss dep.468, f.124.; for official assent see: Asquith to the King, 1 May 12, f.135, Asquith Papers, Box 6.

176. Churchill to Harcourt, 29 Jan 12, Harcourt Papers, f.113, dep.468.

177. Harcourt to Churchill, 1 Feb 12, Harcourt Papers, f.121, dep.468.

178. Robert Borden to Harcourt, 16 May 12, Harcourt Mss, f.21, dep.462.

179. Churchill to War Staff, memorandum marked 'Secret', 15 Feb 12, paragraph two, ADM 116/3099.

180. 'Admiralty Memorandum on New German Naval Law', Churchill, 9 Mar 12, CAB 37/110/43.

181. 'Amendment to the laws of 14 Jun 1900, and 5 Jun 1906, concerning the German Fleet', Churchill, 14 Feb 12, CAB 37/109/21.

182. 'The Naval Situation', Churchill, 25 Jun 12, CAB 37/111/80; 'Manning Requirements for the Navy', Churchill, 26 Jun 12, CAB 37/111/82.

183. Admiralty memorandum, 'Manning the Fleet Committee: remarks on Mr. McKenna's memorandum', printed March 1907, Fisher Papers, FISR8/23, FP4826. (I am indebted to Professor Jon Sumida for bringing this document to my attention.); Also n.b.: The majority of seamen at this time entered the service as boys.

184. Fisher to Churchill, 6 Nov 1911, f.16, Chart13/2 [Sir Winston Churchill Papers: Chartwell Trust, Churchill College, Cambridge]. Fisher to Churchill, 16 Jan 1912, p 11, Chart 13/14.

185. Paul Halpern, *The Mediterranean Naval Situation, 1908–1914* (Harvard University Press, 1971) pp.22–42.; see also additional evidence cited in chapter by: Nicholas Lambert, 'Admiral Sir Francis Bridgeman', in Murfett, M., ed, *The First Sea Lords: From Fisher to Mountbatten* (Praeger: Westport, 1995).

186. For the Navy: Vice-Admiral Prince Louis of Battenberg (Second Sea Lord) and Rear-Admiral David Beatty (Naval Secretary); for the Army, Lieutenant General Sir John French.

187. Churchill to Bridgeman, draft of secret telegram, 1 Jun 12, CAB 1/33.

188. Lord Esher Journals, 6 Jun 12, ESHR 2/12 [Lord Esher Papers: Churchill College, Cambridge].

189. Memoranda: 'Mediterranean', Bridgeman, 9 Jun 12, f.53, ADM 116/3099.

190. Ibid; also 'Naval Situation in the Mediterranean', Churchill, 15 Jun 12, CAB 37/111/76.

191. Bridgeman to Churchill, 1 Jun 12, f.189, CAB 1/33.

192. Asquith to the King, 16 Jul 12, f.156, Asquith Papers, box 6.

193. But see: 'Secret Enclosure' inside: Asquith to the King, 15 Jul 12, f.157, Asquith 6.

194. 'Memorandum to Cabinet', Churchill, 22 Jun 12, Churchill, *Young Statesman*, companion volume

3, 1570.
195. For evidence that Churchill failed to consult Admiral Alfred Winsloe (C-in-C China, 1910–13)
      see: Winsloe to Churchill, 30 Dec 12, f.70, and reply by Churchill dated 16 Jan 13, Chart13/11,
      f.82.; for evidence that his successor was kept no better informed see: Ian Nish, 'Admiral Jerram
      and the German Pacific Fleet, 1913–15', in Mariner's Mirror, 56 (1970).
196. Gordon, *Dominion Partnership*, chapter 11.
197. Bridgeman to Churchill, 1 Jun 12, f.189, CAB 1/33; Minute (Jan 1913) by Churchill, First Lord's
      Minutes, p 168–170.
198. Asquith to Harcourt, 15 Sept 12, Harcourt Mss, f.188, dep.421.
199. Churchill to First Sea Lord, 17 Jan 13, First Lord's Minutes, p 153–4.
200. Churchill to Greene, 14 Oct 13, f.36, ADM 1/8375/108.
201. Ibid.
202. Churchill to Harcourt, 18 Jun 14, f.182; and Harcourt to Churchill, 25 Jun 14, f.185; and
      Churchill to Harcourt, (draft not sent) f.189, all ADM 1/8375/108.
203   Admiralty to Colonial Office, 27 Jan 13, f.119, ADM 116/1270, (my italics).
204. For unserviceable cruisers see: minute by Capt. George Hope (D.O.D.), 8 Mar 13, ADM
      116/1270, f.121; for unserviceable destroyers see: Vice-Admiral Alfred Winsloe (C-in-C China)
      to Admiralty, 31 Jul 10, 28 Mar 11 and 28 Jul 11, ADM 116/3132, 'War Orders, Far East'.
205. Massey to Lord Liverpool, 17 Jul 14, Harcourt Mss, f.250, dep.490.
206. Lord Liverpool to Harcourt, 29 Aug 13, Harcourt Mss, f.167, dep.490.
207. Joseph Cook (P.M. of Australia) to Admiralty via Colonial Office, 28 Feb 1914, ADM
      1/8375/108.
208. Henry Stead (editor: *Review of Reviews*) to Harcourt, 22 Apr 14, Harcourt Mss, f.80, dep.467.
209. Ibid.
210. Vice-Admiral George King-Hall (C.in.C. Australia) to Battenberg, 1 Mar 13, Battenberg Mss,
      MB1/T23/190; and 29 Apr 12, MB1/T18/144; and 2 Jul 12, MB1/T20/130.
211. Borden to Churchill, telegram, 24 Mar 13, Harcourt Mss, dep.462, f.273.
212. Ibid, Vice-Admiral George King-Hall (C-in-C Australia) to Churchill, 26 Nov 12, f.93; and min-
      utes of 'Private Conference held at Government House, Wellington', 27 Aug 13, Harcourt Mss,
      dep.480; see also McGibbon, *Blue Water Rationale*, p 14.
213. Lord Esher's Journal, 5 Jul 12, in *Journals and Letters of Reginald Viscount Esher,* 4 volumes
      (London, 1938) ed, Oliver, Viscount Esher, iii, 100.
214. 'Cabinet Committee on Replacement of Fleet Units other than Capital Ships and Singapore', min-
      utes of meeting held on 27 Feb 1924, Lord Beatty speaking, in *The Beatty Papers: Selections
      from the Private and Official Papers of Admiral of the Fleet Earl Beatty, Volume 2
      (1916–1927)*, Ranft, B, ed., (Navy Records Society, 1993), p 375.
215. 'Battle and Cruiser Squadron Programme', c.May 1914, ADM 1/8383/179.
216.   But see: Minutes (28 Jan 14) by Churchill, and (30 Jan 14) by Battenberg and Jackson on
      'Secret: Proposed Revision of Cruiser and Light Cruiser Requirements in January 1915', Docket
      dated 28 Jan 1914; Battenberg MSS, M31/T29/278, and Nicholas Lambert, 'British Naval
      Policy 1913/14: Financial Limitation & Strategic Revolution', *Journal of Modern History* (Sept
      1995), 67/3, pp 595–626.
217. Donald Gordon, 'The Admiralty and Dominion Navies, 1902–1914', *Journal of Modern History,*
      33(1961), p 421; for summary of operation in the Pacific during 1914 see: Julian Corbett,
      History of the Great War: Naval Operations, volume I, *To the Battle of the Falklands December
      1914*, pp 137–156, 278–319.

The Empire and the USA in British strategy in the spring of 1917

DAVID FRENCH

In 1914 the Asquith Government believed that the war would reach its climax in 1917. They were determined to maximize Britain's gains and minimize Britain's costs by allowing France and Russia to carry the burden of the continental land war until 1917. Meanwhile Britain would make only a token contribution to the land war by sending the British Expeditionary Force to France. Britain's main contribution towards the common cause was to take the shape of the Royal Navy, which promised to strangle the Central Powers' economies, and the economic and financial assistance it intended to grant to France and Russia. Lord Kitchener raised the New Armies in the belief that by the end of 1916 the armies of the continental powers would be spent. But his army would be intact and in 1917 it would intervene on the continent and crush the Central Powers. Britain would then be able to dictate the final peace settlement.[1]

This policy was unrealistic because neither France nor Russia was willing to fight until 1917 without considerable British military assistance. By the autumn of 1915 the Asquith Coalition Government knew that if it did not give its partners that assistance, defeatism might take hold in Paris and Petrograd and politicians might come to power who thought that it was preferable to make a negotiated peace with the Central Powers rather than continue their alliance with Britain. However, it was equally clear that the cost of increasing Britain's commitment to the continental land war might be too high. In the autumn of 1915 the Chancellor of the Exchequer, Reginald McKenna, and the President of the Board of Trade, Walter Runciman, argued that if the British agreed to their Allies' demands to take part in a major allied offensive in France in the summer of 1916, the losses they would suffer could only be sustained if conscription was introduced. If still more men were taken away from the civilian economy, Britain might be bankrupt before the Central Powers had sued for peace.[2] But under growing Allied pressure, their fears were temporarily cast aside. Conscription was introduced and the commitment of the New Armies to the battle of the Somme on 1 July 1916 marked the start of an enormous gamble. The British Government gambled that the Central Powers would sue for peace before Britain had gone bankrupt.

The gamble failed. By December 1916 the Germans were still in occupation of Belgium and northern France and had occupied Bucharest, the capital of the newest of the Entente Allies, Rumania. They showed their determination to continue the war into 1917 by adopting the Hindenburg Programme and the Auxiliary Labour Law, both designed to enable them to double their shell production and treble their gun production by the spring of 1917. Even more disquieting were the reports that the Germans hoped to starve Britain into surrender by launching unrestricted U-boat warfare, for Britain appeared to be in a poor position to reply. McKenna's fears that bankruptcy would arrive before victory seemed about to materialize when the Treasury warned that Britain would soon lack the dollars and gold it needed to purchase essential supplies in the USA.

This was the unpromising strategic situation which the Lloyd George Government inherited. By the spring of 1917 Britain seemed to have only three major strategic assets remaining: its own army, the resources of its Empire and, its policy-makers hoped, the resources of its newest partner, the USA. The War Cabinet, therefore, did its utmost to maximize their potential. At the same time as they attempted to mobilize more of Britain's own resources, they tried to draw more heavily upon the resources of their overseas possessions and made strenuous efforts to ascertain what resources the Americans could throw into the scales and how quickly they could do so. The outcome of their efforts helped to determine the course of British strategic policy for the rest of the war.

By late 1916 Australia and Canada had each raised or were in the process of raising five divisions, New Zealand had raised one and India had raised eighteen, although three of them had already been broken up.[3] The British Government agreed that the most valuable contribution the Empire could make was to supply more soldiers. But the Dominions were not willing to comply. The Canadians protested that already they could not find enough drafts to support the fifth division they were forming, and the South African Government intimated that it was unlikely that they could contribute more men, as the Boer population was unwilling to enlist for service in Europe.[4] There were limits even to what India could do, but in this case they were imposed by the British themselves. In August 1914 the Viceroy succeeded in breaking the colour bar against employing Indian troops in Europe when he persuaded the Cabinet to deploy an Indian Corps in France. But the British continued to be reluctant to recruit beyond the so-called martial races, because according to the Military Secretary at the India Office, 'The educated classes as a rule are not the fighting castes, and it is a great mistake to suppose that in a country like India "caste" is immaterial. Centuries of close and restricted breeding have produced distinct types of human beings just as much as centuries of selection in animals have produced distinct types and characteristics.'[5] The Government of India also found it difficult to recruit European officers who could speak the same languages as their soldiers. Even after they did cautiously extend their recruitment policy, they insisted that a large garrison had to be retained in India, believing that the only thing standing between India and a jihad were the good sense of the Amir of Afghanistan and the three divisions Delhi had mobilized along the frontier.[6]

Before 1914 the British had not regarded Africa as a reservoir of military manpower for use outside the continent. But the losses the army suffered during the battle of the Somme changed that and in late 1916 the Liberal MP Josiah Wedgwood suggested that the British should follow the French example and raise a million black African troops 'because we do not want all the whites killed—to put it bluntly. To slow down the rate of killing of our own men and to eke out the finest race on earth.' But some of the same obstacles which inhibited the British when they considered utilizing Indian manpower also existed in Africa. Some were political; the South African Government was reluctant to arm blacks because on their return from the war they might 'seriously menace the supremacy of the whites'.[7] Others were military; the Colonial and War Offices complained that African soldiers were not properly trained, that they would not survive in the temperate climate of France and that there were too few white officers and non-commissioned officers who spoke their languages.[8]

The Empire had contributed towards the economic cost of the war. Canada, Australia and New Zealand bore the whole cost of the troops they had raised. South Africa had paid the entire cost of the conquest of German South West Africa and met part of the cost of the pay of the troops engaged in German East Africa. The Indian Government lent the imperial Treasury £100 million and the Canadian Government had lent $120 million and arranged that Canadian banks would lend a further $150 million.[9] The Empire also provided a range of strategic raw materials. India supplied saltpetre, manganese, shellac and jute, Australia and New Zealand wool and foodstuffs, and the Canadians furnished wheat and nickel.[10] But the flow of economic assistance was not all in one direction. With the exception of Canada, Britain's overseas possessions could not supply significant quantities of munitions and had to draw upon British manufacturers for the weapons and equipment their troops required at a cost to the Treasury by early 1917 of £126,905,000.[11]

The support given to Britain by its Empire also had a political cost and the war witnessed a significant shift in the relationship between the Dominions and the imperial Government. Before 1914 the imperial Government believed that, whatever other concessions they had to make to colonial autonomy, they could retain control of the Empire's foreign and defence policy. In August 1914 they took it for granted that Britain's declaration of war on Germany would pledge India and the Dominions, and they were correct. The white English-speaking peoples of the Empire were drawn into the war not only by sentimental ties of kith and kin, but also by the realization that if Germany won the war, they would be the spoils of its victory.[12] Only amongst the Boers of South Africa and the francophone population of Canada were serious doubts expressed about whether they should become involved in the war.

Two years later, Britain's growing dependence on India and the Dominions persuaded the new Government that the time for consultations had arrived. The new administration wanted to draw more heavily upon imperial resources, and, as Lloyd George recognized, since 'We want more men from them. We can hardly ask them to make another great recruiting effort unless it is accompanied by an invitation to come over to discuss the situation with us.'[13] He did so in the realization that, much as he might like to do so, he would not be able to confine discussions to matters concerned with mobilizing more men. He would also have to consider war aims, for there was a growing suspicion in the Dominions that, 'they might be asked to make a sacrifice of their conquests in order to make it easier for His Majesty's Government to fulfil its pledges to Belgium and France.'[14] Furthermore, some members of his Government had additional items they wished to add to the agenda. Lord Milner and his acolytes such as Leopold Amery and Philip Kerr, hoped that the Imperial War Cabinet would be the first step in transforming their pre-war dream of a politically consolidated and autarkic empire into reality. The War Cabinet therefore agreed that the Imperial War Cabinet would examine three issues: what India and the Dominions could do to increase the levels of their economic and military effort, what peace terms the British Empire was fighting to achieve and what should be the postwar constitution of the British Empire.[15]

The first session of the Imperial War Cabinet held fourteen meetings between 20 March and 2 May 1917. The British were represented by the members of the War Cabinet. The Empire's representation was a more complicated matter. The New Zealand Government had been formed by a fusion, rather than by a coalition of the two main parties and the New Zealand Prime Minister, W. F. Massey, insisted that his fellow party leader, Sir Joseph Ward, had to be present. Sir Robert Borden, the Canadian Premier, demanded that one of his ministerial colleagues, Sir George Perley, the Minister of the Overseas Military Forces of Canada, must accompany him.[16] The Newfoundlanders were represented by their Premier, Sir E. P. Morris, the South Africans by their Minister of Defence, Jan Smuts, and India by the Maharajah of Bikaner and Sir S. P. Sinha. Australia was not represented, because the Australian Premier, Billy Hughes, was in the middle of a major political crisis and could not travel to London.

The War Cabinet was right to think that the Dominions suspected that they were ignoring their interests. By late 1916 the heavy losses their forces had suffered at Gallipoli and on the Somme made colonial leaders anxious to have some say in directing the Empire's strategy and war aims. Smuts and the New Zealanders came to London determined to insist that under no circumstances would they relinquish the German colonies which their forces had captured. Others were reluctant to accept Milner's agenda for the post-war organization of the Empire. Borden, like Lloyd George, was an exponent of the 'knock-out blow', but he was at one with Smuts in being determined to resist any British attempts to impose closer imperial unity upon the Dominions.[17]

Lloyd George tried to persuade his colonial colleagues that they must increase their military efforts if the Entente was to win the war in 1918. On 20 March he warned them that the cost of victory would be expensive. 'To be ready for 1918', he concluded, echoing the determination of the Asquith Government to secure a peace settlement which would ensure its security against all-comers, 'means victory, and it is a victory in which the British Empire will lead. It will easily then be the first Power in the world.'[18] The assembled leaders accepted the British timetable for victory. They agreed that the Empire should make the biggest possible effort in 1917 to force Germany to accept their peace terms but as they were unlikely to succeed they would repeat the process in 1918 when victory would be more certain.[19]

But although the colonial leaders accepted Lloyd George's timetable for victory, they were not so willing to listen to his pleas for more resources. They insisted that there were limits to what they could do. There were francophones in Canada, the Boers of South Africa and the Irish in Australia, 'to whom the purposes of the war do not appeal so strongly as to other portions of our population.'[20] Canada, New Zealand and South Africa promised to do little more than maintain their existing forces at their present strength. It therefore seemed that only India could provide a significantly larger supply of manpower.[21]

Lloyd George remained committed to the programme of restitution, reparations and effective guarantees against repetition which he had outlined shortly after becoming Prime Minister in December 1916. But he had considerable difficulty in persuading the Dominions to agree. On 20 March he explained that the first of these objectives could be achieved if the Germans were driven from all occupied Allied territory and if Poland were established as an independent state. But laying the foundations of a lasting peace would not only necessitate the redrawing of the European map along lines of nationality, it would also require the Entente to achieve a military victory over Germany to demonstrate that military aggression would always bring a just measure of punishment and 'the democratisation of Europe' because democracy was 'the only sure guarantee of peaceful progress.'[22] If the British settled for less, it would mean that their sacrifices had been in vain and that the burden of eliminating the German menace would fall on a future generation.[23]

Borden, who had no territorial ambitions for Canada, agreed it was necessary to teach not only the German Government but their people 'that an unprovoked aggression cannot be profitable to them...' and accepted that the interests of the Entente demanded a victory in Europe since the European settlement would ultimately determine Germany's future ability to menace Britain and its Empire.[24] But some of Lloyd George's listeners did have territorial ambitions of their own and they were disturbed when Lloyd George hinted that if the war ended in a military stalemate they might have to return some of Germany's colonies.[25]

Lloyd George's critics were not imperial isolationists who believed that Britain could safely ignore the European balance of power. They were men like

Smuts and Amery, who thought that it was unlikely that the Entente could ever inflict on Germany a military defeat such that it would be compelled to accept all their desiderata, including a democratic regime, and that the price of attempting to do so might be too high.[26] They thought that Germany had two objectives, to establish a German Middle European empire embracing Central Europe and the Near East, and to create an overseas empire by absorbing the British Empire. Britain's overriding objective should be to forestall Germany's second aim, but to do so it would also have to block its path towards a Middle European empire. Britain's immediate aim, therefore, should be to deprive Germany of control of those parts of the globe—France, Belgium, Syria, Palestine, Mesopotamia, south and east Africa and the Pacific—from whence it could menace Britain's imperial communications. For Smuts, Amery and their colleagues these were the irreducible minima to safeguard Britain's own security. Other objectives, such as the reduction of German power in Central Europe, the satisfaction of the national aspirations of the subject nationalities of the Austro-Hungarian Empire, and the achievement of French aims in Alsace-Lorraine, were of secondary importance. Even though the Entente's efforts might fall short of the total victory that Lloyd George sought, Britain could rest content, Amery argued, if it secured a 'just equilibrium' on the continent and if it wrested control of both the Channel coast and the Turkish Empire from Germany.[27]

As a first step towards imposing their priorities on the War Cabinet, Milner, Smuts and Ward pressed Lloyd George to establish an inquiry into the relative importance of the Empire's war aims. But Lloyd George, the exponent of the 'knock-out blow', refused to agree until 12 April when he received a telegram from the Russian Chief of Staff, General Alexieff, informing the Allies that the Russian army would be in no condition to mount an offensive until June, and calling into question the Entente's ability to inflict catastrophic defeat on Germany.

The inquiry took the form of two committees, the first under Milner to discuss non-territorial war aims and the second under Curzon to consider territorial war aims.[28] Some of the spade-work for the Curzon committee had already been performed by an earlier committee established in 1916 under the chairmanship of the former Ambassador to Turkey, Sir Louis Mallet. It had recommended that the German colonies in the Pacific south of the equator should be retained by Australia and New Zealand and that Japan should be permitted to keep those north of the Equator.[29] This last concession was forced on the British Government by the Japanese, who otherwise refused to provide further naval assistance to the Entente. Given the sensitivity of Australia and New Zealand concerning Japanese expansion in the Pacific, the Imperial Government took care to keep them informed and had insisted that Japan give reciprocal promises concerning Germany's colonies south of the Equator.[30] The disposal of Germany's African colonies also caused dissension. The Admiralty, India Office and Colonial Office representatives wanted to retain all captured German colonies. They were a threat to the security of the British Empire, the cost of reconquering them in another war would be high and their indigenous populations supposedly preferred British to German rule. Retaining them would also add to the Empire's economic resources and improve imperial communications. But Sir George Macdonogh, the Director of Military Intelligence and the War Office's representative on the committee, argued for a more far-sighted policy. He questioned whether fighting to retain still more square miles of real estate was worth the cost in blood and treasure, and he believed that it would be unwise to deprive Germany of all of its colonies and thus to leave it with a permanent grievance against Britain. Looking beyond the present war, he noted that the existing grouping of the powers might not be permanent and that in a few years Britain might welcome a strong and well-disposed Germany as an ally against an over-mighty Russia.[31]

Such prescience found no echo in the Curzon committee. Massey warned that if the British tried to return Germany's colonies, it would have an adverse effect on public opinion in the Dominions which had occupied them.[32] Long gave him voluble support, telling the War Cabinet that retrocession would harm the prestige of Botha's Government in South Africa 'thereby endanger[ing] the British connection', would deal a damaging blow to British prestige amongst the indigenous populations of Britain's colonies to the north and would add to the cost of defence after the war.[33] Amery, as co-secretary of the Curzon committee, drafted its report.[34] It concluded that the extent to which it would be possible to secure acceptable peace terms would depend upon the Entente's military success. If these were not decisive, allied statesmen might have to retract some of their public statements. The committee accepted that the restoration of occupied Allied territory were, 'essential conditions of any peace', but distanced itself from any attempt to wage the war to democratize Germany or to crush Prussian militarism, arguing that, 'even in the event of the most complete military success, it should not be the purpose of British policy to destroy the national existence of any of the enemy Powers, or to set up a condition of resentment and unrest which would tend to revive the competition of armaments and eventually bring about another European war.'[35] The committee's commitment to the cause of nationalism in Central and Eastern Europe was only lukewarm, for the settlement of the Alsace-Lorraine, Polish and Austro-Hungarian questions were of more concern to the Allies than to Britain. But the committee 'had been impressed with the extreme importance of securing an effective barrier to the extension of German power and influence, both political, economic and commercial, over the Near East.'[36] They believed this could be achieved by a settlement of the Balkan question which would meet Serbian aspirations, by Russian occupation of Constantinople and the Straits or by securing a separate peace with either Bulgaria or Turkey.

Outside Europe the committee wanted to establish 'a Monroe doctrine for the southern half of the Empire'.[37] If Britain did achieve an overwhelming victory, it should retain all of Germany's colonies and destroy the Ottoman

Empire, for otherwise they would constitute a permanent threat to the security of the Empire, and a threat which would become even more acute in the future, as the capabilities of aircraft and submarines were further developed or if the Germans raised a large Black African army.[38] It was a measure of the committee's determination to safeguard the Empire that even in the event of a less-than-total victory, it was only willing to return Togoland and the Cameroons to Germany. Nor was it accidental that both colonies were of more concern to France than to Britain.

The Milner committee took equal care to fashion a report designed to safeguard Britain's post-war interests, although it was a little more ready to balance the need to pursue them against the need to meet Britain's wartime obligations to its Allies. In the light of the backsliding of several of the Allies and the known hostility of the United States to the Paris Economic Resolutions of 1916, which were designed to create an exclusive trading bloc centred on the Entente alliance, the committee agreed that there had to be further negotiations between the members of the Entente to ensure a common policy towards the enemy during peace negotiations. It also recommended that Britain should resist the inclusion of any clauses in the peace treaty preventing the Governments of the Empire from co-operating to develop their own economic resources. Indemnities for the destruction wrought by the Germans in Belgium and northern France and to Allied and British merchant ships by U-boats should be extracted in kind rather than in cash. Support for a post-war League of Nations had been growing slowly in Britain before 1916, but it received a new respectability when President Woodrow Wilson told the US Senate on 22 January 1917 that he advocated a programme for peace based on democratic justice, an end to entangling alliances, self-determination, freedom of the seas, all to be sustained by a League of Nations.[39] Exactly what form the League could take remained unclear. The Minister of Blockade, Lord Robert Cecil, suggested that it could become an international court of arbitration or a system of conferences. The committee preferred the latter option, but also wanted further guarantees, fearing that another European war might produce 'the complete destruction of civilised society'. They therefore wanted to discuss with the USA and the Allies before the conclusion of the present war the insertion into the peace treaty of a clause providing that none of its signatories would resort to war again without first submitting their disputes to a conference of the powers. However, their idealism only went so far and they were easily persuaded by Sir Eyre Crowe of the Foreign Office that Britain's future security could not be laid to rest on a disarmed Germany alone. It must also depend upon Britain's own military and naval strength and the preservation of a balance of power in Europe. Consequently, the committee wanted no truck with Wilson's cherished aim of securing the 'Freedom of the Seas'. Any concession on that point would threaten the foundation of Britain's post-war imperial security, the dominance of the Royal Navy.[40] The Royal Navy was a powerful deterrent, for 'the existence of our own dominating sea-power, coupled with

the sea-power of America, was undoubtedly the best guarantee for peace;...'
But beyond agreeing that any discussions with the USA concerning a future
League of Nations ought also to include some consideration of how to bring
about an international agreement on the reduction of armaments, the Imperial
War Cabinet failed to agree on any course of future action.[41]

Lloyd George was willing to overrule French objections to the British establishing a protectorate over Palestine. British, not French forces were responsible for expelling the Turks and only the British were capable of ruling over a
mixed population of Moslems, Jews, and Roman Catholics.[42] But he was otherwise critical of the extreme annexationist programme embodied in the Curzon
report, pointing out that although the report embodied 'what we ought to aim at
in the case of complete victory' it provided no guidance to British delegates, 'if
they had to face a Conference under conditions which left Germany still in
possession of a great deal of Allied territory. It had not quite faced the difficulty which would arise if France or Russia asked us to surrender some of our
conquests in order to release their territory.' With Borden's support, he successfully insisted that Britain had wider interests in the European settlement
and ensured that Curzon's recommendations should be regarded only as a
guide, and not as an agreed blue-print for a settlement.[43]

The results of the imperial War Cabinet fell short of Lloyd George's hopes.
Although each member had promised to put forth its maximum effort in 1917
and again in 1918 if necessary, it had discovered few hitherto untapped imperial resources which could be mobilized in the short term to assist the war effort.
But it had given the Dominion Governments an opportunity to insist that the
imperial Government underwrite their own local imperial ambitions in Africa
and Asia. This occurred at the very moment when it was becoming apparent
both that French and Russian efforts were declining and that the Entente might
not be able to inflict the 'knock-out blow' on Germany. Even so, their territorial objectives remained remarkably extensive, both inside and outside Europe
and threatened to throw them into conflict not only with the USA but with
those of their own peoples who favoured a Wilsonian peace settlement. The
Imperial War Cabinet's final deliberations included a formula which seemed to
commit Britain and the Empire to fighting on until they had secured guarantees
against Germany's future behaviour, but they did not define the exact nature of
those guarantees. Some ministers, although not Lloyd George, were willing to
consider abandoning any attempts to democratize Germany provided they
could secure territorial war aims sufficient to end Germany's present bid for
hegemony. At their penultimate meeting on 1 May, the representatives agreed
on a compromise resolution which embodied most of the objectives Lloyd
George and his imperialist critics sought but left undecided which were the
most vital. They agreed that they were fighting not only for 'the re-establish-
ment of liberty and public right in Europe and on the high seas', but for a
European political settlement based on self-determination, the liberation of the
oppressed nationalities of the Turkish Empire, and 'the security and integrity of

the British empire'. Although the final resolutions contained no explicit references to the need to democratize Germany, it did assert that Britain was fighting to achieve 'the framing of measures for the preservation of lasting peace in concert with our Allies'.[44]

It seemed equally unlikely, at least in the short term, that the War Cabinet would be able to find the extra resources it sought from across the Atlantic, for the US Government not only had its own war aims, it also had its own strategic policy. Only a few days after Wilson's speech of 22 January the Germans declared unrestricted U-boat warfare and on 3 February the USA broke off diplomatic relations with Germany. But, to the exasperation of the British, Wilson refused to declare war on Germany unless its U-boats actually attacked American shipping.[45] When they did so, pressure from shipowners and a growing section of public opinion compelled Wilson to ask Congress for authority to arm American merchant ships. By early March the USA, suspended awkwardly between war and peace, was waging armed neutrality in the Atlantic.[46] What tipped the balance in favour of war was the ability of the Admiralty's cryptanalysts in London to read the diplomatic telegrams which emanated from Berlin and the fact that they revealed a German plot to inveigle Mexico into an alliance to wage war against its northern neighbour.[47]

It now remained for the US Government to determine what form their intervention should take. Until the eve of war, the US administration had given little thought as to how they might co-operate with the Entente in the war against the Central Powers. On 13 February Herbert Hoover, who was in charge of the Belgium Relief Commission, had suggested to Wilson's confidant, Colonel E. M. House, that if the USA did enter the war it should forbear joining the Entente alliance. Initially it should restrict its assistance to providing its associates with merchant shipping, destroyers, money and food. Eventually, a powerful US army could be sent to Europe at an opportune moment so as to assure Wilson a powerful voice at the peace conference.[48] Wilson approved of Hoover's ideas and on 2 April embodied several of them in his address to Congress asking for a declaration of war. Like Lord Kitchener in 1914, Wilson was determined to give his new partners only just enough help to prevent their defeat until such time as he could mobilize a large army and so secure a dominant voice at the peace conference.[49]

Wilson's war aims conflicted with those which the Imperial War Cabinet had tabulated in several key respects. Although the President shared the British distaste for Prussian militarism and feared that a German victory would end his hopes for the future reconstruction of the world community, he also had a large measure of distaste for Allied imperialism and British 'navalism'. Wilson did not commit the USA to the restoration of a European balance of power, nor did he express any sympathy towards the Entente's territorial war aims. 'We have', he told Congress on 2 April, 'no selfish ends to serve. We desire no conquest, no dominion.' Rather, he insisted, the war should be fought 'To make the world safe for democracy.'[50] Wilson refrained from signing the Pact of

London which bound the Entente allies together, and the USA became an Associated Power, not an ally of the Entente. That left Wilson in a powerful bargaining position. Without any formal diplomatic ties, he could threaten his partners with a withdrawal of US assistance if they did not comply with his wishes, a threat he actually used on the eve of the armistice negotiations with Germany in 1918. Sir William Wiseman, a British diplomatist who established a close relationship with House, summarized the public support for Wilson's stance in America when he reported that 'the sentiment of the country would be strongly against joining the Allies by any formal treaty. Sub-consciously they feel themselves to be arbitrators rather than allies.'[51]

Within days of hearing that the USA had broken diplomatic relations with Germany, British policy-makers began to speculate about the material assistance they wanted from across the Atlantic. Lord Eustace Percy, who had previously served in the Washington embassy and was now in the Foreign Office's War Department, prepared a shopping list of goods and services. Provided, he wrote in a condescending tone which was soon to be shattered, the British took the initiative, for 'The United States understands little or nothing of the way in which a war is conducted', the US Government would be willing to provide merchant shipping, money, munitions and military manpower. But what the British neither expected nor wanted was an American trained and led army in France. In February 1917 Macdonogh reported that the US regular army numbered less than 95,000 officers and men. It had no trained reserve and the National Guard could only muster two-thirds of its nominal establishment of 150,000. Remembering their own difficulties in raising and training the New Armies in 1914–15, the War Office believed that the American army's existing staff was quite inadequate to deal with a sudden expansion of the army and within six months of the start of the war would be able to place only six divisions in the field. What both Macdonogh and Percy did want from the Americans was large numbers of American volunteers who could be absorbed into Allied divisions. 'An American Expeditionary Force of any size', insisted Percy, 'can neither be trained, armed nor transported in time to make itself felt. The only sound war policy the United States can pursue is to encourage enlistment in the British and French Armies.'[52] Such a policy would also overcome the Ministry of Munitions, fears that the raising of a huge American army would cause the US Government to divert supplies of munitions destined for the British to their own army.[53] The absorbtion of US manpower into the British army was to become an obsession for many British policy makers for much of the remainder of the war.

On 5 April, having been warned by the British Ambassador in Washington, Sir Cecil Spring-Rice, that the US Government 'will do everything it can to avoid any joint or concerted action';[54] the Imperial War Cabinet decided to send a mission to Washington to assess exactly what assistance they could secure. Balfour was selected to lead it, and he was accompanied by representatives of the War Office, the Admiralty, the Treasury, the Royal Commission on

Wheat Supplies, the Ministry of Blockade and the Ministry of Munitions.[55] The Balfour mission left convinced that the USA was an enormous repository of the raw materials of war, just waiting to be tapped, and willing and capable of making good the losses which the Entente had suffered following the slackening of the efforts of France and Russia. They returned home somewhat wiser. The mission arrived in Washington on 22 April and spent approximately a month in the USA. It did indeed confirm the War Cabinet's belief that their new partner had potentially enormous resources which it could throw into the struggle. But it also highlighted the political and practical problems in the way of mobilizing that potential in accordance with *British* strategy and in pursuit of *British* war aims.

In public Balfour and his colleagues tactfully insisted that they had come to the USA not to offer advice, unless it was requested by their hosts, but to explain to the administration the needs of Britain and its Allies. During his conversations with politicians and officials, Balfour was impressed by the fact that 'with one possible exception, [he found] the greatest eagerness to do all that was possible to help the Allied cause.'[56] Even so, his mission met with only mixed success and many of the high hopes which the War Cabinet had entertained were disappointed. On the positive side the representatives of the Ministry of Blockade and the Wheat Commission met with considerable success. In the spring of 1917 the blockade of Germany was still far from being watertight. This was partly due to the propensity of British traders, long habituated in peacetime to trading in international markets, to place profits before patriotism and to trade with Germany through contiguous neutrals. But it was also due to the refusal of some neutrals, including the USA, to stop trading with Germany. The Ministry of Blockade's representatives went far towards overcoming American scruples about the legality of certain aspects of the blockade and the British left satisfied that their new partners would co-operate in enforcing it more rigorously. Henceforth, customs officers in American and Allied ports played an increasingly important role in implementing the blockade, and from June 1917 the 10th Cruiser squadron, which had enforced the North Sea blockade, could be disbanded.[57] The Wheat Commission's negotiations were also successful. Hoover, whom Wilson had made head of the US Food Administration, agreed with the British representatives on the need to establish a Wheat Executive which would purchase all wheat in the USA and sell any surplus to the British Wheat Export Company.[58]

The Munitions, Treasury, and Shipping missions were less successful. Before the mission arrived in Washington, the War Trade Intelligence Department had already concluded that 'the United States Shipping board appear anxious to build up an American merchant marine at our expense.'[59] Nothing that transpired in Washington caused them to alter this conclusion. The head of the US Shipping Board, William Denman, was convinced that British requests to the USA to provide tonnage to supply France and Russia, to increase merchant ship building and to control the chartering of merchant ships by private individuals, were part of a British plot to lure US ships into the path of German U-boats. At the end of the war the American merchant fleet would be depleted and Britain would remain the world's dominant maritime power and control the world's carrying trade. Thus he refused to acquiesce in British demands.[60] Similarly the representatives of the Ministry of Munitions failed both to persuade the US Government to determine production priorities between the needs of their own army and those of Britain and the other Entente partners, or to adopt British-calibre artillery and thus ensure that there was no interruption in the supply of munitions to Britain.[61]

The Treasury mission's task was made more difficult by the continued tension between Sir Hardman Lever, the Financial Secretary to the Treasury, and the Governor of the Bank of England, Lord Cunliffe. On 9 April Lever told the Chairman of the Federal Reserve Board that Britain required $500 million at once to cover French and Russian commitments in the USA. But the US Government now had to fund its own war effort, and the Treasury Secretary, William McAdoo, refused to permit the British to raise a further loan in the USA until his Government had raised its own Liberty Loan. Lever had to wait until 25 April before he received $200 million to meet Britain's immediate needs. Meanwhile Cunliffe made his job of securing long-term financial assistance much more difficult by informing the Americans that the British still retained some gold which they could ship across the Atlantic. Thus, when Lever asked the USA for a loan of $2000 million designed to last until the end of 1917, or for $1100 million plus a $400 million overdraft at their own bankers, J. P. Morgans, the most McAdoo would promise was $200 million to be paid in three instalments. J. M. Keynes, the Treasury official in charge of overseeing the exchange situation with the USA, described the outcome 'as anxious but not by any means desperate'.[62] McAdoo was determined to maximize US influence by keeping America's new partners on a short financial leash.

But the biggest disappointments were conjured up by the military and naval missions. The leaders of the British and French military missions, Lt-General Sir Tom Bridges and Marshal Joffre, did awake Wilson to the need to send large numbers of American troops to Europe. But they were handicapped in doing more by Wilson's refusal to discuss military matters with them.[63] Bridges believed that this reflected the fact that the US Government had no settled policy on the issues the military mission wished to discuss and had tried to hide the fact by offering their guests lavish hospitality.[64] But Bridges' greatest failure, to persuade the War Department to despatch half-trained American troops to France where they could complete their training then be used as drafts in depleted British units, required no such elaborate explanation. The US administration and its General Staff were determined to train and equip their own army before despatching troops to France. Whatever the other lacunae in their thinking, they recognized, as had the British in 1914, that their objective was not only to win the war, but also to win the peace. America's influence over the final peace terms would depend to a large extent on the size of its contribution to the land war. In their opinion, if the European Allies were short of men, they should remain on the defensive to husband their resources until the Americans arrived. The most that Bridges and Joffre could extract from the War Department in the short term was an agreement to send a small force of regulars to France as soon as possible as a token of American involvement in the war and to boost Allied morale.[65] At the end of the Balfour mission the General Staff correctly concluded that, although the US Government had extensive industrial capacity and manpower reserves at its disposal, a lack of prior planning meant that they would not be able to transform that potential into divisions capable of taking their place in the line until 1918 at the earliest.[66]

The naval mission also revealed the extent to which the USA was both a partner and a rival. It persuaded the US navy to increase from six to forty-eight the number of destroyers it was willing to send to European waters but it did not persuade them to increase destroyer production.[67] In 1916, as part of a preparedness campaign intended to give the USA a major voice in the peace settlement, the United States navy had embarked upon a fleet-building programme designed to provide it with a superiority in capital ships over every other navy in the world, including the Royal Navy.[68] That meant in the short term that American shipyards could not build the destroyers the Entente needed to counter German U-boats, and in the long term that the American navy threatened the Royal Navy's supremacy. When Balfour raised the matter with House, the latter suggested that a way around the obstacle could be found if Britain and the USA signed a secret naval treaty. If the British agreed to safeguard American interests in the Pacific against Japan, they would release the Americans from the need to build so many capital ships, and they could devote more shipbuilding capacity to destroyers. When Balfour returned to London he suggested to the War Cabinet that Britain, France, Italy and Japan should engage to assist each other against any maritime attacks for four years after the termination of the present war. It was an indication of how low Anglo-Japanese relations had sunk, and how dependent the War Cabinet believed they were upon the USA, that they permitted him to begin negotiations. However, Wilson eventually quashed the proposal. For the moment that did not matter, for in July 1917 the US Government unilaterally postponed capital ship construction and did begin to lay down 200 more destroyers, but in the longer term the episode demonstrated that Britain's maritime security might not be assured even if Germany was defeated.[69]

Finally, the Balfour mission highlighted how far apart were the political objectives for which Britain and the USA were fighting. At the Imperial War Cabinet on 26 April Borden told the assembled representatives that 'the United States and the British Empire in agreement could do more than anything else to maintain the peace of the world.'[70] In Washington Balfour impressed his hosts with his amiability and statesmanship, and helped to diminish some of the anti-British sentiments which had prevailed there before the USA entered the war.[71] But he did not succeed in binding Woodrow Wilson to the Entente, nor did he persuade the President to underwrite Britain's war aims. When Balfour met Wilson and his Secretary of State, Robert Lansing, on 23 April, Wilson told Balfour that although he was determined to see the war through to a successful conclusion, he did not think that it would be expedient to tie the USA to the Entente by a treaty of alliance.[72] Balfour discussed peace terms and the treaties which Britain had signed with its Allies with House and the President on 28 and 30 April. The Foreign Secretary also sent House a copy of the memorandum on British war aims he had written in October 1916, forwarded to Wilson copies of the secret treaties Britain had signed since the start of the war, and presented Lansing with a copy of the lengthy statement that he had made outlining British foreign policy to the Imperial War Cabinet on 22 March 1917.[73] Balfour had two further meetings with the President, on 17 and 21 May and, although there was no formal record of what was said, it is likely that they again considered possible peace terms.[74] Wilson was affronted, for their conversations left him no doubt about the rapacity of his partners, and Balfour was disquieted because the President left him in no doubt that several features of his agenda for the post-war world, particularly his pursuit of 'freedom of the seas' and his distaste for all forms of European imperialism, ran counter to British interests. In the second half of 1917 the British tried to solve this predicament by trying to win the war before the Americans were fully mobilized and able to exert significant influence over them. The French adopted a different policy. Following the mutinies which swept their army in the early summer of 1917, the new French Commander-in-Chief, General Pétain, decided to avoid any further major offensives until the arrival of the American army in strength in 1918. After lengthy debate, the British opted for a more dangerous policy. They launched the third battle of Ypres on 31 July 1917 in the hope that Haig could win the war before their dependence upon the Americans reached a dangerous level.[75] The gamble failed and the result was that in 1918 their need for American assistance grew, and with it their recognition of the fact that the cost of gaining American help might be the emergence of a new and potentially even more powerful rival across the Atlantic.

By May 1917 many of the early promises which had sustained the Lloyd George Government had been dashed. At home it had been unable significantly to accelerate the mobilization of British manpower. At sea, the U-boats were making growing inroads into British and Allied tonnage. On the Eastern front, the ability of the Russian army to sustain its resistance to the Central Powers was increasingly being called into question, whilst on the Western front the Nivelle offensive failed. It was therefore inevitable that the British looked across the oceans, to their own Empire and to their newest partner, for material assistance, but in the short term they were disappointed. Neither the USA nor the Empire appeared to be willing or able to provide them with ships, soldiers, money and food quickly, and the help they did proffer carried a heavy price.

Although the Dominions agreed to sustain their existing efforts, only India seemed capable of providing more manpower. But, in return the Dominion Governments had committed the Lloyd George regime more heavily than ever to the pursuit of their own local imperialist war aims in Africa and the Pacific. That was a source of growing embarrassment for the British Government for the rest of the war, for their objectives ran directly counter to those of Britain's newest partner—and potential rival—the USA. The Balfour mission demonstrated that the British could expect very considerable material assistance from the USA, but it also discovered that the Wilson Government intended to provide that assistance in its own way, according to its own timetable, and in pursuit of its own objectives. The first session of the Imperial War Cabinet and the Balfour mission therefore left the British Government to perform a delicate balancing act as, for the rest of the war, they tried to reconcile the competing political objectives of the Dominions and the USA while extracting the largest possible quantities of manpower and economic resources from them to pursue their own political objectives.

NOTES

1. D. French, 'The meaning of attrition, 1914–1916', *English Historical Review*, 103, 407 (1988), pp 385–405.
2. T. Wilson, (ed.), *The Political Diaries of C. P. Scott 1911–1918* (London, 1970), p 137.
3. Historical Section, *Committee of Imperial Defence, Divisional Distribution Chart* (London, nd), passim.
4. Minutes of War Cabinet, 15 Mar 1917, CAB 23/2/WC97, [Public Record Office, Kew, Surrey. Henceforth PRO]; 'Note on the available resources of manpower, both white and coloured in the overseas Dominions and dependencies of the Empire', R. H. Brade, 9 Jan 1917, CAB 23/1/WC41 [PRO].
5. G. Martin, 'The influence of racial attitudes on British policy towards India during the First World War', *Journal of Imperial and Commonwealth History*, 14, 1 (1986), pp 91–109; 'Proposal for raising territorial units in India, 19 June 1917', E. G. Barrow, 19 June 1917, CAB 37/150/5 [PRO]; 'Additional Military Assistance from India', E. G. Barrow, 2 Jan. 1917, CAB 24/6/GT22 [PRO]; ; Monro to Robertson, 28 Dec 1916, Robertson mss I/32/51 [Liddell Hart Centre for Military Archives, King's College London. Henceforth LHCMA].
6. 'Imperial War Conference. Memorandum on the military assistance given by India in the prosecution of the war', India Office, 11 Mar 1917, CAB 24/7/GT152 [PRO].
7. 'Question of raising native troops for imperial service', A. Bonar Law, 18 Oct 1916, CAB 37/136/19 [PRO].
8. D. Killingray, 'The idea of a British imperial African army', *Journal of African History*, 20, 4 (1979), pp 425–6; D. Killingray, 'Repercussions of World War One on the Gold Coast', *Journal of African History*, 19, 1 (1978), pp 39–50.
9. 'Financial assistance rendered by the Dominions and India to His Majesty's Government. Memorandum issued by the Treasury in connection with Imperial War Cabinet sittings', [nd but *c.* 14 Mar 1917] CAB 24/7/GT172 [PRO].
10. 'Imperial War Conference. Memorandum on the assistance given by India in supplying commodities essential to the prosecution of the war', India Office, 5 Mar 1917, CAB 24/7/GT197 [PRO]; 'Memorandum on assistance in the war rendered by the Dominions other than naval and military (including munitions) or financial assistance', Imperial Conference Secretariat, 13 Mar 1917, CAB 24/8/GT203 [PRO].
11. 'Imperial War Cabinet. Memorandum', Ministry of Munitions, [nd but *c.* 20 Mar. 1917] CAB

24/8/GT232 [PRO]; 'Financial assistance to the Dominions by H. M. Government', the Treasury, [nd but *c.* 13 Mar 1917], CAB 24/7/GT173 [PRO].

12.   R. Hyam, 'The Colonial Office mind, 1900–1914,' *Journal of Imperial and Commonwealth History,* 8, 1 (1979), pp 31–55; P. Hayes, 'British foreign policy and the influence of Empire, 1870–1920', *Journal of Imperial and Commonwealth History*, 12, 1 (1984), pp 112–13.

13.   D. Lloyd George, *War Memoirs* (London, 1936), vol 2, p 1026; N. Mansergh, *The Commonwealth Experience. Volume I. The Durham Report to the Anglo-Irish Treaty* (London, 1969/82), p 198.

14.   Minutes of War Cabinet, 22 Dec 1916, CAB 23/1/WC15 [PRO].

15.   Minutes of War Cabinet, 10 Feb 1917, CAB 23/1/WC67 [PRO].

16.   Hankey diary, 1 Mar 1917, Hankey mss HNKY 1/1 [Churchill College, Cambridge. Henceforth CCC]; L. Amery, *My Political Life. Vol. Two. War and Peace 1914–1929* (London, 1953), pp 105–106.

17.   G. L. Cook, 'Sir Robert Borden, Lloyd George and British military policy, 1917–1918', *Historical Journal,* 14, 2 (1971), p 371; D. C. Watt, 'Imperial defence policy and imperial foreign policy, 1911–1939. A neglected paradox?', *Journal of Commonwealth Political Studies,* 1, 3 (1961–63), p. 268; J. Turner, *Lloyd George's Secretariat* (Cambridge, 1980), p. 127; Mansergh, *The Commonwealth Experience,* vol. I, pp 195–8; K. Ingham, *Jan Christian Smuts. The Conscience of South Africa* (London, 1986), pp 90–1.

18.   Minutes of Imperial War Cabinet, 20 Mar 1917, CAB 23/40/IWC–1 [PRO].

19.   Minutes of Imperial War Cabinet, 23 Mar 1917, CAB 23/40/IWC–3 [PRO].

20.   Minutes of Imperial War Cabinet, 20 Mar 1917, CAB 23/40/IWC–1.

21.   Minutes of Imperial War Cabinet, 30 Mar 1917, CAB 23/40/IWC–6 [PRO]; Chamberlain to Viceroy, 28 Mar 1917, CAB 24/9/GT317 [PRO]; Viceroy to Chamberlain, 11 Apr 1917, CAB 24/10/GT443 [PRO].

22.   Imperial War Cabinet, 20 Mar 1917, CAB 23/40/IWC–1 [PRO].

23.   Ibid.

24.   Ibid.

25.   Cook, 'Sir Robert Borden', pp 374–5; V. H. Rothwell, *British War Aims and Peace Diplomacy 1914–1918* (Oxford, 1971), p 127; Minutes of Imperial War Cabinet, 22 Mar 1917, CAB 23/40/IWC–2 [PRO]; L. S. Jaffe, *The Decision to Disarm Germany. British Policy Towards Postwar German Disarmament, 1914–1919* (London, 1985), p 55.

26.   Minutes of Imperial War Cabinet 22 & 23 Mar 1917, CAB 23/40/IWC–2 & IWC–3. ; Barnes and Nicholson (eds.), *The Leo Amery Diaries,* pp 146–7; Hankey diary, 23 Mar 1917, Hankey mss HNKY 1/1 [CCC]; Turner, *Lloyd George's Secretariat,* p 151; Ingham, *Jan Christian Smuts,* p 83; 'Notes on possible operations in 1917', Amery [nd but *c.* 16 Jan 1917], CAB 21/88 [PRO].

27.   'Notes on possible terms of peace', L. Amery, 11 Apr 1917, CAB 24/10/GT448 [PRO]; Amery, *My Political Life,* vol. 2, pp 104–5; Cook, 'Sir Robert Borden', pp 375–77; G. Smith, 'The British government and the disposition of the German colonies in Africa, 1914–1918', in Gifford, P. and Roger Louis, Wm (eds.), *Britain and Germany in Africa: Imperial Rivalry and Colonial Rule* (New Haven, Conn., 1967), p 288.

28.   Minutes of Imperial War Cabinet, 27 Mar & 12 Apr 1917, CAB 23/40/IWC–4 & /IWC 9 [PRO]; Barnes and Nicholson (eds.), *The Leo Amery Diaries,* pp 147–8.

29.   Rothwell, *British War Aims,* p 67.

30.   Wm. Roger Louis, *Great Britain and Germany's Lost Colonies 1914–1918* (Oxford, 1967), pp 78–79; I. Nish, *Alliance in Decline: A Study in Anglo-Japanese relations 1908–1923* (London, 1972), pp 202–209; L. F. Fitzhardinge, 'Australia, Japan and Great Britain, 1914–1918: a study in Triangular diplomacy', *Historical Studies,* 14 (1970), pp 257–8; Minutes of War Cabinet (29 Jan & 1, 5 & 27 Feb 1917), PRO CAB 23/1/WC47, /WC51, /WC54, & /WC63; FO to Governor Generals of Australia and New Zealand, 2 Feb 1917, PRO FO 800/383.

31.   Jaffe, *The Decision to Disarm Germany,* pp 48–9; Committee on territorial changes. Report and proceedings, 1916–1917, PRO CAB 16/36.

32.   Minutes of Imperial War Cabinet, 20 Mar. 1917, PRO CAB 23/40/IWC–1.

33.   Objections to retrocession of German East Africa to Germany', Long, 14 Feb 1917, PRO CAB 24/6/GT27.

34.   Barnes and Nicholson (eds.), *The Leo Amery Diaries,* p 149.

35.   Minutes of the Committee of the Imperial War Cabinet on territorial desiderata in the terms of peace, 17 Apr 1917, PRO CAB 21/77.

36.   Ibid.

37. Barnes and Nicholson (eds.), *The Leo Amery Diaries*, p 149; C. à Court Repington, *The First World War 1914–1918* (London, 1920), vol. 1, p 516.
38. Committee of Imperial Defence. Sub-committee on Territorial Changes. Second Interim report, 22 Mar 1917, CAB 24/3/G-118; Imperial War Cabinet, Report of committee on terms of peace. Territorial desiderata, 28 Apr 1917, CAB 21/77; Sykes to Balfour, 8 Apr 1917, FO 800/210/124; 'Cameroons. Note by Colonial Office', [nd but *c.* 28 Apr 1917], CAB 24/11/GT592; Roger Louis, *Great Britain and Germany's Lost Colonies,* pp 81–85; W. B. Fest, 'British war aims and German peace feelers during the First World War (December 1916–November 1918)', *Historical Journal,* 15, 2 (1978), pp 293–4; J. Nevakivi, *Britain, France and the Arab Middle East 1914–1920* (London, 1969), p 47; Smith, 'The British government and the disposition of the German colonies in Africa', pp 288–89.
39. J. M. Cooper Jr., *The Warrior and the Priest. Woodrow Wilson and Theodore Roosevelt* (Cambridge, Mass, 1983), pp 312–314.
40. Report of a committee on terms of peace. Economic and non-territorial desiderata, 24 Apr 1917, CAB 21/71; `Memorandum on proposals for diminishing the occasion of future wars', Cecil, *c.* Apr 1917, CAB 24/10/GT484; 'Notes by Sir Eyre Crowe on Lord R. Cecil's proposals for the maintenance of future peace', Eyre Crowe, 12 Oct 1916, CAB 24/10/GT484A; K. Middlemas, (ed.), *Thomas Jones. Whitehall Diary. Vol. I 1916–1925* (Oxford, 1969), pp 29–34; Jaffe, *The Decision to Disarm Germany,* p 66; G. W. Egerton, *Great Britain and the Creation of the League of Nations: Strategy, Politics and International Organization, 1914–1919* (London, 1979), pp 47–54.
41. Jaffe, *The Decision to Disarm Germany,* pp. 67–71; Minutes of Imperial War Cabinet, 26 Apr & 1 May 1917, CAB 23/40/IWC–12 &IWC–13.
42. Bertie to Hardinge, 22 Apr 1917, FO 800/176/Pal/17/3.
43. Rothwell, *British War Aims,* p 71; Minutes of Imperial War Cabinet, 1 May 1917, CAB 23/40/IWC–13.
44. Minutes of Imperial War Cabinet, 1 May 1917, CAB 23/40/IWC–13.
45. Hardinge to Bertie, 2 Feb 1917, FO 800/181/US/17/3; Lord Riddell, *Lord Riddell's War Diary 1914–1918* (London, 1933), p 238.
46. A. S. Link, *Wilson the Diplomatist. A Look at his Major Foreign Policies* (Baltimore, 1957), pp 82–5.
47. P. Beesly, *Room 40. British Naval Intelligence 1914–1918* (London, 1982), pp 204–23; B. W. Tuchman, *The Zimmermann Telegram* (London, 1959), passim.
48. D. R. Beaver, *Newton D. Baker and the American War Effort, 1917–1919* (Lincoln, NB, 1966), pp 25–6.
49. D. F. Trask, *The United States in the Supreme War Council: American War Aims and Inter-Allied Strategy, 1917–1918* (Middletown, CN, 1961), p 7; I. Flotto, 'Woodrow Wilson: War aims, peace strategy and the European left', in Link, A. S. ed., *Woodrow Wilson and a Revolutionary World, 1913–1921* (Chapel Hill, NC., 1982), pp 135–6.
50. J. B. Scott ed., *Official Statements of War Aims and Peace Proposals, December 1916 to November 1918* (Washington, 1921), p. 91; E. B. Parsons, 'Why the British reduced the flow of American troops to Europe in August–October 1918', *Canadian Journal of History,* 12, 2 (1977–78), pp 176, 182; Link, *Wilson the Diplomatist,* pp 87–89.
51. Cecil to War Cabinet and enc., 21 Aug 1917, CAB 1/25/12; D. R. Woodward, *Trial by Friendship. Anglo-American Relations 1917–1918* (Kentucky, 1993), pp 26–43.
52. Riddell, *Lord Riddell's War Diary,* pp 238, 249; Repington, *The First World War 1914–1918,* vol. I, p 449; Maclay to Balfour, 3 Apr 1917, FO 800/208/224; Percy to Balfour, 4 Apr 1917, FO 800/208/220; 'Note on the military forces of the US', General Staff, War Office, 5 Feb 1917, WO 106/1511 [PRO].
53. 'Production of Munitions by America. Manner in which USA can best render assistance in event of their entry into the war', Addison, 12 Feb 1917, CAB 24/6/GT12.
54. Spring-Rice to Hardinge, 23 Feb 1917, FO 800/242/313.
55. Minutes of Imperial War Cabinet, 3 & 5 Apr 1917, CAB 23/40/IWC–7 & IWC–8; Minutes of War Cabinet, 6 Apr 1917, CAB 23/2/WC115. The best published account of the mission is Woodward, *Trial by Friendship,* pp 44–68.
56. Balfour to Lloyd George, 23 June 1917, Lloyd George mss F/116 [House of Lords Record Office].
57. J. McDermott, 'Total war and the merchant state: aspects of British economic warfare against

Germany, 1914–1916', *Canadian Journal of History*, 21, 1 (1986), pp 61–76; A. J. Marder, *From the Dreadnought to Scapa Flow. The Royal Navy in the Fisher Era, 1904–1919. Volume 4. 1917: Year of Crisis* (Oxford, 1969), p 41; K. M. Burk, *Britain, America and the Sinews of War 1914–1918* (London, 1985), pp 108–110.

58. Burk, *Britain, America and the Sinews of War*, pp 114–115; 'The food question', Cecil, 16 Apr 1917, CAB 24/10/GT474; Minutes of War Cabinet, 18 Apr 1917, CAB 23/2/WC122.
59. 'Summary of blockade intelligence', War Trade Intelligence Department, 30 Mar–6 Apr 1917, CAB 24/9/GT387.
60. Burk, *Britain, America and the Sinews of War*, pp 111–112.
61. Burk, *Britain, America and the Sinews of War*, pp 119–121. An excellent study of the mobilization of the US army, and its employment in 1918 is D. F. Trask, *The AEF and Coalition War Making 1917–1918* (Kansas, 1993), passim.
62. Burk, *Britain, America and the Sinews of War*, pp 127–34; Keynes to Chambers, 30 May 1917, T 172/427 [PRO].
63. Sir T. Bridges, *Alarms and Excursions. Reminiscences of a Soldier* (London, 1938), pp 176–7.
64. Bridges to Robertson, 27 Apr 1917, Robertson mss I/21/63. [Liddell Hart Centre for Military Archives, King's College London].
65. Burk, *Britain, America and the Sinews of War*, pp 123–4; Beaver, *Newton D. Baker*, pp 39–48; Bridges to Robertson, 29 Apr 1917, CAB 24/13/GT717; Bridges to Robertson, 3 May 1917, CAB 24/13/GT785; Bridges to Robertson, 19 May 1917, CAB 24/13/GT786; J. J. Pershing, *My Experiences in the Great War* (Blue Ridge Summit, PA, 1931; repr. 1988), vol. I, pp 31–3.
66. 'The present situation in regard to military assistance by the USA', General Staff, War Office, 17 May 1917, CAB 24/13/GT744.
67. Minutes of Imperial War Cabinet, 26 Apr 1917, CAB 23/40/IWC–12; Foreign Office to Spring Rice, 26 Apr 1917, CAB 24/11/GT560; Minutes of War Cabinet, 2 May 1917, CAB 23/2/WC130.
68. J. A. S. Grenville, 'Diplomacy and war plans in the United States, 1890–1917', in Kennedy, P. M., ed, *The War Plans of the Great Powers, 1880–1914* (London, 1979), pp 35–6; A. S. Link and J. Whiteclay Chambers II, 'Woodrow Wilson as Commander in Chief', *Revue Internationale d'Histoire Militaire*, 69 (1990), p 322.
69. Nish, *Alliance in Decline*, pp 215–19; Minutes of War Cabinet, 22 May 1917, CAB 23/2/WC142; Minutes of War Cabinet, 19 June 1917, CAB 23/3/WC163; Balfour to Wiseman, 5 Jul 1917, FO 800/209/188; 'Notes on interview between President Wilson and Sir W. Wiseman', Wiseman, 13 Jul 1917, FO 800/209/203; 'Future naval construction in the United States', Balfour, 22 Jun 1917, CAB 23/3/WC174. Appendix: GT1138; Minutes of War Cabinet, 11 Jul 1917, CAB 23/3/WC181; 'The submarine campaign. Draft telegram under instructions of War Cabinet minute 195 (11) to Lord Northcliffe or Sir C. Spring Rice', War Cabinet, 2 Aug 1917, CAB 24/21/GT1539 & GT1539A; 'Admiralty memorandum resulting from recent discussions with US Naval officers as to the form of future naval assistance from the USA', Naval Staff, Admiralty, 27 Sept 1917, ADM 116/1806 [PRO].
70. Minutes of Imperial War Cabinet, 26 Apr 1917, CAB 23/40/IWC–12.
71. R. F. Mackay, *Balfour. Intellectual Statesman* (Oxford, 1985), pp 313–14; S. Gwynn (ed.), *The Letters and Friendships of Sir Cecil Spring Rice* (London, 1929), vol. 2, p 400.
72. Burk, *Britain, America and the Sinews of War*, pp 104–105.
73. Balfour to Wilson, 18 May 1917, FO 800/208/8; Spring Rice to FO, 3 May 1917, and minute by Oliphant and Hardinge, FO 371/3081/89749; Drummond to House, 28 Apr 1917, FO 800/208/16; Department of State, *Papers Relating to the Foreign Relations of the United States. The Lansing Papers 1914–1920* (Washington, 1940), pp 18–32.
74. Burk, *Britain, America and the Sinews of War*, pp 105–106.
75. D. French, *The Strategy of the Lloyd George Coalition, 1916–1918* (Oxford, 1995), pp 94–123.

For diplomatic, economic, strategic and telegraphic reasons: British imperial defence, the Middle East and India, 1914–18

KEITH NEILSON

It may seem odd to give much consideration to British imperial defence during the First World War and its immediate aftermath. While the Empire was an important contributor to Britain's war effort, and while there was fighting in both Africa and the Middle East closely linked to Empire, the obvious focus of Britain's war effort was the defeat of the Central Powers in Europe.[1] But this should not blind us to the fact that considerations of Empire helped shape British policy and war aims during the First World War.[2] The former was not made solely, nor (it may be argued) even primarily as a result of British thinking concerning the fate of Europe.[3] Instead, much of British policy was determined by imperial issues, and much of British planning during the First World War can be understood clearly only if viewed from the imperial angle. British war aims, British policy concerning intervention in Russia, and British policy in the Middle East become more coherent when considered in the context of imperial defence. Equally, such an approach also has other rewards. It demonstrates a central tenet of imperial defence. British thinking about imperial defence from 1914 to 1918 was not based solely on matters having to do with Britain's wartime position. Nor was it fashioned solely to counter the possible depredations of Britain's wartime enemies. Instead, it was created to safeguard long-term and long-standing British interests against *all* comers, both in war and peacetime.

The most difficult aspect of British imperial defence before 1914 was the defence of the north-west frontier of India. This was due to at least three factors. The first was that Britain had to defend India without the prospect of aid from any allies. This ensured that defence would be costly, and would weaken Britain's ability to defend her other interests (as had happened during the Boer War). The second factor was the open-ended nature of the commitment. Did the defence of India begin on the frontiers of India, or did it extend beyond these borders, into Afghanistan, Persia and the Middle East? The third factor was linked to the second. The defence of India necessarily involved the entire

British system of imperial defence, including the Royal Navy, since the Royal Navy would be called upon to ferry troops and supplies to India.[4] In all cases this meant that lines of communication to India (primarily through the Suez Canal, but also around the Cape) had to be secure. But, if the defence of India were thought to extend beyond India's borders, then the Royal Navy's task was expanded, and the security of the Persian Gulf needed to be considered. And, if the Persian Gulf needed to be secure, then the control of its hinterland was an issue of some importance. Clearly, India was ubiquitous in imperial defence planning.

Before 1914, the defence of India meant defending it against Russia.[5] This was thought to be militarily difficult, if not impossible. Equally, any stable, long-term political settlement of the matter was felt, given Russian ambitions, by many to be unlikely. 'There is no greater fallacy in contemporaneous politics', George Curzon, the Viceroy of India, wrote in 1902, 'than the idea that England can come to an agreement with Russia over Asia. It is not possible except at the price on our side of surrendering the outlying bulwarks of the Empire .... The reason does not lie merely in the ingrained duplicity of Russian diplomacy, but also in that fact that an agreement of whatever kind means the drawing of a line somewhere to Russian ambitions, and that she does not want to set any limit to them whatsoever.'[6] As the British and Russian Empires clashed in the Far East, on the north-west frontier of India and in the Persian Gulf such a belief was understandable. Nonetheless, in 1907, much of this enmity was temporarily ended by the signing of the Anglo-Russian Convention, although, on the eve of war, the convention was in need of rene-gotiating, as Anglo-Russian relations in Persia deteriorated.[7]

All of these issues arose in March 1915 as a result of the Russian insistence that the Entente formally acknowledge that Constantinople would be Russian in any post-war settlement.[8] The matter was discussed at the War Council on 10 March and again on 19 March, and the Government appointed a committee to determine British interests in the face of the Russian demand.[9] Even before this committee met, there was discussion as to the repercussions for imperial defence of the Russian acquisition of Constantinople. Lord Kitchener, the Secretary of State for War and a man with long experience in both India and Egypt, argued that if Russia were at the Straits, she would then be in a position to threaten Egypt and the British line of communication to India.[10]

But, Kitchener did not stop there. He argued that, if Britain contemplated taking Mesopotamia as her share of the deal, the port of Alexandretta also should become part of the British desiderata. His reasons for believing this spoke directly to the interlocking nature of British imperial defence. In a war with Russia, when the latter held Constantinople, both Egypt and Mesopotamia would need to be reinforced. This could be accomplished either from India or from Britain. However, should India not be able to send troops, forces from Britain could get to Mesopotamia from Britain much faster via Alexandretta and the railway connections to the Gulf region than could seaborne troops moving via the Suez Canal. Equally, British troops situated at Alexandretta and Aleppo would be perfectly placed to threaten the flank of a Russian force advancing on Mesopotamia from Armenia and Kurdistan.

And, Kitchener's reasons as to why Mesopotamia should be acquired in the first place also spoke to imperial defence. The first was simple: 'if we do not take Mesopotamia, the Russians undoubtedly will sooner or later'. This would be unacceptable, since the British position in the Persian Gulf would be made untenable. Thus, it was 'imperative' that, should the Ottoman Empire collapse, 'Mesopotamia should become British'. Other advantages would accrue: Mesopotamia was potentially a valuable agricultural area and could provide an area of settlement for Indian emigration; it contained large amounts of oil for the Royal Navy; and its possession would assure direct land communication between the Mediterranean and the Gulf. The disadvantages of acquiring it were the mirror image of its acquisition. A British line stretching from Alexandretta to the Gulf would provide a tempting flank to a Russian attack. But, Kitchener termed this 'a choice of evils', since the alternative was to abandon to Russia the 'great line of communications to India'.

Kitchener's appreciation was supported by the Admiralty. If Russia held Constantinople, then Britain must play 'Babylon against Byzantium' and hold Mesopotamia as a check against the relative decline of the British position in the region.[11] The Admiralty further contended that Mesopotamia 'must be brought to the shores of the Mediterranean' by means of the acquisition of Alexandretta. 'With Mesopotamia under our control', Their Lordships declared, 'and with access to it at Alexandretta, we have at our feet a complete solution of the new situation'. This new situation was made more difficult by the fact that the Admiralty no longer accepted the position that they had advanced in 1903—that Russian possession of Constantinople 'would not fundamentally alter the present strategic position in the Mediterranean'[12] —and now stated that this would 'make our communication through the Mediterranean with Egypt and India almost impossible.'[13] Thus, by the time that the Cabinet committee, headed by the former British Ambassador to Vienna, Maurice de Bunsen, met in April, the imperial defence parameters of the British position concerning the Middle East were already evident.[14]

The proceedings of the de Bunsen committee were dominated by considerations of defence. But, there were varying departmental points of view concerning this matter. While the India Office professed itself satisfied with an annexation in Mesopotamia only as far north of the Persian Gulf as a line drawn from Hit on the Euphrates to Tekrit on the Tigris, this was insufficient for the War Office.[15] Noting that what Britain always had to 'bear in the mind in the future was the possibility of a war with Russia', Major-General Sir Charles Callwell, the Director of Military Operations (DMO), insisted that the British territory had to include the strategic line of hills to the north of the *vilayet* of Mosul. Further, if the British were to take this region, then an outlet on the Mediterranean was 'essential', since reinforcements for Mesopotamia would almost certainly not be able to come from India, as the subcontinent likely would be another theatre of operations against Russia. As to which Mediterranean port was required, Callwell was not insistent on Alexandretta. He was aware that French claims for Turkish territory might include that port, and opined that Haifa, properly linked by rail to the Baghdad railway, would serve British interests.[16]

The Admiralty's arguments were based on different reasoning than were Callwell's, but supported the DMO's position. As the Admiralty insisted on the taking of Mesopotamia as far north as the *vilayets* of Basra and Baghdad in order to safeguard the oil supplies of the Royal Navy, this meant that Callwell's earlier strictures about the need to annexe Mosul came into effect. Indeed, at a subsequent meeting, the Admiralty modified its own view, and also called for the annexation of Mosul due to its significance as a potential oil-producing region.[17] Rear-Admiral Sir H.B. Jackson, the Admiralty's representative on the committee, did not feel that Haifa was a suitable naval base, but agreed that it would serve Callwell's purposes as a point for the disembarkation of troops destined for Mesopotamia.

The final recommendation of the de Bunsen committee was to avoid partitioning the Ottoman empire.[18] Instead, a scheme of decentralisation was favoured, for the latter would avoid Britain's having to assume any permanent responsibilities and largely satisfy her strategic concerns. Besides, some of these concerns had already been put to rest when the Russians had agreed that the neutral zone of Persia, created by the 1907 Anglo-Russian Convention, would be given to Britain as compensation for the Russian acquisition of Constantinople.[19] But the enduring strategic concerns of Britain were not lost sight of in the war. In the subsequent negotiations with the Arabs (the so-called 'McMahon–Hussein correspondence'), the French (the Sykes–Picot agreement) and the Russians (the Anglo–French–Russian discussions in the spring of 1916) over the division of the Ottoman Empire, the British retained the essence of what had been outlined in the de Bunsen committee.

In August 1916, a related imperial issue was raised. This concerned the extension of the British Indian railway system from Quetta to Seistan.[20] This extension, which had the potential to allow the Russian Trans-Persia line to link up with the British line, had long been opposed by the Indian military authorities due to the threat that it posed to the security of the subcontinent. However, the need to deal with the German and Turkish forces in Persia, which threatened the stability of Afghanistan and hence India, made it necessary to reconsider the issue. The Chief of the Imperial General Staff (CIGS), Sir William Robertson, opposed moving large numbers of troops to an area as remote as Baluchistan while the fate of Europe hung in the balance. He preferred instead to ensure India's security by moving reinforcements to south Persia, where they could act as a bulwark against the Turkish push towards India and yet still be readily available for deployment in Palestine or even Europe if necessary.[21] However, his general remarks about the proposed extension underlined long term concerns about imperial defence and how they transcended the present situation:

> we cannot say how long the present grouping of the European powers
> may continue, and it should not therefore affect our military railway
> policy in Persia. This policy should continue to be guided by the strate-
> gical principle which influenced the General Staff before the war in
> condemning proposals for railway lines from the Indian system to
> Seistan.

Curzon was at odds with Robertson's argument.[22] For the former viceroy, in
typical fulsome and overdetailed argument, whether the line should be built
was contingent on

> our future position and policy in Eastern Persia, on our relations with
> the Russian sphere of influence in Khorasan, on a possible ulterior
> junction of the proposed railway ... with other railways of the future,
> Russian or Persian, on the development of trade between India and
> Persia, on our future action in Seistan itself, and finally upon the
> defence of India itself.

In all cases, imperial considerations were to be dominant. This having been
said, Curzon was convinced that all these issues pointed towards the need to
construct the Quetta–Seistan line, since this alone could ensure India's security.
For him, the issue to be decided was one of timing.

Curzon's view was accepted, and in late August 1916 the building of the
Quetta–Nushki line was approved.[23] As a result of the collapse of the Russian
army in 1917, the situation in Persia became more perilous, as the British
found themselves deprived of their ally's assistance in holding back the
Germano-Turkish forces. As a result, the British railway line was extended fur-
ther westward, from Nushki, to Dalbandin and hence in the direction of
Mirjawa on the Persian frontier. In April 1918, the Indian government proposed that the line should be built even further, angling northwards from
Mirjawa along the Persian–Afghanistan border. This was suggested with the
aim of stabilizing eastern Persia and throwing a protective palisade between
Persia and Afghanistan. When this proposal was considered in London on 3
May, it was rejected, not only on the basis that construction would be opposed
by both the Persians and the Amir of Afghanistan, but also on the basis that the
line would be indefensible and that it would weaken, not strengthen the British
position in the area.[24]

However, in August 1918 this decision needed to be reconsidered in view of
the rapid expansion of German forces in the region as a result of the treaty of
Brest-Litovsk. For the General Staff, the danger, if not the future of the situation was evident:

> Today Germany is in undisputed command of the Black Sea; her
> troops have advanced to within 60 miles of the Volga, and it can only

be a question of time before German troops enter Baku. It is impossible to foresee to what extent Germany's present position in Russia and the Middle East will be reversed at the end of the war, but in considering the future security of India, it is necessary not only to calculate as hitherto for railway enterprise being directed against India with hostile intentions, but to allow for such enterprise being backed by German energy, German skill and German resources. This may be an overstatement of the dangers of the case, but until the future of the Middle East is clearer than at present, it will be as well to frame our strategical conceptions on these premises. This being so the arguments adduced in the past against our countenancing any railway projects tending to bridge the gap between the Indian and Russian systems hold good today but with added force.[25]

Regardless of potential opponent, imperial considerations remained paramount. However, it was reluctantly agreed that the first 90 miles of the line angling northwards from Mirjawa towards Meshed should be begun.[26]

The collapse of the German threat to the region at the end of the war ended the General Staff's toleration of the project. In December 1918, the entire issue of Persian railways was reconsidered.[27] The conclusion was that construction of the northern extension should immediately end. Further, *all* efforts that would connect the Russian Trans-Persian line to the Indian system should be rejected on the traditional grounds of Indian defence. However, should it be decided, for reasons of high policy, to link the two lines, the General Staff was insistent that the only acceptable way to effect this juncture was first to bring the Russian line down to the Gulf, where it was 'more easily controlled from the sea.' This illustrates clearly how imperial defence was thought of in systemic terms: naval and military means should be combined to carry out the goal of defending the Empire.

Leaving railways aside, it is necessary to return to 1917, where, by the spring, the imperial position seemed strong. The British had gained Allied agreement to British control of two key regions: the Persian Gulf and its hinterland to just north of Baghdad and Palestine (including the port of Haifa). French sensibilities had been propitiated by agreeing to their holding Syria (including Alexandretta) and a diminishing wedge of territory stretching eastward to Kurdistan. The oilfields at Mosul were outside the area of direct control of either Britain or France, but inside a zone of French influence. This was an economic loss; however, it meant that French territory now stood as a buffer between British and Russian interests in the Middle East. The report of a special sub-committee of the imperial War Cabinet, chaired by Curzon, which met in April 1917 to consider British territorial desiderata at the end of war, accepted this situation, utilizing strategic arguments that had not altered since 1915.[28]

The Russian revolution in March 1917 created what David French has termed a 'new strategic geography' for Britain.[29] This had its implications for imperial defence. As Robertson noted in May, the Russian collapse threatened to allow the Germans to concentrate all their forces in the West.[30] This would mean that Britain, at whatever cost to the Empire, would have to go on the defensive in areas such as Palestine and Mesopotamia. Such a view was supported by the Admiralty. Sir John Jellicoe, the First Sea Lord, argued that Russia's defection would make the Black Sea a Turkish lake and worsen the British naval position in the eastern Mediterranean.[31] As a result, the British would have to improve the railway systems in Asia Minor in order to supply Allied forces in Mesopotamia. Others did not agree. Curzon contended instead that Britain would now have to be willing to accept less than absolute victory, focus less on Europe and concentrate her efforts more on ensuring that imperial interests were settled in Britain's favour.[32] Further, the Russian proposals concerning peace 'without annexations' had to be treated carefully. While the British could show substantial sympathy towards this idea, if 'no annexations' suggested national self-determination, such a concept could not be accepted outside Europe.[33]

Despite such arguments, Robertson continued to assert that Russia's collapse meant that, out of sheer military necessity, the British position in the Middle East and Persia would have to take a distinct second place to preventing a German victory in Europe.[34] To placate his imperial critics, Robertson was willing to shut down the British commitment at Salonika—in any case, long one of his *bêtes noires*—in order to find troops for a British attack in Palestine.[35] Such an assault, the CIGS believed, would prevent any action being taken against the British position in Mesopotamia. Meanwhile, discussions of war aims centred around the possibility of denying Russia Constantinople and the Straits in the hope of using this as lure to induce Turkey to agree to a separate peace. But this idea foundered on the fact of British and French claims to *their* portions of the carcass of the Ottoman Empire.[36] By September 1917, as the Passchendaele offensive ground on with mounting casualties, opinion in the War Cabinet turned more towards a concentration of forces against the Turks in order both to reduce losses in Flanders and to shore up the British imperial position in Mesopotamia, despite the logistical difficulties inherent in the latter.[37] The collapse of the Russian army had led to anarchy in all parts of the Russian Empire, and this was bound to affect both Britain's imperial position and the position of the Entente generally.[38]

The Bolshevik revolution of November 1917 served to make worse the problems that had emerged after the March revolution. After the Bolsheviks had concluded the armistice of Brest-Litovsk in mid-December, the British no longer felt bound to observe the provisions of tentative post-war settlements that had been worked out in 1915 and 1916. On the other hand, Bolshevik Russia loomed as a possible threat to Britain's domestic stability, the loss of Russia as an ally made defeat or stalemate in the First World War more likely and the collapse of Tsarist power created disorder and unrest along the periphery between the Russian and British Empires in Central Asia. New possibilities were everywhere.

There were complications from other directions. The first was that the British and French had signed an agreement on 23 December 1917 dividing Russia into zones of influence for the purpose of co-ordinating their efforts to help elements loyal to the Allies maintain the eastern front and to deny the Germans access to the raw materials of Russia.[39] The British were allotted the Cossack lands to the east of the Black Sea, along with the region of the Caucasus, while the French looked after the Ukraine, Bessarabia and the Crimea. Given the British military involvement in Persia and the Middle East, this was logical, but meant that actions in the Black Sea would necessarily have to be co-ordinated with the French. The second complication was the matter of war aims. The German–Bolshevik negotiations at Brest-Litovsk in December, which referred favourably to the concepts of national self-determination, pushed the British Prime Minister, David Lloyd George, into making a statement on 5 January 1918 of the British position.[40] The Prime Minister's lip service to the idea of self-determination meant that future British war aims would have to be couched in terms commensurate with this concept.

The signing of the treaty of Brest-Litovsk in early March 1918 created complex problems for Britain. Russia's leaving the war made it likely that Rumania also would make peace.[41] A derivative of this was the likelihood that Germany would thus gain rail access to the Black Sea, thereby establish herself at Batoum, Baku and hence advance to Persia.[42] Since the situation in the Caucasus was 'absolutely chaotic' and that in Persia was 'as unintelligible as usual', this had implications for British imperial defence.[43] This meant that the British kept a close eye on the Russian Black Sea fleet since if it fell into German hands, the Central Powers would have a seaborne line of supply into the Caucasus.[44] It was also evident, in the face of this situation, that the cumbersome system of ad hoc committees that had sprung up during the war to co-ordinate British dealings with Russia was inadequate to deal expeditiously with the complexities of the problem.[45] As a result, on 11 March the War Cabinet authorized Lord Curzon to draw up terms for a new committee to take charge of the matter.[46] While Curzon did this, events demonstrated the need for action. On 21 March, the War Cabinet discussed the thorny issue of Japanese intervention in Siberia.[47] There was little hope expressed that the Japanese could re-open the eastern front; however, should Japan gain control of the trans-Siberian railway as far west as Cheliabinsk, it could prevent the Germans from gaining entry into Turkestan and thus into Persia.[48] This linkage between Japanese intervention and imperial defence had been remarked upon earlier. On 26 February 1918, Lord Milner, the influential minister without portfolio in the War Cabinet, had argued that Japan's intervention in Russia had to be obtained, not least because of its effect on Persia: 'we must stop the wave of German influence sweeping right into the heart of Asia. Only Japan can do this in the North & only we in the South.'[49] Since, in the words of Sir Henry Wilson (CIGS), if Persia were to be occupied by the Germans, 'our whole position in India would be imperilled', the War Cabinet was quick to authorize the new body—to be called the Eastern Committee—that Curzon proposed.[50]

While all eyes were fixed on the German offensive that was launched on the Western front in late March, the Eastern Committee began its work. On 24 April, the question of the future of Mesopotamia was discussed.[51] Curzon pointed out that the concept of 'self determination' and Lloyd George's statement—contained in his speech of 5 January—that the fate of Mesopotamia would be decided at a post-war peace conference meant that the committee's deliberations were somewhat constrained. However, Curzon posited that in the case of Allied victory, Britain should 'construct a State with an "Arab Facade," ruled and administered under British guidance'. The region of Basra, given 'the political and commercial interests involved', should be kept 'entirely in British hands'. Immediately, the sort of strategic thinking that had motivated the de Bunsen committee earlier began to re-appear. The Director of Military Intelligence (DMI), Major-General Sir G.M.W. Macdonogh, suggested that the area around Basra be extended northward and towards Persia to create a 'defensible strategic frontier'.

It was the latter country that consumed the interest of the Eastern Committee in May. Since the 1915 agreement with the Russians, the British and the Tsarist forces had been working together to prevent Persia's being taken over by a Turkish force stiffened with German advisers. In tandem with the Russians, the British concentrated on defending a line Kerman–Hamadan–Kasvin, but the withdrawal to the Caspian Sea of the Russian forces prompted General Dunsterville, the British officer commanding in the region, to propose that he, too, should move northward.[52] The discussion of this on 31 May made clear the complicated nature of imperial defence in the region. If Dunsterville were to abandon his defensive line, then all of Persia would be open to a Turkish advance through Kurdistan; however, if he should not go either to Enzeli or Baku, then the Caspian fleet might fall into the hands of the Germans and be used to transport troops to Krasnovodsk, an equally unpleasant circumstance, as this would open the way into Central Asia. In this situation, the committee decided to take what Curzon termed a 'gigantic gamble', and authorized Dunsterville to take a mission to Baku, leaving the Kermanshah–Hamadan–Kasvin line to be held by the remainder of his force. A week later, however, the committee reversed itself, and decided that Dunsterville should not go to Baku until he had sufficient resources to secure the road from Kasvin to Enzeli.[53] With only limited information available to them, and with rumours flying that Turkish and German troops were on their way to Baku, on 11 June the committee authorized Dunsterville to move 4.7 inch guns to Enzeli and to lay mines in the harbour there in case the Caspian fleet fell into enemy hands.[54] Further, Dunsterville was to destroy the oil supplies at Baku and Grozny if possible.

Towards the end of June, the ambit of imperial defence in the region was made wider. The rapid advance of German troops to Tiflis and the presence of large numbers of German prisoners of war in Turkestan triggered fears for the stability of Afghanistan.[55] Sir Henry Wilson pointed out that the British policy throughout the war had been to put a 'ring fence' around Afghanistan in order to insulate it from the conflict. This was no longer possible, and Wilson suggested that the British should attempt to bring the Amir of Afghanistan into the war by offering him arms and ammunition, plus a slice of Russian territory. Unless this were done, the CIGS believed that the Germans would offer the Afghans a larger portion of Russian territory and the consequent pro-German orientation of Afghanistan would have serious consequences for the defence of India.

Wilson's suggestion was a point of contention: Arthur Balfour, the Secretary of State for Foreign Affairs, felt it presumptuous to promise Russian territory, but others argued to the contrary. Edwin Montagu, the Secretary of State for India, argued that it was more efficacious to make an alliance with Persia, since it would require too many British troops to keep the Turks out of Persia now that Russian assistance had been lost. Balfour raised a similar alternative to Wilson's line of thinking. He stated that he would prefer not to abrogate the Anglo–Russian Convention in order to gain Persian support, since the latter would, in any case, likely result in Britain's being committed to assist in a Persian attempt to regain the lost territories of Azerbaijan in exchange for military assistance of dubious value. While the committee reached no decision in either case, the debate underscored the link between Britain's policy towards Russia and the realities of imperial defence.

During late August and early September 1918, the sprawling nature of the British war effort in the Middle East was underlined by a proposal by Montagu that the military operations in this area, with the possible exception of Palestine, be placed under the Indian army.[56] Montagu's suggestion was part of a larger scheme for re-organising the control of British policy in the region generally, but his arguments were based on the fact that the Indian army was better suited by specialized knowledge and experience to exercise this authority.[57] The War Office, not surprisingly, objected.[58] Wilson pointed out that the campaigns in Mesopotamia and Palestine were too closely connected to divide, that the British forces in north-west Persia were linked to and based on the Mesopotamian command and that the military situation in Turkestan derived from the general military situation in Russia and Siberia. 'These considerations', the CIGS concluded, 'make it impossible to enlarge the sphere which has been allotted to the Indian Government for military control'.

But the importance of the war effort in the Middle East caused the matter to be raised again in September. Arguing the need for a unity of command, the commander-in-chief of the Indian army, General Sir Charles Monro, proposed that all British forces in Mesopotamia, trans-Caspia and Persia be placed under his control.[59] This position was supported by Montagu, but General Macdonogh reiterated the War Office's opposition to 'dual control', arguing that this was not practical because 'all theatres were so inter-dependent'. The matter did not die there, largely because of the support that it was given in the War

Cabinet by Lieutenant-General Jan Smuts, the prominent South African politician and military man.[60] Smuts argued that, while the Germans were in retreat elsewhere, in the Middle East and Central Asia they were advancing. Continued German success might result in a situation where the British war effort in 1919 'would [be] cripple[d] ... from Palestine and Salonica to Central Asia.' To prevent this, Smuts suggested that General Monro be moved from India and be given control of all the British forces 'from Baghdad to Meshed'.

Debate on this matter, in the Eastern Committee on 18 September, turned into a rambling discussion of the British position in the area and the competence of those in command in the field.[61] Smuts repeated his arguments concerning the need for Monro to assume command, and added his belief that the present British commander in Mesopotamia, General William Marshall, lacked strategic vision.[62] Sir Henry Wilson argued hard against Smuts' suggestions, denying Marshall's faults and asserting that unity of command was best achieved by placing the British troops in Persia under the command of Marshall or his successor. In essence, this was a battle over authority, with Wilson wishing to keep command of the entire theatre in the hands of London and out of the hands of Simla. The flow of the meeting went against Wilson: Arthur Balfour shared the general view that Marshall did not realize the significance of the Caspian and Turkestan regions, and Lord Robert Cecil, the Assistant Secretary of State for Foreign Affairs and in charge of a section newly created at the Foreign Office to deal with Middle Eastern issues, opined in a letter that there was urgent need for a more unified command structure. While the issue was left unresolved, its very nature illustrated the intricacies, both military and bureaucratic, of imperial defence in the region.

By early October 1918, with the prospect of victory in sight, the Eastern Committee began to examine carefully the spoils of war. A first item was a reconsideration of the terms of the Sykes–Picot agreement of 1916.[63] Curzon contended that the latter was now 'out of date and unscientific and that it was desirable to get rid of it'. Sykes, who himself was one of the representatives of the Foreign Office at the meeting, pointed out that the Mesopotamian aspects of the agreement might be revised, and noted that the French had been given Mosul in 1916 at the behest of the Secretary of State for War, Lord Kitchener,

> to establish something in the nature of a buffer-state between the area in Mesopotamia in which we were mainly interested and the Russian area in Kurdo-Armenia. Unofficially, he had always impressed upon M. Picot the impossibility of the French sphere going to Mosul.

This, of course, was a return to the position advocated in the de Bunsen report, and reflected the imperial needs of Britain. Curzon, indeed, took the need for revision a step further. The chairman of the committee pointed out that he objected to the 'surrender of a monopoly position in Alexandretta, Mersina and Adana to the French, and he thought that the whole question of the future of Armenia should be raised'. Clearly, now that French sensibilities and Russian interests did not need to be considered so delicately, British interests were to be paramount. In the War Cabinet, Curzon took the issue further.[64] On 14 October, he informed his cabinet colleagues of the Eastern Committee's deliberations, and made it clear that in the new circumstances the post-war settlement in the Middle East would have to be considered afresh.

The impending armistice pushed British policy. On 18 October, the War Cabinet discussed post-war British policy towards Russia.[65] The Cabinet reached no decision, prompting the calling of an inter-departmental conference, held at the Foreign Office on 13 November. At this meeting, it was agreed that Britain could not 'embark on an anti-Bolshevik crusade in Russia'.[66] However, Milner noted that this did not mean an indiscriminate withdrawal of British forces, for 'considerations both of honour and of interest demanded that we should keep Bolshevism from the regions East of the Black Sea, i.e. the Caucasus, the Don country, and Turkestan.' Such a sentiment was echoed at the Foreign Office, but the concern there was with the post-war situation. As a memorandum drawn up by the influential Eyre Crowe noted, it would be 'dangerous' for Britain to give 'advice and support' to the fledgling Caucasian states, except sufficient to avoid anarchy, as to do so would undoubtedly antagonize a recrudescent Russia.[67] Instead, Crowe recommended that France be given a mandate to deal with Armenia and the Caucasus. The ambiguity inherent in all of these pronouncements was reiterated at the War Cabinet on 14 November.[68] The opposition to an 'anti-Bolshevik crusade' was accepted, but so, too, was a principle, espoused by Milner, that any 'friendly anti-Bolshevik Government which it was to our advantage to support' should be aided. This had particular relevance to the Caucasus, where British troops occupied the Baku–Batoum railway in support of the fledgling governments in the region.

After the end of the war, the Eastern Committee turned its attention to determining British desiderata in a more systematic fashion.[69] At the first meeting held to consider them, on 27 November 1918, Curzon made clear the seriousness of the deliberations and the relevance to the Empire.[70]

> Upon the fate of these territories, and the way in which our case is presented at the Peace Conference, and the form of administration to be set up, will depend not only the future of the territories themselves, but also the future of the British Empire in the East.

The problem that soon emerged was the Sykes–Picot agreement, which Curzon characterized as having 'been hanging like a millstone round our necks' since it was signed. For Curzon, the fact that the agreement had been 'concluded under conditions wholly different from those existing now' was enough to vitiate it, but Cecil, for the Foreign Office, believed the French to be in 'an unassailable position' and argued that the agreement could be got rid of only 'by buying off the French with some other concession' or by getting the Americans to pressure the French to accept a British solution. With these points in mind, the Committee decided that Basra and Baghdad should have, in Cecil's words, 'a British-controlled Government, and I do not think there is any question at all that it ought to be in the form of an Arab Government'. The only question left open was to what extent that the Arabs themselves should be consulted as to whether they wanted a single government for the two (possibly three if Mosul could be wrested away from the French) areas and what Arab figure-head should be put in charge of the government. The strategic thinking behind this decision was left unspoken, having changed not at all since 1915.

This was not the case with respect to the Caucasus and Armenia.[71] Here, with the collapse of Russia, the British felt themselves not bound by the provisions of previous agreements. At the Eastern Committee on 2 December, Curzon put the British position clearly: 'we want to have an independent Armenia'. Beyond altruism lurked strategic interests. An independent Armenia would serve as a 'palisade ... against the Pan-Turanian ambitions of the Turks, which may overflow the Caucasian regions and carry great peril to the countries of the Middle East and East'. Equally, it would provide 'something like an effective barrier' against the future expansion of any other power that might wish to expand in that direction. The size of the new Armenia was a matter of some contention. The Foreign Office proposed a 'large' Armenia, stretching from Mersina and Alexandretta on the Mediterranean to a point west of Trebizond on the Black Sea, with its eastern boundary abutting Persia. While this meant putting some Turks under Armenian rule, the alternative of a 'small' Armenia meant the reverse and failed to provide 'a barrier from the Black Sea to the Mediterranean', the object of the exercise.

But this needed to be considered in light of the fate of the Caucasus. This was a complex issue, given the historic enmities of the peoples involved, but its strategic significance for Britain was plain. As Curzon put it, a 'hostile force in possession of the region of the Caucasus would turn the flank of the British position in Asia, as it very nearly did in Persia and Trans-Caspia in the course of the past six months'. For him, the key was the port of Batoum, with its rail access—the 'spinal cord of the country'—to the oil reserves of Baku and hence into Persia. Curzon suggested that Batoum revert to its status of a free port—its position prior to Russia's annexation of it—and that the railway line to Baku be placed under the control of some tutelary power. Baku itself should be internationalized.

The question that remained was how, and who should do this. Smuts suggested that the answer was to put both Armenia and the Caucasus under the League of Nations and to let some Power act as a mandatory. For him, there were only two candidates, France and the United States, and he favoured the latter as being the more disinterested. Curzon readily agreed that the Americans would be preferable to the French:

> I must say that I am very much alarmed at the idea of the French being there. If you have France there, with a control which will extend from

the eastern corner of the Mediterranean right across to the Caspian, our
position will be very assailable in the East. Trouble in Persia means trouble
in Afghanistan, and then you are brought right up to the borders of India.

Indeed, Curzon went further, and argued that 'the great Power from whom we
may have most to fear in the future is France, and I almost shudder at the possibility of putting France in such a position'. However, for the time being,
given the chaos in the region, the Committee was in favour of continued
British occupation of Batoum and Baku.

This was neither a satisfactory nor a complete decision. A week later, on 9
December, the Eastern Committee reconsidered the matter.[72] This time the
imperial tocsin was sounded by Sir Henry Wilson. Wilson argued that having
the French in control of such a large area would irretrievably weaken the
British position, and suggested that if France were to be made the tutelary
power then Armenia should be split in two, with France controlling only the
westerly, Turkish portion. The reason for this was clear. If France held all of
Armenia, she would have a 'protectorate stretching from Alexandretta to
Baku'.[73] Trumpeting the traditional line of imperial defence, the War Office
argued that such an occurrence

> would be most undesirable for the approaches to India from South
> Russia, the Black Sea, and Turkey in Asia which converge at Baku,...
> [would] be placed at the disposal of an ambitious military Power,
> which, although friendly to us at the moment, is our historical world
> rival. In fact, it does not appear to the General Staff that any other
> Great Power except herself can be permitted by Great Britain to func-
> tion in this matter.

The War Office concluded that the ideal solution would be to create 'a
self-contained bloc in the Middle East between Russia and a French sphere of
influence on the one hand and between any potential Western combination and
the Caspian on the other hand.' To do so, the General Staff called for the creation of three independent states: Georgia, Azerbaijan and Russian Armenia.
Britain could aid in their creation by keeping Constantinople and the Straits
open, thereby permitting the use of Batoum as a British base against any future
Russian advance down the western shore of the Caspian.

Lord Robert Cecil demurred. He believed that this was too complicated, and
suggested instead that the key was sea power:

> If we have control of the Black Sea that is all right, and nobody can go
> to Batum without our leave. If we have not, then we evidently cannot
> defend Georgia at all. If we have control of the Caspian, which I think
> we ought to retain, and also cut off that route a little further on, it
> seems to me our proper course is to abide by our traditional policy, to
> go in for supremacy on the sea in the Black Sea and the Caspian, and
> let anybody who likes have the intervening bit of land, which does not
> matter to us at all.

Wilson and Rear-Admiral G. P. W. Hope, the Deputy First Sea Lord, did not agree. They argued that it would be impossible to exert such control without having ports, and that ports required military occupation. This was too much for Balfour, whose experience in these matters went back to the heated debates about the defence of India in 1903–05:

> when we come to the point of the defence of India, I hope the General Staff will be a little careful about the demands they make upon us about India. Every time I come to a discussion—at intervals of, say, five years—I find there is a new sphere which we have got to guard, which is supposed to protect the gateways of India. Those gateways are getting further and further from India, and I do not know how far west they are going to be brought by the General Staff.

These remarks were a red flag to Curzon, himself a veteran of Indian defence and the arguments about it that had surrounded the negotiation of the Anglo-Russian Convention. The chairman contended that the war had shown the need to defend India at the Caspian, and that, *faute de mieux*, the British were best placed to ensure the security of the entire region. Balfour riposted that the best solution would be for all the Powers to withdraw from the region and let the local inhabitants 'cut each other's throats'.

This sanguinary suggestion perhaps had merit, but Montagu wished to tackle the military assumptions of Wilson and Curzon. For the Secretary of State for India, the idea either that France could utilize a position in the Middle East for an assault on India or that a militarized Armenia could do likewise was implausible in the extreme. Montagu asked plainly, 'what is the strategical danger to India in supposing the worst came to the worst', that is, should the Caucasian states not govern themselves, France should take them on and turn hostile? Wilson answered that in peacetime Britain would not likely keep a force 'worth talking about' in either India or Mesopotamia, but contended that the situation Montagu had outlined would 'ruin Mesopotamia to a great extent' and that, due to the oilfields, this would be unacceptable to the Admiralty. 'Do not think for a moment', he concluded, 'that you would reduce your dangers, and therefore the number of troops you must keep by bringing the danger nearer to India.'

The defence of India had other aspects. This was evident from discussions in late 1918 about the future of Constantinople. The General Staff pointed out that Constantinople was important both as '(a) a land bridge and, (b) a sea passage'.[74] The former was of lesser importance for purely British interests, but in its latter aspect, Constantinople 'gives access to the main door of Russia and to an important line of advance on India'. Concerns about the latter had played on British policy throughout the nineteenth century and, more recently, had given the Turks a bargaining lever during the negotiations for an armistice in 1918.[75] However, once the immediate challenge to the British position in the Middle East and Persia had subsided, there was a determination to ensure that

Constantinople would in future be held by a power that would not threaten British interests. The key point was as follows: 'the importance of Constantinople to an Empire such as ourselves, with great interests in the East, is clear, and it is there that any future naval expansion based on a reconstituted Russia must be throttled'. British concerns did not, however, end with Russia. No strong, or potentially strong, sea power—the United States, France or Italy —could be considered as mistress of Constantinople. It was 'essential that Constantinople and the Straits be held by a weak naval power.' This concern was similar to those held about mandatory powers for a future Armenia— British imperial security came first. While the Admiralty merely wanted the Straits internationalized, fortifications there razed and an international commission to administer the waterway, the General Staff also wanted no bridges over or tunnels under that convenient moat.[76] In fact, the General Staff's ultimate aim was that Britain should administer the whole of Turkey, for in this way not only would the Straits be controlled in a fashion favourable to British interests, but also Britain would control a 'ready-made Turkish garrison to bar the road to the East'. This would mean that two of the routes to India—via Asia Minor and through the Caucasus—would be secure, leaving only the Orenberg–Tashkent railway as a threat to the defence of India 'for such time as we now see into the future'. And, in case that Constantinople alone was not sufficient to guarantee the British imperial position, Cyprus should be retained in order to guard the far-flung lines of imperial communications.[77]

What can we conclude from the above? The defence of what Leo Amery, the acting British Colonial Secretary, termed that 'Southern British World which runs from Cape Town, through Cairo, Baghdad and Calcutta to Sydney and Wellington' clearly was a difficult task.[78] And, this 'Southern British World', particularly in the Middle East and Central Asia, had quite elastic frontiers. Nor was there unanimous agreement as to where these frontiers should be placed. For example, the gap between Curzon's position (largely supported by the military and naval authorities) and that held by Montagu (largely supported by people like Balfour and Cecil) was never bridged. The need to protect imperial lines of communication, the Admiralty's particular interest in oil and the requirement for strategic frontiers all continually pushed the British defensive umbrella further away from India. Montagu deplored this attitude. He wrote disparagingly and sarcastically that there were many kinds of Britons who favoured increasing the size of Empire,

> And then there is the rounded Lord Curzon, who for historical reasons of which he alone is master, geographical considerations which he has peculiarly studied, finds, reluctantly, much against his will, with very grave doubts, that it would be dangerous if any country in the world was left to itself, if any country in the world was left to the control of any other country but ourselves, and we must go there, as I have heard him say, 'for diplomatic, economic, strategic and telegraphic reasons.'[79]

While much of this attack was personal and resulted from Curzon's pompous and pedantic manner (the antipathy between the two men was to culminate in Montagu's being forced out of office in 1922[80]), was it accurate? This is a moot point. Recent research argues that Russia never intended to invade India, but simply wished to use the *threat* of invasion as a diplomatic lever against Britain.[81] However, British military planning was always based on such a possibility, and thus the Russian threat, real or imagined, was an important factor in imperial defence. However, imperial defence was against all comers, not just Russia, and the deliberations of the Eastern Committee show that, from a strategical point of view, a well-situated France was deemed just as big a threat as her erstwhile alliance partner had been. Further, Britain's 'associated Power', the United States, also was felt to be a potential threat to Britain's interests, particularly given the American threat to build a fleet 'second to none' and their awkward attitude concerning freedom of the seas and belligerent rights. Even the Italians, a far less formidable potential foe, needed to be kept well away from British imperial communications. And, of course, if wartime allies needed to be kept away from the approaches of India, this was doubly true of wartime enemies. The British were determined that Germany would not be able to forge a victory in the Middle East or Persia that would either deny Britain her share of the spoils of war or, worse, leave Britain facing a new powerful enemy at the gates of India.

The ubiquity of naval considerations also looms large. Defending the 'Southern World' depended on sea power. The defence of the north-west frontier of India was not merely the result of the strength of arms of the Indian army reinforced by British troops. Instead, the Royal Navy was central to all planning. Which line of railway communications in Mesopotamia was favoured was determined by naval considerations: the need to ensure a secure supply of oil and the necessity to shuttle troops between the two secure depots in England and India. And, in related fashion, war aims concerning the Middle East were dependent on British desires to ensure that the Royal Navy held bases such that the Russian fleet (or a French fleet) in the eastern Mediterranean could be dealt with before it threatened the Suez Canal. Also, great effort was made to ensure that all possible future Russian rail links to India passed near the British naval positions in the Persian Gulf, where the Royal Navy could be brought to bear on them in a fashion impossible if the Russian lines were situated in the interior. Finally, after the collapse of Russia, the future of Constantinople and the Straits was to be settled so that the Royal Navy could operate in the Black Sea and deny the Caucasian route to India to either a recrudescent Russia or any other Great Power that had established itself in the region.

The most evident point, however, is the inadequacy of dealing with British policy during the First World War from a purely 'continental' perspective. British policy was formulated with considerations of Empire just as firmly in mind as were considerations of the Continent. This was only natural. As a

Great Power whose geographic position gave her a certain immunity from direct attack and whose strength was based on the linked factors of Empire, the Royal Navy and economic power, Britain naturally had a wider variety of concerns than did the other belligerents when it came time to determine her course of actions. Only a comprehension of the dual nature of the British position permits a full understanding of Britain's actions in the First World War.

NOTES

1. By far the best studies of Britain's effort in the First World War are the two volumes by David French: *British Strategy and War Aims 1914–1916* (London, 1986) and *The Strategy of the Lloyd George Coalition* (Oxford, 1995).
2. Some evidence can be found in V. H. Rothwell, *British War Aims and Peace Diplomacy 1914–1918* (Oxford: Clarendon, 1971), John Gooch, 'Soldiers, Strategy and War Aims in Britain 1914–1918', in Hunt, B. and Preston, A., eds., *War Aims and Strategic Policy in the Great War* (London: Croom Helm, 1977), 21–40 and Lorna S. Jaffe, *The Decision to Disarm Germany* (London: Allen & Unwin, 1985), but none of these authors considers their evidence in the Imperial context.
3. A start has been made to remedy this defect; see Benjamin Schwarz, 'Divided Attention: Britain's Perception of a German Threat to Her Eastern Position in 1918', *Journal of Contemporary History*, 28 (1993), pp 103–22. Also important is J. Darwin, *Britain, Egypt and the Middle East. Imperial policy in the aftermath of war 1918–1922* (London: Macmillan, 1981), pp 143– 61.
4. 'The Oversea Transport of Reinforcements in Time of War', Report of the Standing Sub-Committee of the Committee of Imperial Defence, 16 Jun 1910, Cab[inet Office] 4/3/116–B, [Public Record Office, Kew, England—hereafter, PRO].
5. I have discussed this elsewhere; see Keith Neilson, *Britain and the Last Tsar. British Policy and Russia 1894–1917* (Oxford, 1995), pp 110–46. Also important is John Gooch, *The Plans of War. The General Staff and British Military Strategy c.1900–1916* (London: Routledge & Kegan Paul, 1974), especially pp 198–237.
6. Curzon to Lansdowne (British foreign secretary), 16 Mar 1902, Curzon Papers, MSS Eur F111/161 [India Office Library and Records, London—hereafter, IOLR].
7. D. W. Sweet and R. T. B. Langhorne, 'Great Britain and Russia, 1907–1914', in Hinsley, F. H., ed., *British Foreign Policy under Sir Edward Grey* (Cambridge: Cambridge University Press, 1977), pp 251–5.
8. Neilson, *Britain and the Last Tsar*, pp 344, 357–60; G. Paget, 'The November 1914 Straits Agreement and the Dardanelles–Gallipoli Campaign', *Australian Journal of History and Politics*, 33 (1987), pp 253–60; A. L. Macfie, 'The Straits Question in the First World War, 1914–18', *Middle Eastern Studies*, 19 (1983), pp 43–74.
9. Rothwell, *British War Aims*, pp 26–8; meetings of the War Council, 10 and 19 Mar 1915, Cab 42/2/5 and 14 [PRO].
10. 'Alexandria and Mesopotamia', Kitchener, 16 Mar 1915, Cab 24/1/G–12 [PRO].
11. 'Alexandretta and Mesopotamia', Admiralty, 17 Mar 1915, Cab 24/1/G–13.
12. 'Report by Mr. Balfour of the Conclusion Arrived at on February 11 1903, in Reference to Russia and Constantinople', Balfour, 14 Feb 1903, Cab 2/1 [PRO].
13. 'Russia and Constantinople', Admiral A. K. Wilson (1st Sea Lord), 15 March 1915, Cab 24/1/G–17. The Admiralty also objected strongly to Alexandretta's being held by any other naval power; see 'Alexandretta. Its Importance as a Future Naval Base', Admiral H. B. Jackson, 18 Mar 1915, Cab 24/1/G–15.
14. The best study of the de Bunsen committee is J. Nevakivi, *Britain, France and the Arab Middle East 1914–1920* (London, 1969), pp 18–25.
15. The following two paragraphs, except where otherwise noted are based on minutes of the 2nd meeting of the de Bunsen Committee, 13 Apr 1915, Cab 27/1 [PRO].
16. For French concerns about British motives, see George H. Cassar, *The French and the Dardanelles. A study of failure in the conduct of war* (London, 1971), pp 50–60.

17. Minutes of the 3rd meeting of the de Bunsen committee, 15 Apr 1915, testimony of Vice-Admiral Sir E. J. W. Slade, Cab 27/1.
18. 'British Desiderata in Turkey in Asia. Report', de Bunsen committee, 30 Jun 1915, ibid.
19. This and the rest of the paragraph are based on David Stevenson, *The First World War and International Politics* (Oxford: Clarendon, 1988), pp 125–31; Nevakivi, *Britain, France*, pp 26–44; A. S. Klieman, *Foundation of British Policy in the Arab World* (Baltimore, 1970), pp 4–17, and E. P. Fitzgerald, 'France's Middle Eastern Ambitions, the Sykes–Picot Negotiations and the Oil Fields of Mosul, 1915–1918', *Journal of Modern History*, 66, 4(1994), 697–725.
20. A. Chamberlain to Chelmsford (viceroy, India), 10 Aug 1916, Chelmsford Papers, MSS Eur E 264/2 [IOLR]; 'Quetta–Seistan Railway', 4 Aug 1916, Cab 6/4/107–D [PRO]. The latter contains a short history of the proposal upon which the following is largely based.
21. 'Extension of the Quetta–Nushki Railway to Seistan', Robertson, 16 Aug 1916, Cab 6/4/108–D.
22. 'Nushki–Seistan Railway', Curzon, 17 Aug 1916, Cab 6/4/110–D.
23. See the history of this in 'The strategical aspect of railway construction in Persia, with special reference to the extension of the Sistan Railway', Macdonogh (for Sir H. Wilson, the CIGS), Aug 1918, Cab 27/30/EC 1116.
24. Ibid.; minutes of 6th meeting of the Eastern Committee, 3 May 1918, Cab 27/24.
25. 'The strategical aspect of railway construction in Persia with special reference to the extension of the Sistan Railway', Macdonogh (for Sir H. Wilson, the CIGS), Aug 1918, Cab 27/30/EC 1116.
26. Minutes of the 27th meeting of the Eastern Committee, 20 Aug 1918, Cab 27/24
27. 'Railway Policy in Relation to General Military Policy in the Middle East', General Staff, 8 Dec 1918, Cab 27/33/EC 2766.
28. 'Minutes of the Committee of the Imperial War Cabinet on Territorial Desiderata in the Terms of Peace, Held at 2, Whitehall Gardens', ns (but chaired by Curzon), third meeting, 19 Apr 1917, Cab 21/77.
29. French, *Strategy of the Lloyd George Coalition,* p 175.
30. 'Military Effect of Russia Seceding from the Entente', Robertson, 9 May 1917, Cab 24/12/GT–678.
31. 'Naval Effect of Russia Seceding from the Entente', Jellicoe, 10 May 1917, Cab 24/12/GT–688.
32. 'Policy in View of Russian Developments', Curzon, 12 May 1917, Cab 24/13/GT–703.
33. 'Memorandum on Russian Statement of War Aims', Intelligence Bureau, Department of Information, 15 May 1917, Cab 24/14/GT–844.
34. 'Palestine', Robertson, 19 Jul 1917, Cab 27/7/WP 45 [PRO].
35. 'The Present Military Situation in Russia and its Effect on Our Future Plans', Robertson, 29 Jul 1917, Cab 24/21/GT–1549; Robertson to Maude, secret and personal, 17 Aug 1917, Robertson Papers, I/34/31 [Liddell Hart Centre for Military Archives, King's College London].
36. See, for example, Bertie to Balfour, private and confidential, 25 Aug 1917, Bertie Papers, Add MSS 63047 [British Library].
37. Robertson to Haig, 24 Sept 1917, Robertson Papers, I/23/53; 'Provision of additional Sea-Transport for the Movement of Troops', Robertson, 17 Sept 1917, Macdonogh Papers, WO 106/1515 [PRO].
38. For a cogent summary of such problems, see G. M. W. Macdonogh (DMI) to General Shore (Tiflis), 7 Nov 1917, WO 106/5128.
39. R. H. Ullman, *Anglo-Soviet Relations, 1917–1921,* vol. I, *Intervention and the War* (Princeton, 1961), pp 53–7.
40. Rothwell, *British War Aims,* pp 147–55. The significance of the matter of self-determination on public opinion in Russia and elsewhere can be seen in Buchanan (British ambassador to Russia) to FO, tel 7, 2 Jan 1918, FO 371/3436/1671 [PRO] and Balfour to Spring Rice, private and secret tel, 5 Jan 1918, Balfour Papers, FO 800/205 [PRO].
41. 'Memorandum', Balfour, 7 Mar 1918, Cab 24/44/GT–3840.
42. On this, see U. Trumpener, *Germany and the Ottoman Empire, 1914–1918* (Princeton, 1968), chapters 6 and 7.
43. R. Cecil to Balfour, 8 Jan 1918, Balfour Papers, Add MSS 49738 [British Library].
44. Balfour to Admiral Hope, 29 Apr 1918, Balfour Papers, FO 800/205; ibid, 'Reference G.T. 4344', Naval Staff, Admiralty, 29 Apr 1918, and 'Future of the Russian Fleets. Admiralty Memorandum for the War Cabinet', E. Geddes (First Lord of the Admiralty), 25 Apr 1918, Cab 24/49/GT–4344.
45. On the early committees, see Keith Neilson, 'Managing the War: Britain, Russia and Ad Hoc Government', in Dockrill, Michael and French, David, (eds), *British Strategy and Intelligence in*

the First World War (London, 1995). On the need for a new organisation, 'The Present Situation in Russia & The Near East', Sir Henry Wilson (Chief of the Imperial General Staff — CIGS), 7 Mar 1918, Cab 24/44/GT–3834.

46.   Minutes, WC 363, 11 Mar 1918, Cab 23/5 [PRO].
47.   The rest of this paragraph, except where noted, is based on the minutes, WC 369, 21 Mar 1918, Cab 23/5.
48.   For a wider examination, see 'Note by the Chief of the Imperial General Staff on Memorandum T.21169 of the 7th March 1918...(G.T. 3840)', Wilson, 11 Mar 1918, Cab 24/44/GT–3891 and Milner to Curzon, 26 Feb 1918, Curzon Papers, MSS Eur F112/122a.
49.   Milner to Curzon, 26 Feb 1918, Curzon Papers, MSS Eur F112/122a; see also, Hardinge to Bertie, 5 Mar 1918, Bertie Papers, Add MSS 63049 [British Library].
50.   For the Committee's mandate, see 'Eastern Committee', Curzon, 13 Mar 1918, Cab 24/45/GT–3905. For an interesting commentary on the Committee's composition, see R. Cecil to Curzon, 7 Apr 1918, Curzon Papers, MSS Eur F112/121a.
51.   Minutes of the 3rd meeting of the Eastern Committee, 24 Apr 1918, Cab 27/24 [PRO].
52.   8th and 10th meetings of the Eastern Committee, 10 and 28 May 1918, Cab 27/24.
53.   Minutes of the 12th meeting of the Eastern Committee, 5 Jun 1918, Cab 27/24.
54.   Minutes of the 13th meeting of the Eastern Committee, 11 Jun 1918, Cab 27/24.
55.   'British Policy in Afghanistan and Turkestan. Note by the C.I.G.S.' Wilson, 21 Jun 1918, appendix to the 16th meeting of the Eastern Committee, 24 Jun 1918, Cab 27/24. The rest of this paragraph is based on Wilson's memo and the minutes of the 16th meeting.
56.   'The War in the East', Montagu, 5 Jul 1918; minutes of the 24A meeting of the Eastern Committee, 13 Aug 1918, both Cab 27/24.
57.   On the wider aspects, see Ephraim Maisel, The Foreign Office and Foreign Policy, 1919–1926 (Brighton, 1994), pp 208–12.
58.   'Note on Mr. Montagu's Memorandum "The War in the East.", Henry Wilson, 15 Jul 1918, Cab 27/24.
59.   Minutes of the 30th meeting of the Eastern Committee, Cab 27/24.
60.   'The Military Command in the Middle East', Smuts, 16 Sept 1918, Cab 24/63/GT–5700.
61.   Minutes of the 32nd meeting of the Eastern Committee, 18 Sept 1918 and appendices, Cab 27/24.
62.   Marshall had a similarly low opinion of the strategic vision of the Eastern Committee; see his memoirs, Memories of Four Fronts (London, 1929), 282–3.
63.   Minutes of the 34th meeting of the Eastern Committee, 3 Oct 1918, Cab 27/24.
64.   Minutes, WC 485, 14 Oct 1918, Cab 23/8; and see 'Future Government in the Middle East,', R. Cecil, 12 Oct 1918, Cab 24/66/GT–5955.
65.   Minutes, WC 489, 18 Oct 1918, Cab 23/8.
66.   'Minutes of the Proceedings of a Conference held at the Foreign Office on November 13th, 1918 at 3.30 p.m.', ns, 13 Nov 1918, Cab 27/36/EC 2392.
67.   'Memorandum on a Possible Territorial Policy in the Caucasus Regions', E. Crowe, 7 Nov 1918, secret, Cab 27/36/EC 2359.
68.   Minutes, WC 502, 14 Nov 1918, Cab 23/8.
69.   There is an excellent account of this in Erik Goldstein, Winning the Peace. British Diplomatic Strategy, Peace Planning, and the Paris Peace Conference 1916–1920 (Oxford: Clarendon, 1991), pp 150–90. My different reading of the documents reflects an interest in Imperial defence rather than a more general view.
70.   Minutes of the 39th meeting of the Eastern Committee, 27 Nov 1918, Cab 27/24.
71.   The following is based on the Annexe to the minutes of the 40th meeting of the Eastern Committee, 2 Dec 1918, Cab 27/24.
72.   Minutes of the 42nd meeting of the Eastern Committee, 9 Dec 1918, 'Annex', Cab 27/24.
73.   This and the following quotations are from 'Future Settlement of Trans-Caucasia. (The military aspect of the case.)', General Staff, WO, secret, 5 Dec 1918, Cab 27/36/EC 2243.
74.   'The Strategic Importance of Constantinople to the British Empire', secret, General Staff, WO, 22 Dec 1918, Cab 27/39/EC 2824. The rest of this paragraph and the quotations in it, except where otherwise noted, are from this document.
75.   Neilson, Britain and the Last Tsar, pp 112–17; G. Dyer, 'The Turkish Armistice of 1918: 2 – A Lost Opportunity: The Armistice Negotiations of Moudros', Middle Eastern Studies, 8, 3(1972), pp 313–16; French, Strategy of the Lloyd George Coalition, pp 263–5.
76.   'Memorandum by Admiralty', Admiralty, 21 Dec 1918, Cab 27/39/EC 2825; see also

'Constantinople and Internationalisation', L. Mallet (FO), 25 Dec 1918, Cab 27/39/EC 2964, and 'The Future of Constantinople', Curzon, 2 Jan 1919, Cab 27/39/EC 3027.
77. 'The Future of Cyprus', Curzon, 3 Jan 1919, Cab 27/39/EC 3028.
78. Amery to Lloyd George, 8 May 1918, as cited in Jeffery, *Crisis of Empire*, p 133.
79. Montagu to Balfour, private and personal, 20 Dec 1918, Balfour Papers, Add MSS 49748.
80. See Goldstein, *Winning the Peace*, pp 168–9.
81. William C. Fuller, Jr., *Strategy and Power in Russia 1600–1914* (New York: Free Press, 1992).

'It is our business in the Navy to command the Seas'

The last decade of British maritime supremacy, 1919–1929

'The decline of the Navy means the decline of the Empire'
(Admiral David Beatty, 1921[1])

JOHN FERRIS

According to the conventional view, British sea power declined steadily during the 1920s. In 1919, so the story goes, Britain was as strong at sea as ever, but between 1920 and 1922 the 'One Power Standard' and the Washington Naval Treaty produced parity in strength between the Royal Navy and the United States navy. These events are usually seen as a turning point for British sea power, and the beginning of its end. Most scholars agree that between 1922 and 1929 every government let British maritime power wither to dangerously low levels.[2] Historians have explained these phenomena through four arguments. The first focuses on economics. Navies are a rich man's weapon. Only wealthy countries can maintain large fleets and by 1919 Britain was an 'exhausted island kingdom', inferior in financial and industrial capacity to the United States.[3] This is closely linked to a second argument, that fear of antagonizing this greater power led Britain to cut its naval strength.[4] The third argument addresses attitudes. It assumes that the British public and elite no longer believed in armed force or realist ideas, and hence let their sea power slide: liberalism sank the Royal Navy.[5] The fourth centres on the politics of strategic policy, especially on the Treasury's attacks against the navy and the unwillingness of politicians to support naval programmes which would preclude policies of social reform.[6]

Each of these arguments has force: they have been merged in sophisticated forms. Yet still this conventional view is blinkered. It assumes that naval policy was a stable matter, produced by static causes. In fact, that policy changed constantly and so did the significance of the causes which shaped it. This view refers to proof only of weakness while overlooking all signs of strength, falling victim to what David Edgerton calls the fallacy of 'inverse whiggism'.[7] It emphasizes Britain's vulnerability to attack across the globe while ignoring the corollary—that Britain alone could project naval power across the globe. It notes that the Royal Navy was limited in size throughout the 1920s, but not that Britain had the largest and the most modern fleet in the world, a unique network of overseas bases and unchallenged dominance of maritime trade. This view mentions the decline of British industry, but not that Britain retained the best and largest naval armament capacity on earth. It overestimates British fear of the United States and distaste for naval expenses. It underestimates British determination to maintain its maritime security and the Royal Navy's strength. Above all, this view does not explain the matter at hand. In 1919 Britain possessed the world's greatest fleet and naval armament capacity and the ability to master any threat at sea; so too did it in 1929. By 1939, all of these characteristics had vanished. This change occurred in 1920–1930.

The period 1919 to 1929 was the last decade of British maritime supremacy. It did not continue without challenge, but continue it did, only to vanish abruptly. In 1919, the Royal Navy possessed a three power standard in warships. This level of power was almost unprecedented—Britain had possessed anything like it only once before, during the years immediately after the Napoleonic wars[8] —and it did not survive past 1922. On the other hand, Britain had no need to maintain such a level of strength simply for its own sake. As one First Lord argued in 1901, 'to ensure ourselves against any possible (however improbable) hostile combination, to adopt a four power standard or a three power standard is unnecessary and impossible'.[9] In the nineteenth century Pax Britannica at sea often rested on a one power standard. Neither was there a steady decline in British naval power between 1919 and 1939. During that time the only consistent thing about naval policy was its inconsistency, its abrupt reversals of direction. In the first of these periods, 1919–21, Britain waited on events with security. During the second, 1922–29, Britain remained secure at sea and its maritime power was on the rise. During the third, 1930–35, only in the best of cases could Britain fight an effective war in the Pacific against the imperial Japanese navy. It would be hard pressed to win a war against virtually any two naval powers. Its fleet moved from being as modern as any to one of the oldest among the naval powers. This legacy crippled British naval strength throughout the 1930s and left it near disaster in 1941. Even so, during the fourth of these periods, 1936–39, Britain rearmed at sea more thoroughly and speedily than any other power. Had war not broken out when it did, Britain might well have healed its self-inflicted wound of 1929–30 and restored the days of its maritime supremacy. That British sea power had declined forever did not become a certainty until 1940. The question is how and why it became a possibility.

Any enquiry into that point must begin where decision makers did. Sea power, Austen Chamberlain once said, 'was our great strength and decisive weapon'.[10] Without it, Britain would cease to be an independent power, a European great power or a world power; neither the British elite nor its public would tolerate such a slip in status. Yet that strength did not have a simple nature. The story of British sea power after 1815 is often told in terms of steady decline from Pax Britannica, to the recall of the legions around 1900,

the one power standard, and then to shipwreck. This story is not history. First
of all, it misrepresents the nature of Pax Britannica at sea. The latter had existed for two reasons—the nature of British power and of the actions required to
challenge it; before 1815 it did not exist.

Between 1692 and 1793, the Netherlands and the Bourbon powers often
maintained navies comparable to those of Britain, while several other states
possessed significant fleets. One diplomatic decision by two powers could put
British sea power to the challenge; one by three could put it at risk. Given the
'Family Compact', Britain always had to reckon on naval co-operation
between France and Spain if it fought either state. As the maritime campaign
of the American Revolutionary war showed, even when loosely combined, the
Dutch, Spanish and French fleets could not defeat the Royal Navy, but they
could cripple the British Empire. Again, between 1804–12 the fleets of
Napoleon presented a serious danger to Britain. That Britain could stand off
the combined fleets of Europe proved its superiority in seapower: because such
a threat existed Britain could not turn naval superiority to maritime supremacy.

For decades after 1815, however, Britain possessed the largest standing fleet
in the world, an extraordinary strength of warships in reserve and the financial
and shipbuilding capacities to outbuild any other state whenever it wished to
do so. As Germany's experience before 1914— in fact, the entire history of the
interwar years—showed, no single state could or would match British sea
power on its own. The Royal Navy could be matched only if at least two powers systematically and simultaneously expanded their maritime strength. Such
challenges could succeed only if these powers could continue to co-operate in
the lengthy pursuit of a difficult, costly and risky objective, if Britain could not
or would not buy one of them off, or outbuild both or find other means to
counter them. As Winston Churchill once put it, 'Always in the past, when
Great Britain had been faced with burdens which were difficult to bear, she had
had recourse to combinations with other countries'.[11] These conditions were
unlikely. Consequently, until around 1885 no powers cared or dared to take the
steps required even to begin to challenge British sea power. Pax Britannica
rested on the deployment of a remarkably small fleet at sea—Britain was the
strongest naval power in the Pacific Ocean simply because it was the only one
there—often a dangerously small one. During the 1830s the Mediterranean station, one of Britain's central squadrons, usually possessed just five sail of the
line, or half the strength of Russian and French fleets at Toulon or Sevastopol.
On occasion this weakness crippled Lord Palmerston's diplomacy, despite his
blithe assumption that any one British battleship equalled any two it might
encounter.[12] Pax Britannica remained afloat for one reason: other navies were
even smaller.

Between the 1880s and 1914, several powers did expand their navies. This
returned Britain to the strategic circumstances of the eighteenth century: a
challenge at sea now stood just one diplomatic decision by two states away.
That immediately cost Britain its control of certain waters, most notably the

Black and Baltic and Caribbean and East China Seas, and its shadowy supremacy over the Pacific Ocean—not that anyone dominated that ocean until 1944. But the actions of Britain's Government, combined with the nature of its naval position, ensured that it lost nothing else. Diplomacy kept some naval powers on Britain's side. Its economy outbuilt the rest. Between 1890 and 1918 Britain's naval strength returned toward the level of 1815, far above the norm for Pax Britannica. Nor did Britain slip below that norm between 1919 and 1929; in some ways it improved on it. Britain continued to control all the waters which it had done in 1900, and acquired the ability to enter Eurasian seas which had been beyond its reach for a generation. It was relatively as strong in European waters as ever during the heyday of Pax Britannica and more able to project power into the Pacific Ocean than ever before. Britain's share of the world's fleets was scarcely different in 1925, 1905 and 1895. The new order of sea power which began in the 1880s vanished only in the 1940s, when all of the conditions needed to destroy Britain's maritime power finally emerged. It fought a long and single-handed war against two naval powers, and then had to face a third and to call for support from a fourth. During 1941–42 British maritime strength failed to overcome two deadly threats—the U-boat campaign and the southward thrust of the imperial Japanese navy—while for the first time the United States systematically tapped its industrial resources for maritime purposes. Thus, for the first time in centuries, British naval power was inadequate to its needs and outstripped in its scale.

Their history of power, rather than our story of decline, shaped British views of their strength and their needs at sea. Nor did decision makers have one view on these matters. David Beatty, Chief of Naval Staff (CNS) between 1919 and 1927, once said that any country's 'authority ... in the counsels of the world depends primarily on her naval strength'. When necessary he denied that the Admiralty 'aimed at superiority in all seas', but in fact this was his aim and that of other admirals, such as his successors, Charles Madden, and Ernle Chatfield. In 1929 Madden wrote 'The Navy is the chief sanction of our Foreign Policy; it is hardly an exaggeration to say that every Foreign Office telegram is backed by it.' The Admiralty did pursue the ability to destroy any and every other fleet, including those of the United States and imperial Japan, in their home waters.[13] The Admiralty did wish to recreate Pax Britannica. It saw the seas as indivisible: they must be wholly commanded or wholly lost, and that was the whole of power.

Few outside the Admiralty wanted such power, because most Britons knew that Britain had never possessed it. Even wiser First Lords recognized, as Bolton Eyres-Bonsell noted in 1934, 'We never had had command of all the seas, nor had we ever entertained that idea'.[14] Statesmen thought of defence, not of attack, of security at sea rather than supremacy over it, of the empirical ability to use specific oceans for particular ends. They were Corbettians by instinct. They did not aim to restore Pax Britannica but to control those seas which were directly linked to British security—those which Britain had controlled since the 1890s. Politicians like Churchill and David Lloyd George defined Britain's needs for sea power by one simple criterion—that the British Empire be able to defend its 'special seas' or 'home waters'.[15] A few decision makers, Treasury officials such as George Barstow and Labour politicians like Philip Snowden, went even further, arguing that any naval power beyond the minimum necessary to defend home waters would endanger Britain. Thus, Snowden in 1924:

> Fleets are required by nations primarily as defensive weapons. They can neither invade a territory nor capture a trade. They can destroy a trade, but they cannot build one up. It is for Defence, and not for Offence, that Great Britain, the United States of America, even Germany before the war, equipped their fleets ... Means of Defence are necessary because of the fear of attack. So long as the principal naval powers are uncertain of each other's intentions, they will not dare to reduce their scales of defence. Each defensive development they undertake is capable of being misinterpreted as a preparation for attack. Hence they get into a vicious circle of armaments.[16]

Navalists and radicals alike stood outside the mainstream of British views on sea power. The elite and the general public were annoyed when other powers built fleets which Britain found inconvenient. They believed that Britain had unique rights to sea power. They remained adamant about maritime security and certain of its significance. As Eyres-Bonsell stated in 1934, 'If it was really true that we could not afford to maintain our seapower, then the matter ought to be looked at in a big way and the whole question should be considered as to whether we were, in fact, prepared to give up our Empire'.[17] These points are best illustrated by the statesmen who most challenged naval programmes between 1919 and 1927. In 1919 Robert Cecil informed the advisor to President Wilson, Colonel House, that 'if I were British Minister of the Navy and I saw that British naval safety was being threatened even by America, I should have to recommend to my fellow country men to spend their last shilling in bringing our fleet up to the point which I was advised was necessary for safety'. Cecil was one of few ministers to support the Admiralty's original construction programmes of 1925.[18] As Prime Minister in 1920–21, Lloyd George saw no need for a naval construction programme, which he feared might create an arms race with the United States and 'bankruptcy or war'. He held that America would 'never tolerate our being superior in naval power in seas in which they had the greatest interest'.[19] Neither would he tolerate an American threat to maritime security. He told House that Britain 'could not, whatever the cost, permit any other Power to get ahead and be in a position to starve her out in the event of war'. Instead, Lloyd George wanted the United States and Britain each to rule out the other as an enemy and each to pursue supremacy in its own 'special seas'. He defined Britain's 'special seas' rather broadly—including 'the North Sea, the Mediterranean, the Indian seas, etc'. As he told the

American ambassador in 1920,

> ...whenever the word came that Great Britain's Navy was no longer
> first in the world, a shudder would creep down the backs of the British
> people and they would spend their last shirt in order to regain their
> position: that no Government could withstand the demand. For this
> reason he viewed with the greatest apprehension the programme of
> competitive building between the two countries. He thought there was
> no desire to have a larger navy than America but it must at least be
> equal and predominant in European waters leaving to America, if she
> chose, the preponderance in American and Pacific waters.[20]

Again, in 1920 Churchill argued that 'Great Britain, since the most remote
times, had always been supreme at sea. It would be a terrible day for the country when she ceased to be thus.' In 1921, he accepted parity on paper between
the Royal Navy and the US navy because he believed the American Government would never maintain that status once this was granted, while Britain
could meet its maritime needs on that standard. In a speech of 1929 Churchill
claimed that at the Washington Conference Britain had abandoned 'altogether
that supremacy at sea which we had enjoyed for at least 100 years [and] which
we had never abused...we accepted the new principles that Britain and the
United States should be equal Powers upon the sea'. But, this decision did not
imply 'a mere numerical measure of two fleets, each the replica of the other...
Then we should not have equality, but under the guise of equality an absolute
and final inferiority'. Britain absolutely needed an absolutely larger fleet than
that of the USA. 'The safety and power of the country, and the whole life and
cohesion of the British Empire' rested on one condition—'the maintenance of
the British Navy at the minimum strength necessary to enable us to guarantee
the security of our food supplies and our trade, and to preserve the necessary
contact with the world spread Dominions and Possessions of the British
Crown'.[21] Such statements resound throughout his official minutes and state
papers of the 1920s.

Between 1919 and 1928, even the politicians who most opposed Mahanian
doctrines and Admiralty policies demanded that Britain remain secure at sea,
and they defined that security in spacious terms. In its pursuit all governments
let the Navy execute large programmes. When in positions of power only two
bodies, the Treasury and the Labour Party, rejected this consensus, and during
1924 even the first Labour Government authorized a large construction programme. Granted, other aims, especially the desires to reduce expenditure and
to reform society, hampered naval estimates. Most politicians accepted the theory of arms races and held that too rapid and too large preparations might
alarm other powers and create unnecessary dangers at sea. Nonetheless, during
the 1920s the Royal Navy had room to manoeuvre. It used that room to establish an ambitious policy.

That policy emerged from Britain's response to American and Japanese naval construction from 1919 to 1921. British statesmen believed that while these programmes were directed against each other, each put Britain at risk. They knew that the United States was potentially the strongest power on earth, and its greatest industrial state. They preferred to avoid an arms race with it, for fear that this would antagonize the United States and, perhaps, make it tap its resources in an attempt to outmatch Britain at sea. Lloyd George feared that such a competition 'might in the end ruin us': his Chancellor of the Exchequer, Austen Chamberlain, believed that Britain could only hope to win one by attacking the United States before 1923, 'which Heaven forbid'. The Treasury denied that Britain could ever compete with American financial capacity. As Barstow put it, 'Their resources are so much greater than our own that for every ship we lay down they can afford to put down two.' Even the Admiralty's war plans of 1921 conceded that 'Time all on side of U.S.A.' and that in order to win (as against draw) Britain must force a quick and decisive fleet action.[22]

Yet there was more to the matter than fear in London. Statesmen knew that the United States could only threaten Britain if it took an unprecedented and unlikely action, to devote systematically and for a sustained period its economic resources to sea power. They held that this would happen only if Britain provoked the United States; indeed, that if denied a British bogeyman, the US navy would always remain second to one. Lloyd George and the leader of the Conservative Party, Andrew Bonar Law, made these points in 1920. They echoed in Whitehall until 1939.[23] Nor, if fear proves power, can Britain be written off. To judge from the surviving record, between 1919 and 1921 Colonel House and the American Chief of Naval Operations, Admiral Benson, feared Britain more than any Briton did the United States.[24] When assessing a hypothetical Anglo-American war, both the Royal Navy and the US navy foresaw a prolonged and inconclusive struggle at sea. The only Cabinet committee to consider the issue at all concluded 'the operations would result in a stalemate in which neither side could obtain decisive victory'.[25] Above all, Britain did not wish to fight the United States or treat it as an enemy, nor need it unless America were to force its hand. Britain could safely let the United States and Japan command the waters off their coasts which they had been controlling for 30 years. British statesmen conventionally regarded the United States not as a country like the others, but as a liberal power, one most realistically managed through liberal means. They were right.

Between 1919 and 1921 Britain was sufficiently wise to play a waiting game, and sufficiently powerful. Even the Admiralty, confident in 'our relative Naval superiority over any possible combination of Powers', conceded that Britain had no need to rearm until 1921.[26] Britain's aim was simple—to maintain its security while avoiding an arms race, which would at best leave it holding what it held at greater cost, and at worst might produce enemies or a war. Statesmen hoped to avoid these dangers by deferring construction so long as it was safe and by engaging the United States in maritime diplomacy. This policy failed in 1919–20 because of the chaos in American decision making. That forced Britain toward the first step in its post-war naval policy, the public enunciation of the one power standard. This standard was loosely defined, but it had three components—that Britain did not regard any other power as a threat, but that the navy 'should not be inferior to the Navy of any other power', specifically including the USA, and that the navy's 'strength and standard of efficiency' must always 'enable it to do its duty by the Empire'.[27] Lloyd George authorized this statement for political reasons. It would define Britain's bottom line to the American Government and the British public. As it stood, however, that standard had no specific meaning while Britain had no naval policy. The Admiralty had defined one but it had not been authorized.

The basis for naval policy was determined at the Washington Conference of 1921–22. Here the maritime rivalry of 1919 came to an end, giving Britain virtually everything which its statesmen had pursued, in return for some sacrifices. The Japanese and American Governments abandoned their construction programmes, scrapping many partly completed 'capital ships', while Britain destroyed larger numbers of its oldest warships.[28] This trade-off was equitable enough. These British vessels were obsolete and inferior to the warships of the '1916' programme, even if the latter were noted more for cost than quality. It did, however, sacrifice one of Britain's strengths, large numbers of third class battleships in reserve. The Washington Naval Treaty also defined a practical basis for British maritime strength—a one power standard with the United States, and, in effect, a two power standard at their selected moment against Japan and any one European state. It established a 5:3:1.75 ratio in 'capital ships' and aircraft carriers between Britain and the United States, Japan, and France and Italy. After the signatories had finished their scrapping and completed their authorized programmes by 1926, Britain would have twenty battleships and battle cruisers totalling 580,450 tons; the United States, eighteen of 525,850; Japan, ten of 301,320; France, ten of 221,170, and Italy, ten of 185,500 tons. With a few exceptions, no new 'capital ships' would be laid down during a ten-year building holiday. Between 1933 and 1945 the signatories would replace these vessels according to a defined schedule and reduce their number to 15, 15 and 10 for Britain, the United States and Japan. All of these new battleships and battle cruisers, including two British ones to be laid down in 1922–23, *Nelson* and *Rodney*, were limited to a size of 35,000 tons and 16-inch guns. Britain and the United States could maintain an aircraft carrier strength of 135,000 tons; Japan, of 81,000; and France and Italy of 60,000 tons each. No limits were placed on the numbers of other categories of warships, though a maximum size of 10,000 tons and 8-inch guns (the 'Washington standard') was defined for cruisers.[29]

This agreement angered the admirals. They believed that British prestige had been shaken, that Yankee upstarts should have been publicly slapped down, that the warships in Britain's '1921' programme utterly outclassed those in the '1916' programme while the Royal Navy would have whipped the US navy in arms race or war. The Admiralty warned the Government that the building holiday and the limits on the size of battleships and battle cruisers 'implies a break in the continuity of our naval development, from the point of view alike of construction and of naval tactics and training, so serious as to place in uncertainty the whole future basis of our sea power'. One admiral pledged to tell Beatty his opinions of the Washington Treaty and of negotiations with Sinn Fein 'when we meet in London next spring, provided of course that H.M.G. has not handed over London to the Chinese and the Admiralty and War Office to the Turks'. Years later Chatfield held that Britain 'had gained nothing but lost in every direction' at Washington: 'we had lost prestige and it had resulted in our dividing the rulership of the sea with America'.[30]

The truth of the matter was more complex. In principle, it was dangerous for a seapower to define its strength by words rather than needs. In practice, the Treaty was far from perfect for Britain and parts of it were damaging. The building holiday endangered the naval armament industries of every country but especially British ones, greater than their Japanese or American counterparts and needing more orders to survive. The Treaty, conversely, hampered the quality and quantity of Britain's fleet less than those of the other signatories. Few of Britain's 'capital ships' were sufficiently modern in design to have incorporated the lessons of the great war at sea, but here the Royal Navy was better placed than any other navy. It had the world's only post-Jutland warships, *Nelson* and *Rodney*, while few other ships matched the modernized pre-Jutland battle cruiser *Hood*. The rest of Britain's 'capital ships' were still young, having entered service between 1914 and 1916. Their quality was comparable to any others at sea in 1922, and for several years Britain understood better than any other how to upgrade such warships during refits.

The Admiralty later claimed that the Naval Treaty had eliminated Britain's 'commanding superiority in material'.[31] Such views still lurk in the minds of some commentators. They are dubious. That superiority did not vanish, it simply slipped a few notches from the almost unprecedented status of 1919; nor did the Treaty itself weaken Britain's position. The USA and Japan cut their fleets and construction to roughly the same degree as did Britain; but the latter maintained as favourable a balance in 'capital ships', at a lower level of strength, as it would have retained by 1925 had there been no Treaty and had the Admiralty's proposals of 1920–21, the American '1916' and the Japanese '8-8' programmes all been completed without further escalation. Under these circumstances, Britain would have had all eight of the world's post-Jutland 'capital ships'. Compared to these vessels, *Hood*, the best of the navy's other battleships (the 'Revenge' and 'Queen Elizabeth' classes) and the warships in the '1916' and the '8-8' programmes, would have become second class. The Royal Navy would have been numerically inferior to the US and the Japanese navies in such warships, the mainstay of battle fleets, but greatly superior in third class battleships. Such a fleet, the Admiralty conceded in 1920, would have been little stronger than the US navy. Meanwhile, other powers might have trumped the British ace by increasing the size and the gunpower of their 'capital ships'. Years later Chatfield held that 'the greatest accomplishment of the Washington Treaty was not in limiting numbers or total tonnages but in stopping the principle of going one better'.[32] By 1925 Britain's 'commanding superiority' in material would have vanished to precisely the degree that it did after Washington unless some new factor had intervened. The most obvious of these factors, further British construction or an Anglo-Japanese alliance directed against the United States, were dangerous. They would have risked war with a stronger country or else might have made Americans systematically pursue naval superiority against Britain. Nor was any of this necessary. The Treaty did give Britain superiority in 'capital ships' and, in effect, it also made cruisers into third-class battleships. Britain held an overwhelming advantage in modern cruisers. Thus, after Washington the Royal Navy retained a sizable superiority in large warships over the US Navy or any other two powers.

There were no such gains to balance other losses caused by the Treaty. As Japan and Italy immediately began to cheat on parts of it, especially the tonnage of cruisers, Britain's maritime position became slightly worse than envisaged in Washington. The Treaty automatically might give rise to further dangers by the later 1920s. In particular, the Royal Navy equalled any two naval powers excluding the United States because the European fleets were obsolete. This position might decline, perhaps down to a two power standard only on paper, if France and Italy were to build modern warships as the Washington Treaty entitled them to do during the later 1920s, while Germany and Russia might also expand their fleets. As Britain's 'capital ships' were older on average than those of Japan and the US, it would suffer most of all should the building holiday ever be extended. Worst of all, the Anglo-Japanese Alliance was abandoned, and the third strongest naval power, uncomfortably close to the richest and worst defended portions of the British Empire, ceased to be an ally and became a potential threat.

Substantial these problems were, but not decisive. The Treaty did not alter which seas a naval power could dominate, nor did it produce a new order of sea power. It simply confirmed that order which had emerged between 1888 and 1906 and it left Britain the greatest power at sea. The US navy gained a larger share of world sea power, but Britain's portion did not decline. It continued to dominate maritime trade and shipbuilding. Britain was the only sea power with the strength and bases to be a world power. It could project fleets to places other navies could not reach, and those fleets remained the strongest and best balanced in the world. Britain had a decided lead in naval aviation and cruisers and, according to the Naval Staff, a 'slight superiority' over the US in the real strength of 'capital ships'.[33] It could easily overawe any two naval powers in Europe and deter any threat from Japan. In 1933, Chatfield held that the Washington Treaty had created

approximately a two-power standard as regards Japan and France ... It had been the idea that if we found it necessary to despatch the fleet to the East, we should be able to retain sufficient naval forces in European waters to act as a deterrent against any trouble starting in Europe.[34]

Not, for that matter, that Japan even began to regard England as an enemy until 1936. Meanwhile, by eliminating the British bogeyman, the Treaty becalmed American sea power—immediately, the US navy's strength and construction slipped behind the British standard. For the five years following the Washington Conference, Britain was more secure at sea than it had been at any time since 1888. There were deficiencies in its position, to be sure, but ample time to overcome them, while its strengths outweighed its weaknesses.

American observers provide the best testimony for these facts. Men ranging from House to Benson, institutions including the State Department, the Military Intelligence Division and the US navy, all agreed that Britain was the most ruthless and dangerous state on earth, concerned above all else with the preservation of its maritime trade and power, one which traditionally smashed its rivals on the seas through tenacity and treachery. They agreed that Britain would defend its position against its American rival through its practised policies, and that it possessed formidable means to do so.[35] Thus in 1924 Captain C.L. Hussey, the American Naval Attache to Britain, told the United States Navy War College that the personnel and material of the Royal Navy were 'highly efficient' and in many ways superior to their American counterparts. Britain possessed a 'margin of supremacy in sea power ... by virtue not only of superior naval strength in ships and personnel, but also of the strategical value of naval bases, fuelling stations, Merchant Marine, and systems of world communication'. 'The British are still supreme on the sea and are the dominating influence in world affairs. Their power and prestige were never greater. Changing conditions threaten that dominance'.[36] Similar views marked strategic analyses conducted at the United States Army War College in 1929 to assist the formulation of war plans against the British Empire, and so did the plans themselves.[37]

The strength of Britain's position stemmed from the Washington Treaty and the decisions which followed it. This event forced Whitehall to define a naval policy. In the months after that conference, the Royal Navy faced great pressure. Lloyd George's Government forced sizable reductions in naval manpower and spending—respectively, by 17% and 25% from the level of 1921—and flirted with more radical cuts. The Treasury opposed all of the navy's policies and even wanted to cancel the two Treaty battleships Britain was authorized to build. Ultimately, however, the Cabinet concluded that in order to maintain security, naval strength could be cut no further while all of the components of the navy's policy must be authorized. In particular, it accepted the Admiralty's argument that Japan threatened imperial security.[38] Then, between 1922 and 1924, Britain entered a period of unstable Government. The Admiralty turned this chaos to its favour. Through resolute and skilful politics, it gained authorization for all of its policy.

This policy was ambitious. It rested on a sophisticated assessment of Britain's position as a world power, of maritime strategy and the lessons of the great war at sea. During the Washington Conference, the Admiralty began to recast its war plans of 1920–21, which had assumed that Britain could somehow force an enemy to fight a quick and decisive fleet engagement.[39] It turned its attention toward the case of a prolonged war with a major naval power based outside Europe, the problems of the defence of empire and trade and the application of inter-continental blockade, and the role of one warship class, the cruiser. It realized that for years after any such war began, the enemy could easily keep its main fleet in being, avoiding battle and maintaining easy access to the high seas. Then, its main fleet would neutralize Britain's while its cruisers could reinforce the battle fleet or else raid maritime trade. Among the naval powers, Britain relied most heavily on this trade and was uniquely exposed to world-wide danger, yet it also had an unmatched capacity for blockade.[40] In 1930, Madden provided a classic exposition of these circumstances.

> Our special problems of defence arise from the unique conditions of the British Empire; its world-wide distribution; the fact that all parts of it are to a greater or lesser extent dependent upon communication by sea for their well-being or in some cases for their very existence, and that in the last resort it is on the transport of adequate forces by sea that the Empire relies to resist aggression and ensure the security of our interests and integrity of our territory. Thus it is that the security of sea passage to and from all parts of the Empire forms the basis and foundation of our system of Imperial Defence, without which all other measures of defence can be of little avail.
>
> The surest method of ensuring security of sea passage is to remove, or failing removal, to render innocuous, that which threatens it. Hence the primary aim is the destruction or, failing destruction, the neutralisation of the enemy's fleets and squadrons. Destruction is not readily attained, and the most usual situation is one in which the enemy conserves his naval force by refusing decisive action and neutralisation becomes necessary. Thus the struggle for sea supremacy is prolonged, and supremacy is seldom absolute.
>
> Our naval strategy, therefore, is based on the principle that a fleet of adequate strength, suitably disposed geographically and concentrated against the enemy's fleet, provides the 'cover' under which security is given to widely dispersed territories and trade routes. The security cannot be given by the same strength of fleet dispersed to afford local protection to particular territories or trade routes. Such dispersion would leave the enemy free initiative and would invite the destruction of these detached forces by an enemy concentration. Dispersion of the

main fleet, therefore, merely defeats its own object.

Whilst, however, the main fleet is the basis upon which our naval strategy rests, naval requirements are not satisfied solely by its provision. The 'cover' it can provide is rarely complete, and instances have occurred in all wars of units detached by the enemy evading the main fleet and carrying out attacks of a sporadic nature on territories and trade.

To deal with these sporadic attacks cruiser squadrons are required over and above those forming part of the main fleet. It may be sufficient to maintain these squadrons cruising in the various areas liable to attack, but if this system fails or after experience is thought likely to fail, it will be necessary to resort to the 'convoy' system to provide adequate security.

The measures for protecting our own trade are adapted also to the attack on the enemy trade, so that, to summarise, the measures by which we protect our own sea communications and attack those of the enemy consist of 'cover', 'cruising' and 'convoy'.[41]

The Admiralty sought to create a navy which could sustain imperial defence and world power. Such a force required an elaborate infrastructure of logistics and bases to deploy, concentrate and maintain its forces in all seas essential to the Empire, a main fleet able to provide 'cover', and a large and additional strength to defend British trade and attack foreign commerce. The long term aim was to defend British maritime interests against all comers through to the 1940s—senior sailors like Chatfield, Dudley Pound and Roger Keyes wanted to be able to prepare for war even with the United States.[42] The immediate aim was to match the threat of the imperial Japanese navy in the Pacific. The two objectives were linked. The Admiralty did see a Japanese threat, but it also distorted that danger so to rationalize the greater aim. This phenomenon emerged right after the Washington Conference.

In July 1922 the imperial Japanese navy announced that over the next six years it would replace most of its lighter warships, 117 of them. In particular, it would build four Washington standard cruisers and four 7100 ton cruisers with 8-inch guns. This programme was not aimed at Britain, but it plausibly could be seen as a threat. The Admiralty, however, exaggerated the matter to suit its political needs. When this announcement was made, Whitehall was battling over naval policy. Immediately, the Admiralty announced that this programme proved that Japan intended to threaten British security and showed how it would do so. In particular, the Royal Navy interpreted the construction of 8-inch gun cruisers as proof that Japan was preparing for a *guerre de course* against Britain through surface warships. In fact, judging from their designs and Japanese doctrine and strategy, these warships were intended to bolster the Japanese battle fleet against the US navy. In any case, the Admiralty argued, Britain could match this threat only by developing the logistical means to redeploy the fleet to Singapore and through construction of its own. Beatty soon offered the CID a taste of warnings it would hear for years: that Japan was likely to attack India or Australia, that the navy alone could restrain these 'aggressive tendencies' and that until the fleet could operate in the Pacific, the Empire would exist on Japan's 'sufferance'. Given Whitehall's use of the term 'sufferance', Beatty was claiming that Japan endangered not just Britain's maritime security, but its very status as a great power.[43]

Around the argument of a Japanese threat, the Admiralty created a coherent and expansionist policy. It interpreted the so-called Ten Year Rule to mean that every naval preparation for a major war must be completed by 1929. It used that rule to justify increasingly large expenditure on its programmes.[44] It also told the Cabinet that if any of its programmes were delayed, the Government must publicly abandon the one power standard.[45] This, of course, was impossible for political and diplomatic reasons. Then, the Admiralty used the Japanese menace to justify the development of two means to project great offensive power to every sea. The first was to complete the fuel oil reserve and the Singapore base needed for the fleet to operate in the Pacific Ocean, off the coasts of Malaya—or of Japan. The second was to maintain the world's greatest fleet. The Admiralty intended to reconstruct its 'capital ships' between 1931–41, according to the schedule defined by the Washington Treaty. By its interpretation, Britain was legally bound to this schedule. In 1925, the Board of Admiralty concurred that 'we are involved' in the replacement programme 'by the Washington Treaty following on the ten years' holiday'.[46] This programme would absorb much of Britain's naval armament capacity and increase Naval Estimates. Consequently, before 1931 the Admiralty intended to lay down as many new vessels as possible in the warship classes which were not regulated by the Treaty. It defined a massive construction programme which would not end until 1940 when, in turn, those vessels laid down in the 1920s would have to be replaced. In effect, the Admiralty wanted future naval construction to follow the rate of 1888–1914, the most expensive programmes which Britain had ever followed in peacetime.

The programmes of the 1920s centred on cruisers. Until one understands why that should have been the case, the naval policy of this decade will be incomprehensible. Contrary to conventional views and its own claims, the Royal Navy did not value cruisers primarily for trade defence. It wanted them not just for defence, but for victory. For much of the 1920s it believed that cruisers would give a relative advantage to the Treaty fleet; they were always fundamental to a central component of naval policy—the waging of inter-continental economic warfare. During the First World War, blockade and trade protection alike had been exercised by cruisers. The Admiralty sought to create the same defensive and offensive capabilities on the oceans.

In 1921, it believed that all new cruisers must be able to serve on the oceans, which would require warships of 10,000 tons with 7.5 or 8-inch guns.[47] Hence, it favoured the establishment of the 'Washington standard' for cruisers. Until 1926 it wanted all of its cruisers to reach those dimensions. Meanwhile, in Washington a new factor entered the equation—the need to strengthen the Treaty battle fleet, with fewer 'capital ships' than in 1918 and a fixed strength in aircraft carriers. This augmentation could easily be done through cruisers, the largest category of ship whose numbers were not restricted by the Treaty. That was the Royal Navy's approach. However unsuccessful the design, Britain's 'Washington standard' warships of the 1920s were intended to have the firepower, speed and range needed to catch and destroy the strongest foreign cruiser anywhere at sea and to fill some functions of 'capital ships' for the fleet.[48] The Admiralty had a ratio for the cruisers 'required for work with the main Fleet ... For every 3 battleships, 5 cruisers are required'.[49]

By 1926, however, it sought to limit the construction of new 8-inch gun cruisers by the world's navies and became willing to impose the 5:5:3 ratio on them. This change occurred largely for financial reasons, but also because the Admiralty was learning that no cruiser with a 10,000 ton displacement could be designed to fight effectively with the fleet and wage trade warfare. Oceanic work required endurance and seaworthiness; combat needed speed and gunpower. On 10,000 tons, either demand could be achieved only at the expense of the other and of armour protection. This problem was multiplied because, unlike any other navy, the Royal Navy had to be able to match the wide range of design characteristics for 8-inch gun cruisers adopted by every other fleet. The more 8-inch gun cruisers at sea, furthermore, the greater the chances that a British cruiser designed for trade warfare would unexpectedly confront an adversary better designed for single ship combat. In order to ensure the role of cruisers in economic warfare, the Admiralty had to abandon their use as a means to increase the relative power of the British main fleet.

This ended one aspect of the navy's policy toward heavy cruisers, but it did not mark a retreat to passive defence. The Admiralty still demanded large numerical superiority in all other cruisers, ostensibly to protect British trade. To be sure, this task was necessary and that means was essential to it. Cruisers were no less effective platforms than submarines for oceanic economic warfare. Any vessel able to protect oceanic commerce, however, could also blockade it. In particular, the warships and the deployments needed for trade defence were ideally suited for the blockade of Japan, which was second only to Britain in its dependence on maritime commerce. Blockade was fundamental to the Royal Navy's plans for prolonged wars, especially against Japan. The Admiralty's fears of surface *guerre de course* by Japan were a case of projection—an indication of its own offensive strategy for war with that country—and of cynical politics. The Naval Staff knew that Japan could not cripple the trade of any enemy during any war.[50] By acquiring cruisers able to withstand this danger, however, the Royal Navy could gain the means to win a war of attrition against Japan. The cruiser programme of the 1920s was fundamentally part of the Singapore strategy, and the latter rested as much on offensive economic warfare as on the deployment of the main fleet for prolonged operations in the South China Sea. While the main fleet checked the Japanese navy, British cruisers would strangle the Japanese economy, either destroying it or forcing the enemy to accept a decisive battle.

Admirals differed over Britain's numerical needs for cruisers—estimates ranged from 50 to 93—but they settled on an arbitrary, if reasonable figure of 70.[51] Since Britain possessed only 48 cruisers at sea in 1923, just four of which were designed for oceanic operations, substantial construction would be needed. Initially, the navy pursued all these ends simply by completing warships left over on the stocks from 1918. Next, in 1923, it proposed to replace old or obsolescent warships. This programme, estimated to cost £66,771,000 between 1924 and 1931, aimed to build 72 destroyers, 32 submarines, eight Washington standard cruisers and another ten, perhaps smaller, cruisers.[52] It was generally justifiable in technical and strategic terms, although the Naval Staff later concluded that Britain really needed to lay down only 36 destroyers before 1931. In late 1923, however, Stanley Baldwin, the Prime Minister, indicated that for electoral purposes he would favour a larger programme.[53] The Admiralty responded by doubling its size and cost. Under this new programme, Britain would build 117 destroyers and 52 cruisers (at least 17 being of Washington standard) between 1924 and 1935.[54] The Admiralty wished to replace virtually every lighter warship in the fleet, generally years before their time. Many of the arguments it used to justify this programme were dubious. Through various sleights of hand, the Admiralty grossly overstated the size of the Japanese fleet and of the British strength needed to match it. It argued that the main fleet needed a 5 to 3 ratio, plus a 25 per cent margin for security, in 8-inch gun cruisers over all those of the Japanese navy, and also as many 8-inch gun cruisers for trade defence as Japan possessed. The Admiralty then equated ten obsolete Japanese coast defence vessels with Washington standard cruisers. Finally, in effect, it claimed that Britain needed three times as many cruisers as Japan, and two and one half times as many Washington standard cruisers.[55]

'It is our business in the Navy to command the seas', Beatty once said. During the 1920s business was good.[56] The Admiralty did not acquire everything it pursued, but its successes were impressive. Between 1922 and 1926 it laid down more warship tonnage than any other state—almost as much as Japan and the United States combined.[57] While its construction fell short of the maximalist programme given to politicians, the navy acquired most of the warships that it truly wanted. The Sea Lords saw no need to spend more than £10 million a year on construction from 1924 to 1926, or £7 million annually between 1927 and 1931.[58] Until June 1929 it received slightly more money than this for these purposes. The Naval Staff really wanted to lay down 17 to 18 cruisers between 1924 and 1929.[59] It started 17 during that period, while Baldwin's Government authorized the construction of another for 1929. By 1929 the navy laid down all the programme considered necessary in 1923–24, with the exception of one aircraft carrier. It had the largest and most modern fleet of cruisers at sea, virtually the only operational carriers in the world, alongside the best squadrons of 'capital ships'. Despite deferment in the completion date from 1931 to 1936, the navy completed 60 per cent of the fuel oil reserve programme and in 1929 was beginning the three year period in which most of the Singapore base would be completed. Detailed war plans against Japan were defined and practical steps taken to execute them.[60] By 1928 the Admiralty was preparing to project its power to Japan's doorstep. Its planning assumed that the Main Fleet would not stop at Singapore but would sail straight to Hong Kong, and from there operate in Japanese waters, in order to annihilate their navy or starve out the other island empire.[61]

There were problems in naval policy by 1929. The Royal Navy lost its lead in naval aviation, due to British failures and American and Japanese successes. While much of its policy was motivated by the danger of surface commerce raiders, it did not fully recognize the scale of another menace, submarines. Yet it did recognize that the latter problem existed and it did intend to allocate substantial forces, such as 100 destroyers or 50 sloops, specifically against it.[62] The Admiralty's planning against Japan exaggerated the speed and ease with which such a war would be fought. In 1921 it assumed that once the Singapore base was complete, Britain could transfer its entire fleet to the Pacific and win the war almost immediately: two years later the Naval Staff concluded that 'The Japanese Fleet could not face the British Main Fleet in battle'. Herbert Richmond was the only admiral of that era to 'question the assumption that we are able to dominate the Pacific with a Washington standard of strength at sea based upon Singapore'.[63] Between 1927 and 1929, the pace of naval construction fell off and the naval balance moved against Britain, as France, Germany, Italy and the United States, however haltingly, began to rebuild their cruiser fleets. Nonetheless, in 1929 the Royal Navy was as well prepared to defend British maritime interests in Europe as ever before, and better able to do so outside Europe than since the 1890s. It was stronger than the US navy, able to fight an effective war against Japan and any one European navy, and ready to re-enter waters which it had been forced to abandon since the 1890s, be it the east China or the Baltic seas. The age of British maritime supremacy had not ended.

Britain possessed the greatest fleets in the world and the greatest capacity to build them. It is fashionable to overstate Britain's industrial decline and its effect on British power, to note economic weaknesses while ignoring strengths.[64] Between 1870 and 1940, to be sure, Britain's share of world manufacturing declined, and significantly so, but still it remained an industrial power. Only the United States outclassed Britain's economy and it did not use its industrial muscle to challenge the navy—it flexed it for no strategic purposes at all before 1940, and then to Britain's benefit. Until 1939 British armament industries remained world leaders, long after most civilian firms lost that status. Britain possessed one of the largest aviation industries, and the greatest base for mercantile construction. Nor were these sectors backward. Before 1914

Britain easily beat Germany in naval construction; after 1919 it built warships for half the unit cost incurred in the United States.[65] The quality of British military material was high. It made mistakes, its capacity had limits, this was true of every power.

Not that naval arms firms found the 1920s an easy time. After the war, they had more capacity than Britain could use except in a war. Since 1890 they had developed on the basis of large and continual orders; since 1914 they had expanded their plant and worked at full capacity. When these orders declined, those industries had to contract. Nor was this their only problem. All these firms possessed steel and civilian engineering plant or mercantile shipyards, which were linked to sectors in crisis. British steel and engineering firms sagged under external pressure while shipbuilders suffered, as the Treasury put it, from 'an excessive capacity of production in comparison to the world demand, tending to produce cut-throat competition'.[66] Production and profits were soft, unemployment and unused capacity high. From 1921 to 1929, Britain used only one third of its shipbuilding capacity of 1920, and scrapped half of the latter.[67] Yet still it retained the world's greatest shipyards and merchant marine. It never fully recovered its prewar mastery of these sectors, but its position rose significantly through the 1920s, especially against the United States. British yards produced on average 45 per cent of the world's new mercantile tonnage. Forty per cent of the world's mercantile marine flew the British flag, double that of the United States, greater than that of Japan and America combined. By 1929 Britain's mercantile fleet was far more modern than in 1920, and among the youngest in the world; 22.5 per cent of it, or four million tons, was completed between 1924 and 1929, by British yards. Alone of the prewar staple industries, the market share and capacity of British shipbuilding still dominated the world, nor did it lag in competitiveness and innovation. American war planners were uncomfortably aware of the consequences.[68]

The warship building sector could meet large and sudden demands. During the 1920s, the Admiralty continually monitored this to ensure that the industry could handle two fundamental requirements, if necessary at one and the same time—the 'capital ship' reconstruction programmes intended for the 1930s, and whatever crash construction might be needed for emergencies. In case of crisis, during 1920 the Admiralty intended to complete, over a 30 month period, four battleships and battle cruisers, eight cruisers, sixteen destroyers and a host of smaller craft.[69] In 1921 Britain had the power to do so, with one exception: because of a bottleneck in armour plate production, it could fit out no more than three 'capital ships' every three years.[70] The Washington Treaty threatened this power. During that conference Beatty emphasized the imperative need to keep the 'personnel of the Armament and Naval Shipbuilding Firms throughout the Country ... employed at their highly specialised work, without which the art of designing and the production of Capital Ships which are efficiently protected, armed and equipped cannot be effected'. The building holiday, Chatfield the Controller, feared, might mean 'the extinction of British Sea Power'. 'We have got to safeguard our power of building Navies at all costs'. Against a ten-year building holiday followed by large construction between 1931–41, the Admiralty preferred to keep plant and labour in constant use by building the same number of 'capital ships' at a steadier rate between 1922 and 1942. If not, it warned, Britain could only maintain the specialized capacity needed for reconstruction by subsidizing firms by £1 million a year, or else by £500,000 per year while providing another £50 million in capital investment.[71]

These predictions were overly pessimistic—indeed, exaggerated for political purposes—and other authorities had different views. The armament firms preferred a holiday followed by massive reconstruction. The Board of Trade concluded that

> With a large demand upon them likely to arise at end of long holiday period comparatively small subsidy would probably induce private works and yards to keep them in being to sufficient extent and do moderate amount of experimental work. Moreover this [ten year holiday] plan would retain element of competition which would be absent under alternative plan, since that would provide insufficient work for example for more than one armour plate mill. It appears that no great difficulty likely to be experienced in getting together staff and labour to meet large demand even at end of long holiday period. The limiting factor is plant.[72]

The truth lay between these views. With fewer subsidies than the Admiralty estimated, until 1930 firms retained enough plant to meet the 1931–41 reconstruction programme and conducted some expansion and experimentation. By 1930, however, the industry was far more fragile than the Board of Trade had expected. By 1934, after another arms limitation conference, all of the Admiralty's dire predictions came true, while skilled labour became the greatest bottleneck for naval rearmament.

By 1925, the Admiralty's demands for construction during crises had risen. It realized that Britain could not quite meet the worst possible case—the building needed to defeat France and Japan at sea while ensuring that at war's end, the Royal Navy would equal the US navy in size. Even the Admiralty, however, found this requirement unrealistic for 1925. It reduced its demands to the need to defeat Japan while still retaining equality with the USA in 'capital ships'. In the first twelve months of such a war, the Admiralty held, Britain must lay down and complete within a few years seven battleships and battlecruisers, two aircraft carriers, 30 cruisers, 40 destroyers and 32 submarines—more large warships than Britain produced in 1939–45. The Admiralty concluded that even sectors which depended entirely on naval orders possessed just enough capacity to meet these needs. Armour plate manufacturers, for example, could immediately produce 44,000 tons per year, and reach a maximum of 60,000 tons from their existing plant. In two to three years they could easily fit out this emergency fleet. In 1925 warship building capacity could handle the worst case—that was precisely the problem. There was far too much capacity for any lesser circumstance. Thus, the Admiralty calculated that during the 1930s the construction of fifteen 'capital ships' would require 18,000 tons of armour plate per year. It sought to keep enough firms alive to produce 26,000 tons of plate, with a maximum capacity, when plant was fully utilized, of 35–40,000 tons: enough to supply both the reconstruction programme and another simultaneous one of equal size for emergencies. Here it gained an unexpected if temporary bonus. Both in 1922–23 and 1925, when the five armour plate firms were asked to nominate two of their number for closure, all agreed to keep their plant open and to divide the orders. Meanwhile, sufficient capacity existed to meet the navy's needs for optics, directing systems, guns, heavy shell and most kinds of gun mounting.[73]

The Admiralty wished 'to secure retention of the various types of plant through the lean years between the present time and the 1931 replacement programme without undue expense and without losing our powers of expansion in event of war'.[74] Until 1929, by manipulating firms and accounting practices, it did so. Its arrangements varied from not cutting prices to the lowest possible level, or providing subsidies, so as to keep some firms hungry but living; to excluding others from the 'rings' of companies allowed to tender in closed markets; to the careful allocation of orders—concentrating contracts for certain items with specific concerns while dispersing others throughout the trade as a while. Such practices had substantial effects. As compensation to businesses for the cancellation of four battle cruisers after the Washington Conference, the Admiralty provided preferential access to contracts on *Nelson* and *Rodney* and £872,940 in compensation—more profit than those firms were likely to have made had the contracts been completed. In 1923 the Admiralty excluded the lowest bidder for armour plate from the ring of five firms allowed to tender for contracts, driving it from the trade. Later, the Admiralty guaranteed this ring £60,000 per year to maintain its capacity even if it received no orders.[75] During the 1920s many firms and skilled labourers left the warship-building business and the rest went on a diet, but still the Admiralty preserved the capacity to meet any threat. It overcame its only bottleneck—the fact that even when utilized 'under war conditions for production' existing plant could manufacture only the 16-inch gun turrets required for the 1931 replacement programme, with nothing to spare for any emergency programme of 'capital ships' —by convincing Messrs Vickers to double its capacity at its own expense.[76]

During the 1920s the naval arms industry received major orders. Between 1914 and 1920 it enjoyed profits which provided fat for lean times—in 1919 alone, the Admiralty spent £35 million on contract shipbuilding—and gave firms a reason to hold on. Between 1922 and 1926, the Royal Navy carried out large construction, above the norm of the years 1888 to 1914. It laid down on average 60,000 tons of warships per year —two battleships, fourteen cruisers,

two destroyers and ten submarines; at the same time it completed seven cruisers and six carriers left on the stocks. During the 1920s, the navy almost
always gave firms orders of £8 million per year (usually around £10 million)
for contract shipbuilding and naval armaments. Accounting for changes in
prices, this was close to the level between 1885 and 1900, though only about
half of that between 1909 and 1914.[77] To this figure must be added substantial
amounts for compensation and subsidies, which went directly into the profit
columns of companies. In 1926 Armstrong & Whitworth had £8 million in
naval orders on its books. In 1929 one contract to fit two cruisers with armour
gave Vickers £250,000. Such orders kept in profit the armament sections even
at an inefficient firm like Beardmore, while the accounts at its civilian businesses ran blood red. Vickers' gun and gun mountings shops enjoyed boom times.[78]

The Royal Navy's orders were the largest on earth, but so was Britain's warship-building industry, with a £100 million investment in plant during 1921.[79]
On their own, these orders could not sustain that sector. Yet they had to do so,
because the civilian components of warship-building firms collapsed. In 1919,
all these firms diversified, often making large capital investments in civilian
sectors, where they all suffered heavy losses. This, by the middle 1920s, combined with dividends and investment in new armament plant, eliminated the
financial reserves accumulated during the First World War. Meanwhile, foreign
munitions orders slipped and engineering and mercantile contracts barely met
the costs of material and labour. Naval orders alone gave shipbuilders a margin
for profit. The navy still offered 'cost-plus' contracts, paying labour and material costs up to a fixed limit with an allowance for overhead and profit. The latter varied from 5% for the battle cruiser contracts of 1921, to 15% for cruisers
in 1928.[80] After 1926, however, naval orders slackened and the industry sick-
ened. In both 1927 and 1928, only 34,000 tons of new warships started, (three
cruisers, eighteen destroyers and twelve submarines). Although in 1929 the
Baldwin Government authorized the laying down of 45,000 tons, after the election this was cancelled by the Labour Government. Between 1926 and 1929,
Britain used just 40–50 per cent of its naval armament capacity, even less in
specialized plant required only for battleships and submarines.[81] By 1925
Chatfield felt that 'provided peace continues the Armour Plate makers will be
in a very bad way until orders for battleships are started'. He was right. In
1925, armour manufacturers expected contracts for 2,500 tons per year until
1931 while the Admiralty hoped to procure 3,000 tons: in fact, 1133 tons were
ordered each year between 1925 and 1929.[82] Again, during the 1920s the
Admiralty allocated £10 million per year to the Royal Dockyards, but still several yards closed and their labour force shrank from 67,853 in November 1918
to 30,071 by October 1928.[83]

Firms endured these lean times only because they hoped that they would
feast in the 1930s—that the 'capital ship' replacement programme would work
precisely as the Admiralty planned. This, in turn, could happen only if governments continued to accept the Admiralty's policies. If firms did not receive

such a scale of orders, they would cut their capacity. Signs of danger emerged between 1926 and 1929, as difficult times and bad management drove one great firm, Armstrong & Whitworth, to the wall. The Admiralty declined extraordinary steps to help it, regarding most of its plant as surplus to naval needs and encouraging Vickers to absorb the rest. In itself, this decision was reasonable: British sea power could survive that company's wreck. More alarming was the context. Another major warship builder, Beardmore, almost went under for identical reasons. Even strong and efficient firms were weakening. Only the occasional naval order kept the great shipbuilder John Brown from collapse. The overall profitability and value of Vickers sagged by 1925, yet still it overextended itself by expanding capacity at the Admiralty's behest. By 1927 even Vickers could not keep up all its capacity without a guarantee of £300,000 per year in armament contracts or subsidies. Looming behind all this was deadly danger. By early 1929 the Bank of England and the industry were taking the first steps toward the establishment of National Shipbuilders Security Ltd and the scorched earth closure of capacity in the warship-building and allied industries. This would restore profitability for the survivors. It would also gut the industrial basis of maritime supremacy.[84]

An irony was emerging. During the 1920s Britain built as many new warships as it needed to match external threats—arguably, more than it needed. It allocated more money to arms firms than any other country and about half the amount, accounting for inflation, of before the war. Given the collapse of profitability in the civilian markets of the warship-building industry, however, these orders were too few to sustain the mouths to feed. While the short rations of 1927–29 were tolerable for a short period, the process could not continue much longer. The armament industries had grown up on a continual cycle of large orders, just as British naval power had rested on that unmatched capacity. If this cycle were broken for even just five years, that capacity would be cut back, and with it British maritime power. If the virtuous circle between the size of fleet, the scale of orders and the capacity of industry did not continue, a vicious one would emerge. Naval policy would no longer sustain the existing level of armament capacity, which would be cut, endangering Britain's ability to reconstruct the fleet and wrecking the basis of naval policy. By 1929 the navy really faced only two futures, though no contemporary fully recognized the situation. Either the Admiralty's policies would be followed, British sea power would retain its powerful position and build on it; or else catastrophe— naval policy would be overturned, and the finely tuned set of relationships between fleet, industry and security would tumble down. It was for these reasons that, in 1929–30, Britain turned abruptly from maritime security toward dangerous seas.

By 1929 the American Office of Naval Intelligence (ONI) concluded that before 1914, British

public opinion was to a great extent united in the support of whatever

Naval Policy the Admiralty brought forward, and they had little trouble
in obtaining Cabinet and Parliamentary approval of their programs ...
Since the War the power of the Admiralty within the Cabinet, although
still large, appears to have declined.

As proof, the ONI noted that Britain had laid down only 66 per cent of the
cruisers announced in 1924–25 and had accepted a form of parity with the US,
that some British figures advocated a change in blockade policy while the
Labour Party publicly accepted American views on naval limitation and blockade rights.[85] These observations were acute and similar to those proffered by
many British officers. Thus H.F.O. Oliver, commander of the Atlantic Fleet:

The Navy had suffered far greater losses in recent years from its enemies in this country and from apathy and general lack of interest
throughout the Kingdom than it has ever suffered in war since the days
of Charles II. While Naval thought is largely centred on probable
future war in the far East, our Enemies at home, assisted by public
indifference and a large section of the Press which misleads the people,
are steadily sapping the strength and efficiency of the Service.[86]

By 1929 the danger to the navy was internal rather than external, in the
realms of opinion and politics.

The problem was the scale of the Admiralty's programmes, combined with
the absence of threat to justify them. On his appointment as Chancellor of the
Exchequer in 1924, Churchill warned Baldwin of this equation. If enacted, the
navy's policies would

(a) prevent any appreciable relief of taxation during the present
Parliament,

(b) exclude any form of social legislation which involved finances, and

(c) present naval estimates of about 80 millions in 1928–29 as the main
issue for the consideration of the electorate. I believe that if this were
the course of events, we should have taken the most effective steps to
secure the return of the Socialist Administration, and the naval programme for which everything would have been sacrificed would thus
have been broken up before it was complete.[87]

While not right in every detail, this was a good prophecy of the events of
1929. Naval policy was eliminating the room for social reform, it was threatening to create new tensions with the United States and Japan, and it was endangering the chances for a balanced budget, international stability and the electoral success of the Government.

The costs of naval programmes rose steadily and astronomically. Thus, the
Admiralty understated the costs of the Singapore base and pursued a greater
scheme than it admitted. Even so, by January 1924, six months after the
scheme was defined in detail, Beatty recognized that its constant escalation in

expense left the Admiralty in a 'weak position'. While the official cost was estimated at £11 million, by current projections it would reach £21 million— close to the £30 million which the base's opponents claimed it would require. He cut these expenses back to £11 million. The same exercise had to be repeated in 1926.[88] Again, the Admiralty hoped to lay down seven 'capital ships', 21 cruisers, 48 submarines, 63 destroyers and a carrier, between 1931 and 1936, at enormous expense. In 1925–26 it agreed that this programme would cost £161,222,000 over six years, and take Naval Estimates to between £80– £85,000,000; almost 50% above its then level.[89]

Increasingly, the Admiralty concluded that politicians would not finance all these policies, and that something must be cut.[90] It did so first by shaving waste and easing readiness for immediate war, reducing complements for warships in service, placing more vessels in reserve, extending their lives and periods between refits. Still the problem remained. So the Admiralty took more serious measures—to slow the development of naval aviation forces and the Singapore base and to reshape its warships and its fleet. By 1926 the Naval Staff concluded, 'It is becoming evident every day that the Board of Admiralty will find it increasingly difficult in the future to persuade the Government to meet Naval Requirements, if the new men-of-war of the next decade have to be built to designs similar to those of the ships now under construction'. So to evade this dilemma, the Admiralty turned to arms limitation. Through an international agreement to further reduce the size and firepower of battleships and the number of Washington standard cruisers, it hoped to slash the reconstruction programme of 1931–40 by 25% in cost or £5 million per year.[91] The navy no less than Robert Cecil led Britain into the Geneva Naval Limitation Conference of 1927, a turning point for British sea power. One leading member of the Naval Staff justified this conference in words which echoed Churchill's views of 1924.

> ... unless something is done to reduce the estimates they will automatically in a few years reach a total which it does not seem within the bounds of possibility that we should be able to screw out of any Govt ... If we can get something concrete out of this conference it may make things considerably easier for the Admiralty when the next non-Conservative Government comes in.[92]

These efforts did not solve the problem. The Geneva Conference failed, the estimates required to support Beatty's programmes during the 1930s remained high and the level of threat low. In the stable circumstances of the later 1920s, 'liberal' views about international affairs were increasingly plausible among the masses and the elite. Not that 'liberals' were entirely brainless or absolutely dominant in British politics. 'Realists' were equally strong, while 'realist' and 'liberal' views co-existed in the minds of British statesmen. Typically, they thought that arms limitation, social reform, a great Britain and the greatest of fleets were all good things.[93] By the later 1920s, however, the power of 'liberal' views in British politics was rising. The world, it appeared, was at peace and becoming more so every day; the Washington and Locarno conferences seemed to show that 'liberal' means could solve international problems. The apparent need for the Admiralty's policies declined sharply, and those policies came to be seen as a source of danger.

There was an element of prophecy in Beatty's arguments about the Japanese menace: thus, in 1924 he stated that 'Should the whole position in the Pacific be re-considered in [1931], our diplomatic position would be much stronger if we had a base at Singapore capable of maintaining the Fleet.'[94] His case was unshakable regarding Japanese capabilities and the uncertainty of Tokyo's intentions over the long term, but weak in its emphasis on clear and present dangers. Throughout the 1920s, British Naval Attaches to Tokyo reported Japan to be unprepared for maritime aggression in the foreseeable future, and not even preparing for war with Britain. They were right.[95] By 1927 even the Admiralty no longer feared Japan as it had done in 1925. As the plausibility of this case collapsed, so did that of the policy which it had justified, while the sceptics came to be seen as prophets. In 1925 Churchill complained that, on the basis of predictions of 'Japan going mad and attacking us', the Admiralty had created 'far-reaching schemes of alarmist peril and consequential armament': that the Singapore base was simply 'a gigantic excuse for building up arma-ments'.[96] By 1927 this view was common and the consequences were danger-ous. Thus, in 1924–25 the Foreign Office favoured much of Beatty's policy. Even so, it denied that Japan would threaten Britain during the foreseeable future—the Foreign Secretary during Baldwin's second administration, Austen Chamberlain, could 'conceive of no subject which ought to range us in hostile camps, and still less can I think of war between Japan and the British Empire'—and feared that large-scale construction might make Tokyo regard Britain as a threat.[97] On this topic diplomats became increasingly hostile to sailors. By 1926 Chamberlain believed that

> The Admiralty is obsessed with the thought of what is to be done in the case of an imaginary war with Japan. This obsession is dangerous and causes me anxiety for they insist on behaving as if such a war were imminent and I cannot help feeling they had persuaded themselves that it is so.[98]

During 1925–27 the Cabinet rejected the Admiralty's views of Japan and cut the programmes directed against it —which, given Beatty's politics, meant virtually every naval programme. Soon much of Whitehall turned even more sharply against the Admiralty on another issue. Between 1927–29, after the Geneva conference, blockade rights and naval limitation became controversial points in Anglo-American relations and in Whitehall. Again, this directly affected the navy's policies. Baldwin's Government restrained naval construc-tion between 1927 and 1929, partly to cut expenses, mostly to reduce tensions with Washington. During these years it laid down only half the cruisers approved in 1925. Much to the Admiralty's anger, the Cabinet considered radical changes in blockade rights, and planned, had it won the election of 1929, to pursue a settlement with Washington over maritime matters.[99] Meanwhile, the Labour Party came out openly in favour of accepting American terms on these issues.

This did not stem from fear of the United States. Between 1922 and 1928 the Royal Navy laid down three times as many tons of new warships as the USA. No figures in Whitehall or in Baldwin's Government believed that America would spend for superiority; this idea scarcely even affected Labour's views in 1929–30. Officials, admirals and politicians routinely recognized that if it wished, the United States could outbuild Britain: none of them thought that it would. Even the greatest exponents of concessions to Washington, like Cecil, denied that 'any serious student of American ways' could expect the United States to build for superiority in the absence of extreme provocation.[100] The Admiralty evinced some fear of the United States in 1920. It was scornful by 1927. Thus the First Lord, William Bridgeman: 'Possible they will build one as large as ours, which would not be very alarming. Possibly they might go still further and have a larger Navy than ours, but such a course would fall in time of its own weight, as do most megalomaniac policies'.[101] Beatty described the US navy's position at the Geneva Conference as 'the most gigantic bluff on the part of the Americans to acquire Command of the Sea without having to pay for it or fight for it'. Pound and Churchill noted that the US navy demanded parity with Britain in cruisers but knew that it could not receive the money necessary to build up to the British level. Hence, it wanted Britain to cut down to a level which Congress would finance.[102]

Fear of the United States scarcely entered British decisions in 1927–30; neither did any narrow maritime concern at all. The aims, instead, were to nip problems with Washington a decade before they came to bud and to keep up the momentum toward the creation of a liberal, peaceful and stable world. British Governments believed that an arms race over cruisers might begin within a few years, and create dangerous relations with the United States. They were also tempted to buy American diplomatic support for arms limitation and for international reconciliation conducted through the League of Nations by cashing in on some of their high level of security at sea. Under these circumstances, 'liberal' views could easily be reconciled with maritime security—since the dangers had declined, so could the fleet. Indeed, one could plausibly argue that a large and sudden development of naval strength would actually increase the threat. To 'liberals', the greatest dangers to British security were 'realism' and navalism.

Nor was the Admiralty's only problem a sea change in attitudes toward security. Its political position was collapsing. Frequently between the wars, one British department of state acquired extraordinary political power and used that aggressively against the rest, which all countered by joining to smash its pretensions and policy. This happened to the War Office in 1919–21, to the

Treasury and the Foreign Office after 1936, and to the Admiralty in 1928–30. From 1923, the Admiralty's policies and its pretensions to be their only arbiter increasingly antagonized Westminster and Whitehall. It was, in effect pursuing maritime supremacy, when most of the country would settle for security. The Admiralty became notorious for leaking material to the press in order to defeat its rivals and the Board for threatening to resign unless its demands were met.[103] The Admiralty continually and often unfairly attacked the RAF and the Treasury. When politicians challenged naval policy, Beatty's response was intransigent and ill considered. He informed the Labour Government in 1924 that should the navy be forbidden to prepare against either the USA or Japan, 'it would be better to carry out that policy in toto and scrap at least half the British navy and save the taxpayers the cost of upkeep'. In 1925 Beatty reminded ministers that when they disagreed with the Admiralty's policies, they had only three choices—to accept its policy, or replace the Board, or publicly abandon the one power standard. 'We say: "We are very sorry: we say that your policy is an expensive one—you must change your policy and have a cheaper one"'.[104] Four years later they took his advice.

These arguments were dangerous and so was the attitude. They led figures like Warren Fisher and Cecil to complain that the Admiralty rejected the principles of civilian control. Beatty had the power to survive these dangers, but he left Madden in an exposed position. Even right wing Conservative politicians, such as Lord Salisbury and the retired Admiral Reginald Hall, criticized the Admiralty's demands and its manner. As Salisbury said, sailors 'are splendid people, but their notion of an argument closely resembles an order from the quarter-deck, and it puts them off if everybody does not fall in with it'. Cecil, a supporter of the Navy during its troubles in 1919 and 1925, became a bitter foe. The Admiralty enraged even Churchill who, contrary to the conventional view, was the Navy's stalwart friend.[105] These problems were even greater in Whitehall than Westminster. By 1925, in order to avenge past wrongs, the Air Ministry and the Treasury were trying to wreck naval policy. Treasury officials hoped that the Board would honour its threats to resign—as Barstow put it, only thus 'can the Govt. ever hope to control these unruly boys in blue'.[106] Meanwhile, from 1927 the Admiralty and the Foreign Office came to bitter blows over blockade rights and arms limitation.[107] In January 1930 William Tyrrell, just retired as Permanent Under Secretary to the Foreign Office, told the Labour politician Hugh Dalton, 'The Admiralty always tried to have a foreign policy of their own'. Tyrrell recalled how Madden had said ' "You are no better than a pacifist"' during the blockade rights controversy. Dalton also recorded that Cecil, Tyrrell and Arthur Salter, insiders all,

> have all said to me recently that until the Sea Lords are allowed to resign, we shall never see the politicians really on top of the Admiralty. They had always been allowed to bluff so far, and they have learned to calculate, to a nicety, just when and how to threaten

resignation. They are gallant fellows, in the simplest sense, but they are for the most part weak in logic, when it threatens the foundation of their traditions, but less weak in certain kinds of political and press intrigue.[108]

These were precisely the complaints which the Treasury had been making since 1923. By 1929, they were widely expressed across Whitehall and Westminster.

In 1929 all of the challenges to naval policy were embodied in the Labour Government's pursuit of disarmament. Labour, just as it claimed, approached that issue in a new way. The Lloyd George and Baldwin Governments had favoured arms limitation, but only as pragmatic solutions to specific difficulties and only after ensuring that the fine print sustained British interests. Labour acted from ideology rather than expediency. It did not want just arms limitation: it wanted disarmament, which it saw as a universal answer to general questions. Labour's doctrine, in the Gladstonian manner, joined evangelical Protestantism and liberal idealism to ambitious policy. As Prime Minister in 1924, Ramsay MacDonald had hoped that his decision to cancel the Singapore base might spark a World Disarmament Conference.[109] On returning to office in 1929, he picked up where he had left off. He described himself as struggling against 'all the devilish powers' which led to arms races. 'This parity business is of Satan himself'. He wished to reduce international military requirements for security 'to zero by making nations secure by other means than armaments'.[110]

> The question now is whether we are going to welcome the prospect that is offered to us in a wide and generous spirit, or whether, by adopting a purely traditional attitude towards problems which have lost much of the significance of former years, we are going to risk the loss of a mighty accretion to our security and prestige in the years to come.[111]

Similarly, his Foreign Secretary, Arthur Henderson, scorned the Admiralty for pursuing security only through 'ships and guns', for failing to realize

> that national security is not simply the result of an armament situation; it is also a political condition ... True security can only result from the avoidance of war ... Every diminution in the risk of future war gives an obvious increase in national security, and an increase which armaments cannot give ... in the risk of a world-war lies the greatest danger to the integrity and security of the British Empire ... no British Government can now accept the proposition that Imperial security depends upon the possession of a fixed minimum amount of armament or upon the guarantees furnished by our national armaments alone. If we reduce our armaments under International Treaty, our relative position remains as strong as it was before ... the risks of a policy of peace

are less than the risks which future war would bring. Imperial security can best be promoted by the prevention of war through the patient and systematic organisation of peace. To this end a general reduction of national armaments is the most important single measure.[112]

These ministers hoped that further naval limitation would pave the road to a world disarmament conference, and that, they believed, was the only way to establish a better means than force in international affairs. They chose to run risks in pursuit of this aim, and to attack the Admiralty's policies head on. Nor were they without friends. Whitehall's strongest departments, the Foreign Office and the Treasury, wished to see the Admiralty beaten and supported Labour's attempts to do so. The Foreign Office co-ordinated Labour's onslaught in Whitehall. Meanwhile, the Admiralty had no allies beyond a few Conservative politicians like Churchill. It fought with all its strength — Madden did not fail because he was less able and resolute than Beatty, but because he faced too many enemies and a determined Prime Minister. In 1924 MacDonald had beaten Beatty on naval policy. In 1929–30 he did not fear threats that admirals might resign, which Madden's Board did hint at several times.[113]

In June through August 1929 the Board,knowing that it must respond to Labour's insistence on arms limitation, proposed a variant of Britain's position at Geneva in 1927. The Washington Treaty should be altered to ban further construction of 8-inch gun cruisers and to cut the size of new 'capital ships' by one third, to 25,000 tons and 12-inch guns. The Board also hinted at reductions in the numbers of 'capital ships' due to be built between 1931–36. With reluctance, it agreed to reduce from 70 to 60 the cruisers it wanted to be kept in service, by sacrificing ten overage ones in reserve. Madden, however, insisted on 'a definite and steady programme of New Construction' to provide security for Britain and its arms firms. Three cruisers, nine destroyers and six submarines should be laid down every year, and one 'capital ship' every 12 to 18 months. His aim 'is to secure a steady programme on a scale which will eventually produce the number of ships required and subsequently maintain them at that level, accepting the fact that the number of ships under age in certain classes will for a time fall below standard requirements'.[114] In hindsight, this package was reasonable, and close to the optimum for Britain. It would have limited arms while still providing a margin for security. The addition of just a few 'capital ships' to the other warships laid down between 1931–36 would have saved a large part of the warship-building capacity lost during that period. Yet this package did not suit MacDonald. He saw no dangers at sea, he was not impressed by Madden's technical arguments and he did want an arms treaty. That could not be done on Britain's terms of 1927. It might be possible on American terms. So over the coming months MacDonald adopted them: he cut the number of cruisers which Britain would keep in service to 50 and he accepted wholesale American views on 'capital ships'. He also abandoned the

Admiralty's proposals for qualitative limits on battleships and 8-inch gun cruisers rather than clash with Washington over them. He told his First Lord, A.V. Alexander, however, that he might accept the Admiralty's views on other technical points, and continue some new construction.[115]

The Board faced a dilemma. It could not point to any immediate, plausible and major threat—it did not even try to make such a case and agreed that 'under existing circumstances some relaxation of strategical requirements can be accepted'.[116] Yet the Admiralty did not believe that threat was absent just because it was invisible. Madden told the Government that Britain's fleet was 'obsolescent' and 'wearing out'. Since 1927 it had been 'relatively losing ground' in new construction. Other states had 'buil[t] up a modern fleet of the types to meet their special requirements, whilst our programmes had perforce had to be restricted, in spite of the fact that what other Powers build becomes a potential danger to ourselves unless countered by similar craft'. The Royal Navy faced several navies, each tailor-made to pursue specialised aims in specific seas. It had to maintain a large and general purpose fleet able to handle each of these foes at its selected time and place, while simultaneously deterring hostile actions by other powers.

> Our defensive measures compel in us a degree of dispersion and we could therefore scarcely avoid inferiority in the critical theatre. It is clear, therefore, that if the growing strength of other Powers cannot be checked, ours must be increased ... At the present rate the outcome of naval disarmament will be to reduce us step by step to the level of the others, and if we refuse to face the necessity of future construction, we shall finally be inferior ... We are endeavouring to balance good intentions here against naval expansion abroad. Unfortunately the good intentions have nothing behind them.

Other nations were 'building the largest and most powerful types of auxiliary vessels ... we are talking of the Pact of Paris, Disarmament, and lasting peace'.[117] Madden distorted the immediate danger, but he did provide a prescient warning of the risks at stake five years ahead should the disarmament gamble fail. His arguments were not convincing because Britain's immediate maritime position was too strong, as was Labour's faith that its gamble would succeed. Beatty had cried wolf so often that Madden was ignored when at last the beast hove in sight.

The Admiralty disliked MacDonald's negotiating position. It saw the American proposal which initially underlay discussions, the 'Yardstick' to determine the relative value of cruisers, as a trick. Madden feared 'that when we give way to US on Cruiser parity & the Freedom of the Seas, we will be pressed to commercial treaties drafted to suit US & to our disadvantage'.[118] These concerns were strengthened by the bad faith and bad management in Washington's response to MacDonald's overtures and by the nature of his bargaining. MacDonald was more realistic than many of his colleagues, composed, as he said, of '50 per cent. caution and 50 per cent. ideal desire'.[119] He was willing to hear the Admiralty's technical arguments, so long as they accepted his policy. As time went on he gained respect for his admirals. He resented and fought off American attempts to gain still further advantages over cruisers. Yet he was bound on agreement, his bargaining was soft and sometimes he was manipulated. In his meeting with President Hoover of October 1929, so eager for agreement was MacDonald that he almost wrecked British blockade rights: even his leading colleagues Snowden and Henderson vetoed his proposals.[120] The Admiralty understood horse trading and had prepared for it —in January 1929 Madden declined to scrap a few older 'Town' class cruisers simply to retain them 'for bargaining purposes at a naval conference'. Ironically, this increased MacDonald's real embarrassment—the strength of his hand. As he told the American ambassador, 'At the moment the bulk of your cruiser strength is in a programme; ours is on the water'.[121] The Prime Minister could not get an agreement by trading horses, only by shooting them.

MacDonald strove not to strengthen his hand but to weaken it. He suspended two cruisers started in 1928 and cancelled two announced for 1929 in return for the suspension of just two American; later he scrapped two 'Town' class cruisers without demanding any quid pro quo. For bargaining purposes he equated British cruisers at sea with American warships half of which existed only on paper, with half the remainder incomplete. Then, he accepted the basic American demand: to produce parity in cruisers at the maximum number the United States would match rather than the minimum number Britain needed in case of peril. As Alexander and MacDonald realized, 'we could only get down to 50 by 1936 by premature scrapping' —specifically of eighteen 6-inch gun cruisers and four 'Hawkins' class cruisers (mounting 7.5-inch guns).[122] So strong was Britain's position, even after all this massaging of numbers, that mathematical parity with the United States was possible only by scrapping prematurely almost half the British cruisers at sea. This change in the maritime balance sparked new demands from other naval powers and forced Britain to beg concessions from four capitals. In return for these self-imposed difficulties, no other navy scrapped one useful cruiser.

None of this pleased the Sea Lords: neither did their option. If they rejected MacDonald's demands and resigned, they could not change his policy. They might drive him toward ministers who were even more hostile toward the navy, like Henderson and Snowden. MacDonald himself flirted with the idea of abolishing 'capital ships'. He was suspicious of sailors, warning Alexander to beware 'that your experts are not controlling you more than you imagine', fearing that the new construction which the Admiralty insisted on as a condition for limiting its strength to 50 cruisers was 'increasing the fighting efficiency of the Navy so that ... it is more formidable than it would be if we had more ships with a total efficiency for war purposes of a decidedly lower level than our fleet will be in 1936'.[123] Alternately, the Board could accept MacDonald's basic policy and try to prevent further damage in the details, which was

Alexander's approach. With reluctance, sailors accepted the London Naval Treaty as an agreement to last until 1936, after which Britain could pursue its old policy. The Government recognized that the Admiralty regarded this agreement as 'an absolute minimum and acceptable for the purposes of this agreement only in view of the prevailing international conditions'.[124] In political terms this was the Admiralty's best option. MacDonald did abandon some of his radical proposals and he did support some new construction but all this came at a price.[125] The policy which the Admiralty had pursued since 1920 was reversed. British strength at sea declined, that of its potential threats remained constant or else grew, and the navy took the fork in the road leading to maritime peril rather than power.

Judgement on these issues cannot be simple, since they embrace everything from diplomacy to industry, relative strength in several types of warships, perceptions, power, and might have beens. The London Treaty was part of a strategic gamble. By taking a risk at sea, one which seemed small, MacDonald hoped to jump-start a systematic settlement of world troubles through the disarmament conference at Geneva. This explains his soft bargaining with Hoover: concessions on cruisers were intended to buy some American support at Geneva, and it did so. Had this gamble paid off, the gains would have been enormous and the stake recovered. Nor was it doomed to fail. But fail it did and the stake proved greater than MacDonald had assumed. He believed that if the worst came to the worst by 1936, Britain could 'expand our fleet to any standard required before 1939'. He was wrong. He was 'really worried by the industrial aspect' of deferring the construction of 'capital ships' until 1937; he wished to preserve 'a sort of nucleus' in capacity for this purpose.[126] He did not know that this nucleus was near to collapse or that the London Treaty would trigger it. He exaggerated the power of the liberal international order and did not realize that the very fact of his gamble would weaken it. Stability reigned during the 1920s largely because 'liberal' and status quo powers—Britain, the United States, France and Japan—dominated the seas. The London Conference crippled armed liberalism at sea. Japan became a greater sea power but no longer a 'liberal' one; the relative strength of Germany and Italy rose and between 1929 and 1935 debates over disarmament produced more mistrust between Britain and France than any other factor.

In purely naval terms, the London Treaty was a mediocre deal for Britain, though a mixed one. In 1921 arms limitation was an effective means to secure concrete British interests under real challenge. It had not reduced British sea power more than construction by other powers was doing. In 1929 there was no arms race, no concrete challenge to British sea power and no reason to expect either. Britain had no imperative maritime need even for a favourable arms limitation agreement, and the London Treaty was not drafted to suit British interests. It multiplied all the aspects of Washington which were bad for Britain and weakened the Royal Navy more than any other. Again, this worked in a complex fashion, varying with warship type, foreign rival or time period.

The Royal Navy's immediate strength slipped only marginally, but the potential legacy was the possibility of real danger at sea for the first time in a century and a quarter. By 1936, if MacDonald's gamble failed, Britain's margin for security against the Japanese and any European navy would be razor thin. If it came to the worst, it would be condemned to large naval rearmament conducted by weak industrial capacity, and the price of failure would be high.

The London Treaty had no effect on aircraft carriers or Britain's strength in naval aviation. It did, however, gut British power in 'capital ships'. Against the Admiralty's objections, the 'building holiday' was extended to 1936.[127] No new 'capital ships' were to be laid down until 1937, and those which were to have been replaced during that period were, instead, immediately scrapped. This brought the British, US, and Japanese navies to a 15:15:9 ratio in 1930 and compromised Britain's two power standard of 1922. Britain scrapped five battleships and battle cruisers—obsolete, sure enough, but still a match for those of Italy and Germany combined until 1938. It had few 'capital ships' and these were, on average, the oldest among the leading fleets (17.7 years in 1936), followed closely by those of the United States (17 years). At their prime in the 1920s, these British warships had been the strongest at sea. By 1929 their individual strength was on the wane. Excluding *Nelson*, *Rodney* and to some degree *Hood*, they were designed to meet circumstances twenty years gone, and unsuited in incorporate developments in engines, ordnance, armour and airpower. Their design characteristics were well below the state of the art and increasingly difficult to maintain even at their original level. The older the warship, the lower its efficiency, the more its need for refits and the fewer of them in service during crises. Once crises became common, the circle became even more vicious, as the Admiralty was increasingly reluctant to take 'capital ships' out of commission for refits, which hastened the tempo of their decline. Accounting for refits, during the 1920s the navy had 16 to 18 'capital ships' in commission at any one time: only 11 or 12 between 1933–39, with the elimination of 25 per cent of their strength and the greater age of the survivors. When considering the replacement of 'capital ships' after the London Treaty, the Admiralty concluded that *Repulse* and *Renown* would have to be serving when they were 34 years old.[128] Japanese 'capital ships', on average 15 years old during 1936 and still in the prime of their lives, suffered least from these problems among the major fleets. France and Italy remained free under the Washington Treaty to build new battleships and battle cruisers, while Germany or the Soviet Union might also resume the construction of 'capital' or 'semi-capital' ships. The London Treaty sharply reduced Britain's relative strength in 'capital ships'—between 1930 and 1936 it might easily cease to match the Japanese and any European fleet in such warships—and it automatically produced another problem. If MacDonald's gamble failed, by 1937, at the end of their operational lives, these British 'capital ships' would have to race European ones entering the days of their youth and Japanese ones in far better condition. Meanwhile the construction of new battleships might start out years behind those of Italy, France and Germany.

The Treaty also hampered the navy's strength in cruisers, to a lesser degree and in a complex way. Britain agreed to scrap 24 cruisers between 1930 and 1936 and to have only 50 of 339,000 tons in 1936—well below the strength of 1929 or that which the Admiralty hoped to maintain afterward. Yet some of the advantages of 1929 were a wasting asset. Half of its cruisers of 1929 were designed for North Sea service and were wearing out. Even with optimistic assumptions about new construction, the Admiralty believed that in 1936, it would have only 62 cruisers in commission.[129] By January 1929 the Naval Staff saw no point even in trying to extend the lives of the cruisers which were to be scrapped prematurely under the London Treaty, except the four 'Hawkins': 'the really important thing is to get on with new construction, for which all the money that can be obtained should be allocated'.[130] In fact, this assessment was premature. Some of these cruisers were well suited to naval problems in Europe of 1935–40 and had they been lost, judgement would be severe; but this point is moot. When the Treaty was renegotiated in 1936, Britain kept in service the eight best of these 24 cruisers, all it could man. Hence, by 1936 Britain possessed 58 cruisers, rather than 50, almost as many as it had hoped to maintain in that year before the London Treaty and almost as modern. The Treaty authorized Britain to build 91,000 tons of new cruisers between 1930–36 and the Government exercised that right. This level of new cruiser tonnage was not impressive—only 50% of the annual figure between 1924–29 and no more than that which Conservative ministers, including Churchill, had expected to meet between 1929–34 had they won the 1929 election—but it was real.[131]

In 1928 Britain possessed the largest and the most modern fleet of cruisers and superiority in the most powerful of them. It matched the US and Japanese navies in these warships. Under the London Treaty, all of these edges declined. On average, by 1936 its cruisers were smaller and less well armed than those of other powers. The Royal Navy maintained its numerical ratio of 1929 over Japan's 29 cruisers, but not over those of Japan and any European navy. Between 1925 and 1936 all the European fleets built many heavy cruisers. In 1929 France had ten modern cruisers built or building, Italy twelve and Germany five. By 1933 these strengths were, respectively, eighteen, nineteen, and nine. This quantitative problem was multiplied by a qualitative one, the effect of cheating on tonnage by other powers combined with Britain's need to sacrifice armour for range so to meet the 10,000 tons displacement. Admiralty technical staff held that only on a displacement of 13,000 tons could a cruiser carry the armour and guns needed to make an effective fighting platform.[132] This was the tonnage of many German, Japanese and Italian cruisers. Thus, Japan's twelve 8-inch gun cruisers arguably had the same combat value as their fifteen British equivalents. By 1936 Britain's strength in cruisers barely equalled that of the Italian navy and Japan's. Its cruisers were inferior in combat capability to one third of those of Japan, half those of France, Italy and the

United States, and most German ones.

The London Treaty established parity between the Royal Navy and the US navy in main fleets, though not other components of sea power. Its effect, however, is best measured by comparing the Royal Navy to the Japanese and any European navy. Here, Britain's margin for security in heavy surface warships decayed. As Madden noted, 'even preserving a 5:3 ratio, the smaller the total numbers [of 'capital ships'] the smaller would be our margin, and the more serious would be the loss of a single ship'. In order to maintain equality with the IJN in a war launched at its selected moment, Britain would have to despatch 12 'capital ships', five aircraft carriers and 46 cruisers to the Pacific and trade protection/blockade stations. This would leave a fleet in Europe of just four cruisers, one carrier and no 'capital ships' at all until some of those under reconstruction were readied, which might take months.[133] In the early 1930s, Britain could perhaps take this risk against the small French and Italian fleets of obsolescent 'capital ships' or Germany's few 'semi-capital ships'. The tide, however, turned fast. Between 1930 and 1936, Germany, France and Italy each frequently laid down more new warship tonnage per year than Britain. In particular, between 1929 and 1932 Germany laid down the three 'Deutschland' class cruisers while Italy modernized two battleships and started seven cruisers. This situation became even worse in 1934–36, when Italy laid down two new battleships and Germany four, long before Britain could begin to reciprocate under the London Treaty. By this time, despatching to Singapore a fleet equal to the Japanese would be a major risk.

If MacDonald's gamble failed, the London Treaty would start to hamper British security only around 1934. The London standard of strength was tolerable in 1929. Unfortunately, Britain remained frozen at that standard until 1939. It could not begin large scale rearmament at sea until the Treaty ended. Thus, not until 1937 could it start to build 'capital ships' which incorporated the lessons of 1916. Not until 1939 did the first of its post-Treaty warships enter service and the quantity and quality of its fleet began to pass the London standard. The Treaty, of course, was not the only cause of these difficulties, nor did they end with warships. In 1929 the Labour Government cancelled the Singapore base, precisely as it was beginning. Only £1,600,000 of the £8,700,000 authorised had been spent and work on the heart of the base had not begun. About 30 per cent of the £1,991,000 programme for land defences had been spent or allocated. The base, in the Chief of the Imperial General Staff's words, was 'virtually undefended', and the fighting services were divided on how to protect it.[134] All this, followed by the National Government's unwillingness to restore the programme, left the navy no better able to operate in the Pacific during 1935 than in 1925. Its ability to handle even normal problems declined. Between 1929 and 1934 Naval Estimates fell 15 per cent below the average of 1924–29 and expenditure on new construction by 25 per cent. Given the deadweight of non-effective expenses like pensions and the cost of maintenance, the navy had little disposable income to invest in any new areas of policy.

The consequences were dire. In 1929 the British fleet was as modern as any. By 1936 it was among the world's oldest. Warships which had stood top of their class were worn out; a fleet strong enough to meet the most serious of probable threats was so weak that any possible threat was serious. In 1928 there was no German navy while Britain safely could ignore the Italian navy. By 1936 many Italian and German warships were better than British ones and either fleet combined with Japan was a match for Britain. The Royal Navy no longer had the ability even on paper to fight Japan and any one European power simultaneously. The resources required to block a maritime threat in one hemisphere would eliminate the ability to handle a threat in the other. In 1900 only when every other seapower joined forces was Britain at risk. By 1936 any seapower could endanger Britain. Any rival which challenged Britain would find an ally; any crisis with one naval power was likely to trigger another.

This created dangers in case of war and rearmament. By 1936, virtually all the navy's 'capital ships' would suffer from block obsolescence and require replacement as a whole at once. So too would one third of its cruisers and half its carriers and destroyers. The simultaneous replacement of 75 per cent of the Royal Navy's warship tonnage would take some time, during which the fleet would consist of obsolete warships and not enough of them. In 1936, eleven of its battleships would be 20 years old or more and yet they would have to remain the heart of British sea power until 1940. And all this effort would merely replace dying warships—only when that was over could the fleet expand.

In order to handle these needs, Britain would have to lay down far more tonnage per year even than under the original 1931–41 replacement programmes. Its warship-building industries of 1928 could easily have handled that level of orders. By 1930 a combination of the London Treaty, the great depression and National Shipbuilders Security destroyed this capacity. In 1929 the Admiralty warned MacDonald

> how the productive capacity for naval material in this country has shrunk until it depends on the continuance of a few firms who alone possess the specialized plant and the skilled and experienced staff of workpeople required for the purpose. The danger that an entire cessation of naval orders may lead to the extinction of such productive capacity as still exists is one of the most serious matters for consideration in connection with this question.[135]

Since 1921 the Admiralty had encouraged warship-building firms to keep great capacity despite low profits. Firms had tolerated this situation on the assumption that the civilian market could get no worse while major rearmament would begin in 1931. During 1929–30, however, the naval and civilian markets simultaneously collapsed in an unprecedented fashion. Britain's shipbuilding industry was marked by an absence of orders, an increasingly desperate search for business and a direct relationship between naval contracts and the health of a firm.[136] The industry began to vanish: by 1933 new mercantile orders fell to 10 per cent of the level of 1929.[137] Meanwhile, the construction authorized under the London Treaty was too small to substitute for the extension of the building 'holiday'. The industry had expected orders for 75,000 tons of warships or more each year between 1931–36. By 1930 it knew that it could receive 20,000 tons annually, and only if the Government built up to treaty limits—precisely the assumption that had got firms into this fine mess. They responded rationally to these expectations. Half the British shipbuilding capacity was scrapped between 1929 and 1935; for example, the numbers of slipways able to hold warships the size of destroyers and above fell by 57 per cent, from 459 to 266. In 1920 the total workforce in the shipbuilding industry was 338,000; in 1930, over 200,000 and by 1935, 161,000.[138] The naval armaments industry contracted sharply as well.

In 1928 weak warship-building firms were going under: by 1930 strong ones became weak. During 1929, the Admiralty warned that Vickers-Armstrongs had become Britain's sole source 'for the production of much essential Naval material and without whose continued existence it would be almost impossible for the requirements of the Fleet to be met in any serious emergency'. If construction was cut, Vickers might close much of its plant, especially its specialist submarine business and one of its two heavy gun mounting works—just built, under Admiralty pressure, to handle the 1931–41 reconstruction programme— and slash its work force by 4000 men, losing irreplaceable skilled workers and designers. Most of these warnings came true. By 1934, at the start of the rearmament period, Vickers was gravely wounded and yet far stronger than any other arms firm.[139] As with firms, so with capacity. Again in 1929, before Labour entered office, three of Britain's five manufacturers of armour plate merged under Vickers-Armstrong. With the Admiralty's blessing it scrapped 40 per cent of that plant. One year later, after the London Treaty, the Admiralty reduced the capacity which it endeavoured to keep in being by another 25 per cent and encouraged 'the firms to carry out further rationalization, if they desire and find it practicable to do so'. In the space of 18 months Britain's capacity for the production of armour plate shrank from a maximum of 40,000 tons to 18,000 tons per year. Yet by the later 1930s requirements for armour plate surged back toward 60,000 tons per year. The consequences were obvious. Only by working at maximum stretch could the armour plate manufacturers fit out many heavy warships and with no room for error. It could not meet the reconstruction necessary for the worst case without expanding its plant, a task requiring several years.[140] All these developments, in turn, changed the results of the Admiralty's industrial strategy. The latter had preserved massive capacity throughout the 1920s but by starving all the arms firms contributed inadvertently to disaster in 1929–30. These firms lacked the strength to survive a famine. So most of them left the market, two thirds of the way to the time when they would all be needed.

Much of this damage would have occurred without the London Treaty, nor did the latter create all of the former. The Treaty did not prevent the navy from laying down new aircraft carriers, but still it did not do so before 1937. The Treaty, along with the depression, was just one of two blows which hit the navy in 1929. It is hard to distinguish the effect of one blow from the other, and yet each was crippling. The depression alone might have prevented the reconstruction programme from beginning in 1931, and simultaneously have made it even more necessary to the warship-building industry's survival. Nor did the National Government favour large expenditures on rearmament before 1935. With or without the London Treaty, naval construction would not have been particularly sizeable and much armament capacity would have evaporated by 1935. Had Baldwin's Government won the 1929 election, it too would have pursued a naval settlement with Washington, though probably a better one. Nonetheless, without the Labour Government and the London Treaty, the Singapore base would have been further developed by 1934 and naval rearmament might have begun earlier than it did, and on the basis of a larger fleet. Conversely, had the London Treaty occurred but not the great depression, on the average level of mercantile orders of the 1920s more of this warship-building capacity might have survived, easing the rearmament bottleneck of 1936.

Nor did the events of 1929–30 necessarily doom British sea power. In 1934 British maritime power was considerable. The quality of Royal Naval personnel and doctrine was high and that of its equipment tolerable. Britain's ravaged naval armaments industries were still the largest on earth. The downward spiral of sea power had halted and conceivably from that base an upward spiral could have restored the virtuous circle of the prewar era. From 1936 the Admiralty was free to pursue its policies of the 1920s —indeed, more ambitious ones: in effect, a two power standard excluding the US navy, with an additional margin in cruisers. In 1939 the Royal Navy was far stronger than any other single navy and its lead was increasing. Had the Second World War not broken out until 1942, its relative position would have been rather better than it was in 1939; the RN believed that it could virtually restore Pax Britannica at sea by 1950. The problem was that in 1929–30, the margin of maritime strength was cut too far for quick recovery, while the National Government's dithering delayed the start of that process. In the 1930s Britain still possessed the resources needed to re-establish its maritime security. It lacked the time needed to harness them.

The story of British seapower during the 1920s is not the conventional one of continued and unbroken decline. It is a story of marginal rise above the norm between 1890–1914, followed by an abrupt fall. The causes of this phenomenon, too, are less simple than is often supposed—after all, they produced not merely the fall but the rise. Two putative explanations should be thrown on the scrap-heap of historiography. Fear of American power had little to do with British actions, much less so than did Britain's desire to convince Washington to support a liberal and stable world order. Nor did the limits to Britain's economic and financial strength produce the collapse of the navy. The opposite is just as true: it was the navy's collapse which crippled British industrial capacity for seapower.

The greater causes are the effect of ideas, attitudes, and politics, but they require sophisticated treatment. One cannot say, as is often said, that 'liberal' ideas or the League of Nations Union or the power of the Treasury or the desire to finance social reform or naval limitation treaties continually crippled naval policy—indeed, one cannot even say that all of these factors had this effect most of the time. They did not prevent the Admiralty from completing expensive programmes in the 1920s. They simply moderated those programmes, reducing their projected expenditure by perhaps a third, and these projections were larger than necessary in the first place. The Admiralty received all the funding it needed between 1919–21 and arguably so too between 1922–27. 'Liberal' ideas or the desire for social reform always affected naval policy but they really dominated it for only a few years, between 1929 and 1932. Throughout most of the 1920s, they were overborne by two other factors, the Admiralty's political power and the British elite's demands for maritime security. This permitted the Royal Navy remarkable success which, however, contributed to a backlash that wrecked its policy in 1929–30. The success of the navalists in the Admiralty strengthened the hand of the radicals among the politicians for a brief but crucial time. Ultimately, the core contribution to the development of British naval policy were ideas about security and sea power. Throughout most of the 1920s British statesmen spent whatever money they believed was needed to secure imperial 'home waters'. By the later 1920s, their efforts had been so successful and the world seemed so calm that a sizable faction of British decision makers believed they could maintain maritime security through a smaller navy.

They were wrong, because of another fundamental factor in British maritime power. After the First World War Britain could not pursue a moderate course or a rational naval policy. It could not precisely calibrate its navy and construction to the scale of existing threats. Britain was the greatest seapower of the 1920s largely because of its capacity for naval construction. Yet these industries had reached that scale only through a large and continual diet of orders for forty years: without sizeable and steady rations, they would decline and strip Britain of the industrial superiority which produced naval mastery. The only policy which could have preserved that capacity was the Admiralty's policy of the 1920s, and yet that policy was far larger than Britain needed to meet the naval threats of that time. By 1929 British maritime power had to be far stronger or far weaker than Britain needed. It became weaker.

NOTES

I am grateful to Chris Bell, Greg Kennedy, Andrew Lambert, Gordon Martel and Keith Neilson and the participants in a seminar at the North American Conference on British Studies, held at Vancouver in October 1994, for comments on earlier drafts of this paper. I am also indebted to Bryan Ranft for an education in seapower. All primary citations from the ADM, CAB, FO, PRO and T series are taken from material held at the Public Record Office, Kew, and appear by permission of the Comptroller of Her Majesty's Stationery Office. All material cited from the RG series is used with permission of the National Archives, Washington. Material from the papers of David Lloyd George (House of Lords Record Office), Herbert Richmond and David Beatty (National Maritime Museum), Lord Haldane of Cloan (National Library of Scotland); Maurice Hankey, John de Robeck and A. V. Alexander (Churchill College, Cambridge) is cited by permission of the copyright holders.

1. Beatty to Richmond, 26 Feb 1921, Herbert Richmond papers RIC 7/4 [National Maritime Museum].
2. The standard account of modern British maritime history remains Paul Kennedy, *The Rise and Fall of British Naval Mastery* (London, 1976) and for the interwar years as a whole, Stephen Roskill, *Naval Policy Between the Wars*, Volume 1: *The Period of Anglo-American Naval Antagonism, 1919–1929* (London, 1968) and Volume 2, *The Period of Reluctant Rearmament* (London, 1976). For more recent work on the navy during the 1920s, see the relevant sections of John Robert Ferris, *Men Money and Diplomacy, The Evolution of British Strategic Policy, 1919–1926* (Ithaca, 1989) and John R. Ferris, 'The Symbol and Substance of Seapower: Britain, the United States and the One-Power Standard, 1919–1921' in B.J.C. McKercher, (ed) *Anglo-American Relations in the 1920s, The Struggle for Survival* (London, 1991).
3. William Braisted, *The United States Navy in the Pacific, 1909-1922* (Austin, 1971), p 440. cf. Corelli Barnett, *The Collapse of British Power* (London, 1970) pp 258–63 and Paul Kennedy, *The Realities Behind Diplomacy: Background Influences on British External Policy, 1865–1980* (London, 1981), pp 223–36.
4. Kennedy, *Realities*, pp 259–63; Philip Pugh, *The Cost of Seapower, The Influence of Money on Naval Affairs from 1815 to the Present Day* (London, 1986), pp 46–8, 156–7.
5. Barnet, *Collapse*, pp 237–43, passim, and Bernard Semmel, *Liberalism and Naval Strategy: Ideology, Interest and Sea Power During the Pax Britannica* (London, 1986).
6. Roskill, *Naval Policy*, I, p 215, passim.
7. David Edgerton, *England and the Aeroplane, An Essay on a Militant and Technological Nation* (London, 1991), p 6.
8. Andrew Lambert, *The Last Sailing Battlefleet, Maintaining Naval Mastery 1815–1850* (London, 1994).
9. 'Navy Estimates 1901–2', Selborne 17 Jan 1901, CAB 37/56/8.
10. CP 258 (27), CAB 24/189 [Public Record Office].
11. 28th meeting of the CID, 7 Jul 1927, CAB 2/5
12. Lambert, *Naval Mastery* and, idem., *Battleships in Transition. The Creation of the Steam Battlefleet* (London, 1984), offers the best account of British maritime strength in the nineteenth century. Several other works demonstrate the limits to that strength during and after the Napoleonic wars: cf. Piers Mackesy, *Statesmen at War, The Strategy of Overthrow,1798–1799* (London, 1974); *The War in the Mediterranean 1803–1810* (Cambridge, Mass, 1957), and *War Without Victory, the Downfall of Pitt, 1792–1802* (Oxford, 1984); and Edward Ingram, *Commitment to Empire: Prophecies of the Great Game in Asia, 1797–1800* (Oxford, 1981) and *The Beginning of the Great Game in Asia, 1828–1834* (Oxford, 1979). The standard account of British maritime power and policy between 1888 and 1814 is now Jon Sumida, *In Defence of Naval Supremacy, Finance, Technology, and British Naval Policy 1889–1914* (London, 1989), though Arthur Marder, *The Anatomy of British Seapower: A History of British Naval Policy in the Pre-Dreadnought Era, 1880-1905* (New York, 1940) and *From the Dreadnought to Scapa Flow: Volume One, the Royal Navy in the Fisher Era, 1904–14* (Oxford, 1961) still should be read.
13. Memorandum by Beatty, 28 Jan 1924, ADM 1/8666 [Public Record Office]; Beatty to de Robeck, 30 Nov 1919, John de Robeck Papers [Churchill College, Cambridge] 5/13; undated and unsigned memorandum by Beatty, probably late September–early October 1919 by internal evidence, and Beatty to Long, 15 Dec 1920, David Beatty papers [National Maritime Museum] BTY 13/28;

Madden to Beatty, 26 Nov 1918, BTY 13/29; 'Notes by the First Sea Lord', 5 Jul 1929, PRO 30/69/267 [Public Record Office].

14. 55th Meeting of the Defence Requirements Sub-Committee, 24 Jul 1934, CAB 16/109.
15. 134th meeting of the Committee of Imperial Defence, 14 Dec 1920, CAB 2/3; memorandum by Barstow, 18 Jul 1921, T 161/119 S. 9627/1; memorandum by Snowden, Jun 1924, FO 371/9671 [Public Record Office]; first and second meetings of the Birkenhead committee, 2 and 5 Mar 1925, CAB 27/273.
16. Memorandum by Philip Snowden, undated, circa Jun 1924 by internal evidence, FO 371/9617; cf. undated and unsigned memorandum, but by Barstow and circa 29 Jun 1919 by internal evidence, T1/12469; and CP 12 (30), CAB 24/209.
17. 55th meeting of the Defence Requirements Sub-Committee, 24 Jul 1934, CAB 16/109.
18. Memorandum by Cecil, 10 Apr 1919, Lloyd George Papers F/6/6 [House of Lords Record Office]; Martin Gilbert, *Companion Volume, V, 1922–1939* (London, 1976), pp 390–91.
19. This phrase is not found in the official record, but was cited immediately afterward by Beatty to Long, 15 Dec 1920, BTY 13/28.
20. Julia Davis and Dolores A Fleming (eds), *The Ambassadorial Diary of John W. Davis, The Court of St. James, 1918–1921* (Morgantown, 1993), p 357; 134th meeting of the Committee of Imperial Defence, 14 Dec 1920, CAB 2/3; memorandum by Lloyd George, 7 Mar 1919, and Lloyd George to Bonar Law, 31 Mar 1919, Lloyd George papers, F/147/1 and F/30/3, Lloyd George papers [House of Lords Record Office]. For similar views, cf. second meeting of the Cabinet Finance Committee, 11 Sept 1919, CAB 27/71.
21. *The Navy*, Jul 1929, p 193; for similar statements by Churchill between 2929–30, cf. memorandum by Churchill (undated, but Jan–Feb 1928 according to internal evidence), Maurice Hankey papers, HNKY 5/1 [Churchill College, Cambridge]; Report of the Churchill committee, 4 Feb 1922, CAB 27/164; CP 189(27), CAB 24/187; Official Report, Parliamentary Debates, House of Commons, CCXXXVIII, cols. 2102–03.
22. Ferris, 'Symbol and Substance', pp 62–66; cf. minute by Barstow, 4 Jun 1921, T 161/119 S. 9627/1; memorandum by Barstow, 15 Nov 1922, T161/119S.9627/01; memorandum by Barstow, 31 Jan 1924, T 161/227 S. 23175; CP 12 (30), CAB 24/209; 134th meeting of the Committee of Imperial Defence, 14 Dec 1920, CAB 2/3; memoranda by Admiralty Plans Division, 4 Jan 1921, 'War with U.S.A.', Beatty Papers, BYT 8/1.
23. 134th meeting of the Committee of Imperial Defence, 14 Dec 1920, CAB 2/3.
24. *Foreign Relations of the United States, (FRUS), The Paris Peace Conference, 1919,* Volume XI (1943), pp 620–21; Mary Klachko with David F. Trask, *Admiral William Shepherd Benson, First Chief of Naval Operations,* (Annapolis, 1987), pp 131-55, 160–61, passim.
25. Memoranda by Admiralty Plans Division, 4 Jan 1921, 'War with U.S.A.', Beatty Papers, BTY 8/1; Admiralty Board Memorandum No. 755, by Admiral Wemyss, 23 Mar 1919, ADM 167/58; Report of the Sub-Committee on the Question of the Capital Ship in the Navy, 2 Mar 1921, passim, CAB 16/37; Study of Anglo-American naval war in 1925 conducted by the Senior Officers' Course at Greenwich, 1921, ADM 1/86281/120; 'British Imperial Bases in the Pacific', memorandum by Plans Division, 26 Apr 1919, ADM 1/8570; Steven T. Ross, *American War Plans, 1919–1941, Volume 2, Plans for War Against the British Empire and Japan, The Red, Orange and Red-Orange Plans, 1923-1938* (New York, 1992), pp 229–413.
26. Board Minutes 699, 20 Mar 1919 and 939, 22 Sept 1919, ADM 167/56.
27. Ferris, *Evolution*, pp 79–83, passim; Ferris, 'Symbol and Substance', passim.
28. Serious problems surround the term capital ships and the warship classes of battleships and battle-cruisers. In order to avoid them, the text will refer to such warships as 'capital ships'. In principle, capital ships are the strongest combat vessels, those which guarantee any navy's ability to control a given sea and to exercise the functions of seapower there. Neither capital ships, however, nor seabattles, are the whole of seapower. It is easy to make a fetish of the warship types identified as capital ships and to forget the observation of Admiral Herbert Richmond, 'you have to consider the whole of the ships together. They all act in unison. It is not one particular type that is the dominant unit'. (Third meeting of the sub-committee on Capital Ships in the Navy, 5 Jan 1921, CAB 16/37).

In practice, moreover, the term capital ship is identified with battleships and battlecruisers. Today, many view such warships as having been worthless by 1939 and any attention paid to them during the interwar years as a waste. Such views are wrong. During the Second World War, both aircraft carriers and heavy surface warships mounting big guns performed as capital ships. In the process each demonstrated unique strengths and weaknesses. On the high seas, outside the range of land-based aircraft and in the day, aircraft carriers possessed unmatchable combat power. Yet these conditions were hard to achieve, and when they failed so did carriers. In the Pacific Ocean during 1942 carriers ran for home once night fell, in the Mediterranean and North Seas they were easy meat for land based aircraft. Carriers dominated combat in most of the Pacific War. Surprisingly often even here, however, heavy surface warships remained 'capital ships' and they were the only warships with that status in any European sea. Unlike the case of the First World War, however, these heavy surface warships were not fleets of battleships and battlecruisers. They were mixed squadrons of 'capital ships', cruisers and 'semi-capital ships', warships midway between cruisers and battlecruisers in their design characteristics. The conventional distinctions between these types of warship hampers the analysis of naval warfare between 1939–45. During that conflict, battleships and battlecruisers varied dramatically in age and combat power: 'semi-capital ships' were closer in combat strength to 30 year old British 'R' class battleships than the latter were to the Japanese super-battleship 'Yamoto'. 'Capital ships' were far better suited to survive enemy airpower based on land or at sea. They were the most deadly of surface ships but also few in number. Cruisers and 'semi-capital ships' were more numerous, more vulnerable and fought more frequently. Along with smaller warships, they also exercised all of the functions of seapower.

29.   CMD 1627 of 1922.
30.   Fourth meeting of the Defence Requirements Sub-Committee, 18 Jan 1934, CAB 16/109; De Robeck to Beatty, 30 Dec 1921, de Robeck Papers, 8/7; Paul G. Halpern (ed) *The Keyes Papers*, Volume II: *1919–1938*, (London, 1980), p 238; CID Paper 285-B, 21 Nov 1921, CAB 4/7; GRC (D.D.) 4, Appendix One, CAB 27/164.
31.   CP 169/28, CAB 24/195.
32.   Ferris, *Evolution*, pp 60–63; *Documents on British Foreign Policy*, (*DBFP*) Second Series, Volume XIII, (London, 1973), pp 77-78.
33.   Minute by Sperling, 1 Feb 1924, FO 371/9616.
34.   Third meeting of the Defence Requirements Sub-Committee, 4 Dec 1933, CAB 16/109.
35.   Cf. n 24 above; Extracts from M.I.D. Intelligence Summaries, 16 Aug 1929, 3 Jan 1930, C-10-m, 19542 A, RG-38; memorandum by Col Ford, G-2, for Chief of Staff, 'The Attitude of British Official Circles and British Public Opinion Toward the United States', 2 Mar 1929, 2657-a-205, RG-38; memorandum by division of western European affairs, Department of State, 28 Oct 1931, Confidential US State Department Central Files: Great Britain, Internal Affairs, 1930-1939, microfilm, Reel 2; Ross, *American War Plans*, pp 229–413.
36.   Lecture by Captain Hussey 'Great Britain and the British Navy', 15 Dec 1924, F-10-2, 17770, RG 38.   .
37.   For assessments by staff officers of the United States Army and the United States Army War College, cf. Files 382-7A and 362-4B, United States Military History Institute, Army War College Curriculum Archives, United States Army War College Carlisle Barracks, Pennsylvania.
38.   Ferris, *Evolution*, pp 111–24, 133–34.
39.   Memorandum by Naval Staff, 9 Nov 1921, ADM 1/8615; Admiralty Board Memorandum No. 1352, ADM 167/64; memoranda by Admiralty Plans Division, 4 Jan 1921, 'War with U.S.A.' and 'War with Japan', Beatty Papers, BTY 8/1.
40.   CID Paper 285-B, CAB 4/7.
41.   Memorandum by Madden, 14 Jan 1930, 'Basis of British Naval Strategy', ADM 116/2746; this passage subsequently was inserted verbatim into many reports by the Chiefs of Staff Committee. For other statements on these topics, cf. Beatty's testimony to the first meeting of the Birkenhead Committee, 2 Mar 1925, CAB 27/273; 'Naval Staff Notes', undated, circa July 1923, CAB 21/272; M.00469, 7.31, 'War Plan (Eastern)', ADM 116/3118.
42.   Halpern, *Keyes Papers*, II, p. 239; Pound to Richmond, 31 Aug 1924, Herbert Richmond papers, RIC 7/4; CAB 19/109.
43.   165th meeting of the CID, CAB 2/3.
44.   Ferris, *Evolution*, pp 117–21, 132–39.
45.   Ibid, pp 134.
46.   ADM 167/72, Admiralty Board Memorandum, No. 2052, 26 May 1925; cf. ADM 167/71, Admiralty Board Minute No. 2096, 6 Oct 1925.
47.   Minutes by de Brock, 21 Jun 1921, Chatfield, 23 Jun 1921, memorandum by Pound, 14 Sept 1922, passim. ADM 1/8653.

48. Memorandum by DCNS, 30 Jul 1924, passim, ADM 1/9253; memoranda by Director of Gunnery
     Division, 18 Oct 1923, ADM 1/9248; memorandum by Director of Gunnery Division, 18 Jul
     1923, ADM 1/8635; memorandum by Chatfield, 26 Apr 1926, passim, ADM 1/8694. The most
     useful accounts of British cruiser designs and policy between the wars are Alan Raven and John
     Roberts, *British Cruisers of World War Two* (Annapolis, 1980) and D.K. Brown, *A Century of
     Naval Construction. The History of the Royal Corps of Naval Constructors, 1883–1983* (London,
     1983), pp 136, 146–47. The best study of cruiser designs between the wars is Norman Friedman,
     US Cruisers, An Illustrated Design History (Annapolis, 1984). Jon Sumida, 'The Best-Laid Plans:
     The Development of British Battle-Fleet Tactics, 1919–1942', *International History Review*, 14,
     4(1992), pp 661–700, is the most useful account of that topic.
49. CP 193/27, Part 5, CAB 24/187.
50. COS 596, Jun 1937, CAB 53/32; for the role of blockade in Admiralty war plans, cf. n. 25 above;
     Naval Staff memorandum, undated, 'The Naval Situation of the British Empire in the Event of
     War between Japan and the USA', undated, circa Oct 1921, passim, ADM 1/8948; M.00469, 7.31,
     'War Memorandum (Eastern)', ADM 116/3118.
51. Memorandum by DCNS, 18 Mar 1919, ADM 167/57; CID papers nos. 290-B, 295-B, CAB 4/7;
     memorandum by Pound, 12 Jun 1923, ADM 1/8702.
52. Memorandum by Pound, 12 Jun 1923, ADM 1/8702.
53. John Barnes and David Nicholson (eds), *The Leo Amery Diaries*, Volume One: *1896–1929*
     (London, 1980) pp 349–52.
54. Memorandum by Pound, 27 Oct 1923, ADM 1/8653; Admiralty Board Memorandum No. 1754,
     14 Nov 1923; Ferris, *Evolution*, pp 135–36.
55. Ibid., ND (25) 7 & 8, first meeting of the Birkenhead committee, 2 Mar 1925, CAB 27/273.
     Appendix 11 to COS 124, 15 Feb 1928, CAB 43/14, shows that the Admiralty knew that the IJN
     possessed only 23 modern cruisers in 1928, whereas in 1924–25 it sometimes pretended that this
     figure was 39.
56. First meeting of the Birkenhead Committee, 2 Mar 1925, CAB 27/273.
57. During this period Britain laid down two battleships, two aircraft carriers, 14 cruisers and 11
     destroyers and submarines. The United States laid down two carriers and three submarines and
     Japan, two carriers, 8 cruisers and 49 submarines and destroyers. The RN's advantage declined if
     one adds in the completion of warships under construction in 1921: Britain, eight cruisers and one
     carrier, the United States seven cruisers and the finishing touches on two battleships, and Japan
     five cruisers, 33 destroyers and submarines and final work on one battleship. Even so, between
     1922–26 Britain both laid down and completed far more warship tonnage than any other single
     power.
58. Minute by Keyes, 25 Jun 1923, ADM 1/8702; minutes of meeting of the Sea Lords, 28 Jan 1924,
     BTY 8/5.
59. P.D. 01955/24, ADM 1/8672.
60. Ferris, *Evolution*, pp 135–36.
61. Chris Bell, 'Hong Kong and British Naval Strategy Between the World Wars', *Journal of Military
     History*.
62. ADM 167/72, Board Memorandum No. 2086, May 1925.
63. Ferris, *Evolution*, pp 137–39; minutes of a Naval Staff Conference, 15 May 1923, ADM
     116/2397; Richmond to Haldane, 24 Jun 1924, [Lord Haldane of Cloan papers, National Library
     of Scotland] Volume 5916.
64. Paul Kennedy, *The Rise and Fall of Great Powers* (New York, 1987). For recent challenges to
     this view, cf. Keith Neilson,' "Greatly Exaggerated": The Myth of the Decline of Great Britain
     before 1914'; John Ferris, 'The Greatest World Power on Earth: Great Britain in the 1920s'; and
     Brian McKercher, 'Our Most Dangerous Enemy': Great Britain Pre-Eminent in the 1930s' all in
     International History Review, 13, 4(1991) and Sidney Pollard, *Britain's Prime and Britain's
     Decline: The British Economy, 1870–1914* (London, 1989) and Edgerton, *England and the
     Aeroplane*.
65. Gary Weir, *Building the Kaiser's Navy* (Annapolis, 1992); Gregory C. Kennedy, 'The 1930
     London Naval Conference and Anglo-American Maritime Strength 1927–1930', pp 149–71, in
     B.J.C. McKercher, *Arms Limitation and Disarmament, Restraints on War, 1899–1939* (Westport,
     CN, 1992) pp 152 and n. 12; Pugh, *Cost of Seapower*, pp 173–80.
66. CP 53 (29) CAB 24/202.
67. Useful accounts of the development of the British economy between 1870 and 1945 are Sidney

Pollard, *The Development of the British Economy, 1814–1980* (4th ed, London, 1984) and *Britain's Prime*, and Derek H. Aldcroft, *The Inter-War Economy: Britain, 1919–1939* (London, 1970). Four good studies of the shipbuilding and naval armament industries before 1914 are Michael S. Moss and John R. Hume, *Workshop of the British Empire, Engineering and Shipbuilding in the West of Scotland* (Rutherford, NJ, 1977), Hugh B. Peebles, *Warship building on the Clyde: Naval Orders and the Prosperity of the Clyde Shipbuilding Industry*, 1889–1939 (Edinburgh, 1987), Sidney Pollard and Paul Robertson, *The British Shipbuilding Industry, 1879–1914* (Cambridge, Mass, 1979) and Clive Trebilcock, *The Vickers Brothers: Armaments and Enterprise, 1854–1914* (London, 1977). For general studies of the shipbuilding industry between the wars cf. William Hornby, *Factory and Plant, History of the Second World War* (London, 1958), pp 38–39; J. R. Parkinson, 'Shipbuilding', pp 79–102, in Neil K. Buxton and Derek H. Aldroft, *British Industry between the Wars. Instability and Industrial Development 1919–1939* (London, 1979); Edward H. Lorenz, 'An Evolutionary Explanation for Competitive Decline: The British Shipbuilding Industry, 1890–1970', *Journal of Economic History*, 51, 4(1991), pp 911–21; A. Slaven, 'A Shipyard in Depression: John Browns of Clydebank, 1919–1938' in R. P. T. Davenport-Hines, *Business in the Age of Depression and War* (London, 1990) and Sir Allan Grant, *Steel and Ships — the History of John Browns* (London, 1950). For useful accounts of warship building and naval armament firms during the 1920s, cf. John R. Hume and Michael S. Moss, *Beardmore. The Story of a Scottish Industrial Giant* (London, 1979), pp 153–207, and J.D. Scott, *Vickers* (London, 1962). The best survey of the state of the naval arms industry by 1929 is G. A. H. Gordon, *British Seapower and Procurement Between the Wars*, (London, 1988), pp 76–92, and of Britain's mercantile capacity as a source of power, Greg Kennedy, 'Great Britain's Maritime Strength and the British Merchant Marine, 1922–1935', *Mariner's Mirror*, 80, 1(1994), pp 66–77. Useful and easily accessible primary documentation on British shipbuilding are contained in the Board of Trade memoranda in the CAB 24 series and in the various editions of Brassey's Naval Annual.

68. CP 55 (30), CAB 24/210; Kennedy, 'The London Naval Conference', pp 159–60; Ross, *American War Plans*, II, pp 263–66, 296–98.
69. ADM 167/56, Admiralty Board Minute No. 989, 8 Oct 1919, ADM 167/60, Admiralty Board Minute No. 1133, 28 Jan 1920; Halpern, *Keyes Papers*, p 60.
70. Admiralty Board Memoranda No. 1310, 28 Jan 1921 and No. 1351, 9 May 1921, ADM 167/64 and CID Paper No. 310-B, CAB 4/7 of Nov 1921. These estimates differ on one key point — whether British armour plate capacity could fit out two or three 'capital ships' in any three year period. In any case, this problem diminished after 1921, after which battleships became 25% smaller than those the Admiralty had planned to build in 1920-21. By 1925 the Board concluded that British armour plate capacity would outfit two capital ships annually. ADM 167/72. Admiralty Board Memorandum, No. 2052, 26 May 1925. This, however, seems contradicted by the evidence cited in n. 73 below.
71. 34th meeting of the Cabinet Finance Committee, 28 Feb 1921, CAB 27/71; CD papers 285-B, 304–B, 310-B, 314-B, CAB 4/7.
72. London to British Delegation, Washington, No. 21, 18 Nov 1921, ADM 116/3445.
73. Admiralty Board Minutes No. 1441, 2 Mar 1922 and No. 1463, 31 Mar 1922, ADM 167/65; Admiralty Board Minutes, Nos. 2052, 25 Jun 1925 and 2096, 6 Oct 1925, ADM 167/71; Admiralty Board Memorandum, No. 2052, 26 May 1925 and No. 2096, May 1925, ADM 167/72; Admiralty Board Memorandum No. 2219, 19 Jun 1926, ADM 167/74; Admiralty Board Memorandum No. 2749, ADM 167/82; ADM 116/3747, passim; memorandum, 'Armour for London Class', ll Aug 1923, ADM 116/3351.
74. ADM 167/72, ibid
75. Admiralty to Treasury, 20 May 1921, passim, T 161/119 S.9627/1; Admiralty to Treasury, 28 Jul 1923, T 161/119 S. 9627/2, passim; minutes of conferences between Admiralty and armour plate manufacturers, 15 Jul 1923, 6 Nov 1923, passim, ADM 116/3351. For other examples of Admiralty relations with armament firms, cf. Hume and Moss, *Beardmore*, pp 231–32; Yvonne Youngberg, 'Unrecognised Potential: The Relationship Between the Royal Navy and Vickers Armstrong, 1930–39' (University of Calgary MA dissertation, 1994); Gordon, *Procurement*, pp 83–85.
76. Admiralty Board Memorandum, No. 2052, 26 May 1925 and No. 2096, May 1925, ADM 167/72.
77. Figures taken from Vote 8 (iii) and Vote 9 in the ADM 181 series on Naval Estimates. Pollard and Robertson, *Shipbuilding*, p 215 and Sumida, *Naval Supremacy*, Table 6, provide compilations and

analyses of prewar expenses.

78. Minutes by Niemayer and Barstow, 11 Oct 1926 and 12 Oct 1926, T 161/281 S. 32783; memoranda by Alexander, 21 Jun 1929, FS (29), 3, and FS(20) 5, Admiralty 'New Construction Programme 1928: Financial and Employment Aspects'. *CAB* 27/407; Hume and Moss, *Beardmore*, pp 187, 194; Scott, *Vickers*, pp 187.
79. 34th meeting of the Cabinet Finance Committee, 28 Feb 1921, CAB 27/71.
80. Slaven, 'Shipyard in Depression', pp 132–2; Admiralty to Treasury, 20 May 1921, passim, T161/119 S 9627/1; Admiralty to Treasury, 28 Jul 1923, T162/119 S. 9627/21, passim.
81. Undated memorandum, but circa 1927, by William Pleneth, Industrial Chairman, Vickers and Armstrong Joint Committee, CAB 27/353; COS 295, pp 8, CAB 53/22.
82. Admiralty Board Memoranda, No. 2052, ADM 167/72; Admiralty Board Memoranda No. 2749, ADM 167/82.
83. Board Minute No. 940, 23 Sept 1919, ADM 167/56; CP 319 (28), CAB 24/198; cf. figures for Vote 8 (i) and (ii) in the ADM 181 series.
84. Bridgeman to Southborough, 12 Oct 1926, minutes by Niemayer and Barstow, 11 Oct 1926 and 12 Oct 1926, T 161/281 S. 32783; AFC (27) 3, memorandum by Bridgeman, 21 Jul 1927, CAB 27/353; Slaven, 'Shipyard in Depression', pp 132–45; Scott, *Vickers*, pp 156–58; Hume and Moss, *Beardmore*, pp 198–219.
85. 'Memorandum for Director of Naval Intelligence, Some Factors to be Considered in Estimating British Policy', 29 Mar 1929, C-10-m, 19542A, RG-38.
86. C-in-C Atlantic Fleet, H.F. Oliver, undated 'remarks', Sept 1925, in Oliver to Field, ADM 1/8700/121.
87. Ferris, *Evolution*, pp 161–62.
88. Admiralty Board minutes, Nos. 1690, 12 Jul 1923 and 1710, 3 Aug 1923, ADM 167/67; Board Memoranda 'Singapore-Proposed Naval Base', 9 Jul 1923 and No. 1710, ADM 167/68; Minutes of meeting of the Sea Lords, 28 Jan 1924, BTY 8/5; P.D. 02544/26, 'Memorandum on Singapore Naval Base by Civil Lord', minutes by Chatfield, 14 Jul 1926 and Field, 8 Jul 1926, ADM 116/2416.
89. First meeting of the Birkenhead Committee, 2 Mar 1925, ND (25) 8, 9 Mar 1925, CAB 27/273; CID paper 304-B, CAB 4/7; 'Revised Forecast', 26 Jan 1926, ADM 181/107; Memorandum by ACNS/DCNS/Controller, 21 Dec 1926, passim, ADM 1/8699/118.
90. Admiralty Board Memorandum No. 2088, 1 Oct 1925, ADM 167/71; Admiralty Board Memoranda, No. 2064, 17 Jun 1925 and No. 2088, 28 Sep 1925, ADM 167/72; Board Minute No. 2211, 8 Jun 1926, ADM 167/73; Bertram Watson to Richmond, 9 Jun 1925, plus enclosure, Herbert Richmond papers, RIC 7/3b; minutes by Egerton, 16 Apr 1926, Field, 21 Apr 1926, Beatty, 28 Apr 1926, and Bridgeman, 29 Apr 1926, ADM 116/2416.
91. Minutes of 227th meeting of the CID, 20 May 1927, CAB 2/5; memorandum by ACNS/DCNS/Controller, 21 Dec 1926, passim, ADM 1/8699/118; ADM 1/9270, passim.
92. Halpern, *Keyes Papers,* p 221.
93. Ferris, *Evolution*, pp 37–52.
94. Seventh meeting of the COSC, 31 Jan 1924, CAB 53/1.
95. For example, British Embassy, Tokyo, to Foreign Office, No. 82, 19 Feb 1924, covering Naval Attache, Japan, Report No. 3, 18 Feb 1924, FO 371/10309.
96. 215th meeting of the CID, 22 Jul 1926, CAB 2/4.
97. Minute by Ashton-Gwatkin, 19 Feb 1924, FO 371/10299; memoranda by Victor Wellesley, 'Singapore', 1 Jan 1925 and 'The Improbability of War in the Pacific', 1 Jan 1825, FO 371/10958; Austen Chamberlain to Eliot, FO 800/256, 17 Dec 1924; 193rd meeting of the CID, 5 Jan 1925, CAB 2/4.
98. Minute by Chamberlain, 11 Aug 1925, FO 371/11233; cf. minute by Chamberlain, 8 Aug 1926, FO 371/11885.
99. Over the past decade, a voluminous literature has emerged on Anglo-American relations and naval arms limitation during the later 1920s. The most important volume is B.J.C. McKercher, *The Second Baldwin Government and the United States, 1924–1929, Attitudes and Diplomacy* (London, 1984). Excellent recent accounts with good bibliographies are Gregory C. Kennedy, 'The 1930 London Naval Conference and Anglo-American Naval Strength, 1927–1930' in McKercher (ed), *Arms Limitation and Disarmament*; Orest Babij, 'The Second Labour Government and British Maritime Security, 1929–1931', *Diplomacy and Statecraft* (forthcoming) and Richard Fanning, *Peace and Disarmament, Naval Rivalry and Arms Control,*

1922–1933 (Lexington, 1995). Some useful primary documents on the topic include CP 258 (27), CAB 286 (27), CAB 24/189; CP 179 (38), CAB 24/195; CP 358 (28), CP 367 (28), CAB 24/199; CP 32 (29), CAB 33 (29), CAB 35 (29), CAB 24/201; CP 71 (29), CAB 24/202; FO 800/260, FO 800/261, FO 371/10633, FO 371/12036, FO 371/12040, FO 371/12041, FO 371/12049.

100. Cecil to Chamberlain, 17 Jul 1927; Howard to Chamberlain, 21 Jul 1927, FO 800/261.
101. CP 35 (29), CAB 24/201.
102. Halpern, *Keyes Papers*, pp 225, 227; memorandum by Churchill (undated, but January–February 1928 according to internal evidence), Maurice Hankey papers, HNKY 5/1, Churchill College, Cambridge; Philip Williamson, *The Modernisation of Conservative Politics, The Diaries and Letters of William Bridgeman, 1904–1935*, (London, 1988) pp 206–08, 223–4.
103. For discussions of this issue, cf. John Ferris and Uri Bar Joseph, 'Getting Marlowe to Hold his Tongue: The Conservative Party, the Intelligence Services and the Zinoviev Letter', *Intelligence and National Security*, 8, 4(1993), pp 102–21; Roskill, *Naval Policy*, I, pp. 378–82; CP 373 (23), undated but c. July 1923, T 172/1309 (a Cabinet Paper weeded from the CAB 24 series), passim. The diaries and letters of the editor of *The Times* between 1923 and 1927 provide illuminating references to leaks from the Admiralty regarding the Cabinet's lengthy debates about naval policy: cf. Geoffrey Dawson's diary, Bodleian Library, Volume 27, entries 26–27 July 1923, Volume 29, entries 17 Feb 1925, 9 Jul 1925, 19 Jul 1925; Bridgeman to Dawson, 1 Jul 1927 and memorandum by Bridgeman, 1 Jul 1927, Volume 72. Orest Babij, a DPhil candidate at Oxford, has provided persuasive evidence to indicate that from middle 1928, the Admiralty became far more accommodating in its politics. I am grateful to him for allowing me to read a draft chapter on that topic.
104. Second meeting of the Singapore Committee, 3 Mar 1927, CAB 27/236; first meeting of the Birkenhead committee, 2 Mar 1925, CAB 27/273.
105. Cecil to Chamberlain, 12 Apr 1927, Salisbury to Austen Chamberlain, 15 Apr 1927, FO 800/269;   Ferris, *Evolution*, 158–69; John Ramsden (ed), *Real Old Tory Politics, The Political Diaries of Robert Sanders, Lord Bayford, 1910–1935* (London, 1981), p 221. These arguments have been extended in an important forthcoming article by Jon Sumida. For proof that nothing but study can eliminate myth, cf. David MacGregor, 'Former Naval Cheapskate: Chancellor of the Exchequer Winston Churchill and the Royal Navy, 1924–1929', *Armed Forces and Society*, 19, 3(1993), pp 319–33.
106. Ferris, *Evolution*, p 6, 169–78; minute by Warren Fisher for Chancellor of the Exchequer, 29 Dec 1923, T 161/217 S. 21914; minutes by Warren Fisher, 30 Jul 1923, 5 Feb 1924, T 172/1309.
107. McKercher, *Second Baldwin Government*.
108. Ben Pimlott (ed), *The Political Diary of Hugh Dalton, 1918–40, 1945–60* (London, 1986), pp 87, 89–90.
109. Fourth meeting of the Cabinet committee on the Singapore base, 11 Apr 1924, CAB 27/236.
110. MacDonald to Dawes, 1 Aug 1929, 23 Sept 1929, PRO 30/69/267.
111. CP 312 (29), CAB 24/207.
112. Memorandum by Henderson, 'London Naval Conference 1930, Proposals for the British Commonwealth Delegation', 23 Jan 1930, ADM 116/2746.
113. For a useful, if partial, account of MacDonald's views, cf. David Marquand, *Ramsay MacDonald* (London, 1977) pp 504–17.
114. Admiralty Board Minute, No. 2589, 3 Jun 1929, ADM 167/79; 'Notes by the First Sea Lord', 5 Jul 1929, PRO 30/29/267; First meeting of the Cabinet Committee on the Fighting Services, 25 Jun 1929, CAB 27/407.
115. Alexander to MacDonald, 18 Feb 1929, AVAR 5/2. Most of the primary documentation exchanged tween the British and American governments, particularly on the cruiser issue, along with much of the internal diplomatic correspondence on the issues, are reprinted in *DBFP*, Second Series, Volume 1 (1947), pp 3–311; *FRUS*, 1929, Volume One (1943), pp 1–316 and Volume Three (1944) pp 1–37. For MacDonald's willingness to let the United States make the running in 'capital ships', cf. *FRUS*, 1930, Volume 1 (1945), pp 3–4, 13–17. Kennedy, 'The 1930 London Naval Conference' and Babij, 'British Maritime Security, 1929–1931', offer persuasive revisionist accounts of the effect of the London Treaty on British maritime power, especially in lighter surface warships.
116. Memorandum by Oswyn Murray, 4 Jul 1929, 'Redistribution of the Fleet', ADM 167/80.

117. FS (29) 16, 11 Nov 1929, CAB 27/407.
118. Minutes by Bellairs, 7 Jun 1929 and Domville, 4 Jun 1929 and Madden, undated marginal comments on M. 3255, 26 Jul 1929, ADM 116/2686.
119. *DBFP*, Second Series, Volume One, (1949), p 80.
120. CP 312 (29), CAB 24/207; *FRUS,* 1929, Volume III, pp 1–5.
121. Minute by Madden, 9 Jan 1929, ADM 116/2423; MacDonald to Dawes, 31 Aug 1929, PRO 30/69/267.
122. Alexander to MacDonald, 18 Sep 1929, A.V. Alexander papers [Churchill College, Cambridge], AVAR 5/2.
123. MacDonald to Alexander, 17 Sep 1929, AVAR 5/2.
124. 'London Naval Conference 1930, Memorandum Respecting Proposals to be submitted', L.N.C. (E) 7, ADM 116/2746; minute by Madden, 28 Nov 1929, ADM 116/2689; minute by Fisher, 4 Jan 1930, ADM 116/2717; 'New Construction Programme 1929/30', ADM 167/80; COS 238, 23 Jun 1930, CAB 53/21.
125. Keith Middlemas (ed), *Thomas Jones, Whitehall Diary*, Volume II, *1926–1930* (London, 1969), pp 232–34; MacDonald to Alexander, undated ('Wed'), 17 Sep 1929, Alexander to MacDonald, 18 Sep 1929; MacDonald to Trevelyan, 1 Apr 1930, AVAR 5/2; MacDonald to Alexander, 31 Aug 1929, PRO 30/69/1753/4; Macdonald to Alexander, 2 Jun 1930, PRO 30/69/676; Henderson to Campbell, 26 Nov 1929, ADM 116/2689.
126. MacDonald to Alexander, 31 Aug 1929, (unsigned but in MacDonald's handwriting), PRO 30/69/1753/4; *FRUS*, 1930, Volume I, p 4; *DBFP*, Second Series, Volume I, p 34.
127. Memorandum by Madden, 14 Jan 1930, 'Basis of British Naval Strategy', ADM 116/2746; minute by Madden, 2 Oct 1929, meeting of Sea Lords, 20 Dec. 1929, passim, ADM 116/3372.
128. COS 310, 10.33, CAB 53/23; memorandum by Pound, 12 Jun 1923, ADM 1/8702; 'Battle Fleet–Large Repairs to 1940', memorandum to Director of Naval Contracts, 1934, ADM 1/8774, cited in Youngberg, Unused Capacity, pp 29-30. For precisely these reasons, the Naval Staff, though not Chatfield, opposed a 15–15–9 ratio at the Washington Conference (Halpern, *Keyes Papers*, pp 61–62).
129. Minute by Bellairs, 2 Oct 1928, ADM 116/2423.
130. Minutes by Backhouse, 25 Oct 1928, and Madden, 7 Jan 1929, ibid.
131. CAB 305/27, CAB 24/190; CP 358 (28), CAB 24/199.
132. Brown, *A Century of Naval Construction*, pp 236, 146–47
133. Memorandum by Madden, 14 Jan 1930, 'Basis of British Naval Strategy', ADM 116/2746; COS 579 (JP), 5.37, CAB 53/31; COS 596 6.37, CAB 53/32; COS 310, 10.33, CAB 53/23.
134. CP 162 (29) CAB 24/204; CP 243 (29), CAB 24/205; CP 254 (29), CAB 24/206; cf. 78th meeting of the COSC, 11 Jun 1929, pp 33–34, 79th meeting, 16 Jul 1929, CAB 53/3.
135. Alexander memo, 21 Jun 1929, FS (29), 3 FS (29) 5, Admiralty 'New Construction Programme 1928: Financial and Employment Aspects' and FS (29) 6 Madden, 3 Jul 1929, CAB 27/407.
136. CP 164 (29), CAB 24/204; CP 211 (29), CP 250 (29), CAB 24/205; CP 281 (29), CAB 24/206; CP 340 (29), CP 270 (29), CAB 24/207; CP 87 (30), CP 129 (30), CAB 24/211.
137. CP 24 (30), CAB 24/209; CP 84 (30), CAB 24/210; CP 87 (30), CAB 24/211; Hornby, *Factory and Plant,* p 37.
138. Hornby, *Factory and Plant*, pp 38–41.
139. Alexander memo, 21 Jun 1929, FS (20), 3, FS (29) 5, CAB 27/407; Youngberg, *Unrecognized Potential*; Hume and Most, *Beardmore*, pp 208–47; Hornby, *Factory and Plant*, pp 58–62; M.M. Postan, *British War Production, History of the Second World War* (London, 1952), pp 50–51.
140. ADM 167/81, Board Minute No. 2749, 7 Oct 1930.

The Royal Navy and the defence of the British Empire 1928–1934

OREST BABIJ

A view persists that during the twenty 'Years of Decay' between the First and Second World Wars Great Britain lost its maritime supremacy and hence its ability to defend the Empire successfully. There are two main components to this argument: first, that the British economy could no longer support the size of fleet which was required to defend the Empire adequately and, second, that British statesmen lacked not just the will to maintain the Royal Navy at a sufficient strength and readiness but also, because they were mired in liberal values, the ruthlessness to pursue an aggressive defensive posture.[1] As a corollary to this view are the writings of those historians, many of whom are American, who look at these twenty years as the culmination of the inevitable rise of the United States Navy to replace the Royal Navy as the world's pre-eminent naval force.[2] Within these viewpoints, however, the years from 1928 until 1934 are notable as the nadir of British defence preparedness in the inter-war period. Expenditure on the navy reached its lowest level in 1932. Whilst much of the censure for this is placed upon a parsimonious Treasury and politicians who, it is claimed, were more interested in the chimera of disarmament than in the reality of defence, the senior leaders of the Royal Navy in these years have also received a great deal of criticism. The two First Sea Lords who served from 1927 until 1933, Admirals Sir Charles Madden and Sir Frederick Field, are widely regarded as intelligent men but with neither the force nor the character necessary to make a strong stand for the Royal Navy.[3] Thus, the conventional view remains that ineffectual leadership on the part of both the Admiralty and British statesmen combined with economic malaise to destroy Britain's maritime power in the years 1928–1934.

While it is an indisputable fact that these years were a low point for the navy, the above views do not present an accurate portrayal of the formulation of Britain's naval policy between the years 1928 and 1934. The prime reason for this is that most historians of British inter-war naval policy begin their study with the Second World War and then project backwards into the 1920s and 1930s.[4] This process might help sustain their arguments as they relate to the war, but it fails to provide a proper understanding of the nature of the development of policy in the inter-war years. It fails to understand Admiralty actions in the late 1920s and early 1930s because it misinterprets the Admiralty's goals and the tactics which senior admirals used to pursue their aims. These aims, in turn, were predicated on the Admiralty's interpretation of its role within the system of imperial defence.

British statesmen of the inter-war years in many respects were no different from those men who had held the same posts for hundreds of years. They were concerned with the defence of their Empire from both internal subversion and external threats and they utilized many of the same military, financial, diplomatic and economic tools as their predecessors to protect the interests of the Empire.[5] Despite this wide array of resources, of central importance to the entire system of imperial defence was the maintenance of the sea communications of the Empire. Along the sea lanes which linked the disparate parts of the Empire, and along many others, flowed the trade that was essential not just to the prosperity, but to the survival of the United Kingdom itself. The main responsibility for the defence of these sea communications rested upon the Royal Navy and involved a modern and efficient main fleet to act as a screen for detached squadrons, trade protection vessels to ply the sea lanes, and a global string of defended naval bases and fuelling stations.[6] These were a few, but not all of the elements which together comprised British sea power. Also of importance were the maintenance of a large merchant marine[7] and the industrial infrastructure to support both a peacetime fleet and rapid wartime expansion.[8] In order to fulfil its designated role, the Royal Navy always endeavoured to maintain these vital components of its strength at the highest level of readiness and to build the most modern and powerful fleet. By the late 1920s and early 1930s, however, admirals found it difficult to enlist support among politicians for the expensive, multi-year programmes they believed were necessary to maintain the navy's readiness when the latter perceived no immediate and dangerous threats to the British Empire which required a response from it. There was also a real need in Britain for a redirection of resources from military expenditure towards the domestic, civilian economy. Thus these were years of severe financial constraints on the naval budget. But this period coincided with pressure from within the Royal Navy for increased expenditure in order to maintain the sinews of its strength. Rapid technological change, constraints on the mobility of the main fleet, and an ageing fleet all called for a response from the Admiralty if the navy's ability to protect the Empire's sea communications was to be maintained.

To preserve the core of its maritime power, the Admiralty pursued an opportunistic policy in order to attain its main aims. This was characterized by a series of temporary compromises to the political and fiscal realities of the day. These were not absolute. Where it could, the Admiralty attempted to secure programmes which would respond to the pressures on its ability to carry out its main functions. Concurrently, and underpinning these tactics, senior admirals prepared plans for meeting the navy's deficiencies which could be brought into play should a suitable opportunity present itself. From 1928 the Royal Navy was forced to make very difficult choices so as to preserve those elements which were most essential to the exercise of British maritime power.

In May 1929, on the occasion of the general election, the Deputy Chief of the Naval Staff, Vice-Admiral William Fisher, prepared a memorandum which summarized the broad aims of Admiralty policy.[9] Overall naval policy, he noted, was predicated on the maintenance of a One Power Standard. The numbers of capital ships and aircraft carriers were set by the Washington Naval Treaty of 1922, but the strength of all other ships was guided by a more general formula which stated:

> ...as regards all other types, that they should be at such strength as will ensure adequate security for British territory, together with freedom of sea passage to and from all parts of the Empire. The Admiralty contends that this standard is not merely a question of numbers of ships, but also of training, efficiency and readiness for war.[10]

By Cabinet decision the Admiralty was not permitted to take the US navy into account when considering the basis of its preparations for war and so 'Japan being the next strongest naval power, requirements in the event of war in the Far East form the general basis on which preparations are made'. Fisher continued to write that the navy was committed to the completion of a naval base at Singapore in 1937 and to the build-up of a reserve of fuel oil equivalent to one year's wartime consumption by the fleet in annual instalments of one-tenth of the total. As far as naval construction was concerned, the aim was to secure a steady programme which eventually would produce the numbers of vessels the navy believed it required and thence to maintain them at that level, 'accepting the fact that the number of ships under age in certain classes for a time will fall below standard requirements'. These aims could be met, he projected, by an annual programme of three cruisers, nine destroyers, six submarines and seven sloops. Mindful of the need to begin new capital ship construction in 1931, Fisher reiterated the long term Admiralty support for a qualitative reduction in these vessels to 25,000 tons displacement with 12-inch guns.[11] Finally, he concluded by stating that it was also the policy gradually to accumulate materials for the underwater defences of ports east of Suez on the route to Hong Kong and for certain ports at home and in the Mediterranean. The Admiralty Board approved this memorandum several days later.[12]

In this paper Fisher elucidated most of the salient features of Admiralty policy as seen by the naval staff, but not all, for it omitted any reference to the most significant change in naval policy which had occurred in the preceding year. Then, the Cabinet had changed the underlying basis determining all service estimates by confirming 'that on any given date there will be no major war for ten years'.[13] This decision made permanent a guideline which had originally been accepted in 1919 by a British Cabinet attempting to formulate post-war defence policy. At the time it had been hoped to use this so-called 'ten year rule' to reduce service expenditure, but over the ensuing six years it had been rarely applied.[14] In 1925, however, the Cabinet had reinterpreted this ruling, in the case of the Royal Navy, to mean that no war against Japan should be expected before 1935 and the navy had been forbidden from preparing offensive plans against that country. But, the navy was permitted to complete various programmes it believed were necessary for maritime security, such as the fuel oil reserve, the Singapore naval base and several other replacement programmes.[15]

The 1928 revision was a reflection of the security of the British Empire within a peaceful international order. However, it had been precipitated by the acrimonious debate between the Treasury and the Admiralty over the size of that year's naval estimates. This, in turn, had been fuelled in part by the fact that each ministry had interpreted the 1925 decision on the ten year rule in a different manner, and in part because the two disagreed over the basis of the navy's estimates, namely the probability of war with Japan. Basically, the two departments were working to two different policies. The Treasury, under the Chancellor of the Exchequer, Winston Churchill, had assumed that the rule would come forward each year and thus each successive year would bring with it a new ten year period. The navy, on the other hand, interpreted the decision to mean that it had to be ready to wage a major naval war in 1935 and based its preparations accordingly.[16] Churchill had also been piqued that the First Lord of the Admiralty, William Bridgeman, had ignored his request in a December Cabinet meeting for all departments to find additional savings in order to prevent an anticipated budget deficit. The Admiralty had been asked to find £2 million in savings, but the estimates contained only £300,000 in reductions.[17] Furthermore, Admiralty officials proved intransigent when the Treasury asked for further compromises on their part.[18] This only served further to anger Treasury officials who already believed that the navy, unlike the army, 'has money to spare'.[19] This belief was based in large measure on the fact that the Treasury discounted the Japanese threat to the Empire, and consequently deprecated any expenditure on preparations for war with that power.[20] As a result, they determined to force the Admiralty to adhere to the Treasury's interpretation of the 1925 decision.[21] Whilst the latter did not achieve this before the 1928 estimates were presented to Parliament, immediately after this, Churchill brought the issue before the Cabinet and the Committee of Imperial Defence (CID).[22]

The entire matter was discussed at a meeting of the committee in early July. The international situation had begun to undermine much of the Admiralty's case for the urgency and necessity for its programmes. In April 1927 the Foreign Office reported that Japan 'should not be regarded as a menace to peace in any quarter'.[23] Since 1924 the Foreign Office had been engaged in a delicate diplomacy to ensure that the balance of power in the Pacific did not turn against British interests and by 1928 this policy was paying great dividends.[24] In Europe, the Locarno Treaty, signed in 1926, had ushered in a new period of stability and goodwill which secured British interests on the continent.[25] Britain's world situation was so secure that the Foreign Secretary, Sir Austen Chamberlain, felt justified in reporting to this meeting of the CID that the 'one outstanding uncertainty was Russia' but added that this danger was not imminent nor would it be impossible to avoid.[26] Thus, by the late 1920s there appeared to be no immediate and plausible threats to the British Empire. Based on this, the CID recommended that the assumption of ten years' peace should be placed on a daily revolving footing and the Cabinet officially adopted this policy later that month.[27]

In large measure Madden and the Admiralty were to blame for this decision. Since 1924 the Admiralty had sought expensive and ambitious programmes and had fought for them very aggressively.[28] This had continued to be the approach that Madden and Bridgeman had taken with the Treasury. But, at an early stage in the negotiations Churchill had been willing to compromise for he had been worried 'about the Navy in view of the Yankee menace'.[29] Compromise at this point would have been on terms favourable to the Admiralty, but its intransigence only served to harden the attitude of Churchill and his officials, to the ultimate detriment of all three defence services.

Yet, whilst this decision extended the Treasury's power over service expenditure, it also forced a change in the Admiralty as it altered its policy, albeit reluctantly to meet the new situation. The aggressive pursuit of its interests, accompanied with threats of Board resignation, which had marked the earlier 1920s, declined and was replaced with a period of retrenchment and more subtle tactics. Above all, the Admiralty had to decide which programmes it believed were most important. It sought compromise in some areas, gave way in others but still hardily pursued its interests in those areas it judged to be most important. Its policy now was guided by the consideration of 'what is actually possible of accomplishment with the resources available'.[30]

Nonetheless, the naval staff had already begun to consider how to respond to the fact that the international situation was undermining the primary justification for their policies, but they found themselves unable to agree on an alternative framework. From as early as 1920 the navy had concluded that the next greatest threat to the Empire would be faced from Japanese desires to expand in the Far East and the first tentative war plan against Japan was drawn up that year.[31] The need to be able to fight a war in the Far East against a first class naval power, the Imperial Japanese Navy, became the central justification for setting the levels of Admiralty stores, material and personnel.[32] That navy also became the standard by which the Royal Navy judged the strength of its fleet, both qualitatively and quantitatively. By mid-1928, however, Fisher saw that 'Far Eastern war plans appear to be becoming less attractive to the Cabinet', and pondered whether a new basis for the navy's requirements could be found.[33] Later that year he proposed a new and broader formula which he hoped would be of more general application and thus 'more convenient and politic to follow'.[34] As a result of his proposals Madden asked the Director of Plans, Roger Bellairs, to investigate what would be the Royal Navy's cruiser requirements in a war with the United States or with France.[35] Apart from this investigation no action was taken to reorientate the basis of naval war plans, and hence of Admiralty expenditure, and these remained wedded to the concept of a Far Eastern war. Madden believed that the policy which Fisher had briefly outlined was the correct one, but he also felt that it was not one which the Admiralty could aim for at that time. Oswyn Murray, the long-serving Permanent Under-Secretary of the Admiralty, added that a Far Eastern war was the most difficult one the navy might be called upon to engage in and so, if it were taken as the basis for planning, the navy would also be prepared for any other 'ordinary emergency'.[36] His view prevailed for, while a Far Eastern war had lost favour with politicians, the fundamental fact remained that it was still the best justification which the Admiralty could muster for the maintenance of a world-wide system of bases and the other elements of its system of imperial defence. A broader proposal like Fisher's would have been capable of various interpretations and could have been used with ease by the Treasury against the Admiralty to reduce expenditure on the navy. Japan had to remain the principal enemy.

Notwithstanding this and as a result of the expansion of the ten year rule, there were immediate effects on several long term Admiralty policies which had been designed to modernize its warships and to provide the world-wide mobility of that fleet. The latter point was built on two main foundations: the fuel oil reserve and a world-wide string of properly defended naval bases and fuelling stations. The modernization programmes were centred around the steady replacement of the navy's rapidly ageing, war-built cruisers, destroyers and submarines, the modernization of its capital ships to meet new forms of attack and lastly the ultimate start to a programme of capital ship replacement.

Since the end of the First World War the navy had been concerned about the defences at its ports both at home and throughout the Empire. Responsibility for their defence was divided. The navy provided all the local seaward defences, such as anti-submarine nets, anti-torpedo nets and minesweeping facilities whilst the War Office was responsible for the gun defences of the ports. Most of the latter had been built before the war and they had not kept up with the technological advances in warship gunnery.[37] This point was brought home in 1928 when, at a series of gunnery trials at Portsmouth and Malta, the coastal defence guns scored almost no success against a target ship.[38] As a result the Chiefs of Staff concluded that the majority of the Empire's coast defences were obsolete. Although this situation had perplexed the minds of the Admiralty and the Chiefs of Staff throughout the 1920s, the 1928 decision placed the highly expensive enterprise of remedying this strategic problem at an even lower level of priority. In addition, almost no ports possessed any anti-aircraft defences and those bases east of Suez which were vulnerable to attack in the early stages of a Far Eastern war contained an inadequate amount of anti-submarine or anti-torpedo defences and few minesweeping facilities. The 1928 decision also provided further arguments for deferring the accumulation of the full amount of the fuel oil reserve.[39]

Moreover, since the Washington Conference, the Admiralty had worked on a basis of attempting to complete as many as possible of these long term programmes before 1931. In that year, according to the provisions of the Washington Treaty, capital ship construction was to recommence and the Admiralty realized that the expense of that programme would make it very difficult for it to carry on with other large programmes.[40] For example, the 1928 naval estimates had included a large provision for the addition of a new anti-aircraft gun specifically designed to deal with the problem of low level attack by torpedo bombers.[41] The Admiralty hoped to complete this modernization process in a four year programme ending in 1932.[42] This had been one of the items on that year's estimates which had so annoyed the Treasury and as a result the original programme was scaled back tremendously.

Thus, Fisher's memorandum in the spring of 1929 was an attempt to summarize Admiralty objectives in the new international and domestic atmosphere. The election of a minority Labour government under James Ramsay MacDonald, however, confronted the Admiralty with a new set of challenges and, as it would turn out, a new set of opportunities. Early on the new Government made it known that it intended to question the continuation of the Singapore naval base, that it was desirous of achieving a naval agreement with the United States and that it hoped to cut service expenditure across the board. The Admiralty responded by mounting a spirited defence of the principle of the maintenance of the current proposals for the Singapore base, and by attempting to utilize the dawning Anglo-American naval negotiations to secure both a favourable cruiser balance and a steady replacement programme. To secure these objectives, Madden had to give way over the size of the naval estimates. As a result, in order to finance new construction, the Admiralty had to defer many of its other desired programmes, such as the fuel oil reserve, the expansion of the fleet air arm, the modernization of its capital ships and the accumulation of stocks of war reserves.

The construction of a major naval base in the Old Strait in Singapore was the fulcrum of the Admiralty's maritime defences in the Far East. During the tenure of the second Baldwin Government, it worked assiduously first to secure agreement in principle to a scheme for the base, then to begin construction and lastly to equip it with adequate defences. By 1929 basic work on the base area had been completed, a floating dock had been sent, the contract for the main construction work had been let out and authority had been given to begin the first stage of the main gun defences.[43] Now, all these accomplishments appeared to be in jeopardy. Previously in 1924 the first short-lived Labour Government had cancelled the base and in 1929 the party maintained its opposition to the base.[44] Thus, Admiralty policy from the summer of 1929 above all was to save the base from extinction. In this endeavour it succeeded, although it was forced to compromise heavily by slowing down parts of the construction and suspending most of it.

Securing a steady, long term replacement programme had been an Admiralty aim since 1923, for strategic, financial and industrial reasons.[45] At this time the majority of British cruisers were small 'C' class cruisers of 3,500–4,000 tons displacement armed with 6-inch guns. These were outclassed by projected Japanese models and had been designed for North Sea service; as a result they were not suitable for patrolling long distances in tropical weather. In addition, the majority of British cruisers, destroyers and submarines had been batch-built within the space of a few years during and after the war and the naval staff forecast that they would become obsolete within a few years of each other, most likely sometime in the mid 1930s.[46] Thus, the possibility loomed that the navy would be confronted in the 1930s with a choice of either another, sudden, expensive batch-building programme or else a severe diminution in its total of efficient auxiliary vessels. To prevent both these possibilities, to save money in the long term and to provide steady employment in the dockyards, the naval staff continually argued for steady, long-term building programmes.[47] But, during the 1920s it proved difficult to bring such programmes to fruition and it was only when Madden took advantage of the opportunity afforded by the London Naval Conference of 1930 that a multi-year programme was finally secured.

Throughout the summer and early autumn of 1929 there occurred a series of complex negotiations between MacDonald and the American Ambassador, Charles Dawes, whose purpose was to settle the outstanding naval differences between the two countries before a second five-power naval conference which was to take place in 1930.[48] At the beginning Madden again presented MacDonald with the usual Admiralty claim for seventy cruisers.[49] Very quickly, however, MacDonald realized that if he was to achieve any agreement with the Americans then the Royal Navy would have to back down from this figure. He pressured Madden and the Admiralty Board to accept a figure of fifty cruisers and in August they capitulated. As a quid pro quo, however, Madden demanded a low limit to the US Navy's numbers of large 8-inch gun cruisers and a high limit for smaller British 6-inch gun cruisers. In addition, and of crucial importance, he succeeded in getting MacDonald's agreement to incorporate into any agreement a replacement programme of fourteen cruisers between the years 1929 and 1933. Despite pressure from the Americans and protests from the Foreign Office, Madden's desiderata were approved and eventually incorporated into the London Naval Treaty of 1930.[50]

This was a significant achievement for the Admiralty. By incorporating a steady replacement programme into the treaty, the Admiralty succeeded for the first time in decoupling its justifications for a steady building programme not just in cruisers, but also in destroyers and submarines, from the need to fight a war in the Far East. The navy was now able to argue that the provisions of the treaty themselves needed to be fulfilled and this provided an entirely new justification for its cruiser construction programme. This did not prevent the Treasury from challenging the Admiralty's construction programmes after the conclusion of the conference. Indeed, both in the spring of 1930 and in the winter of 1931 Philip Snowden, the Chancellor, attempted to scale back the overall construction programme. But, by separating this issue from that of the need to respond to Japanese construction, in both years Madden and the Admiralty were able to play on MacDonald's suspicion of French policy and on a growing, broader suspicion among the Cabinet that Britain was not being taken seriously on the continent because it refused to spend money on its navy.[51] In each case the Admiralty received the programme for which it had asked.

As a result, from 1930 until 1933 the Cabinet sanctioned the yearly construction of three cruisers, nine destroyers and three submarines.[52] This was the longest and largest steady programme since the end of the First World War and it occurred in a period of the most acute political and financial strain on the British Government.[53] Yet there were costs to this. First of all, the London Naval Treaty postponed new capital ship construction until 1937. By setting the building programme as its priority the Admiralty was forced to make large sacrifices in other areas, especially in its maintenance budget. In 1930 alone the naval estimates were cut by £4 million. This meant that the navy had to forego its fuel oil, battleship modernization and port defence programmes. Yet, without these sacrifices it is doubtful that the Admiralty would have achieved any of its aims. By appearing to co-operate with the Government over its desire to cut defence expenditure, Madden and Frederick Field, his successor as First Sea Lord, succeeded in maintaining their most important programme. Had they resisted these cuts more strongly it is doubtful that they would have achieved more. Indeed, it is very likely that a spirited Admiralty defence of more than its highest priority programme would have undermined its case and more of its strength would have been cut.

In early December 1931 a Fleet Committee of the Admiralty, composed of all the sea lords, met for the first time in order to consider naval policy in light of the financial effects of the sterling crisis the previous summer. This investigation was based on the premise that in the present financial state there was not enough money to fund a building programme, purchase reserves and keep maintenance costs on the present scale. The committee's purpose was to find savings in the annual maintenance cost of the fleet in order to release money for the first two objects.[54] It did so by placing more ships in reserve, by reducing their complements and by increasing the number of ships at home, rather than on foreign stations. The brunt of these cuts fell on the Atlantic and Mediterranean fleets. Outlying foreign stations, such as China, East Indies, Africa and America and West Indies, were unaffected due to their importance in maintaining national and imperial prestige. Having completed this part of their investigation, the committee went on to consider naval building policy and the navy's reserves of war material. The members of the committee felt that the navy's position in regard to cruisers, destroyers and submarines was becoming stabilized as long as it adhered to its annual programme. In regard to capital ships, however, the situation was far from satisfactory, and the committee was emphatic that the replacement of Britain's capital ship fleet could not be delayed beyond 1937. As far as war material was concerned, the committee again noted the serious position of the navy's reserves and recommended that this should be ameliorated by a steady yearly programme.

From the results of this meeting it is possible to see that Admiralty policy remained constant throughout the financial upheavals of the previous year. The main priority continued to be the maintenance of a steady building programme in cruisers, destroyers and submarines and to fund this by sacrificing on the maintenance budget and by foregoing expenditure on improving the mobility of the fleet and in repairing the defences of the navy's imperial bases. Field and the other members of the Admiralty Board, while far from content, accepted this state of affairs until autumn 1932, when they set out to attempt to change Cabinet policy.

Events over the previous year had exposed the weaknesses of Britain's over-all defence posture.[55] In particular, Japan's aggressive actions in Manchuria and in Shanghai had revealed that the Royal Navy's bases in the Far East were largely unprotected from attack by modern craft and that the main fleet's world-wide mobility was severely hampered by shortages in every area, including personnel, depth charges, torpedoes, fuel oil and aircraft. Moreover, the crises in Manchuria and Shanghai had developed extremely quickly and thus had undermined previous planning assumptions that there would be time during a slow build-up of international tension to prepare adequate defences in the Far East. Already in the early spring of 1932, the Chiefs of Staff and the newly appointed Deputy Chiefs of Staff Sub-Committee had investigated the overall deficiencies in Far Eastern defensive measures and had submitted rec-ommendations for improving the situation.[56] These had prompted the CID to recommend that the assumption that there would be no major war for ten years from any given date should be cancelled and that a start should be made, before the end of the Disarmament Conference, to provide for purely defensive commitments with priority given to the Far East.[57] In considering what policy to adopt as a result of the CID recommendations, the Cabinet did not dissent from the views expressed therein, but refrained from setting out any new, more definite policy.[58] However, one result of the CID recommendations was that the Cabinet finally authorized the start of the first stage of the main Singapore defences.[59]

With no specific direction from the Cabinet, the naval staff embarked in the autumn on the development of their own interpretation of the CID's recom-mendations. Vice-Admiral Sir Frederick Dreyer and other members of the naval staff began to examine in detail the navy's deficiencies in reserves over a large number of areas.[60] The results of their endeavours were accepted by Field and were presented to the Admiralty Board in early December 1932.[61] This well argued and highly detailed memorandum mapped out a programme which was intended to make up the Admiralty's deficiencies in armament and supply stores, fuel oil, local defence measures and to provide for the modern-ization of its capital ships and projected a cost of £28,377,500 up to 1942.

Field's memorandum also laid out a concurrent naval construction programme with an additional expected cost of £64,900,000.

By enumerating the expenditure necessary to raise the navy up to a requisite standard of efficiency, Field hoped to strengthen the Admiralty's bargaining power over future estimates. Indirectly, he hoped to use this memorandum to secure from the Cabinet the widest possible interpretation of the CID's March 1932 recommendations and to push the Cabinet to replace the ten year rule with a new decision which would sanction the gradual build up of reserves.[62] The immediate question, however, was how high a figure should be added to the 1933 sketch estimates to begin this process. When the Admiralty Board met to consider this question, however, the Sea Lords shied away from adding too large a figure to the estimates and agreed only to an extra £318,000, mostly for additions to the fuel oil reserve.[63] Together this was far less than the £2,213,110 per annum which Field's paper had projected would be necessary if the scheme was to be completed by 1942. Instead, the Admiralty Board opted for a very conservative, gradualist policy.

Field retired before the 1933 estimates were finalized and was replaced by Sir Ernle Chatfield, who has been described by one historian as the finest officer the Royal Navy produced between the wars.[64] The new First Sea Lord faced an immediate challenge because the Treasury, whilst it accepted that some increase in the 1933 naval estimates for new construction was inevitable, refused to sanction any of the additional expenditure for the build up of reserves and opposed this policy in principle.[65] In response Chatfield met with his sea lords and together they stressed to the First Lord the need to begin making up some of the ground that had been lost in previous years. The order of priority they set for 1933 was defensive equipment and war reserves, fuel oil storage, new flights for the fleet air arm and fuel oil.[66] To support this tough stance, Chatfield had Field's memorandum re-examined. This new report laid out the broad weaknesses of the navy's position. Chief amongst these were the poor strategical position in the Far East due to a lack of defended bases, a general lack of anti-submarine warfare equipment, the restricted mobility of the fleet due to the incomplete fuel oil reserve, little equipment for the defence of the merchant fleet and, finally, a general lack of stores for ships in reserve and for minesweeping. However, this memorandum concluded that these deficiencies could be made good for only £22,580,000.[67]

The Admiralty's refusal to give in on the question of war reserves and fuel oil meant that this whole issue was brought before the Cabinet in February 1933.[68] Bolton Eyres-Monsell, First Lord of the Admiralty, pressed the Cabinet both to sanction the provision of an additional £464,000 in the naval estimates for war reserves, fuel oil and the fleet air arm and to adopt some new assumption as a replacement for the ten year rule. Neville Chamberlain, the Chancellor of the Exchequer, remained opposed to any such increase and reminded the Cabinet that the CID had advised expenditure only on defensive commitments with priority on the Far East. MacDonald agreed with the First Lord that a time assumption was convenient for planning, but added that in his view the current world situation made it difficult to fix any definite assumption. As a result the Cabinet did not sanction the Admiralty's desired expenditure and concluded that the Government's policy should be that which the CID had recommended in March 1932. Thus the Admiralty failed in its first attempt to secure a new policy which would allow for a gradual increase in the navy's reserves and hence its ability effectively to provide for the security of Britain's sea communications in the Far East. For the most part this was due to the fact that the financial situation remained difficult and that the Disarmament Conference was still in progress. Given the above two factors, many Cabinet members found it difficult to accept a policy which seemed to imply naval expansion. Yet, by examining its needs and preparing a detailed programme for meeting them, the Admiralty placed itself in a position where it would be prepared to capitalize on any opportunity which might appear in an ever more threatening international environment.

Notwithstanding this setback in Cabinet, in late February 1933 Chatfield set out to press his colleagues on the Chiefs of Staff Sub-Committee to adopt a more determined stance to have the deficiencies in the Empire's defences rectified. He was spurned on by renewed Japanese aggression in the northern Chinese province of Jehol, and by a secret intelligence report of a planned Japanese attack on Singapore. Both these incidents underscored the defenceless state of the main base at Singapore and motivated the First Sea Lord to make significant alterations in the Admiralty's Far Eastern war plan.[69] The intelligence report, especially, reinforced Chatfield's belief that Singapore was vulnerable to a Japanese *coup de main* and that as a result immediate measures had to be taken to improve its defences.[70] Under his tutelage the Chief of Staff prepared a report which, using the 15 February Cabinet decision as a guideline, detailed how to improve and to speed up the completion of the Singapore defences.[71] The Treasury, though it remained sceptical of Chatfield's belief in the urgency of the measures, approved all the expenditure on Singapore, except for the provision of a new aerodrome, and the Cabinet gave their approval.[72]

Later, in May, Maurice Hankey, the ubiquitous Cabinet Secretary, brought the question of the Empire's coastal defences back to the attention of the Chief of Staff. One of the CID sub-committees, the Joint Defence Committee, had been drawing up a plan for the defences of Malta, but had decided that it needed further guidance from the COS. Hankey suggested that the latter should provide a priority list for coast defence in order to put together a general programme. He added that this might not be possible until after the Annual Review had been submitted. Chatfield agreed with this suggestion and further stated that he believed that they should concentrate on the Far East, but cautioned that, apart from Singapore, they should not submit demands in isolation which could not be implemented in the immediate future. The other committee members concurred with this and agreed to await the annual Foreign Office review before they set any priorities.[73]

The FO, however, believed that by the late spring of 1933, the situation in the Far East had stabilized somewhat but that Europe, especially Germany, was becoming more problematic.[74] This pronouncement had the potential to undermine the urgency which Chatfield and the Admiralty placed on remedying their exposed position in the Far East. Indeed, in the ensuing COS meeting in late June, both the Chief of the Imperial General Staff and the Chief of the Air Staff brought up this review in order to emphasize the deficiencies for the conduct of European operations.[75] The Admiralty response to the Foreign Office pronouncement was to accept it in principle but to ignore it in reality. At the COS meeting, Chatfield, as chairman, steered the discussion toward preparing a list of general deficiencies. He succeeded in obtaining the concurrence of the other two Chiefs of Staff to the preparation of an Annual Review based on a framework of each service pointing out its commitments and then illustrating the means it actually possessed to carry these out. The three major commitments they were to consider were the Far East, Locarno, and the defence of India, although no mention was made of priorities between these.[76] Within the Admiralty, when the DCNS, Charles Little, prepared the yearly memorandum which guided the estimates of each Admiralty department, he reaffirmed that a war in the Far East remained the basis for planning. The Foreign Office review, he mentioned, had 'inclined the finger towards Europe again', but slyly added that it was not desirable to draw attention to this 'as it would seriously affect estimates'.[77]

Under Chatfield's pressure, the Annual Review for 1933 became a very broad document which reviewed defence deficiencies over a wide area. It pointed to the ever-present Japanese threat in the Far East and to the growing, potential danger posed by Germany in Europe. In general, the review stated that the priority for defence expenditure should be based first on the defence of British possessions and interests in the Far East, secondly European commitments, and thirdly the defence of India against Soviet aggression. Lastly, the COS requested that the Cabinet formulate a new and more wide ranging guideline to replace the ten year rule than hitherto it had seen fit to sanction.[78] When this report was considered by the Imperial Committee in early November, it accepted the COS request that a new policy guideline be drawn up and took the priority recommendations embodied within the report as the basis for future policy. In order to co-ordinate any spending which might accrue as a result of the new policy, the CID also recommended that a committee composed of the three Chiefs of Staff, Maurice Hankey, and the Permanent Under Secretaries of the Foreign Office and the Treasury be created.[79]

This new body—the Defence Requirements Sub-Committee—met from late November 1933 until the end of February 1934, when it submitted to the Cabinet its recommendations for remedying the worst defects in the Empire's defences. Much has been written about this committee, which is viewed as a turning point in British inter-war defence policy. One of the most widely held opinions of its deliberations is that under pressure from Sir Robert Vansittart and Sir Warren Fisher, respective Permanent Under Secretaries at the Foreign Office and Treasury, the defence priorities as set out in the COS 1933 Annual Report were rearranged; Germany was placed first, with consequent effects on grand strategy and defence expenditure. However, a closer reading of the report brings out the fact that it was a significant victory for the Admiralty and the culmination of a line of policy it had pursued for several years.

Throughout 1933, the naval staff had continued with their consideration of naval deficiencies and their revision of the figures contained within Field's 1932 memorandum. This study culminated with the issue of a replacement statement at the end of November 1933, which further refined the totals from the previous year.[80] An abridged version of this paper was presented as the naval proposals to the DRC which accepted them *in toto*. They contained programmes for the expansion of the fleet air arm, the modernization of the navy's capital ships, the completion of the fuel oil reserve, the completion of the Singapore base and money for the build up of reserves, stores, local seaward defences, etc.[81] In addition to these, the report contained large items of expenditure for the army and the air force which were primarily for the defence of Britain's possessions in the Far East. The army section included a large outlay for the modernization of the gun defences at the primary ports and fuelling stations throughout the Empire, whilst the RAF requirements included large provision for strengthening the air units at Hong Kong, Singapore, and other Far Eastern ports.

The entire report was an attempt to compromise between those on the DRC who favoured placing preparation for war against Germany above that required for a Far Eastern war, and those who believed that Japan posed the more immediate threat since Germany had only just begun to rearm. Yet, this compromise contained proposals for remedying all the weaknesses in the Empire's naval defences which had vexed Admiralty planners for so long. As such it was an imperial document which embodied the Admiralty's strategic vision. Strategically, the report advocated an immediate policy of 'showing a tooth' in the Far East in order to buttress the exposed British position. Having thus deterred Japan, the report then advocated that 'long range' policy should focus on Germany, 'the ultimate potential enemy'.[82] Thus, the DRC report should be viewed as the culmination of the policy which the Admiralty had pursued since the Washington Conference. It did not, however, survive Ministerial scrutiny.

When the report went before the Ministerial Disarmament committee it was vigorously opposed by the Chancellor of the Exchequer, Neville Chamberlain. He remained far more concerned with the threat posed to the British Isles by a resurgent Germany and was willing to discount the immediacy of danger in the Far East. This view complemented his belief that some diplomatic accommodation with Japan could be found which would obviate the need for expensive defensive preparation in the Far East. He proposed to scale back the provision for the navy and the army in order to increase the RAF in response to the threat he perceived from German air rearmament.[83] Chatfield was infuriated with this proposal and wrote to the First Lord:

> The Chancellor has invented an entirely new Imperial Defence policy ...
> I am sure this looks as if the Chancellor's views are supported we shall
> have come to the parting of the ways as regards Imperial Defence. A
> bogus navy inadequate to its responsibilities is not one which any
> Admiralty could, in my opinion, be responsible for.[84]

However, as opinion in the committee began to solidify behind the
Chancellor, Chatfield abandoned the DRC scheme. He deferred further consideration of the new construction programme in light of the approaching second
London Naval Conference. Further, he withdrew from a multi-year programme
for remedying the navy's deficiencies and instead opted to ask for a £4 million
increase in the 1935 estimates in this regard.[85] In doing so he both departed
from Madden and Field's previous policy of attempting to secure long term
programmes, and followed their opportunistic pursuit of the Admiralty's strategic aims. By making the deficiency programme just another component of the
annual estimates Chatfield hoped to secure more in the long term than the
Ministerial committee had been willing to sanction.

Charles Madden and Frederick Field were not perfect chiefs of the naval
staff. Madden overplayed the Admiralty's hand on the 1928 estimates whilst
Field's miscalculations over the implementation of the 1931 cuts in naval pay
led to the Invergordon mutiny. Yet both were intelligent men who, after the
1928 debacle and in the difficult atmosphere of the early 1930s, realized that
they could not afford to be as aggressive in Whitehall as their predecessor,
David Beatty, in the 1920s. Instead Madden made the difficult choice of sacrificing a variety of programmes he believed were a fundamental necessity in
order to secure the construction programme he viewed as a vital necessity. His
skilful diplomacy during the Anglo-American discussions and the London
Naval Conference placed this programme in such a form that later he was able
to defend it successfully from constant Treasury attack.

Field continued and built upon the policy set by Madden. He guided the
construction programme safely through the budget-cutting first National
Government in 1931, although at the expense of a further cut in the naval estimates. Given Japan's aggressive actions in the Far East, however, Field began
to push the Government to place Britain's defensive posture in that part of the
world on a higher footing. To this end he succeeding in speeding up the completion of the Singapore naval base and beginning the construction of its main
gun defences. More generally he and his staff launched an investigation into
those deficiencies in reserves which limited the navy's ability to pose a credible deterrent in the Far East.

Chatfield by temperament was far more aggressive than either Madden or
Field and immediately upon assuming office he injected a renewed urgency
into war preparations within the Admiralty and into the deliberations of the
COS. His aggressive spirit, however, was appropriate for the time, as from the

beginning of his appointment Britain's security position appeared to decline and become worse than its financial position. In this atmosphere he was the right man to push for the political acceptance of the general need to buttress the Empire's defences and especially to counter the Admiralty's weaknesses.

Thus, from 1928 until 1933 Admiralty policy reverted to basics as its senior officers struggled to preserve their highest priority items. From 1933 Chatfield built on the groundwork that had been laid by his predecessors. The sacrifices Madden and Field had to make hampered the Admiralty's immediate ability to pose a credible deterrent and consequently to expand rapidly. Yet, without these sacrifices, Chatfield would have had a far more difficult task as he set out to build the Admiralty's material resources that would allow it finally to be ready to defend the Empire's lines of sea communications.

NOTES

1.   This is often termed the declinist school of British history. See: Paul Kennedy, *The Rise and Fall of British Naval Mastery* (London, 1976), pp 267–298. The phrase "Years of Decay" is the title of this chapter. idem., *The Rise and Fall of the Great Powers* (New York, 1988), pp 355–446, passim; F.S. Northedge, *The Troubled Giant* (London, 1966); Correlli Barnett, *The Collapse of British Power* (London, 1972); B.B. Schofield, *British Sea Power* (London, 1967); James L. Stokesbury, *Navy and Empire* (London, 1983).

2.   Christopher Hall, *Britain, America and Arms Control, 1921–1937* (London, 1987); Raymond G. O'Connor, *Perilous Equilibrium: The United States and the London Naval Conference* (New York, 1972); George T. Davis, *A Navy Second to None* (New York, 1940); Michael Vlahos, *The Blue Sword: The Naval War College and the American Mission, 1919–1941* (Newport, R.I., 1980) are among the examples of this genre.

3.   Schofield, *British Sea Power*, pp 107–108; Kennedy, *Rise and Fall British Naval Mastery*, p 279; James Neidpath, *The Singapore Naval Base and the Defence of Britain's Eastern Empire, 1919–1941* (Oxford, 1981), p 114; Barry D. Hunt, *Sailor-Scholar: Admiral Sir Herbert Richmond, 1871–1946* (Waterloo, Ont., 1982), pp 169–179, passim. Field receives some especially harsh criticism, see: Paul Haggie, *Britannia at Bay: The Defence of the British Empire Against Japan, 1931–1941* (Oxford, 1981), p 21; Stephen Roskill, *Naval Policy Between the Wars:v.1: The Period of Anglo-American Antagonism, 1919–1929* (London: 1968), p 48.

4.   Roskill's two volume *Naval Policy*, is an example of this kind of examination.

5.   Gregory Kennedy, 'Holding on to Empire: Anglo-American Relations in the Far East, 1933–1939', a paper given at the Canadian Historical Association Learneds, June, 1994 in Calgary, Alta, Canada.

6.   'A Review of Imperial Defence, 1926, by the Chiefs of Staff Sub-Committee', 22 Jun 1926, C[ommittee of] I[mperial] D[efence] 701-B, CAB[inet Records] 4/15, [Public Record Office (PRO), Kew, London]; 'Some General Principles of Imperial Defence', Memorandum by the Overseas Defence Sub-Committee (ODC) of the CID, 12 Mar 1928, CAB 5/7; 'London Naval Conference, 1930, Memorandum by the Chief of the Naval Staff (CNS), Admiral of the Fleet Sir Charles Madden, Basis of British Strategy', 17 Jan 1930, LNC (E) 10, ADM[iralty Records] 116/2746, [PRO, Kew, London]. All these memoranda offer an exposition of the Royal Navy's view of its role within the overall system of Imperial Defence.

7.   Greg C. Kennedy, 'Great Britain's Maritime Strength and the British Merchant Marine, 1922–1935', *The Mariner's Mirror*, 80, 1(1994), pp. 66-76.

8.   For an excellent re-examination of the relationship between the Royal Navy and its industrial base see: G.A.H. Gordon, *British Seapower and Procurement between the Wars: A Reappraisal of Rearmament* (London, 1988).

9.   'Summary of Admiralty Policy', 31 May 1929, ADM 167/80.

10   Ibid., and any subsequent quotations.
11.   This view had been held since at least 1924: 'Further Limitation of Naval Arms', Plans Division, 23 Apr 1924, PD 02001/24, ADM 1/8683/131.
12.   Admiralty Board Meeting, 3 Jun 1929, ADM 167/79.
13.   CID 236 Mtg, 5 Jul 1928, CAB 2/5.
14.   John Ferris, 'Treasury Control, the Ten Year Rule and British Service Policies, 1919–1924', *Historical Journal*, 30, 4(1987), pp 859–883.
15.   Cabinet Meeting, 6 May 1925, CAB 23/50.
16.   W.R. Fraser to A. Waterfield [Treasury officials], 8 Feb 1928, T[reasury Records] 161/285/33101/3, [PRO, Kew, London].
17.   W. Bridgeman to W. Churchill, 21 Dec 1927, T 161/285/S.33101/3; W. Churchill to W. Bridgeman, 16 Jan 1928, T 161/285/S.33101/3.
18.   Minute (17 Feb 1928) by R. Upcott, T 161/285/S.33101/4.
19.   Minute (29 Dec 1927) by W.R. Fraser on W. Bridgeman to W. Churchill, 21 Dec 1927, T 161/285/S.33101/3.
20.   Minute (3 July 1928) by R.V.N. Hopkins [Second Secretary, Treasury], T 175/48.
21.   Minute (3 Jul 1928) by G. Upcott on 'Basis of Service Estimates', Sir Maurice Hankey, 2 Jul 1928, CID 892-B, T 175/35.
22.   'The Basis of Navy Estimates', W. Churchill Memorandum, 25 Jun 1928, CID 891-B, CAB 4/17.
23.   'Extracts from Japan Annual Report 1926, 13 April 1927', Sir J. Tilley [British Ambassador to Japan], 28 Jun 1927, CID 810-B, CAB 4/16.
24.   B.J.C. McKercher, 'A Sane and Sensible Diplomacy: Austen Chamberlain, Japan, and the Naval Balance of Power in the Pacific Ocean, 1924-1929', *Canadian Journal of History*, 21(1986), pp 187–213.
25.   For the security of Britain's position in the world in the late 1920s see: David French, *The British Way in Warfare*, 1688–2000, (London: 1990), pp 185–188.
26.   CID 236 Mtg, 5 Jul 1928, CAB 2/5. For a general overview of the effect of the Soviet threat to India on British strategic policy in the inter war years see: Keith Neilson, '"Pursued by a Bear": British Estimates of Soviet Military Strength and Anglo-Soviet Relations, 1922–1939', *Canadian Journal of History*, 28(1993), pp 189–221.
27.   Cabinet Meeting, 18 Jul 1928, CAB 23/58.
28.   John Ferris, *Men, Money and Diplomacy: The Evolution of British Strategic Policy, 1919–1926*, (Ithaca: 1989), pp 166–69.
29.   Minute (15 Jan 1928) by W. Churchill on Treasury memoranda, T 161/285/S.33101/3.
30.   Minute (13 Nov 1928) by R. Backhouse [Controller] on 'Basis of Naval Estimates', Plans Division, 15 Oct 1928, M.03152/28, ADM 116/3629.
31.   'War Memorandum', Plans Division, 20 Jan 1920, M.00340/20, ADM 116/3124.
32.   'Basis of Naval Estimates', Plans Division, 15 Oct 1928, M.03152/28, ADM 116/3629. This decision was first made in 1923.
33.   Minute (17 Apr 1928) by W.W. Fisher [DCNS] on 'The Total Number and Type of Cruisers required by the British Empire', Plans Division, 15 Mar 1928, PD 02984/28, ADM 116/2607.
34.   Minute (7 Nov 1928) by W.W. Fisher on 'The Basis of Naval Estimates', Plans Division, 15 Oct 1928, M.03152/28, ADM 116/3629.
35.   Minute (23 Apr 1928) by Madden on 'The Total Number and Type of Cruisers Required by the British Empire', Plans Division, 15 Mar 1928, PD 02984/28, ADM 116/2607; 'Cruiser Requirements-France and America (Preliminary Notes Only)', Plans Division, 11 Jun 1928, PD 03048/28, ADM 116/2607.
36.   Minutes (16 Nov 1928 and 18 Nov 1928) by Madden and Murray on 'The Basis of Naval Estimates', Plans Division, 15 Oct 1928, M.03152/28, ADM 116/3629.
37.   On the overall position of British coastal defences see the summary in 'Appendix II-Coast Defence' in 'Appreciation of the General Naval Situation in 1931 by the First Sea Lord', 10 April 1931, CID 1047-B, CAB 4/21; Jon Tetsuro Sumida, '"The Best Laid Plans": The Development of British Battle-Fleet Tactics, 1919–1942', *International History Review*, 14, 4(1992), pp 681–700.
38.   'Interim Report on the Results of the Coast Defence Practices Held in 1928', War Office Memorandum, 18 May 1929, Appendix to: COS 78 Mtg, 11 Jun 1929, CAB 53/3. See also the

COS discussion at this meeting.

39. 'Oil Fuel Reserve-Agreement Between the Admiralty and Treasury', 18 Jan 1929, CID 930-B, CAB 4/18

40. Minutes (12 Jun 1923 and 25 Jun 1923) by Dudley Pound and Roger Keyes on 'Programme of Construction and Reconstruction', 12 Jun 1923 Plans Division, PD 01813/23, ADM 1/8702/151; Minute (2 Sep 1927) by Dudley Pound on 'British and Japanese Cruiser Strength', 15 Aug 1927, Plans Division, PD 02905/27, ADM 116/3440.

41. 'The Multiple Pom-Pom as a Counter to Torpedo Aircraft-Note by the First Sea Lord', 26 Jun 1928, CID 893-B, CAB 4/17.

42. Ibid.

43. Neidpath, *Singapore,* passim.

44. Ibid, p 117.

45. 'Programme of Construction and Reconstruction', Plans Division, 12 June 1923, PD 01813/23, ADM 1/8702/151.

46. See: 'Notes on the Naval Construction Programme', Plans Division, 20 Nov 1929, PD 03430/29, ADM 116/2606.

47. The first such programme was mooted in 'Programme of Construction and Reconstruction'", Plans Division, 12 Jun 1923, PD 01813/23, ADM 1/8702/151, and a far more ambitious programme was presented in 'Ten Year Building Programme', 6 Mar 1925, PD 02171/25, ADM 1/8685/152. The arguments for a long steady programme were presented in these memos and can also be found in these memoranda and accompanying minutes: 'The Total Number and Type of Cruisers Required by the British Empire', Plans Division, 15 Mar 1928, PD 02984/28, ADM 116/2607; 'Cruiser Requirements-France and America (Preliminary Notes Only)', Plans Division, 11 Jun 1928, PD 03048/28, ADM 116/2607; 'Notes on the Naval Construction Programme', Plans Division, 20 Nov 1929, PD 03430/29, ADM 116/2606.

48. The history of the lead up to these negotiations has been set out in an excellent manner in the following: B.J.C. McKercher, *The Second Baldwin Government and the United States, 1924-1929: Attitudes and Diplomacy* (Cambridge: 1984); idem, 'From Enmity to Cooperation: The Second Baldwin Government and the Improvement of Anglo-American Relations, November 1928-June 1929', *Albion* 24, 1(1992), pp 65–88; idem 'No Eternal Friends or Enemies: British Defence Policy and the Problem of the United States, 1919–1939', *Canadian Journal of History* 28(1993), pp 257–293.

49. For the details of these negotiations and the aftermath see: Orest Babij, 'The Second Labour Government and British Maritime Security, 1929-1931', *Diplomacy and Statecraft,* 6, 3 (1995), pp 645–71

50. 'International Treaty for the Limitation and Reduction of Naval Armament, Apr 22, 1930' Cmd. 3556, (London: 1930),

51. FS [Fighting Services Committee] (29), 11 Mtg, 3 Jun 1930, CAB 27/407; FS (29), 14 Mtg, 26 Jan 1931, CAB 27/407; FS (29) 15 Mtg, 29 Jan 1931, CAB 27/407; For MacDonald's suspicions of French policy it is instructive to read his diary entries on the subject: MacDonald MSS, PRO 30/69/1753, [PRO, Kew, London].

52. Roskill, *Naval Policy, v.1,* Appendix C, pp 580-585.

53. For an excellent treatment of the political and economic upheavals of the time see: Philip Williamson, *National Crisis and National Government: British Politics, the Economy and Empire, 1926-1932* (Cambridge, 1992).

54. Fleet Committee–First Report', 7 Dec 1931, M.02946/31, ADM 116/2860. The remainder of this paragraph is based on this report.

55. Haggie, *Britannia,* pp 24–52, passim.

56. 'Report by the Deputies to the Chiefs of Staff Sub-Committee on the Situation in the Far East', 22 Feb 1932, DCOS 1, CAB 54/3; 'The Situation in the Far East-Report by the Chiefs of Staff Sub-Committee', 3 Mar 1932, COS 296, CAB 53/22; 'Imperial Defence Policy-Annual Review for 1932 by the Chiefs of Staff Sub-Committee', 23 Feb 1932, CID 1082-B, CAB 4/21.

57. CID 255 Mtg, 22 Mar 1932, CAB 2/5.

58. Cabinet Meeting, 23 Mar 1932, CAB 23/70.

59. CID 256 Mtg, 9 Jun 1932, CAB 2/5; Cabinet Meeting 11 Oct 1932, CAB 23/72.

60. Admiral Sir Frederick Dreyer, *The Sea Heritage,* (London: 1955), pp 297–298.

61. 'Memorandum by the First Sea Lord–Review of the Present Condition of the Navy and General Remarks on Future Policy', 14 Nov 1932, ADM 167/87; Admiralty Board Meeting, 7 Dec 1932, ADM 167/85. The remainder of the discussion on this subject is taken from these two sources.
62. The priority for the build up of naval stores was set out in a separate memorandum: 'Provision of Reserves of Naval Stores – Priority', Plans Division, 17 Nov 1932, PD 04196/32, ADM 116/3434
63. B. Eyres-Monsell to N. Chamberlain, 14 Dec 1932, ADM 167/87.
64. Arthur Marder, *Old Friends, New Enemies: The Royal Navy and the Imperial Japanese Navy, Strategic Illusions, 1936–1941* (Oxford, 1981).
65. N. Chamberlain to B. Eyres-Monsell, 10 Jan 1933, T 161/580/S.35171/33.
66. E. Chatfield to B. Eyres-Monsell, 16 Jan 1933, ADM 167/89.
67. 'Notes on Navy Estimates for 1933', Plans Division, 14 Feb 1933, ADM 116/3434.
68. Cabinet Meeting, 15 Feb 1933, CAB 23/75.
69. Admiralty telegram to Commander in Chief China Station, 25 Apr 1933, ADM 116/3472; 'Memorandum on Naval Dispositions in the Far East in Emergency', 26 Apr 1933, ADM 116/3472.
70. See Chatfield's comments at the 107th, 108th and 109th meetings of the COS, 28 Feb 1932, 27 Mar 1932, 11 Apr 1932, CAB 53/4.
71. 'The Situation in the Far East', COS Report, 31 Mar 1933, CID 1103-B, CAB 4/22.
72. Treasury minutes, nd. no author, T 175/48; Cabinet Meeting, 12 Apr 1933, CAB 23/75.
73. COS 110 Mtg, 2 May 1933, CAB 53/4.
74. 'Memorandum on the Foreign Policy of His Majesty's Government in the United Kingdom', 19 May 1933, CID 1112-B, CAB 4/22.
75. COS 111 Mtg, 20 Jun 1933, CAB 53/4.
76. Ibid.
77. Minute (2 Aug 1933) by C. Little on 'Basis of Navy Estimates', 20 Jul 1933, ADM 116/3629.
78. 'Annual Review (1933) by the Chiefs of Staff Sub-Committee', 12 Oct 1933, CID 1113-B, CAB 4/22.
79. CID 261 Mtg, 9 Nov 1933, CAB 2/6.
80. 'Naval Defence Requirements, DR, Memorandum by the First Sea Lord', 30 Nov 1933, ADM 167/89.
81. 'General Account of Proceedings up to and Including the Report of the DRC (February 1934) and the Navy Estimates 1934', nd. (spring 1934), ADM 116/3434; 'Defence Requirements Sub-Committee, Report', 28 Feb 1934, DRC-14, CAB 16/109.
82. 'Defence Requirements Sub-Committee, Report', 28 Feb 1934, DRC-14, CAB 16/109.
83. The Chancellor's views were most succinctly brought out in: 'Memorandum by the Chancellor of the Exchequer', 20 Jun 1934, DC(M) 120, CAB 16/111.
84. E. Chatfield to B. Eyres-Monsell, 21 Jun 1934, ADM 116/3434.
85. E. Chatfield to W. W. Fisher, 2 Aug 1934, CHT [Chatfield Papers] 4/5, [National Maritime Museum, Greenwich].

1935: a snapshot of British imperial defence in the Far East

GREG KENNEDY

Britain's position in the Far East in 1935 was an extremely complex and Gordian affair. Peace in the Pacific had been established with some firmness, in 1922 at the Washington Conference and in 1930 at the London Naval Conference, on a basis of the political structure stemming from the Covenant of the League of Nations and a rough balance of power in the region.[1] Japanese aggression in Manchuria in 1931 and at Shanghai in 1932 and the failure of the League of Nations to be able to curb such action, signalled that League of Nations' diplomacy in the Pacific had, by 1935, been replaced by the diplomacy of power similar to the situation which had existed in Europe prior to 1914.[2] As for further naval discussions, most British departments of state and the individuals concerned with such matters recognized that the chances of keeping Japan involved in further naval limitation talks and continuing the capital ship building holiday were not at all likely. At best, perhaps some 'gentlemen's agreement' could be worked out.[3] For the British Empire this reversion to a pre-1914 balance of power situation meant that three elements were crucial to the continued maintenance of Britain's position in the Far East: the interwoven political and economic relationship between the British Empire, China and Japan; a subtle and complex British foreign policy in the region; and a revitalized British military programme that would provide the sinew to back up that foreign and economic policy. British policy makers believed that even though the balance of power in the Pacific was in a state of flux, such fluctuation did not automatically indicate that the British position was unbearably weak, nor, more importantly, was any perceived weakness irreparable. The key to protecting the integrity of the Far Eastern elements of the Empire was a co-ordinated utilization of these three key aspects of imperial defence: financial and economic power, naval power and a foreign policy that strove to maintain the *status quo*.[4] This study will provide a snapshot of the attempts to co-ordinate these elements, which took place within the British Foreign Office (specifically the Far Eastern Department), in association with Cabinet, the Treasury, the Defence Requirements Committee (DRC), the Committee of Imperial Defence (CID), the Chiefs of Staff (COS), and the Royal Navy (RN).

The Foreign Office and the Treasury

By 1935, Britain's trade and commerce in the Far East was entering a new phase of development, particularly in China. One of the main features of this changing situation was the growing commercial competition with Japan.[5] The importance of the Chinese market in actual cash value was limited. China ranked sixteenth as a customer and absorbed only some 2.5 per cent of Britain's total export trade.[6] Investment in the country represented barely 5 per cent of Britain's total foreign holdings.[7] By 1934 Britain received only 11 per cent of China's foreign commerce. However, Britain was still the largest supplier of manufactured goods and British investments in China were estimated at £240 million (gold), surpassing those of any other country.[8] Working from *Foreign Investment in China*, a study by an American economist, C.F. Remer, that showed the position in China as of January 1931, the Foreign Office revealed that of the total foreign investment in China, pegged at £660 million, Britain's share was 36.7 per cent, with Japan's the next closest at 35.1. No other nation's investment exceeded 9 per cent. As for business investments, Britain's share was 38 per cent and Japan's 36 per cent, with no other country after them being over 11 per cent.[9] After the severance of Manchuria in 1931, the total foreign investment was reduced from £666 to £485 million, which by geographic distribution revealed that British-controlled Shanghai held 47 per cent, the rest of China 26 per cent, with 27 per cent being undistributed. Total business investment was reduced from £520 to £352 million, with the British share being 56.2, the Japanese 21, and no other country's exceeding 10 per cent.[10]

In the opinion of the Foreign Office, China's economic future as it affected the British Empire depended somewhat on better railways, roads and waterways to the interior opening up some newer markets, but more importantly:

> This expansion of external trade will in all likelihood be a slow process: it will probably be accompanied by a gradual increase of foreign investments in China. At present the infiltration of money from abroad is checked by unfavourable political conditions, but *pari passu* with the removal of this obstacle, foreign capital should tend to flow into China indirectly in the form of the supply of manufactured products— principally equipment goods—on credit, and directly by the financing of industrial and governmental projects, such as the construction of factories, bridges, &c. In the meanwhile, it seems likely that, whatever happens, the growth of the world's trade with China (and with it that of British exports thither) will be steady rather than spectacular.[11]

As had been the case since the age of Marco Polo, the worth of China lay in the future, particularly in areas of development such as railways, land and buildings, banking, insurance, shipping, factories, roadbuilding, and so on.[12] It was the future development of these areas in which British investors and industrialists were most interested. Louis Beale, the Commercial Counsellor in Shanghai, was certainly of the opinion that Britain was

> ready and able to embark on a very considerable expansion of trade and industry in China. This is particularly true of what I may term the construction and capital side of commerce—shipbuilding, railroads,

machinery, equipment and such basic industries as are suitable for operation in China (textiles, chemicals, paint making and possibly certain forms of iron and steel production, electric light and power, and so on).[13]

This vision of the future required that investors and industrialists be given an answer to the question of whether His Majesty's Government was going to continue to practise a *laissez faire* attitude towards increasing Japanese competition, or was the Government going to take a more active role in protecting and supporting business in the Far East?

The Cabinet agreed with Beale's reading of the situation. One of the first noticeable actions taken by the British Government to try to assist traditional British interests against Japanese competition was the granting of approval for Walter Runciman, President of the Board of Trade, to prepare a bill which would provide £2 million in 'defensive' shipping subsidies for British tramp steamers.[14] Of still greater importance was the formation on 13 February 1935, of the Cabinet Committee on Political and Economic Relations with Japan, made up of the Prime Minister—Ramsay MacDonald, the Chancellor of the Exchequer— Neville Chamberlain, the Secretary of State for Foreign Affairs— Sir John Simon, the Secretary of State for War—Viscount Hailsham, and Walter Runciman.[15]

The formation of this committee reflected an increasing interest in the future of developing Britain's oil industry in the region, as well as a concentration on high capital, finished products for the modernizing Chinese markets.[16] The trouble with Japan over oil, the question of the future of the Government's greater involvement with commercial issues and the formation of the committee also reflected not only how important those economic ties of empire were, but also revealed the interconnection of economic, political and military issues. The committee resulted from three separate events which had their origins in late 1934. The first was the aggressive Japanese threat to British oil interests in the Far East. The second was the report of the Federation of British Industry (FBI) mission led by Lord Barnby on Britain's trade and commerce in relation to Japanese competition. The third was the silver crisis that enveloped China when the American Silver Purchase Act became law in June 1934.[17]

On 27 March 1934, the Japanese Government passed the Petroleum Industry Law. This threatened foreign oil interests, such as the British Asiatic Petroleum Company, in a number of ways. Articles 5 to 7 of the law revealed that, in effect, the Japanese Government intended to maintain strategic reserves of oil (up to two years' worth) at the expense of the foreign importers.[18] Those articles also allowed the Japanese Government the right to buy any quantity of oil they required at a price fixed by them and to regulate the equipment of the companies as they saw fit.[19] Foreign oil companies were also being threatened in Manchukuo where a puppet government controlled by the Japanese Kwangtung army had '...for reasons of national defence and economic development and in the interests of the inhabitants, ... decided to establish an oil monopoly'.[20] Any oil monopoly would be exercised through the Manchukuo

Petroleum Company, a state-controlled concern in which the South Manchuria Railway Company had large interests. Companies like the Asiatic Petroleum Company argued that a monopoly of sales implied a monopoly of imports, and that the high proportion of shares to be held by the South Manchuria Railway, which also happened to operate a large petroleum refinery at Fushun, would weight the scales in favour of the Japanese national.[21] To the British policy makers and oil industry representatives, these actions represented a violation of the 'open door' policy. Such Japanese actions against oil interests were discouraging for British policy makers, especially when looked at in the larger context of the Amau Doctrine.

The Amau declaration of April 1934—a statement of a Japanese-style Monroe Doctrine—warned other nations, particularly Britain, against trying to assist China in any way without first gaining Japanese approval or assistance in the project.[22] This new aggressive Japanese stance coincided with the FBI mission to Manchuria, whose task it was to see how Anglo-Japanese trade relations could be improved.[23] The ensuing report from that mission revealed the differences in opinion between the Foreign Office and the Treasury on both trade issues and whether the solving of those trade problems could bring about a return to closer relations between Japan and the British Empire. However, that discussion of different views on the use of trade to gain political advantage highlighted the common view of both departments, that trade and political issues could not be separated, especially when those political issues were so intimately connected to the larger question of the defence of the Empire. The Foreign Office strategy for dealing with the oil monopoly problem and the Amau Doctrine also reflected one of the fundamental dilemmas that British policy makers faced when dealing with Far Eastern issues: would they avoid formal entangling alliances that gave the appearance of Britain leading any type of anti-Japanese bloc, or, would they attempt to woo and control Japan through closer relations.

The Foreign Office view was that no alliances were possible. The price of such a formal relationship with any power in the region would be too high and it would achieve very little in terms of creating greater security. In fact, it believed that the repercussions of such relations would only hasten the decline of the British position in the Far East. One or more of the other powers with Far Eastern interests would certainly feel threatened by such an act and retaliate in some fashion. Thus, the Foreign Office advocated the 'no bloc' approach, which called for multilateral action, but not formal British support for any bilateral agreement, especially one that would aggravate Japan's sensitivity about its isolation. The Treasury on the other hand supported business and industry interests in China which called for a 'strong policy' that required the British Government to take a firmer stand in support of these interest groups, especially when issues collided with Japanese competition. More importantly, this Treasury/business/Board of Trade alliance—'the Treasury view'—saw some sort of Anglo-Japanese *rapprochement* as the most effective way of securing British interests in the Far East. The important strategic question was which of these two paths would be used in defence of imperial interests in the region.

The difficulty of maintaining a 'no-bloc' policy toward Japan was not lost on the Foreign Office. Sir John Simon, Secretary of State for Foreign Affairs, was always cognizant of the need not to arouse further anti-British attitudes in Japan through any economic or political association with other countries that would alarm the isolated Japanese.[24] However, the Amau statement disturbed Simon because it appeared to be a direct breach of the Nine Power Treaty. But analysis by the Far Eastern Department of the Foreign Office pointed out that the declaration could be aimed at a number of events in China: the German military mission of General von Seeckt to China, the proposed international loan to China that French negotiators were attending but from which Japanese participation was excluded, or the preparation of public opinion for a firm Japanese stand in the forthcoming naval negotiations.[25] It was therefore hard to be certain that this statement had indeed been directed specifically at Britain. Seen in such a context the Amau statement was a potential anti-Japanese rallying point for powers with interests in China. However, later incidents over the oil monopoly issue in 1935 revealed the possible dangers such actions could have for Britain. The Far Eastern Department, primarily under the guidance of Sir A.A.H. Victor Wellesley, Deputy Under-Secretary of State, and the Head of the Foreign Office Far Eastern Department, C. W. Orde, again advised that while co-operation by American companies in lodging actions against the Japanese would be the best strategy, there was no desire to give any official sanction to the withholding of oil supplies by British or American companies.[26] Japan's sensitivity over her strategic oil reserves, concerns over tensions between Russia and Japan, and uncertainty as to the validity of American governmental support if negotiations got rough, dictated a continuance of the Foreign Office 'no bloc involvement' policy.

Those members of the Federation of British Industries (FBI) mission, and later the leading British firms in China, whose petitions to the British Government for some sort of action there prompted the Leith-Ross mission,[27] had found allies within the Treasury. This alliance was based on a common belief—held by Neville Chamberlain, Walter Runciman, and industrialists such as Sir Guy Locock, Director of the FBI, Lord Barnby, a former head of the Federation, and Sir Julian Piggot of British Iron and Steel—that within the Japanese Government there existed a group of powerful men whose views on Japanese strategic policy were moderate.[28] The hope of the Treasury and this group was that, with encouragement and a firm stand from Britain against any further unilateral action, these Japanese moderates could be persuaded to form better ties with Britain.[29] However, neither the industrialists nor Chamberlain advocated giving Japan a 'free hand' in China:

> Clearly we could not contemplate giving Japan a free hand in China or

in Shanghai or in the Dutch East Indies or to do what she thought fit by way of aggression against the Soviet. In the future we were bound to be much concerned with the position of China. It might be doubtful what the designs of Japan on China were, but it was clear that if we are to preserve our own position in China we ought to act now .... Mr. Hirota would have to indicate that in any such pact we must have assurances that our important interests will not be prejudicially affected.[30]

What they did advocate was a more sympathetic attitude towards the interpretation of Japan's ultimate goals in the region and a belief that an agreement in everyone's (Japan's and Britain's) interests could be struck. When situations arose where better Anglo-Japanese relations might be furthered, such as when the Japanese Minister for Foreign Affairs, Hirota Koki, hinted at a possible bilateral non-aggression pact, the Chamberlain faction was simply more inclined to believe that such talks would bring about a better understanding between the two nations.

The Foreign Office on the other hand was less hopeful and enthusiastic that anything worthwhile would be agreed. In this way, the infamous and oft-quoted joint Simon–Chamberlain memo to Cabinet on 'The Future of Anglo-Japanese Relations', reflected that Chamberlain–FBI enthusiasm, but was at all times tempered by Simon and the Foreign Office's bigger imperial view, as well as their wait-and-see attitude towards Japan's true intentions, even with the new spur of possible European conflict with a resurgent Germany.[31] The result was a memo that did little more than show what good relations between the two countries would produce, but did nothing to dispel the latent distrust over Japan's true intentions, nor did it undermine the Foreign Office 'no bloc' policy.[32]

During his 1934 tour of important industrialists and politicians in Britain, Louis Beale had the opportunity to observe how such calls for closer relations to Japan and a firmer stand had implications that ran counter to each other. Beale's comments to Sir Alexander Cadogan, Ambassador in Peking, on a meeting between the industrialists and Simon indicated a number of the policy problems:

> Sir John then ... told his visitors that H.M.G. were determined that the UK should 'stay in China' and that all their legitimate enterprises there would receive the full support of H.M.G. ... Sir John also referred to the difficult problem facing us from the plans and ambitions of Japan in North China and implied that while we were not in a position to resist Japan's incursions, he felt that a satisfactory solution of our economic participation in China in harmony Japan was quite possible and certainly desirable .... However that may be, I believe that we can and should go ahead with all our might in China in trade and industry and I believe that Japan could be led into harmony with such policy. I have

never believed that Japan possessed the resources necessary to develop
a great country like China. The United Kingdom and the British
Empire, however, possess all the resources needful for such a gigantic
enterprise ... How long will the Army dominate the Civil life and
actions of Japan?[33]

The Foreign Office members in London (from Simon, through to the
Permanent Under-Secretary of State, Sir Robert Vansittart, Wellesley, Orde)
and the British diplomats abroad (the British Ambassador in Tokyo, Sir Robert
Henry Clive, and his key adviser, George Sansom, the Commercial Counsellor)
both wanted harmony and a better understanding with Japan. However, they
were adamantly opposed to any view that supposed there was an influential
moderate party in Japan that would protect existing and future British interests
in China.[34] The common Foreign Office vision of the 'no bloc' approach to
Japan and the question of 'moderates' was evident in the minutes surrounding
Sir Clive's despatch of 9 February 1935 to Simon, a document that at Vansittart's
direction soon rose to Cabinet Paper rank.[35] The despatch itself, as well as the
minutes, explained why an understanding with America directed against Japan
would be dangerous for Britain:

> we cannot and must not bank on U.S. co-operation with us against
> Japan, and that it is quite wrong to imagine that this illusory plan will
> strengthen the non-existent 'moderate' or 'civilian' party in Japan in
> opposing anything calculated to favour Japan's vital interests.[36]

Both Orde and Wellesley echoed this view of America's influence in the Far
East, as well as the point on the usefulness of the 'moderates' in any future
policy. Wellesley advised that the Empire's relations with Japan were good
now because it suited Japan, and so '... we should make the best of it for as
long as possible. A time may come when she will no longer fear political isolation and then our only lever will be force.'[37]

Vansittart agreed on these points. He also saw an opportunity to discredit
men such as Lord Lothian, Lord Lytton, General Smuts and Lloyd George[38]
who called loudly and often in public for closer ties with the United States
against Japan. Vansittart considered these men amateurs attempting to discredit
the professional Far Eastern Department people 'who see more clearly and
know their job better'.[39] He also resented the confusion the public utterances
of these men created in Japanese policy-making circles. The Japanese perception of Western government and democracy caused non-Governmental persons
such as Lothian, Lloyd George, Lytton and Smuts to be taken for more than
they really were, thereby muddying the Japanese picture of the true British
position.[40] Sir Robert Clive and his advisors had an 'excellent grip on reality',
according to Vansittart, and for this reason he advised Simon to circulate the
despatch to Cabinet and use it to counteract Lord Lothian and company.[41] As
to the greater question of a policy of opportunism and 'no blocs' safeguarding

Britain's interests in the Far East, he remarked that:

> We are all keenly concerned to keep on good terms with Japan. We
> have no illusions whatever about her: she means to dominate the East
> as Germany means to dominate Europe. We have to play for time and
> to avoid clashes in our own interests. After very careful examination
> we are united in finding that there is no golden road in this policy. We
> have to feel our way carefully from day to day and year to year. The
> ideas, and expressions, of Lord Lothian ... cut definitely across this
> policy.... We have a very difficult and delicate task ahead of us and
> must persevere in the balance of our policy, despite outside interven-
> tion and abuse. Our national safety depends on not giving way to these
> illusionists.[42]

Foreign Office views on the role of the 'moderates' gained even more credibil-
ity when Clive reported that Joseph C. Grew, the American Ambassador to
Japan (with whom Clive was on very good terms) supported this 'no moderates' view. Vansittart thought that 'It is interesting that the American
Ambassador—who has now been in Japan for some time and knows his job—
bears out the view of our own embassy.'[43] Clearly the Far Eastern Department's
role in the policy-making process for a Far Eastern strategy would be a dominant one.

The Foreign Office and strategic policy
    The Foreign Office was responsible for balancing the diverse interests of an
imperial foreign policy. For the Far Eastern Department this meant keeping the
Secretary of State for Foreign Affairs informed of the strategic options applicable to the region, as well as trying to maintain an awareness of where Britain's
imperial interests fitted in with the foreign policies of the other powers in the
region. Operating as an institution responsible for gauging and evaluating
information and situations, these men and the technical experts in their employ
(such as academic specialists who were called in for special consultation) were
the acknowledged experts on Far Eastern affairs.[44] Their specialized skills and
knowledge of a very foreign country gave them an autonomous position in
British foreign policy-making that was not seen in the operations of other
departments. While other FO personnel could claim a knowledge of the situation in departments where they did not even work—the German, French,
American or even Northern departments—because of a general knowledge of
relatively similar cultures and more familiar languages, those who could challenge the Far Eastern Department's view on Far Eastern affairs and mount a
cogent and accurate argument were few in number. Even those within the higher reaches of the office, such as Vansittart, would have to tread carefully in
their dabblings in Far Eastern policy, as we shall see.
    Simon's ideas concerning the Far East, and how a wary balance-of-power
game was to be played out in that region, originated with the Far Eastern

Department staff of the Foreign Office, and other senior staff. Simon's views reflected the information and policies that were recommended to him, through the Permanent Under-Secretary of State, by Sir Victor Wellesley, and especially Orde, Clive, Cadogan, Sansom and senior clerks such as Frank Ashton-Gwatkin and Sir John Pratt (of the Consular Service). Both Simon and Vansittart considered Sir George Sansom, the Commercial Counsellor at the Tokyo embassy, to be the undisputed expert on the Japanese, and therefore to some extent, Chinese affairs. Neither Simon nor Vansittart showed a ready inclination for straying too far from Sir George's advice and analysis. Simon thought Sansom the 'greatest living authority on Japan', and in debates with the Treasury or the Board of Trade over British policy regarding Japan, Sansom's voice would be authoritative.[45] Vansittart's admiration went so far that: 'My own view has been for some time that Sir G. Sansom should be the next Ambassador. He has carried several in his day and should end by having his own day. He is one of the most distinguished men in Asia...'[46] These were the men and ideas behind the policies that Sir John would take to the highest levels of British policy-making.

Simon began his assessment of relations between the British Empire and Japan from the point of view that they were generally good.[47] They were not as close as they once had been, but neither was there a dangerous level of tension.[48] Simon understood that the vital question was how to balance Britain's world-wide interests in a Far Eastern context.[49] For him, the fulcrum in this balancing act was China. It was not so much the direct relationship between Britain and Japan that was the problem, it was rather how to balance British imperial interests in China with Japan's desire to dominate and expand into China. Was there some special action that was required to improve Anglo-Japanese relations in this regard? Into this equation came also the attitudes of the Chinese Governments and people, which were not necessarily in line with British interests. If there was a price to pay to either the Chinese or the Japanese, Simon wondered, what would that price be, and could the Empire afford it?[50] Unavoidably linked to the central feature of Sino-Japanese relations were Britain's own trade interests, as well as other important relations with Russia, Holland, the United States, the British Dominions, France and the growing problem of a conflict with Germany or Italy erupting in Europe.[51] To Simon, the question of the protection of British interests in the Far East was a matter of high policy, not merely economic or trade policy.[52] Simon's proposed solution to this knotty problem was a multilateral agreement between China, the United States, Great Britain and Japan that was based on a large dose of *realpolitik*.

Only Chinese action and acceptance, Simon argued, could solve the twisted problems that the USA, Britain and Japan had with regard to the new challenges to the 'open door' that the invasion of Manchukuo had provoked. They could not be remedied by the creation of anti-Japanese blocs. Recognition of Manchukuo could not be achieved without China's consent. If the Chinese would accept an agreement that allowed them to 'save face,' that amounted to a recognition of the *de facto* position in Manchukuo, combined with a reaffirmation of respect for Chinese integrity inside the Great Wall, many problems would be removed.[53] Then:

> The United States could hardly pretend to be more Chinese than China or at any rate could not complain if we followed China's lead. An agreement on the outstanding question of Manchukuo would perhaps help to get America's consent to a system of agreed naval programmes. Both China and the United States would get some satisfaction from the re-affirmation as to the independence of China proper and as to the continuance of the Open Door both for China and for Manchukuo. If this could be combined with some solution of China's difficulty over the silver question, this would be an added inducement for China ... And, of course, Japan would consider herself as much reassured if better relations between herself and the United States were brought about by such a multilateral agrrangement ...[54]

Simon believed that China had accepted the reality of the Japanese invasion and was 'saving face' in a fashion that indicated that not even the Chinese expected the invasion of Manchukuo to be reversed:

> She claims to treat the independent state of Manchukuo as non-existent, and yet she has postal arrangements with that area under which she accepts letters carrying a Manchukuo stamp. There is an international train service between the two capitals .... China has even set up Custom houses along the Great Wall for the purposes of taxing goods coming in from Manchukuo. Individuals living in Manchukuo who are regarded by China as Chinese subjects none-the-less resort to the Manchukuo courts and are punished by them; and there is an increasing immigration of Chinese into Manchuria.[55]

These Chinese attitudes indicated to Simon that a day would come when the facts of the invasion would have to be recognized and 'a *de facto* change of sovereignty be transformed into a *de jure* recognition'.[56] Therefore, because of the interconnected nature of the Chinese situation, Simon and the Foreign Office strongly rejected any bilateral movement towards *anyone*, especially the Japanese.

In the Cabinet meetings that were a precursor to the setting-up of the PEJ committee, Simon had used Sansom's reputation to discredit the FBI report which had suggested just such a thing:[57] closer formal relations with Japan. Sansom was scathing in his attack on the report of the FBI mission which painted Japan as the rising economic powerhouse in the Far East. He considered the mission a collection of duped, ignorant amateurs:

> ... I cannot help feeling that in Japan they, or some of them, were a little carried away by their enthusiasm, and mistook the genuine hospitality

of their Japanese hosts for a display of willingness to come to terms in the matter of Anglo-Japanese competition. There may be willingness, but there is no determination. Certainly the F.B.I. mission was made welcome, as other trade missions have been and will be made welcome. But the Japanese are glad to see a trade mission here looking out for favours; not because they mean to give more, but because they hope that the mission, having understood the Japanese point of view, will ask less. Indeed, I am convince that the underlying motive of all these rather vague bids for commercial 'co-operation' is in reality political, and that what the Japanese are aiming at is a bargain in which we shall furnish them with political advantages in return for unspecified commercial benefits.[58]

He called the FBI report 'a slovenly document' that contained 'inexcusable blunders', with only the saving grace that it made up for the even more deplorable FBI memorandum of 1932 on Japanese competition. There were also a few reasonable proposals for solutions to Anglo-Japanese trade problems.[59] The central weakness of the FBI report, however, was that while some of its financial aspects were worthy of consideration, the portrayal of the Japanese economic situation was far too generous and ignored major weaknesses in Japanese finances and economic strength. Sansom felt that:

> The fact is that Japan cannot afford to abandon voluntarily any valuable amount of the export trade she had gained. It would require a very strong inducement from us to persuade the Japanese Government that sacrifices must be made by Japanese trade, and a very powerful drive, indeed, by the Japanese Government to exact those sacrifices from their traders. It would therefore, seem that damage resulting from Japanese competition should be dealt with by first-aid methods, or minor operations, and that a radical cure should not at present be attempted, lest it lead to complications. Time is, I think, in our favour; and, meanwhile, if I may venture an opinion on this aspect of the question, it would, in my view, be a grave mistake for us to play with the idea of reaping commercial benefits from a political deal. I am sure that we should lose on both sides of the transaction.[60]

The Ambassador, Clive, lent his support to the anti-FBI salvo, endorsing what Sansom had to say and adding:

> ... it would be unfortunate if, as a result of the mission, the opinion gained ground in the United Kingdom that Japanese commercial competition would be alleviated or other substantial economic advantage be gained by some change in the political relations between the two countries .... I am afraid that on political grounds alone no Japanese Government, however willing, could impose restrictions upon their country's industrial and commercial expansion sufficient to relieve

substantially the strain of Japanese competition .... any new political understanding with Japan, should His Majesty's Government be in favour of one, must be justified on the wider grounds of Imperial policy rather than on the nebulous expectation of commercial advantage.[61]

The Far Eastern Department's denunciation of the Barnby mission's report was pursued in London by Charles Orde.

Orde believed that the FBI's calls for greater efforts to turn commercial negotiations into better political relations with Japan reflected the fact that the mission failed to realize the importance of China's perception of British actions in the Far East.[62] While noting the challenges presented by having to balance Japanese pressures with American interests, Orde was concerned that any suggestion of co-operation with Japan in dividing up China would only lead to irreparable damage to Sino-British relations: 'The fundamental questions to consider are the nature of Japanese ambitions in China and the extent to which we can afford to become identified with them in the minds of the Chinese. It is difficult to do good trade with a hostile people, and we can hardly hope to do so with a hostile China.'[63] Orde echoed other senior Foreign Office members in his assessment of Japan's overall strategy (which he thought generally aggressive in nature) especially with regard to Russian interests in the Far East and the role that Japan's anti-Russia attitude would have on her policy of keeping China weak.[64] Japan would not be able to conquer the Chinese, and the tensions, boycotts and use of force by the Japanese to solve their Chinese problems would continue. His prognosis for the future of Sino-Japanese relations favoured an exasperation on Japan's part, with the probability of another 'Twenty-one Demands' and a repeat of the rape of Manchuria at some point in the future.[65] Britain could not morally afford to associate itself with the exponent of such policies. Orde's solution was to continue to engage in good relations with the Chinese, without weakening British resistance to China's less reasonable demands, because Japan would never be able to dominate and control China as it did Manchuria. This, Orde believed, was demonstrated by the strain put on Japan's resources in her attempts to rule in Manchukuo.[66] His conclusion was therefore similar to Sansom's and Clive's: that it was poor policy to defend the Chinese markets with a political understanding that would link Britain to Japanese policy in the Far East. In addition, Orde felt that: '... China is at present politically and administratively incoherent, but she is too vital to have coherence imposed on her from without, and our policy on the foundation of sympathetic recognition of legitimate Chinese aspirations, ... must, I believe, remain for the present of an opportunist nature.'[67] Orde's assessment of the Chinese problem was fully endorsed by Alexander Cadogan.

The British Ambassador in Peking held the same opinion as Orde about any type of understanding with Japan that linked British interests to Japanese policy.[68] As to what Britain could do about the situation, in a manner uncharacteristic of a diplomat, Cadogan admitted there was not much:

... the situation is that the Japanese are in an unassailable position in this part of the world. They can do what they like with China: they need not get into trouble with Russia: they think they have nothing to fear from us, and I believe they are as convinced as I am that America would never intervene actively.... If they take the bit between their teeth, we can't stop them in China, because I assume that we are not prepared to fight them even if we thought the situation called for the arbitrament of arms. Our policy in these circumstances can only be the rather undignified one of waiting on events.[69]

Japan could not be irritated over unnecessary issues, but British face had to be kept by a show of solicitousness for British interests. Flagrant breaches of treaty obligations by Japan could be remonstrated against, and, where a perceived legitimate British action was desirable to assist the Chinese, such as a loan, then that action should be taken without being paralysed by fear of Japan's response.[70] Cadogan's advice was a mixture of cautious opportunism and careful resistance to Japanese bullying, without Sansom's insights into Japanese economic or financial strengths.[71] These various opinions on common threads of what Britain's strategy should be in the Far East revealed the enormous complexity that surrounded the issue. That complexity led to the formation of the Cabinet Committee on Political and Economic Relations with Japan.

At the first meeting of that committee, Simon quickly outlined the complicated nature of the issues involved in British relations with Japan in China. Purely economic or trade matters, as proposed by the 'strong policy' representatives Runciman and Chamberlain, did not dominate discussions. Nor was China the only question, as Chamberlain argued, although it was a central point of focus due to the silver question and whether there would be a loan to her or not.[72] Instead, Simon used Chamberlain's point about the need to negotiate with the United States and Japan now that no British loan would be forthcoming for the Chinese, and how these Powers complicated matters over the silver price/loan issue, to demonstrate the fragility of Far Eastern policy.

Chamberlain wanted to leave China out of initial negotiations because he feared she would play one power off against another.[73] Simon, using the expertise of Orde Mouw, Adviser for Far Eastern Affairs in the Dutch East Indies, and Mr Archibald Rose of the British American Tobacco Company, pointed out that China could not be left out of the initial discussions about such matters because these talks would be of great importance to her. If the Chinese were left out then they would have every reason to think that some division of China, in the manner reminiscent of the 'open door' discussions, was in progress. Chinese fears over Japan's being given a dominant position in Chinese affairs would be raised, creating an atmosphere that was unlikely to produce any fruitful negotiation.[74] The result would be an antagonized China, which in itself was a serious threat to British Far Eastern interests. At the same time, British policy would have to be wary of provoking any unnecessary Japanese antagonism by challenging Japan's assertion that she held a dominant position *vis-à-vis* China. And, if American co-operation on regulating the price of silver was to be obtained, then their Far Eastern position would have to be included in the equation.[75] What Simon was advocating was the same multi-lateral approach that he had recommended in his memo on Anglo-Japanese relations in late 1934. The conclusions of this first meeting of the committee reflected Simon's influence, for it was agreed that they would:

> ... say *to China* that, whilst we regretted inability to grant her a loan, we wished to assist her in any way possible, in co-operation with the other Governments concerned, and we would welcome any suggestions or observations from China in this regard; and that we had had an enquiry from Japan, to which we had replied on certain lines.
>
> That we should inform *Japan* that we have communicated with China on the above lines, and that when we obtained a reply from China we proposed to approach Japan and the United States of America.
>
> That we should send copies of all the above communications to our Ambassador in *Washington* for his information.[76]

At the second meeting of the PEJ committee, Chamberlain and Runciman continued to press for greater assistance to British trade interests in China.[77] While these petitions on behalf of the industrialists produced both the elevation of the Peking post from Consul to Ambassador (which would have probably occurred in the near future anyway) and the eventual sending of the infamous 'big-gun' Leith-Ross to the Far East to look at China's financial situation, in the Foreign Office view there was little in either manoeuvre that would threaten the delicate balance of power in the Far East.[78] While Simon and the Foreign Office were willing to assent to such shallow gestures, they had staved off the 'strong policy' advocates who could have created a confusing and embarrassing diversion in the Anglo-Japanese discussions, just as Lothian, Lloyd George and Smuts had threatened to do.[79] The Far Eastern Department's 'no bloc' and opportunist policies remained the dominant theme of Britain's Far Eastern diplomatic strategy at the highest level of political decision making.[80] There was no effective dual diplomacy.

The Foreign Office and the Far Eastern Department's views on how to handle the other powers in the Far East were based not only on having to counter Treasury interference in Far Eastern affairs, but were closely linked with imperial defence policy. The union between diplomacy and naval strategy was a relationship that was critical for not only Britain's imperial interests, but was central to the entire scheme of what David French has called the 'British way in warfare'.[81]

The Defence Requirements Committee had identified the material weaknesses in the British Empire's defences in 1934 and what the cost of making good those deficiencies would be. The report had also defined Germany as the 'ultimate potential enemy', but it continued to rank Japan as the nation posing the most immediate and most likely threat to the British Empire.[82] The Chiefs of Staff Sub-Committee played an important role in drafting the Defence Requirement Committee's report and had early on recognized the need for closer co-operation between the diplomatic service and the military services if efforts to defend imperial interests were to be succesful.[83] Both the Foreign Office and the Treasury also recognized that if effective defence planning and rearmament was going to take place, close co-operation by all three groups would be required. As for the Far Eastern situation, the linkage between diplomacy and naval preparation would have to move together in close harmony, keeping potential enemies calm in a period of rearmament, while also working to ensure that both real and potential allies remained viable in defence planning options.

British naval strategy in any war with Japan in the Far East was centred around a defensive campaign. The First Sea Lord and Chief of Naval Staff, Sir Ernle Chatfield, was very critical of any planning that assumed British actions would be offensive in nature, attempting to wrestle Japan's position in China away from her. In fact, Chatfield was most critical of the China C-in-C, Admiral Sir Frederic Dreyer, whom Chatfield thought:

> ... seemed rather obsessed by the principle which had grown up since the War that our final objective would be to defeat Japan and force her to abandon her machinations in China .... It had always, therefore, been assumed that when Hong Kong had either been relieved or recaptured, the war would be carried on into a third stage involving the occupation of Japanese waters and attempts to interfere with their communications with China .... Personally, he thought this third stage was a very difficult and even, perhaps, impracticable one.[84]

Not only did the naval aspects worry Chatfield and Montgomery-Massingberd, Chief of the Imperial General Staff, but there was also the attitude of the United States to be taken into consideration. Only if the USA respected a blockade of Japan or China would the Royal Navy have a realistic hope of applying the traditional pressure of sea power through blockade. Chatfield emphasized that operations in the Far East could not be offensive, unless China or the United States played the role of ally, and even then a great effort would be required in order to throw Japan out of China.[85]

Chatfield and the Chiefs of Staff had recognized the need to keep Japan calm until 1939, while British naval and air rearmament took place.[86] This support for 'appeasement' was a natural extension of the strategic naval planning process that should not be confused with any legacy of the 'guilty men' syndrome or some of the other less flattering definitions of appeasement.[87] But this request by the Admiralty was not out of fear that they could not defeat the Japanese, or the Germans, or the Italians, one at a time. It was the appearance of a number of possible simultaneous naval commitments in 1935 that caused the COS to ask for diplomacy to buy them time to rearm and prepare. And, if it was at all possible, to reduce the risk of having to face a numbr of enemies simultaneously through diplomatic manoeuvring.[88]

Added to these considerations were major concerns over the Japanese rearmament programmes. The Chief of Staff estimates picked 1936 as the 'critical year' for any possible war to occur with Japan and Chatfield emphasized that a careful watch on relations with that country would have to be kept between 1935 and 1937:

> The Naval Conference might have definitely broken down by then; Japan would have completed her battleship modernization programme and her expansion of the naval Air Arm. After 1939 our position would improve because by then we might have got our routes established, enabling reinforcing aircraft to fly direct to Hong Kong, and Singapore would be in a better position. He would like to call particular attention to 1936 as being a critical year, one during which the Foreign Office must, at all costs, try and keep us out of a war.[89]

The use of force was thought likely to be the final arbiter in the Far East, therefore time was needed to modernize and expand the Royal Navy, the cornerstone of defence for any part of the Empire.

At the end of July 1934, the recommendations of the DRC were found wanting in respect of the Royal Navy's estimates and building programmes. Walter Runciman, First Lord of the Admiralty, Sir Bolton Eyres-Monsell, and the Lord President of the Council, Stanley Baldwin, all agreed that the report was a serious blow to Britain's naval power.[90] Although the estimates and exact amounts which the Navy was to receive were still to be decided in separate negotiations between Monsell and Chamberlain, Monsell made it very clear to Cabinet that he was not at all happy with the Treasury's ideas about the future of British naval power:

> The Treasury proposed, apparently, to alter the whole basis of Imperial Defence, in which the Dominions were closely concerned. The defence of our Empire necessitated as a minimum the maintenance of a one-Power standard. Our annual building programmes were formulated, and our existing deficiencies had been calculated with strict reference to that standard. If our building programmes could not be carried out, and equally if our deficiencies could not be made good, the one-Power standard could not be maintained. If that standard were to be abandoned we could not defend the Empire and we might as well have no Navy at all. Short of that standard the Admiralty would not know what to ask for, and the Chancellor of the Exchequer would not know what to give.[91]

The Foreign Office, believing in Japan's ultimate intention of dominating the Far East and eliminating British competition in that region, were natural allies of the Royal Navy in the funding battles of 1935. Both institutions operated from the principle that at some point weight of weapons and use of force would have a decisive role in Far Eastern affairs. In further discussion that dealt with the ongoing rearmament process, the Treasury, with ideas of an Anglo-Japanese understanding, found itself increasingly facing an alliance of the Royal Navy, the Foreign Office and Sir Maurice Hankey, Secretary of the CID, that demanded recognition of the *realpolitik* facing the British Empire in the Far East.[92] Confronted with such powerful opposition, the Treasury's position was not readily accepted as being expert.[93] Furthermore, three major events at the end of September that changed the strategical requirements of the navy in the programme set out at the July 29th meeting of the Defence Policy and Requirements sub-committee.[94] Those events were: the Anglo-German Naval Treaty that allowed Germany to build up to 35 per cent of the Royal Navy's strength; fear that League membership might lead to a war at short notice, thereby not allowing a period of deterioration for rearmament; and Italy's recent hostility over the Italo-Abyssinian conflict which created a possible threat to the British Empire's Mediterranean sea lines of communication.[95]

By October 1935, having taken into account these new developments, even the Treasury appeared to support the rebuilding of the Royal Navy to safeguard imperial interests:

> Hankey: ... we ought to have a Navy which could provide a safe defensive in the Far East and also maintain our position *vis à vis* Germany? Mention had been made at the last meeting of the danger of Italy and our lines of communication. He was inclined to leave out consideration of Italy's strength in assessing the requirements of the Navy as he felt that Italy will be exhausted after the present trouble, and in any case it should be possible for this country to get on comfortable terms with her again within a reasonable period of time. The proposals by the Admiralty were compatible with existing Treaties, but these would not remain in their present form much longer and he was inclined to suggest to the Committee that they should open their mouths wider when putting forward proposals to the Government. No risk could be taken in the Far East. If Japan could defeat us there she could overrun the East and we should be in an impossible position with Australia and New Zealand at the mercy of Japan and India cut off. The whole security of the Empire and maintenance of our prestige in the world depended on the possession of a defence which without risk could leave us in a strong defensive position in the East in the event of trouble in the West. He felt it was well worth paying extra insurance to create a greater deterrent to Japan.

> Sir Warren Fisher said he was entirely of the same mind.[96]

What Hankey and Chatfield proposed was the building of a two-ocean navy, that could cover Britain's imperial interests in the Far East and still deal with either Germany or Italy. This call for a return to a two power standard now had the apparent approval of the Treasury's professional head. Vansittart certainly approved of such preparations, for he believed that 'our weakness was the reason we could count on no one'.[97] He also recommended rearmament take place at an accelerated pace, as he could not guarantee that the Empire would be protected through diplomatic means after 1939.[98]

Sir John Simon and Sir Samuel Hoare, Secretary of State for India, and Secretary of State for Foreign Affairs after 7 June 1935, acknowledged on 22 November 1934, at a meeting of the CID that 1936 would indeed be a critical year. Particular effort had to be made to avoid ill-feeling with Japan before then and until 1939.[99] With special consideration of Japan's place in Imperial Defence firmly in mind, the Foreign Office summed up their assessment of the Far Eastern problem for the COS in March 1935, and explained their 'no bloc' and opportunistic approach to giving the services the diplomatic protection they required for the completion of their rearmament programmes.[100] Russia was the acknowledged primary enemy of Japan and as such was a vital balance against further Japanese aggression.[101] China was the main source of wealth and the object of Japan's ambition, but it was unlikely that Japan would ever be likely to have complete control of China. Therefore, the FO position was that:

> Our interests seem, therefore, likely to be best served by cultivating friendly relations with both China and Japan, avoiding taking sides with either against the other, displaying neither undue jealousy towards Japanese aims, so long as they do not directly conflict with our own interests, nor too unsympathetic an attitude towards China's aspirations to be treated as a modern State in which foreigners must live on the same terms as its native population.[102]

The naval staff's response to the Foreign Office position was one of warning— not to be too ready to think the Japanese willing to accommodate British interests. Listing a series of incidents where Britain's, and particularly the navy's, patience and prestige had been besmirched, the naval staff emphasized their belief that Japan saw Britain as an obstacle to her expansion that had to be eliminated.[103] In their mistrust and appreciation of the ultimate motives behind Japan's national policy, the navy and the Foreign Office saw practically eye to eye.[104]

Now the 'no bloc', opportunistic approach of the Far Eastern Department's strategy served three purposes: protecting British trade and commerce against Japanese and Chinese pressures, exerting diplomatic influence on both Japan and China in the balance-of-power environment, and as a shield, utilizing the balance of power in the region to buy time for the rearmament and reorganization of the defence forces of the Empire. As long as this balance of power remained in the Far East, two elements of the traditional 'British way in warfare' would have an opportunity to take effect: the creation of a dominant maritime force for use in Europe and the Far East, and, time, over which perhaps a new government or fiscal problems would temper Japan's aggressive attitude. One incident of the Foreign Office's own making, however, threatened this critical Far Eastern balance of power in 1935: the suggestion of creating closer relations with Russia through the granting of a loan.[105]

While it was possible that Russia would find some terms of agreement with Germany, the close ties between Germany and Japan cast doubts on such a likelihood. However, because they were viewed as both a European and an Asian power the Russians posed some unique problems for all British strategical planning. Lawrence Collier, Head of the Northern Department in the Foreign Office, stated the reality of the situation clearly when he wrote:

> There is, however, a possibility that, if M. Litvinov who is already somewhat disgruntled at recent developments in Europe, makes up his mind that the French and ourselves are going to leave him without support in face of German "Drang nach Osten", he may throw in his hand altogether in the Far East in order to be able to turn his undivided attention to the West. This, of course, would not suit our book at all, any more than the reverse situation—which is also a possibility though a more remote one—in which a Soviet-German detente in Europe might be brought about through Soviet fear of isolation in the face of Japan in the Far East. The moral for us seems to be that we should handle M. Litvinov very carefully in the next few months.[106]

Both Vansittart and Eden agreed with Collier's analysis. Still, under pressure from what he perceived was a worsening European situation, Vansittart attempted to reach some understanding with Russia over Germany.[107] Vansittart's Europe-first vision caused a near-serious blunder which posed a serious threat to the very fabric of the 'no bloc' strategy that safeguarded Britain's Far Eastern interests.

Because Russia was the main deterrent to Japanese aggression in China, continued pressure on that flank was vital for British diplomacy to continue to balance the one against the other. That balance would involve not only Eastern questions, but would have links to the three countries' relations with Germany as well. The Far Eastern Department realized the tensions that underlay the Russo-Japanese relationship and the prognosis for future relations between the two did not look peaceful.[108] The Foreign Office counted on those Russo-Japanese tensions as their principal weapon of influence, especially if Japan should begin to look south at British possessions.[109] But if diplomacy was to fail, the growing power of the Russian military in the Far East was a comfort as well, and that powerful force was not to be alienated unncessarily.[110]

Any British arrangement with Russia over any issue, no matter economic, commercial, political or military, would give Japan cause to fear the beginning of an anti-Japanese bloc being created by Britain. The result would in all likeli-

hood be a Japanese move southward against those British interests.[111]
Vansittart's attempts at securing European security through an agreement with
Russia cut across the 'no bloc' strategy of opportunism. His approach tended
towards trying to create a sterile environment around the disease (Japan),
rather than dealing directly with the problem, as was Simon's wont to do
through the multi-lateral approach. Given the importance and vulnerability of
the Far East in imperial affairs, the perception of greater volatility from Japan,
and the need to respect the coming of the critical year, 1936, such a disruption
of the balance of power in the Far East could not be tolerated. Just as an
Anglo-Japanese *rapprochement* would have increased suspicions of Britain in
Moscow, thereby perhaps eliminating a potential British ally in the contain-
ment of Germany, Vansittart's ambitions had little chance of success due to the
absolute importance of a 'loose' Russia at this time in the Far Eastern balance
of power. This reliance on an unaligned Russia coincided with the need to
avoid any unnecessary action that might possibly provoke Japan. Victor
Wellesley's instructions to Clive summed up the situation regarding the attitude
of Britain towards Russia and her place in the Far Eastern strategy for defending the Empire. In the most diplomatic of terms, Wellesley, at Orde's and the
Northern Department's request, screamed at Clive to not promote the idea of
better Russo-Japanese relations to the Japanese during this 'critical' period:

> War between Japan and Russia is of course far from our desire. Apart
> from the evils resulting by repercussion from any war a Russo-
> Japanese war would destroy for the time being a balancing factor
> against Germany, our greatest source of anxiety. Our desire to main-
> tain good relations with Russia, both for their own sake and from the
> standpoint of her influence against Germany, has caused us to assure
> her in all sincerity, that we do not wish Japan to attack her. We also of
> course are most anxious to maintain good relations with Japan but she
> is a danger to our interests in the Far East and it is difficult at present
> to see how she is to be checked. We can place no reliance on American
> co-operation against her or, in spite of Litvinov's language to Eden, on
> concerted help from Russia. But nervousness in Japan about Russia
> may be useful as a check on Japanese aggression further South and the
> ideal state of things seems to us to be one in which such nervousness
> should continue but without any commitment of Russia's strength in
> the Far East which could not quickly be liquidated should the situation
> in Europe render this desirable. We think therefore that it will be best
> not to go out of our way unnecessarily to sooth Japan's fears of Russia,
> though naturally we must be careful to negative any impression that we
> *want* ill-feeling between them. Apart from special circumstances this is
> the general line we should like you to follow.[112]

Vansittart apparently had no hand in these instructions, though he later understood what Orde meant when he wrote, 'They [Japan] will probably have to

become more frightened of trouble with Russia before they really try to earn our friendship.'[113] The Far Eastern Department's 'no bloc' strategy had survived another challenge and continued to be the central pillar of imperial foreign policy regarding the Far East. New Secretaries of State would come and go, but the Foreign Office position on this question would remain clearly defined.[114]

Any study of Britain's attempts to maintain her Far Eastern interests must recognize the inseparable connections between political and economic issues, as well as the interdependence of the Far East situation and the European problems in the imperial defence system. Also, the 'no bloc' policy of the Far Eastern Department and their role in the policy-making process has to be recognized as an 'imperial' policy. Their policy was the British way in warfare. This study provides a snapshot of some of the intricate complexities that surrounded British imperial defence and foreign policy in one of the fateful years of the mid-1930s.

Foreign Office strategy was neither easy nor popular. It was an extremely difficult position to make others believe in because of its passive nature. With no solid military alliances that could be counted on to help in the protection of the Far East, British preparations for defending their interests in the region had to assume right up to the actual moment of conflict that such nations as France, Russia, the Netherlands and perhaps America, would play some role in containing any Japanese move against its imperial interests, but the extent of any such assistance was almost completely unknown. These restrictions meant that no alliance planning or co-ordination of action against Japan could be done until very late in the game. Therefore, the 'no bloc' strategy of opportunism created a self-imposed distance on the British Empire, forcing Britain to isolate herself in the same way as Japan, in order to try and influence the volatile Japanese. However, given the limitations of British defences in the Far East and the need to buy time for further defences to be constructed, it appears to have been the most logical, the most effective and the most traditional of methods for gaining security in the Far East. As Ian Nish has said of the Empire's attempts to deal with the myriad of problems that the Far Eastern question presented, 'Variety is perhaps the password.'[115]

NOTES

1. On the Washington Treaty and Britain's maritime interests see John Ferris, 'The Symbol and Substance of Seapower: Great Britain, the United States, and the One Power Standard, 1919–1921', in B.J.C. McKercher ed., *Anglo-American Relations in the 1920s: The Struggle for Supremacy* (London, 1991), pp 55–80. For the 1930 London Naval Conference see, Greg Kennedy, The 1930 London Naval Conference and Anglo-American Maritime Strength, 1927–1930', in B.J.C. McKercher ed., *Arms Limitation and Disarmament: Restraints on War, 1899–1939* (Westport, CN 1992), pp 169–71.
2. Some aspects of these problems are summarized in Ian Nish, *Anglo-Japanese Alienation, 1919–1952* (Cambridge, 1982) chapter 2; Ann Trotter, *Britain and East Asia, 1933–1937*

    (Cambridge, 1975), pp 1–22; and William Roger Louis, *British Strategy in the Far East 1919–1939*, (Oxford, 1971), chapter 6.

3   CAB[inet] Office Records, Public Record Office—hereafter PRO London] 23/79, Cabinet Minutes, Meeting 38, 31 Oct 1934.

4. For a more complete discussion of the elements involved in the defence of the realm, and their coordination see, Greg Kennedy, 'Holding on to Empire: Anglo-American Relations in the Far East 1933–39', a paper given at the Canadian Historical Association Learneds, June, 1994 in Calgary, Alta.

5. For a very complete survey of Japan's trading ability at this time see F[oreign]O[ffice], 371/19355/F4066/288/23 [PRO, London], memo, 'Japanese Trade in Neutral Markets', 22 Jun 1935.

6. CAB 16/111, Defence Requirements Sub-Committee (hereafter DRC) Memoranda, C[abinet] P[aper] 77 (34), 'Situation in the Far East, 1933–34', 15 Mar 1934, No.11, 'Memorandum respecting the British and Japanese Interests in China and the Prospects of a Sino-Japanese Rapprochement.'

7. Ibid. See also Trotter, *Britain and East Asia*, pp 23–31.

8. CAB 16/111, DRC Memorandum, CP 77–A (34), 21 Mar 1934, memo No.11.

9. Ibid, memo No.12.

10. Ibid. On the role of the Shanghai bank and some aspects of this growing rivalry with Japan, see Frank H.H King, *The History of the HongKong and Shanghai Banking Corporation*, Vol.III, (Cambridge, 1988), pp 355–406; Susan Wolcott, 'The Perils of Lifetime Employment Systems: Productivity Advance in the Indian and Japanese Textile Industries, 1920–1938', *The Journal of Economic History*, 54, 2(1994), pp 307–324.

11. CAB 16/111, DRC Memos, CP 77(34), memo No.11.

12. For investments figures see Chi-ming Hou, *Foreign Investment and Economic Development in China, 1840–1937* (Harvard, 1965), p 81.

Foreign Investments in manufacturing in China by country, 1936

	Britain	USA	Japan	Germany	France	(%)
	...........................US $ million................................					(%)
Textiles	64.6	1.2	112.4	3.9	0.0	(54.7)
Metal						
machinery	20.8	3.6	4.1	0.1	0.5	
equipment						(8.8)
Chemicals	63.0	1.7	6.8	2.0	1.0	(22.4)
Lumber						
Printing	0.3	0.3	0.8	0.1	0.0	(0.5)
Food,	23.3	1.1	5.8	0.9	0.5	
Drink,.Tobacco						(9.5)
Other	3.7	1.1	3.3	0.1	0.0	(2.5)
Totals $M	179.7	9.5	134.1	7.1	2.0	—
%	(54.1)	(2.9)	(40.3)	(2.1)	(0.6)	—

13. Louis Beale to Cadogan, (Consul-General in Peking), 21 Jun 1935, Cadogan Papers, FO 800/293 [PRO, London]; see also, William Roger Louis, *British Strategy in the Far East* (Oxford, 1971), pp 235–6 shows that this continued to be the FO's view into 1937.

14. Minutes, Meeting 43, 28 Nov 1934, CAB 23/80.

15. Minutes, Meeting 9, 13 Feb 1935, CAB 23/81.

16. A particularly narrow and superficial work that deals with the British Empire and economic policy without considering the foreign policy or military aspects of Imperial economics is Ian M. Drummond, *British Economic Policy and the Empire, 1919–1939* (London, 1972); idem., *Imperial Economic Policy, 1917–1939* (London, 1974), which claims that the British Empire did not have an oil industry in the inter-war. This would have come as a great surprise to those individuals on the Oil Board, in the Petroleum Department, and who belonged to the Asiatic Petroleum Company, to name just a few. For a useful corrective to some of Drummond's economist

views see, Robert Self, 'Treasury Control and the Empire Marketing Board: The Rise and Fall of Non-Tariff Preference in Britain, 1924–1933', *Twentieth Century British History*, 5, 2(1994), pp 153–82.

17. For a quick overview of these issues see Trotter, *Britain and East Asia*, pp 115–47.
18. R[ecord][G]roup 25, Vol. 1716, file 1935–326, part o, *Monthly Intelligence Summaries Issued by the General Staff the War Office*, Vol.25, No.6, 'Threat to Foreign Interests in the Far East', Oct 1934 [National Archives, Ottawa].
19. Ibid. See also FO 371/19360/F1086/1086/23, 'Annual Report on Japan'.
20. RG 25/Vol.1716, *Monthly Intelligence Summaries*, 'Threat to Foreign Interests'.
21. Ibid. Also FO 371/19350/F94/94/23, 29 Dec 1934.
22. Louis, *British Strategy in the Far East*, p 222; Trotter, *Britain and East Asia*, p 58.
23. Louis, *British Strategy in the Far East*, pp 222–223; Trotter, *Britain and East Asia*, pp 115–131.
24. CAB 23/79, Meeting 17, 25 Apr 1934; FO 371/19353/F7183/94/23, 11 Nov 1935.
25. Minutes, meeting No. 17, 25 Apr 1934, CAB 23/79.
26. FO 371/19350/F156/94/23, 21 Jan 1935; FO 371/19350/F852/94/23, 7 Feb 1935; FO 371/19350/F902/94/23, 9 Feb 1935; FO 371/19350/F1241/94/23, 22 Feb 1935; FO 371/19350/F1822/94/23, 20 Feb 1935; FO 371/19350/F1919/94/23, 23 Mar 1935; FO 371/19351/F2227/94/23, 4 Apr 1935; FO 371/19353/F7183/94/23, 11 Nov 1935.
27. The Leith-Ross mission was a fact-finding mission sent out by the Treasury in August 1935 to investigate China's currency difficulties. Trotter, *Britain and East Asia*, pp 148–167.
28. For a general discussion of these events see Louis, *British Strategy in the Far East*, pp 224–233; Trotter, *Britain and East Asia*, pp 146–167. For specifics on Chamberlain's position on Japan's national policy and his not believing that Japan's interests could be identified, compared to Simon and the Foreign Office position, see, Chamberlain to Simon, 10 Sept 1934, Simon Papers, FO 800/291.
29. Charles William Orde (Head of the Far Eastern Dept.) to Cadogan, 2 Jul 1935, Cadogan Papers, FO 800/293.
30. Minutes, Cabinet meeting no. 2, 25 Sept 1934, CAB 23/79.
31. Memorandum by the Chancellor of the Exchequer and the Secretary of State for Foreign Affairs, 16 Oct 1934, CAB 24/250, CP 223(34).
32. Paul Haggie, *Britannia at Bay: The Defence of the British Empire Against Japan, 1931–1941* (Oxford, 1981), p 63.
33. Beale to Cadogan, 21 Jun 1935, Cadogan Papers, 35/5.
34. Ibid; Minutes, Cabinet meeting no.4, 16 Jan 1935 CAB 23/81; 16 Jan 1935, FO 371/19347/F1245/13/2314 Aug 1935, FO 371/19349/F5289/40/23; 7 Jan 1935, FO 371/19359/F1090/483/23; 28 Feb 1938, FO 371/22180/F3559/71/23.
35. 'Japanese foreign policy', 19 Feb 1935, FO 371/19359/F1090/483/23; 15 Apr 1935 CAB 24/254, CP 80(35).
36. Ibid, A.W.G. Randall, Far Eastern Department clerk minute.
37. Ibid, Wellesley minute.
38. Lord Lytton was a British peer whose report on Japanese actions in China for the League of Nations in Oct 1932 was seen by the Japanese as being central to the League holding Japan responsible for the Manchurian aggressions; South African Field Marshal, Jan Smuts; Lord Lothian, a Liberal Minister, 'idealist, Christian Scientist, internationalist, preacher of the common destiny of the English-speaking peoples, and member of the Round Table', which was a group of politicians, academics and prominent citizens that were linked by the journal on imperialism of the same name; and Lloyd George, former British Prime Minister. Trotter, *Britain and East Asia*, pp 107–108; Correlli Barnett, *The Collapse of British Power* (London, 1972), pp 346–48.
39. Vansittart minute, FO 371/19359/F1090/48.
40. Ibid.
41. Ibid.
42. Ibid.
43. Vansittart minute on 'Japanese foreign policy', 4 Mar 1935, FO 371/19359/F1474/483/23.
44. Ian Nish, '"In One Day Have I Lived Many Lives": Frank Ashton-Gwatkin, Novelist and Diplomat, 1889–1976,' in Ian Nish ed, *Britain and Japan: Biographical Portraits* (Folkestone, Kent, 1994); F.T. Ashton-Gwatkin, *The British Foreign Service* (Syracuse, 1950); Sir John Pratt, *War and Politics in China* (London, 1943); Katherine Sansom, *Sir George Sansom and Japan* (Talahassee, FL, 1972); J. Connell, *The 'Office', A Study of British Foreign Policy and its Makers*

(London, 1958) Trotter, pp 8–10, 35.

45. For Simon's view see his defence of Sansom in minutes, Cabinet meeting no. 4, 16 Jan 1935, CAB 23/81.
46. Vansittart's opinion is found in his minute of 5 Aug 1937, FO 371/21044/F5093/5093/23.
47. For an account of Simon's political career see D.J. Dutton, *Simon: A Political Biography of Sir John Simon*, (London, 1992). By 1935 the British Empire was the chief buyer of Japanese goods:

| Exports from Japan, Percentage of Total Value | | |
To:	1929	1935
British Empire	20.4	28.1
USA and dependencies	44.4	23.6
France and dependencies	2.2	3.2
Netherlands and dependencies	4.4	6.5
China, Manchuria, Kwangtung Leased Territory	21.9	23.1
Others	6.8%	15.5

Figures from Mitsubishi Research Institute, as found in 'Memo – Compiled by his Majesty's Embassy in Reply to Charges that Great Britain has Obstructed Japan's Reasonable Development', 12 Feb 1938, FO 371/22180/F2696/71/23.)

48. Memo on 'Anglo-Japanese Relations', 21 Jan 1935, Simon Papers FO 800/290 [PRO, London]. See also 21 Jan 1935, 'Anglo-Japanese Relations', FO 371/19356/[F]682/376/23.
49. Simon's tenure as Secretary of State has usually been described as a less than brilliant, uninspiring session, with regard to the Far East, Trotter, *Britain and East Asia*, pp 7–11; Peter Lowe, *Britain in the Far East* (London, 1981), pp 139–140; idem, *Great Britain and the Origins of the Pacific War* (Oxford, 1977), p 7. A more favourable assessment is in Louis, *British Strategy in the Far East*, passim.
50. Ibid.
51. Simon to Ramsay MacDonald, 3 Oct 1934, Simon Papers, FO 800/291.
52. Minutes, Cabinet meeting no. 5, 23 Jan 1935, CAB 23/81.
53. Ibid.
54. Ibid.
55. 'Anglo-Japanese Relations', memo, Simon, 21 Jan 1935, Simon Papers, FO 800/290.
56. Ibid..
57. Louis, *British Strategy in the Far East*, p 224–5.
58. 'Report on Economic Conditions in Japan 1933–34', 23 Jan 1935, FO 371/19361/F1116/1116/23.
59. Ibid, p 3.
60. Ibid.
61. Ibid, p.1.
62. Orde to Cadogan, 2 Jul 1935, Cadogan Papers, FO 800/293.
63. Ibid, Orde memo enclosed, pp 2–5.
64. Ibid, p 3.
65. Ibid, p 4.
66. Ibid, p 5. Orde's views were supported by Mr. Mouw, Adviser for Far Eastern Affairs in the Dutch East Indies. Mouw's assessment of the situation was that Russia was Japan's main concern; that Japan was confused and unsure of how to avoid becoming isolated. Japan was weak commercially, financially and in terms of resources. Britain was in the stronger position. Orde thought that, 'It was interesting to find in someone at the exposed point a view so unalarmist and so coincident with our own.' Vansittart also found Mouw's views interesting: FO 371/19353/F149/149/23, minutes and memo of conversation, 4 Jan 1935.
67. Orde to Cadogan, 2 Jul 1935, Cadogan Papers, FO 800/293.
68. Cadogan to Orde, 21 Aug 1935, Cadogan Papers, FO 800/293 index no.35/10.
69. Ibid.
70. Ibid.
71. For further evidence of Sansom's ability and his understanding of his influence on FO policy, see Sansom to Orde, 'Financial currency situation in Japan', despatch, 17 Jul 1950, FO

371/19354/F6595/246/23.

72. 'Committee on Political and Economic Relations with Japan', 18 Feb 1935, FO 371/19356/-F1439/376/23.

73. Ibid, p 2.

74. Ibid, pp 3–4.

75. Ibid, pp 3–10.

76. Ibid, pp 10–11.

75. Ibid, pp 3–10.

76. Ibid, pp 10–11.

77. The second meeting was held May 14, 1935; see 'Political and Economic Relations with Japan', 3 May 1935, FO 371/19357/F2960/376/23; Orde to Cadogan, 21 Aug, 1935, Cadogan Papers, FO 800/293.

78. Orde to Cadogan, 21 Aug 1935, Cadogan Papers, FO 800/293.

79. Ibid.

80. Ibid, record of conversation between Sir John Simon and industrial deputation over HMG's China policy, May 28, 1935.

81. David French, *The British Way in Warfare, 1688–2000* (London, 1990). For a further discussion of the defence of the realm and the British way in warfare, as opposed to the declinist school of Paul Kennedy and Correlli Barnett, see notes 3–7 in Greg Kennedy, 'Holding on to Empire'. The most relevant literature to date on this argument can be found in the articles by Gordon Martel, Keith Neilson, David French, John Ferris, and B. J. C. McKercher, in two special collections of articles: *International History Review*, 13, 4(1991) and *Canadian Journal of History*, 28, 2(1993).

82. The first report and papers that went into that report of the Defence Requirements Committee (DRC) are found in CAB 16/109. See Haggie, *Britannia at Bay*, pp 52–58; Trotter, *Britain and East Asia*, pp 40–42. On DRC and a narrow view of imperial defence regarding Germany as the ultimate potential enemy, see Wesley K. Wark, *The Ultimate Enemy: British Intelligence and Nazi Germany, 1933–1939* (Ithaca, 1985).

83. The Chiefs of Staff (COS)—Admiral of the Fleet, Sir A. Ernle M. Chatfield, Field Marshal Sir Archibald Montgomery-Massingberd, and Air Chief Marshal Sir Edward L. Ellington—were all members of the DRC committee, which was chaired by the Secretary to the Committee of Imperial Defence (CID), Sir Maurice Hankey, and included Sir Warren Fisher, the Secretary to the Treasury, and Sir Robert Vansittart. Contrary to some authors—Brian Bond, *British Military Policy Between the Two World Wars* (Oxford, 1980); Norman Rose, *Vansittart: Study of a Diplomat* (London, 1978), pp 124–125; Michael Howard, *The Continental Commitment* (London, 1972), pp 104–107—who denigrate the ability and efforts of the COS (usually not Chatfield), a thorough and comprehensive reading of the COS minutes and papers, the CID minutes and papers, the DRC minutes and papers, Cabinet minutes and papers, as well as the Foreign Office records for Japan and the United States for the 1930s, reveals that such is simply not the case and that these service chiefs were certainly as capable in their own right as any of their civilian counter-parts.

84. Minutes of COS meeting No. 312, 24 Jul 1934, CAB 53/5.

85. Ibid.

86. On British rearmament programmes see G. Peden, *British Rearmament and the Treasury, 1932–39* (Edinburgh, 1979); R. Shay, *British Rearmament in the Thirties: Politics and Profits* (Princeton, 1977); G.A.H. Gordon, *British Seapower and Procurement between the Wars: A Reappraisal of Rearmament* (London, 1988).

87. Andrew Gordon, *Seapower and Procurement*, chapter 17; idem, 'The Admiralty and Imperial Overstretch, 1902–1941', *Journal of Strategic Studies*, 17, 1 (1994), pp 67–8. On appeasement, particularly Chamberlain's involvement and ideas on it see R.A.C. Parker, *Chamberlain and Appeasement* (London, 1993); and for a different view see Ritchie Ovendale, *'Appeasement' and the English Speaking World* (Cardiff, Unversity of Wales Press, 1975.

88. Minutes, COS meeting No. 132, 24 Jul 1934, CAB 53/5.

89. Ibid. See also, 'Strategical Situation in the Far East with Particular Reference to Hong Kong', 10 Oct 1934, CAB 5/8/C–410. C10 Papers, 'C' series.

90. Minutes of Cabinet meeting No. 31, 31 Jul 1935, CAB 23/79.

91. Ibid.

92. Minutes of 17th meeting of the DRC, 10 Oct 1935, CAB 16/112.

93. For a discussion of how the balance of power worked between the Treasury, the Foreign Office

and the three services see John Ferris, *Men, Money and Diplomacy: The Evolution of British Strategic Policy, 1919–1926* (Ithaca, 1989).

94.   'Naval Defence Requirements', memo by the First Sea Lord and Chief of Naval Staff, 9 Oct 1935, CAB 16/112/DRC–33.

95.   Ibid.

96.   Minutes of the 18th meeting of the DRC, 14 Oct 1935, CAB 16/112.

97.   Minutes of the 17th meeting of the DRC, 10 Oct 1935, CAB 16/113.

98.   Minutes of the 15th meeting of the DRC, 3 Oct 1935, CAB 16/112.

99.   Minutes of the 266th meeting of the CID, 22 Nov 1934, CAB 2/6.

100.   'The Situation in the Far East', 25 Mar 1935, CAB 53/24/COS–368.

101.   As of yet no complete study (in the English language) exists of Russia's role in Britain's defence of the Far East during the interwar. This is a serious lacuna for anyone dealing with British strategic policy in the 1920s and 1930s. However, a very good start has been made by, Keith Neilson, '"Pursued by a Bear": British Estimates of Soviet Military Strength and Anglo-Soviet Relations, 1922–39', *Canadian Journal of History*, 28 (1993), pp 189–221.

102.   'The Situation in the Far East', 25 Mar 1935, Cab 53/24/COS–368.

103.   'Imperial Defence Policy. The Situation in the Far East', 6 Apr 1935, CAB 53/24/COS–370.

104.   The War Office on the other hand was still lobbying along Treasury lines for closer formal relations in early 1936; see 'The Importance of Anglo-Japanese Friendship', Montgomery-Massingberd (CIGS), submitted by the Secretary of State for War, A Duff Cooper, 17 Jan 1936, CAB 24/259/CP 12(36). The Secretary of State for Foreign Affairs, after 22 Dec 1935, Anthony Eden, pointed out to Duff Cooper that '... the FO shared to the full the anxiety of the Chief of the Imperial General Staff for good relations with Japan. It was easier to desire them, however, than to find in current events a good opportunity for promoting them in the general interests'. Minutes of Cabinet meeting No. 3, 29 Jan 1936, CAB 23/83.

105.   Robert Manne, 'The Foreign Office and the Failure of Anglo-Soviet Rapprochement', *Journal of Contemporary History*, 16, 4(1981) pp 725–755; R. Vansittart, *The Mist Procession: The Autobiography of Lord Vansittart* (London, 1958), pp 454–55; Vansittart to Chilston (British Ambassador to Moscow), 21 Feb 1935, FO 371/18826/N1339/55/38; Vansittart minute, 21 Jan 1935, FO 371/19447/N281/1/38; Neilson, 'Pursued by a Bear', pp 209–210.

106.   Collier minute (31 Jan) on Clive to FO, tel, 29 Jan 1935, FO 371/19347/F632/13/23.

107.   Minute by Vansittart and memo from Collier, Wigram and Orde, 12 Feb 1935, FO 371/19460/-N927/135/38.

108.   Conversation between Eden and Stalin, 29 Mar 1935, FO 371/19359/F2096/483/23. Stalin was not hopeful that the sale of the Chinese Eastern Railway will be enough to ensure peace with Japan.

109.   'Soviet-Japanese Relations', Clive to FO, tel, 29 Jan 1935, FO 371/19347/F632/13/23 and minutes; Chancery (Tokyo) to Northern Department, FO, tel 19 Jan 1935, FO 371/19347/F1144/13/23 and minutes; Clive to FO, tel, 19 Feb 1935, FO 371/19347/F1767/13/23 and minutes; Clive to FO, tel, 6 Jul 1935, FO 371/19347/F4366/13/23 and minutes; Clive to FO, 5 Nov 1935, FO 371/19357/F7579/376/23 and minute.

110.   Neilson, '"Pursued by a Bear"', pp 210–211.

111.   'Soviet-Japanese relations', desp, Clive to Simon, 6 Jul 1935, FO 371/19347/F4366/13/23; 'Political Situation in Japan', desp, 20 Jun 1935, FO 371/19349/F4646/29/23; 'Press Summary', 3 Apr 1935, FO 371/19349/F2908/55/23.

112.   'Soviet-Japanese relations', minutes by Orde and Dodd, 6 Jun 1935, FO 371/19347/F4837/13/23.

113.   Vanisttart minute, 12 Dec 1935, FO 371/19357/F8065/376/23; see Alvin D. Coox, *Nomonhan: Japan Against Russia 1939*, (2 vols; Stanford, 1985).

114.   Eden would end the Soviet loan idea officially in Jan 1936; see Victor Rothwell, *Anthony Eden: A Political Biography, 1931– 57* (Manchester, 1992), pp 15–16; Neilson, '"Pursued by a Bear"', p 210.

115.   Ian Nish, 'Japan in Britain's view of the international system, 1919–37', in Nish, Ian, ed, *Anglo-Japanese Alienation, 1919– 1952* (Cambridge, 1982), p 32.

Select Bibliography

Aldcroft, Derek H. *The Inter-War Economy: Britain, 1919–1939* (London, 1970)

Amery, L. *My Political Life*. Vol. Two. *War and Peace 1914–1929* (London, 1953)

Argyll, Duchess of, *George Douglass Eighth Duke of Argyll, Autobiography and Memoirs* (London, 1906)

Ashton-Gwatkin, F. T. *The British Foreign Service* (Syracuse, 1950)

Babij, Orest 'The Second Labour Government and British Maritime Security, 1929–1931', *Diplomacy and Statecraft* 6, 3 (1995) pp. 645–71

Barnes, John and David Nicholson (eds), *The Leo Amery Diaries*, Volume One: *1896–1929* (London, 1980)

Barnett, Corelli *The Collapse of British Power* (London, 1970)

Bartlett, C. J. 'Mid-Victorian Re-appraisal of Naval Policy,' in Kenneth Bourne and D.C. Watts (eds.), *Studies in International History: Essays Presented to W. Norton Medlicott, Stevenson Professor of International History at the University of London* (London, 1967).

Baxter, J. *The Introduction of the Ironclad Warship* (Hamden, 1968)

Beaver, D. R. *Newton D. Baker and the American War Effort, 1917–1919* (Lincoln, NB, 1966)

Beeler, John 'A "One Power Standard?" Great Britain and the Balance of Naval Power, 1860–1880', *Journal of Strategic Studies*, 15, 4(1992), pp 550–67.

Beesly, P. *Room 40. British Naval Intelligence 1914–1918* (London, 1982)

Beloff, Max *Britain's Liberal Empire 1897–1921* (London, 1969)

Bond, Brian *British Military Policy Between the Two World Wars* (Oxford, 1980)

Bonner Smith, D. and A.C. Dewar, *Russian War, 1854. Baltic and Black Sea Official Correspondence* (London, 1943)

Braisted, William *The United States Navy in the Pacific, 1909–1922* (Austin, 1971)

Brodeur, Nigel 'L.P. Brodeur and the Origins of the Royal Canadian Navy', in Boutilier, J., ed, *The Royal Canadian Navy in Retrospect* (Vancouver, 1982)

Brown, D. K. *A Century of Naval Construction. The History of the Royal Corps of Naval Constructors, 1883–1983* (London, 1983)

Burk, K. M. *Britain, America and the Sinews of War 1914–1918* (London, 1985)

Cain P. J. and A. G. Hopkins, *British Imperialism. Innovation and Expansion 1688–1914* (London, 1993)

Calthorpe, S. *Letters from Headquarters; or, the Realities of the War in the*

Crimea (London, 1856)

Cassar, George H. *The French and the Dardanelles. A study of failure in the conduct of war* (London, 1971)

Cheasneau, Roger and Eugene Kolesnik, eds *Conway's all the World's Fighting Ships, 1860–1905* (London: Conway Maritime Press, 1979)

Churchill, Randolph *Winston S. Churchill: Young Statesman* (4 volumes; London, 1967–69)

Clarke, I. F. *Voices Prophesying War, 1763–1984* (London, 1970)

Clowes, W. L. *The Royal Navy. A History from the Earliest Times to the Present* (London, 1901)

Colomb, P. H. *Memoirs of Admiral the Right Honorable Sir Astley Cooper Key* (London, 1898)

Connell, J. *The 'Office', A Study of British Foreign Policy and its Makers* (London, 1958)

Cook, G. L. 'Sir Robert Borden, Lloyd George and British military policy, 1917–1918', *Historical Journal*, 14, 2 (1971)

Cooper, J. M., Jr. *The Warrior and the Priest. Woodrow Wilson and Theodore Roosevelt* (Cambridge, Mass, 1983)

Coox, Alvin D. *Nomonhan: Japan Against Russia, 1939* (2 vols; Stanford, 1985)

Corbett, Julian *History of the Great War: Naval Operations*, volume I, *To the Battle of the Falklands December 1914* (London, 1920)

Curtiss, J. *The Russian Army under Nicholas I, 1822–1855* (Durham, 1965)

Darwin, J. *Britain, Egypt and the Middle East. Imperial policy in the aftermath of war 1918–1922* (London: Macmillan, 1981)

John Darwin, *The End of the British Empire* (London, 1991)

Davis, George T. *A Navy Second to None* (New York, 1940)

Davis, Julia and Dolores A Fleming (eds), *The Ambassadorial Diary of John W. Davis, The Court of St. James, 1918–1921* (Morgantown, 1993)

Dewar, A. C. *Russian War, 1855. Black Sea Official Correspondence* (London, 1944)

Douglass G. and G. Ramsay, *The Panmure Papers* (London, 1908)

Dreyer, Admiral Sir Frederick *The Sea Heritage* (London, 1955)

Drummond, Ian M. *British Economic Policy and the Empire, 1919–1939* (London, 1972)

Drummond, Ian M. *Imperial Economic Policy, 1917–1939* (London, 1974)

Dutton, D. J. *Simon: A Political Biography of Sir John Simon* (London, 1992)

Dyer, G. 'The Turkish Armistice of 1918: 2 — A Lost Opportunity: The Armistice Negotiations of Moudros', *Middle Eastern Studies*, 8, 3(1972)

Earp, G. B. *The History of the Baltic Campaign of 1854* (London, 1857)

Edgerton, David *England and the Aeroplane, An Essay on a Militant and Technological Nation* (London, 1991)

Egerton, G. W. *Great Britain and the Creation of the League of Nations: Strategy, Politics and International Organization, 1914–1919* (London, 1979)

Egerton, Mary Augusta *Admiral of the Fleet Sir Geoffrey Phipps Hornby, G.C.B. A Biography* (Edinburgh, 1896)

Esher, Oliver Viscount, ed *Journals and Letters of Reginald Viscount Esher* (4 volumes; London, 1938)

Fanning, Richard *Peace and Disarmament, Naval Rivalry and Arms Control, 1922–1933* (Lexington, 1995)

Ferris, John 'The Greatest World Power on Earth: Great Britain in the 1920s', *International History Review*, 13, 4(1991)

Ferris, John Robert *Men Money and Diplomacy, the Evolution of British Strategic Policy, 1919–1926* (Ithaca, 1989)

Ferris, John R. 'The Symbol and Substance of Seapower: Britain, the United States and the One-Power Standard, 1919–1921' in B.J.C. McKercher, (ed) *Anglo-American Relations in the 1920s, The Struggle for Survival* (London, 1991)

Ferris, John and Uri Bar Joseph, 'Getting Marlowe to Hold his Tongue: The Conservative Party, the Intelligence Services and the Zinoviev Letter', *Intelligence and National Security*, 8, 4(1993)

Fest, W. B. 'British war aims and German peace feelers during the First World War (December 1916 – November 1918)', *Historical Journal*, 15, 2 (1978)

Fitzgerald, E. P. 'France's Middle Eastern Ambitions, the Sykes–Picot Negotiations and the Oil Fields of Mosul, 1915–1918', *Journal of Modern History*, 66, 4(1994), 697–725

Fitzhardinge, L. F. 'Australia, Japan and Great Britain, 1914–1918: a study in Triangular diplomacy', *Historical Studies*, 14 (1970)

Flotto, I. 'Woodrow Wilson: War aims, peace strategy and the European left', in Link, A. S. ed., *Woodrow Wilson and a Revolutionary World, 1913–1921* (Chapel Hill, NC., 1982)

French, D. *British Strategy and War Aims 1914–1916* (London, 1986)

French, David *The British Way in Warfare, 1688–2000* (London, 1990)

French, D. 'The meaning of attrition, 1914–1916', *English Historical Review*, 103, 407 (1988), pp 385–405

French, D. *The Strategy of the Lloyd George Coalition, 1916–1918* (Oxford, 1995)

Friedberg, Aaron *The Weary Titan: Britain and the Experience of Relative Decline, 1895–1905* (Princeton, 1988)

Friedman, Norman *US Cruisers, An Illustrated Design History* (Annapolis, 1984)

Fuller, William C., Jr *Strategy and Power in Russia 1600–1914* (New York, 1992)

Gallagher, J. and R. E. Robinson, 'The Imperialism of Free Trade', *Economic History Review*, 2nd ser., 6 (1953)

Gibbs, N. H. *Grand Strategy* Vol. I, *Rearmament Policy* (London, 1976)

Goldrick, James and John B. Hattendorf, eds, *Mahan is Not Enough. The Proceedings of a Conference on the Works of Sir Julian Corbett and*

Admiral Sir Herbert Richmond (Newport, RI, 1993)

Goldstein, Erik *Winning the Peace. British Diplomatic Strategy, Peace Planning, and the Paris Peace Conference 1916–1920* (Oxford, 1991)

Gollin, Alfred *The Observer and G.L.Garvin, 1908–1914* (London, 1960)

Gooch, J. *The Plans of War. The General Staff and British Military Strategy c.1900–1916* (London, 1974)

Gooch, J. 'Soldiers, Strategy and War Aims in Britain 1914–1918', in Hunt, B. and Preston, A., eds., *War Aims and Strategic Policy in the Great War* (London, 1977), 21–40

Gooch, B. *The New Bonapartist Generals* (The Hague, 1959)

Gordon, G. A. H. 'The Admiralty and Imperial Overstretch, 1902–1941', *Journal of Strategic Studies*, 17, 1(1994)

Gordon, G. A. H. *British Seapower and Procurement Between the Wars* (London, 1988)

Gordon, Donald 'The Admiralty and Dominion Navies, 1902–1914', *Journal of Modern History*, 33 (1961), pp 407–422

Gordon, Donald C. *The Dominion Partnership in Imperial Defense, 1870–1914* (Baltimore, 1965)

Gowen, Robert 'British Legerdemain at the 1911 Imperial Conference: The Dominions, Defence Planning, and the Renewal of the Anglo-Japanese Alliance', *Journal of Modern History*, 52 (1980) pp 385–413

Grant, Sir Alan *Steel and Ships — the History of John Browns* (London, 1950)

Grenville, J. A. S. 'Diplomacy and war plans in the United States, 1890–1917', in Kennedy, P. M., ed, *The War Plans of the Great Powers, 1880–1914* (London, 1979)

Gwynn, S. ed, *The Letters and Friendships of Sir Cecil Spring Rice* (2 vols; London, 1929)

Hadley, Michael and Roger Sarty, *Tin-Pots and Pirate Ships: Canadian Naval Forces and German Sea Raiders, 1880–1918* (Montreal and Kingston, 1990)

Haggie, Paul *Britannia at Bay: The Defence of the British Empire Against Japan, 1931–1941* (Oxford, 1981)

Hall, Christopher *Britain, America and Arms Control, 1921–1937* (London: 1987)

Halpern, Paul G., ed *The Keyes Papers*, Volume II: *1919–1938* (London, 1980)

Halpern, Paul *The Mediterranean Naval Situation, 1908–1914* (Harvard University Press, 1971)

Hamer, W. S. *The British Army: Civil-Military Relations 1885–1905* (Oxford, 1970)

Hamilton, C. I. *The Anglo-French Naval Rivalry, 1840–1870* (Oxford, 1993)

Hamley, E. *The War in the Crimea* (London, 1891)

Hattendorf, John B. '*Ubi Sumus*? What Is the State of Naval and Maritime History Today?' in John B. Hattendorf, ed, *Ubi Sumus? The State of Naval and Maritime History* (Newport, RI, 1994)

Hayes, P. 'British foreign policy and the influence of Empire, 1870–1920', *Journal of Imperial and Commonwealth History*, 12, 1 (1984), pp 112–13

Heath, L. G. *Letters from the Black Sea during the Crimean War 1854–55* (London, 1897)

Hornby, William *Factory and Plant, History of the Second World War* (London, 1958)

Hou, Chi-ming *Foreign Investment and Economic Development in China, 1840–1937* (Harvard, 1965)

Howard, Michael *The Continental Commitment* (London, 1972)

Hume, John R. and Michael S. Moss, *Beardmore. The Story of a Scottish Industrial Giant* (London, 1979)

Hunt, Barry D. *Sailor-Scholar: Admiral Sir Herbert Richmond, 1871–1946* (Waterloo, Ont., 1982)

Hyam, R. 'The Colonial Office mind, 1900–1914,' *Journal of Imperial and Commonwealth History*, 8, 1 (1979), pp 31–55

Hyde, H. Montgomery *British Air Policy between the Wars 1918–1939* (London, 1976)

Ingham, K. *Jan Christian Smuts. The Conscience of South Africa* (London, 1986)

Ingram, Edward *The Beginning of the Great Game in Asia, 1828–1834* (Oxford, 1979)

Ingram, Edward *Commitment to Empire: Prophecies of the Great Game in Asia, 1797–1800* (Oxford, 1981)

Jaffe, L. S. *The Decision to Disarm Germany. British Policy Towards Postwar German Disarmament, 1914–1919* (London, 1985)

Jeffery, Keith *The British Army and the Crisis of Empire 1918–22* (Manchester, 1984)

Kennedy, Greg 'Great Britain's Maritime Strength and the British Merchant Marine, 1922–1935', *Mariner's Mirror*, 80, 1(1994)

Kennedy, Greg 'The 1930 London Naval Conference and Anglo-American Maritime Strength, 1927–1930', in B.J.C. McKercher ed., *Arms Limitation and Disarmament: Restraints on War, 1899–1939* (Westport, CN 1992)

Kennedy, Paul 'Imperial Cable Communications and Strategy, 1870–1914', in Kennedy, P., ed., *The War Plans of the Great Powers, 1880–1914* (London, 1985), pp 75–98

Kennedy, Paul *The Realities Behind Diplomacy: Background Influences on British External Policy, 1865–1980* (London, 1981)

Kennedy, Paul *The Rise and Fall of British Naval Mastery* (reprint ed., London, 1994, originally published 1976)

Kennedy, Paul *The Rise and Fall of the Great Powers: Economic Change and Military Conflict From 1500–2000* (New York, 1987)

Kennedy, Paul *Strategy and Diplomacy* (Fontana Press, 1984)

Keppel, H. *A Sailor's Life under Four Sovereigns* (London, 1899)

Kerr, Mark *Prince Louis of Battenberg, Admiral of the Fleet* (London, 1934)

Killingray, D. 'The idea of a British imperial African army', *Journal of African History*, 20, 4 (1979), pp 425–6

Killingray, D. 'Repercussions of World War One on the Gold Coast', *Journal of African History*, 19, 1 (1978), pp 39–50

King, Frank H. H. *The History of the Hong Kong and Shanghai Banking Corporation*, Vol.III, (Cambridge, 1988)

Kinglake, A. W. *The Invasion of the Crimea* (Edinburgh, 1863–75)

Klachko, Mary with David F. Trask, *Admiral William Shepherd Benson, First Chief of Naval Operations* (Annapolis, 1987)

Klieman, A. S. *Foundation of British Policy in the Arab World* (Baltimore, 1970)

Lambert, Andrew *Battleships in Transition. The Creation of the Steam Battlefleet* (London, 1984)

Lambert, Andrew *The Crimean War. British Grand Strategy against Russia, 1853–56* (Manchester, 1990)

Lambert, Andrew *The Last Sailing Battlefleet, Maintaining Naval Mastery 1815–1850* (London, 1994)

Lambert, Nicholas 'Admiral Sir Francis Bridgeman', in Murfett, M., ed, *The First Sea Lords: From Fisher to Mountbatten* (Westport, CN, 1995)

Lambert, Nicholas 'Admiral Sir John Fisher and the Concept of Flotilla Defence', *Journal of Military History* 59 (1995), pp. 639–60

Lambert, Nicholas 'The Opportunities of Technology: British and French Naval Strategies in the Pacific, 1905–1909', in Nicholas Rodger, ed, *Naval Power in the Twentieth Century* (London, 1995)

Lambert, Nicholas *A Revolution in Naval Strategy: the Influence of the Submarine Upon Maritime Strategic Thought* (forthcoming)

Lee, Bradford A. *Britain and the Sino-Japanese War, 1937–1939: A Study in the Dilemmas of British Decline* (Stanford, 1973)

Link, A. S. *Wilson the Diplomatist. A Look at his Major Foreign Policies* (Baltimore, 1957)

Link, A. S. and J. Whiteclay Chambers II, 'Woodrow Wilson as Commander in Chief', *Revue Internationale d'Histoire Militaire*, 69 (1990)

Lloyd George, D. *War Memoirs*, (London, 1936)

Lorenz, Edward H. 'An Evolutionary Explanation for Competitive Decline: The British Shipbuilding Industry, 1890–1970', *Journal of Economic History*, 51, 4(1991), pp 911–21

Louis, William Roger *British Strategy in the Far East, 1919–1939* (Oxford, 1971)

Louis, William Roger *Great Britain and Germany's Lost Colonies 1914–1918* (Oxford, 1967)

Lowe, Peter *Britain in the Far East* (London, 1981)

Lowe, Peter *Great Britain and the Origins of the Pacific War* (Oxford, 1977)

McDermott, J. 'Total war and the merchant state: aspects of British economic warfare against Germany, 1914–1916', *Canadian Journal of History*, 21, 1

(1986), pp 61–76

Macfie, A. L. 'The Straits Question in the First World War, 1914–18', *Middle Eastern Studies*, 19 (1983), pp 43–74

McGibbon, Ian *Blue Water Rationale: the Naval Defence of New Zealand, 1914–42* (Wellington, 1981)

MacGregor, David 'Former Naval Cheapskate: Chancellor of the Exchequer Winston Churchill and the Royal Navy, 1924–1929', *Armed Forces and Society*, 19, 3(1993), pp 319–33

Mackay, R. F. *Balfour. Intellectual Statesman* (Oxford, 1985)

Mackay, Ruddock *Fisher of Kilverstone* (Oxford, 1973)

McKercher, B. J. C. 'From Enmity to Cooperation: The Second Baldwin Government and the Improvement of Anglo-American Relations, November 1928–June 1929', *Albion* 24, 1(1992), pp 65–88

McKercher, B. J. C. 'No Eternal Friends or Enemies: British Defence Policy and the Problem of the United States, 1919–1939', *Canadian Journal of History* 28(1993), pp 257–293

McKercher, Brian 'Our Most Dangerous Enemy': Great Britain Pre-Eminent in the 1930s' *International History Review*, 13, 4(1991)

McKercher, B. J. C. 'A Sane and Sensible Diplomacy: Austen Chamberlain, Japan, and the Naval Balance of Power in the Pacific Ocean, 1924–1929', *Canadian Journal of History*, 21(1986), pp 187–213

McKercher, B. J. C. *The Second Baldwin Government and the United States, 1924–1929, Attitudes and Diplomacy* (London, 1984)

Mackesy, Piers *Statesmen at War, The Strategy of Overthrow, 1798–1799* (London, 1974)

Mackesy, Piers *The War in the Mediterranean 1803–1810* (Cambridge, Mass, 1957)

Mackesy, Piers *War Without Victory, the Downfall of Pitt, 1792–1802* (Oxford, 1984)

Maisel, Ephraim *The Foreign Office and Foreign Policy, 1919–1926* (Brighton, 1994)

Manne, Robert 'The Foreign Office and the Failure of Anglo-Soviet Rapprochement', *Journal of Contemporary History*, 16, 4(1981), pp 725–755

Mansergh, N. *The Commonwealth Experience.* Volume I. *The Durham Report to the Anglo-Irish Treaty* (London, 1969/82)

Marder, Arthur J. *The Anatomy of British Seapower: A History of British Naval Policy in the Pre-Dreadnought Era, 1880–1905* (New York, 1940)

Marder, Arthur J. *From the Dreadnought to Scapa Flow* (5 vols; Oxford, 1961–69)

Marder, Arthur *Old Friends, New Enemies: The Royal Navy and the Imperial Japanese Navy, Strategic Illusions, 1936–1941* (Oxford, 1981)

Marder, Arthur G., ed *Fear God and Dread Nought: The correspondence of Admiral of the Fleet Lord Fisher of Kilverstone* (3 vols; London, 1952–59)

Marquand, David *Ramsay MacDonald* (London, 1977)

Martin, T. *The Life of His Royal Highness the Prince Consort* (London, 1877)

Martin, G. 'The influence of racial attitudes on British policy towards India during the First World War', *Journal of Imperial and Commonwealth History*, 14, 1 (1986), pp 91–109

Martineau, J. *The Life of Henry Pelham, Fifth Duke of Newcastle 1811–1864* (London, 1908)

Maurer, J. H. 'Fuel and the Battle-fleet: Coal, Oil, and American Naval Strategy, 1898–1925', *Naval War College Review*, (1981), pp 60–77

Meaney, Nicholas *The Search for Security in the Pacific* (Sydney, 1976)

Mends, B. S. *Life of Admiral Sir William Robert Mends* (London, 1899)

Middlemas, Keith, ed *Thomas Jones, Whitehall Diary*, Volume II, *1926–1930* (London, 1969)

Middlemas, K., ed *Thomas Jones. Whitehall Diary*. Vol. I *1916–1925* (Oxford, 1969

Modelski, George and William R. Thompson, *Seapower in Global Politics, 1493–1993* (Seattle, 1988)

Monger, George *The End of Isolation: British Foreign Policy 1900–1907* (London, 1963)

Moresby, J. *Two Admirals. A Record of Life and Service in the British Navy for a Hundred Years* (London, 1909)

Moss, Michael S. and John R. Hume, *Workshop of the British Empire, Engineering and Shipbuilding in the West of Scotland* (Rutherford, NJ, 1977)

Neidpath, James *The Singapore Naval Base and the Defence of Britain's Eastern Empire, 1919–1941* (Oxford, 1981)

Neilson, Keith *Britain and the Last Tsar. British Policy and Russia 1894–1917* (Oxford, 1995)

Neilson, Keith '"Greatly Exaggerated": The Myth of the Decline of Great Britain before 1914', *International History Review*, 13 (1991), pp 661–680

Neilson, Keith 'Managing the War: Britain, Russia and *Ad Hoc* Government', in Dockrill, Michael and French, David, (eds), *British Strategy and Intelligence in the First World War* (London, 1995)

Neilson, Keith '"Pursued by a Bear": British Estimates of Soviet Military Strength and Anglo-Soviet Relations, 1922–1939', *Canadian Journal of History*, 28(1993), pp 189–221

Nevakivi, J. *Britain, France and the Arab Middle East 1914–1920* (London, 1969)

Nish, Ian 'Admiral Jerram and the German Pacific Fleet, 1913–15', in *Mariner's Mirror*, 56 (1970)

Nish, Ian *Anglo-Japanese Alienation, 1919–1952* (Cambridge, 1982)

Nish, Ian *The Anglo-Japanese Alliance* (London, 1966)

Nish, Ian *Alliance in Decline: A study in Anglo-Japanese Relations, 1908–23* (London, 1972)

Nish, Ian '"In One Day Have I Lived Many Lives": Frank Ashton-Gwatkin,

Novelist and Diplomat, 1889–1976,' in Ian Nish, ed *Britain and Japan: Biographical Portraits* (Folkestone, Kent, 1994)

Northedge, F. S. *The Troubled Giant* (London, 1966)

O'Connor, Raymond G. *Perilous Equilibrium: The United States and the London Naval Conference* (New York, 1972)

Offer, Avner *The First World War: an Agrarian Interpretation* (Oxford, 1989)

Otway, A. *Autobiography and Journals of Admiral Lord Clarence Paget* (London, 1896)

Ovendale, Ritchie *'Appeasement' and the English Speaking World* (Cardiff, 1975)

Paget, G. 'The November 1914 Straits Agreement and the Dardanelles–Gallipoli Campaign', *Australian Journal of History and Politics*, 33 (1987), pp 253–60

Parker, R. A. C. *Chamberlain and Appeasement* (London, 1993)

Parkes, Oscar *British Battleships, 'Warrior' 1860 to 'Vanguard' 1850: A History of Design, Construction and Armament* (London, 1957)

Parkes, Oscar, *British Battleships, 1860–1950* (London, 1957)

Parkinson, J. R. 'Shipbuilding', in Neil K. Buxton and Derek H. Aldroft, *British Industry between the Wars. Instability and Industrial Development 1919–1939* (1979) pp. 79–102

Parsons, E. B. 'Why the British reduced the flow of American troops to Europe in August–October 1918', *Canadian Journal of History*, 12, 2 (1977–78)

Partridge, Michael *Military Planning for the Defence of the United Kingdom, 1814–1870* (New York, 1989)

Peden, G. *British Rearmament and the Treasury, 1932–39* (Edinburgh, 1979)

Pollard, Sidney *Britain's Prime and Britain's Decline: The British Economy, 1870–1914* (London, 1989)

Pollard, Sidney *The Development of the British Economy, 1814–1980* (4th ed, London, 1984)

Pollard, Sidney and Paul Robertson, *The British Shipbuilding Industry, 1879–1914* (Cambridge, Mass, 1979)

Porter, Bernard *The Lion's Share. A Short History of British Imperialism 1850–1970* (London, 1975)

Postan, M. M. *British War Production, History of the Second World War* (London, 1952)

Pratt, Sir John *War and Politics in China* (London, 1943)

Pugh, Philip *The Cost of Seapower, The Influence of Money on Naval Affairs from 1815 to the Present Day* (London, 1986)

Ramsden, John, ed *Real Old Tory Politics, The Political Diaries of Robert Sanders, Lord Bayford, 1910–1935* (London, 1981)

Ranft, Bryan, ed *The Beatty Papers: Selections from the Private and Official Papers of Admiral of the Fleet Earl Beatty*, Volume 2 *(1916–1927)* (London, 1993)

Ranft, Bryan 'The protection of British seaborne trade and the development of systematic planning for war, 1860–1906,' in Ranft, B. (ed.), *Technical Change and British Naval Policy 1860–1939* (London, 1977)

Raven, Alan and John Roberts, *British Cruisers of World War Two* (Annapolis, 1980)

Repington, C. à Court *The First World War 1914–1918* (2 vols; London, 1920)

Robbins, Keith *The Eclipse of a Great Power. Modern Britain 1870–1975* (London, 1983)

Rodger, N. A. M. *The Admiralty* (Lavenham, Suffolk, 1979)

Rodger, N. A. M. 'British Belted Cruisers,' *Mariner's Mirror* 64, 1(1978), pp 23–35

Rodger, N. A. M. 'The Dark Ages of the Admiralty, 1869–1885, Part I, Business Methods, 1868–74,' *Mariner's Mirror* 62, 1(1975)

Rodger, N. A. M. 'The Dark Ages of the Admiralty, 1869–1885, Part II: Change and Decay, 1774–80,' *Mariner's Mirror* 62, 1(1976)

Rodger, N. A. M. 'The Design of the Inconstant,' *Mariner's Mirror* 61, 1(1975)

Ropp, T. (Stephen Roberts, ed.), *The Development of a Modern Navy: French Naval Policy, 1871–1914* (Annapolis, 1987)

Rose, Norman *Vansittart: Study of a Diplomat* (London, 1978)

Roskill, Stephen *Naval Policy Between the Wars* (2 vols; London, 1968–76)

Ross, Stephen T. *American War Plans, 1919–1941*, Volume 2, *Plans for War Against the British Empire and Japan, The Red, Orange and Red–Orange Plans, 1923–1938* (New York, 1992)

Rothwell, Victor *Anthony Eden: A Political Biography, 1931–57* (Manchester, 1992)

Rothwell, V. H. *British War Aims and Peace Diplomacy 1914–1918* (Oxford, 1971)

Rowland, K. T. *Steam at Sea: A History of Steam Navigation* (Newton Abbot, 1970)

Sandler, Stanley, *The Emergence of the Modern Capital Ship* (Newark, Delaware, 1979)

Sansom, Katherine *Sir George Sansom and Japan* (Talahassee, FL, 1972)

Sarty, Roger 'Canadian Maritime Defence, 1892–1914', *Canadian Historical Review*, 71, 4 (1990), pp 462–490

Schofield, B. B. *British Sea Power* (London, 1967)

Schurman, Donald M. *A Bishop and His People: John Travers Lewis and the Anglican Diocese of Ontario 1862–1902* (Kingston, Ont., 1991)

Schurman, Donald M. *The Education of a Navy: The Development of British naval strategic thought, 1867–1914* (London: Cassell, 1965)

Schurman, Donald M. 'Imperial Defence, 1868–1887' (Ph.D. dissertation, Cambridge, 1955)

Schurman, Donald M. 'Imperial Naval Defence: Then and Now', in K. Neilson and E.J. Errington (eds), *Navies and Global Defence* (Hamden, CN, 1995), pp 9–23

Schurman, Donald M. *Julian S. Corbett, 1854–1922: Historian of British Maritime Policy from Drake to Jellicoe* (London, 1981)

Schwarz, Benjamin, 'Divided Attention: Britain's Perception of a German Threat to Her Eastern Position in 1918', *Journal of Contemporary History*, 28 (1993), pp 103–22

Scott, J. D. *Vickers* (London, 1962)

Scott, J. B. ed., *Official Statements of War Aims and Peace Proposals, December 1916 to November 1918* (Washington, 1921)

Seaton, A. E. *A Manual of Marine Engineering: Comprising the Design, Construction, and Working of Marine Machinery* (London, 1907)

Self, Robert 'Treasury Control and the Empire Marketing Board: The Rise and Fall of Non-Tariff Preference in Britain, 1924–1933', *Twentieth Century British History*, 5, 2(1994), pp 153–82

Semmel, Bernard *Liberalism and Naval Strategy: Ideology, Interest and Sea Power During the Pax Britannica* (London, 1986)

Shay, R. *British Rearmament in the Thirties: Politics and Profits* (Princeton, 1977)

Slaven, A. 'A Shipyard in Depression: John Browns of Clydebank, 1919–1938' in R. P. T. Davenport-Hines, *Business in the Age of Depression and War* (1990)

Smith, G. 'The British government and the disposition of the German colonies in Africa, 1914–1918', in Gifford, P. and Roger Louis, Wm, eds, *Britain and Germany in Africa: Imperial Rivalry and Colonial Rule* (New Haven, Conn., 1967)

Stevenson, David *The First World War and International Politics* (Oxford: Clarendon, 1988)

Stokesbury, James L. *Navy and Empire* (London, 1983)

Strachey, L. and R. Fulford, *The Greville Memoirs 1814–1860* (London, 1938)

Sulivan, H. N. (ed.), *Life and Letters of the late Admiral Sir Bartholomew James Sulivan* (London, 1896)

Sumida, Jon Tetsuro '"The Best Laid Plans": The Development of British Battle-Fleet Tactics, 1919–1942', *International History Review*, 14, 4(1992), pp 681–700

Sumida, Jon *In Defence of Naval Supremacy: Finance, Technology and British Naval Policy, 1889–1914* (London, 1989)

Sweet, D. W. and R. T. B. Langhorne, 'Great Britain and Russia, 1907–1914', in Hinsley, F. H., ed., *British Foreign Policy under Sir Edward Grey* (Cambridge, 1977)

Thorne, Christopher *Allies of a Kind: The United States, Britain and the War Against Japan, 1941–1945* (New York, 1978)

Trask, D. F. *The AEF and Coalition War Making 1917–1918* (Kansas, 1993)

Trask, D. F. *The United States in the Supreme War Council: American War Aims and Inter-Allied Strategy, 1917–1918* (Middletown, CN, 1961)

Trebilcock, Clive *The Vickers Brothers: Armaments and Enterprise,*

1854–1914 (London, 1977)

Trotter, Ann *Britain and East Asia, 1933–1937* (Cambridge, 1975)

Tuchman, B. W. *The Zimmermann Telegram* (London, 1959)

Tucker, Gilbert *The Naval Service of Canada* (Ottawa, 1952)

Turner, J. *Lloyd George's Secretariat* (Cambridge, 1980)

Ullman, R. H. *Anglo-Soviet Relations, 1917–1921*, vol. I, *Intervention and the War* (Princeton, 1961)

Vansittart, R. *The Mist Procession: The Autobiography of Lord Vansittart*, (London, 1958)

Vlahos, Michael *The Blue Sword: The Naval War College and the American Mission, 1919–1941* (Newport, RI, 1980)

Wark, Wesley K. *The Ultimate Enemy: British Intelligence and Nazi Germany, 1933–1939*, (Ithaca, 1985)

Watt, D. C. 'Imperial defence policy and imperial foreign policy, 1911–1939. A neglected paradox?', *Journal of Commonwealth Political Studies*, 1, 3 (1961–63)

Weir, Gary *Building the Kaiser's Navy* (Annapolis, 1992)

Wellesley, F. A. *Secrets of the Second Empire. Private Letters from the Paris Embassy* (London, 1929)

Williams, H. N. *The Life and Letters of Admiral Sir Charles Napier, K.C.B. 1786–1860* (London, 1917)

Williamson, Philip *The Modernisation of Conservative Politics, The Diaries and Letters of William Bridgeman, 1904–1935* (London, 1988)

Williamson, Philip *National Crisis and National Government: British Politics, the Economy and Empire, 1926–1932* (Cambridge, 1992)

Wilson, T., ed *The Political Diaries of C. P. Scott 1911–1918* (London, 1970)

Wolcott, Susan 'The Perils of Lifetime Employment Systems: Productivity Advance in the Indian and Japanese Textile Industries, 1920–1938', *Journal of Economic History*, 54, 2(1994), pp 307–324

Woodward, D. R. *Trial by Friendship. Anglo-American Relations 1917–1918* (Kentucky, 1993)